THE LATIN AMERICA READERS

Series edited by Robin Kirk and Orin Starn

THE ARGENTINA READER
Edited by Gabriela Nouzeilles and Graciela Montaldo

THE BRAZIL READER
Edited by Robert M. Levine and John J. Crocitti

THE CHILE READER
Edited by Elizabeth Quay Hutchison, Thomas Miller Klubock,
Nara B. Milanich, and Peter Winn

THE COSTA RICA READER
Edited by Steven Palmer and Iván Molina

THE CUBA READER
Edited by Aviva Chomsky, Barry Carr, and Pamela Maria Smorkaloff

THE DOMINICAN REPUBLIC READER
Edited by Eric Paul Roorda, Lauren Derby, and Raymundo González

THE ECUADOR READER
Edited by Carlos de la Torre and Steve Striffler

THE GUATEMALA READER
Edited by Greg Grandin, Deborah T. Levenson, and Elizabeth Oglesby

THE MEXICO READER
Edited by Gilbert M. Joseph and Timothy J. Henderson

THE PARAGUAY READER
Edited by Peter Lambert and Andrew Nickson

THE PERU READER, 2ND EDITION
Edited by Orin Starn, Iván Degregori, and Robin Kirk

THE RIO DE JANEIRO READER
Edited by Daryle Williams, Amy Chazkel, and Paulo Knauss

THE WORLD READERS
Series edited by Robin Kirk and Orin Starn

THE ALASKA NATIVE READER
Edited by Maria *Shaa Tláa* Williams

THE BANGLADESH READER
Edited by Meghna Guhathakurta and Willem van Schendel

THE CZECH READER
Edited by Jan Bažant, Nina Bažantová, and Frances Starn

THE GHANA READER
Edited by Kwasi Konadu and Clifford C. Campbell

THE INDONESIA READER
Edited by Tineke Hellwig and Eric Tagliacozzo

THE RUSSIA READER
Edited by Adele Barker and Bruce Grant

THE SOUTH AFRICA READER
Edited by Clifton Crais and Thomas V. McClendon

THE SRI LANKA READER
Edited by John Clifford Holt

The Rio de Janeiro Reader

THE RIO DE JANEIRO READER

HISTORY, CULTURE, POLITICS

Daryle Williams, Amy Chazkel, and Paulo Knauss, editors

DUKE UNIVERSITY PRESS   *Durham and London*   2016

Library of Congress Cataloging-in-Publication Data
The Rio de Janeiro reader : history, culture, politics /
Daryle Williams, Amy Chazkel, and Paulo Knauss, editors.
pages cm—(The Latin America readers)
Includes bibliographical references and index.
ISBN 978-0-8223-5974-6 (hardcover : alk. paper)
ISBN 978-0-8223-6006-3 (pbk. : alk. paper)
ISBN 978-0-8223-7506-7 (e-book)
1. Rio de Janeiro (Brazil)—History. 2. Rio de Janeiro
(Brazil)—Civilization. 3. Rio de Janeiro (Brazil)—
Politics and government. I. Williams, Daryle, [date]
editor. II. Chazkel, Amy, [date] editor. III. Mendonça,
Paulo Knauss de, [date] editor. IV. Series: Latin America
readers.
F2646.3.R568 2015
981'.53—dc23
2015022350

Cover art: People gathered on the Escadaria Selarón (Selaron's Stairs),
a mosaic tile stairway in Rio de Janeiro, Brazil. Photo © Jan Sochor.

Contents

A Note on Translations, Spelling, and Monetary Units   xi

Place-Names and Way-Finding   xiii

Acknowledgments   xvii

Introduction: The Marvelous City   1

I   *Colonial Rio*   9

THE EARLY COLONIAL PERIOD, 1502–1720S

A Navigator's Diary, *Pero Lopes de Sousa*   17

On "Brazilian Savages," *Jean de Léry*   19

Channeling the Carioca River, *Municipal Chamber*   24

The Cachaça Revolt, *Salvador Correia de Sá e Benevides and Others*   26

French Corsairs Attack, *René Duguay-Trouin and Jonas Finck*   30

Mapping the City's Defenses, *João Massé*   33

The Wages of Indigenous Labor, *Municipal Chamber*   35

THE VICEREGAL PERIOD, 1763–1808

The Customary Rights of Market Women, *Quitandeiras of Rio de Janeiro and Carlos Julião*   37

Valongo, a Notorious Slave Market, *Bráz Hermenegildo do Amaral and Jean-Baptiste Debret*   41

Fire and Reconstruction of an Asylum for Women, *João Francisco Muzzi*   45

Whaling in Guanabara Bay, *Leandro Joaquim*   48

Lettered Men under Investigation, *Conde de Resende and José Bernardo da Silveira Frade*   50

Cultivating Cinnamon in Late Colonial Rio, *Bernardino António Gomes*   55

THE TRANSFER OF THE PORTUGUESE COURT, 1808–1820S

Eagerly Awaiting the Royal Family, *Padre Perereca*   59

"Infectious Disorders" of the Port, *W. Sidney Smith*   66

The Passeio Público, *John Luccock*   69

II   *Imperial Rio*   73

THE INDEPENDENCE ERA, 1820S–1830S

The Feast of the Holy Spirit, *Henry Chamberlain and G. Hunt*   79
The Emperor Dissolves the Constitutional Assembly, *Henry Chamberlain and Dom Pedro I*   82
Views of the Palace Square, *Jean-Baptiste Debret*   86
The Night of the Bottle-Whippings, *O Republico*   92
Mapping the Capital of Imperial Brazil, *E. de la Michellerie*   97
The Slave Dance Called Candomblé, *Eusébio de Queiroz*   99

A NEUTRAL MUNICIPALITY, 1834–1889

From the Dungeon to the House of Correction, *Eusébio de Queiroz*   101
Photography Arrives in Rio, *Louis Compte and Jornal do Commercio*   103
Transient Laborers of the Fazenda Santa Cruz, *Paulo Barboza da Silva*   106
Recollections of Nineteenth-Century Women, *Adèle Toussaint-Samson*   108
Workers, for Sale or Rent, *Diário do Rio de Janeiro*   112
Maria Angola Denounces Illegal Enslavement, *Maria Angola and Miguel Paes Pimenta*   116
The Capoeira Gangs of Rio, *João Jacintho de Mello*   119
French-Language Classifieds, *Courrier du Brésil*   121
Public Entertainment in Imperial Rio, *Joaquim Manoel de Macedo*   126
Sex Trafficking in the Imperial Capital, *759 Citizens*   130
Visualizing "A Carioca," *Pedro Américo de Figueiredo e Melo*   132
A City Celebrates Slave Emancipation, *A. Luiz Ferreira and Machado de Assis*   134

III   *Republican Rio*   139

THE FEDERAL DISTRICT, 1889–1930

Making the Federal District, *Constituent Assembly*   147
The Legendary Festival of Our Lady of Penha, *Alexandre José de Mello Moraes Filho*   149
The Animal Game, *Francisco José Viveiros de Castro*   155
An Allegation of Infanticide, *Margarida Rosa da Assumpção and Others*   158
The Hotel Avenida, *Brasil-Moderno*   163
Rio's Kiosks, *Augusto Malta*   167
The Cult of Nostalgia, *João do Norte*   170
Anarchists under Arrest, *Corpo de Investigação e Segurança Pública do Distrito Federal*   174

Demolition of the Morro do Castelo, *Carlos Sampaio*   179
Exhuming Estácio de Sá, *Various Notables*   182

THE FEDERAL DISTRICT, 1930–1960
Gaúchos Take the Obelisk, *Anonymous*   185
"Flying Down to Rio," *Louis Brock*   187
Bertha Lutz Goes to Congress, *Bertha Lutz*   191
The Fount of the Queen, *Armando Magalhães Corrêa*   195
A Writer's Brazilian Diary, *Stefan Zweig*   198
Rio and World War II, *U.S. War Department and Walt Disney Studios*   203
A Fond Farewell to Praça Onze, *Herivelto Martins*   206
Avenida Presidente Vargas, *Hélio Alves de Brito*   208
Introducing the "Civilized Indian" João José Macedo, *Cândido Mariano
     da Silva Rondon*   211
Madame Satã, a Grifter in Lapa, *João Francisco dos Santos and Others*   213
A City's Crushing Defeat at the World Cup, Jornal do Brasil *and*
     Correio da Manhã   218
Carmen Miranda Shines in "Ca Room Pa Pa," MGM *Studios*   222
"Soldiers of Fire," *Getúlio Vargas*   224
Censoring *Rio, 40 Graus, Ralph Benedicto Zumbano*   227
The Diplomacy of Samba, Jornal do Brasil   230

IV   *Recent Rio*   235

THE CITY AND STATE OF GUANABARA, 1960–1975
The Ephemeral State of Guanabara, *Federal Congress*   247
Recreation in the Parque do Flamengo, *Ethel Bauzer de Medeiros and
     Others*   251
This House Is Yours!, *Carlos Lacerda*   258
An Act of Student Protest, Correio da Manhã *Staff Photographer*   261

AFTER THE FUSION, 1975–1980S
Dancin' Days, *Nelson Motta with Ruban Sabino*   263
Burger Wars of 1979, Jornal do Brasil   266
Barra da Tijuca, Boomtown (but Not for All), *Israel Klabin; Angela Coronel
     and Heloisa Perez*   270
State Terror in the Early 1980s, *James J. Blystone and Joaquim de Lima
     Barreto*   275
The Consumer Spectacle of BarraShopping, *Cora Rónai*   281
A Weekend at Maracanã, *João Baptista Figueiredo*   285

The Spider Woman Kisses Rio, *Tânia Brandão*   288

Rallying for Direct Elections, *Ricardo Kotscho*   292

A Summer Up in Smoke, *Chacal*   297

CONTEMPORARY RIO, 1990S–2015

Female Planet, *Claudia Ferreira*   301

From Favela to Bairro, *Fernando Cavalieri*   304

Adeus 2-2-6!, *Paulo Mussoi*   308

In Praise of a Modernist Monument, *Gilberto Gil*   311

Venerating Escrava Anastácia, *Kelly E. Hayes*   317

Campaigning for a "Rio without Homophobia," *Rio de Janeiro State
    Secretariat for Human Rights*   320

The Last Night at Help, *Flávia Lima*   325

(Re)Constructing Black Consciousness, *Benedito Sérgio and
    Ailton Benedito de Sousa*   327

A *Quilombo* in Lagoa, *Marcelo Fernandes*   333

An Oral History of Brazilian Jiu-Jitsu, *Ben Penglase and Rolker Gracie*   337

Whatever Your *Fantasia*, Always Use a Condom, *Ministry of Health*   341

"Pacification," *Adam Isacson and Observatório de Favelas*   344

An Open Letter from a Massacre Survivor, *Wagner dos Santos*   354

Reading and Writing the Suburbs, *Biblioteca Parque de Manguinhos;
    Samuel M. Silva and Alex Araujo*   357

A Century of Change at the Port, *Halley Pacheco de Oliveira
    and Unknown Photographer(s)*   362

Suggestions for Further Reading and Viewing   367

Acknowledgment of Copyrights and Sources   375

Index   383

A Note on Translations, Spelling, and Monetary Units

In translating the original documents that appear in *The Rio de Janeiro Reader* from Portuguese, French, or Spanish to English, we have endeavored to maintain the content, spirit, and voice of the source material as originally written. Nonetheless, we have also tried to render the documents legible to contemporary English-language readers. Wherever it was necessary to preserve a keyword or phrase in the original, an English translation appears in brackets that immediately follow.

Original place-names for most landmarks, topographic features, streets, and neighborhoods appear in modernized Brazilian Portuguese (e.g., Praça XV de Novembro instead of Fifteenth of November Square; Avenida Rio Branco rather than Rio Branco Avenue). Exceptions include Guanabara Bay rather than Baía de Guanabara. Corcovado Mountain appears in the simplified form of Corcovado.

Honorific titles, military ranks, and the like generally have been translated into their English equivalents. One exception is "Dom/Dona," the honorific that appears before the given name of high-ranking personalities, such as the Luso-Brazilian royals.

The spelling of Portuguese names and words has varied considerably over the past five hundred years. With the exception of original titles of published works, the editors use standardized contemporary orthography for Brazilian Portuguese. With regard to proper names, we have generally adopted spellings used in official cataloguing of the Fundação Biblioteca Nacional (Brazilian National Library) and the Library of Congress.

Over the course of the more than five centuries that this volume covers, numerous official currencies and monetary denominations have circulated in Brazil. From the colonial period through the mid-twentieth century, the principal monetary unit was the real (réis in the plural, abbreviated as rs.). By the nineteenth century, the declining purchasing power of the real led to the common usage of the mil-réis (1,000 réis, written 1$000, or shortened to 1$) and the conto (one million réis, written 1:000$000, or shortened to

1:000$). The mil-réis was in use until 1942 when a new currency called the cruzeiro (written Cr$) was introduced. The second half of the twentieth century was a period of economic instability, marked by periods of high inflation and numerous currency devaluations. Monetary units changed from cruzeiro to cruzeiro novo (NCr$, 1967), cruzado (Cz$, 1986), cruzado novo (NCz$, 1989), cruzeiro (Cr$, 1990), and cruzeiro real (CR$, 1993). Macroeconomic reforms undertaken during the presidency of Itamar Franco brought the return of the real (R$), or reais in the plural, in circulation since July 1994.

All monetary figures in *The Rio de Janeiro Reader* appear in their original currency. In expressing monetary sums, the editors have refrained from the tricky business of approximating their value in present-day U.S. dollar figures or other monetary denominations. Historical exchange rates are available on such internet sites as http://www.globalfinancialdata.com.

Place-Names and Way-Finding

Many place-names in the Marvelous City, including the name "Rio de Janeiro," are artifacts of Portuguese colonial rule. The names of colonial-era Portuguese authorities and the saints prominent in Iberian Catholicism loom large in the landscape. Even natural features and regions that acquired indigenous names (e.g., Guanabara Bay, the Carioca River, Andaraí, Tijuca) carry with them the legacies of colonial naming practices. These toponyms of the colonial era still orient today's reader within a spectacular landscape of massifs, hills, lowlands, and waterways that has undergone a half millennium of urbanization. Nonetheless, Rio's postcolonial history has added infinite complexity to local place-names. Modern nomenclature for neighborhoods, regions, squares, and streets evoke local notables, real estate speculation, historical dates, and the convenience of municipal administration. Popular naming practices have added more layers of richness to the vocabulary used to demarcate place and orient movement through urban space.

The Rio de Janeiro Reader uses local place-names, written in modernized Brazilian Portuguese. Exceptions include toponyms that have acquired common currency in English (e.g., Sugarloaf Mountain, Copacabana Beach, Guanabara Bay, Corcovado). We also follow local conventions of dividing the city into the historic center city (Centro) and three major zones (Zona Sul, Zona Norte, and Zona Oeste). Finally, *The Rio de Janeiro Reader* follows local conventions to reference the municipalities that surround Guanabara Bay.

Given the importance of place-names and cardinal directions used throughout *The Rio de Janeiro Reader*, some key way-finding tips follow.

The CENTRO is the urbanized historic core of Rio de Janeiro. Although very little of its earliest edifications survive into the twenty-first century, the Centro originated in Portuguese land grants that date from 1567. Colonial-era projects of fortification, earthworks, and lowland drainage, followed by the progressive demolition or disfiguration of numerous hills (e.g., Senado, Castelo, Santo Antonio) in the nineteenth and twentieth centuries, produced a semiregular street grid bounded by the port district (today's Praça

Mauá, Saúde, Gamboa, and Santo Cristo), the parade grounds of Campo de Santanna (also known as the Praça da República), and landfill that now houses Santos Dumont Airport. The Centro is the financial and commercial nerve center of the city as well as home to many, including the residents of the working-class Bairro de Fátima and the Morro da Providência, where the city's first favela took root.

The Centro's main public squares include Praça XV de Novembro (formerly the Largo do Paço), Praça Tiradentes (formerly Praça da Constituição), Largo da Carioca, and Praça Floriano (more commonly known as Cinelândia). All have been sites of some of the city's great historic gatherings. The verdant Passeio Público offers one of the Centro's few respites from dense urbanization. Yet, like the rest of downtown Rio, the eighteenth-century pleasure park has been separated from Guanabara Bay by a series of ambitious public works and feats of engineering that have extended the built city well past the historic shoreline known to the Indians, Portuguese, and Africans who constructed the embryo of today's downtown.

The ZONA SUL, which begins at Praça Paris and follows the bay shore along the Aterro do Flamengo, was lightly populated until the middle of the nineteenth century. Until the early twentieth century, the zone's famous oceanfront promenades of Copacabana, Ipanema, and Leblon were isolated from the central city by the valleys and hills that radiate outward from the forested peaks of the Maciço da Tijuca. Development accelerated with the arrival of tram lines and the construction of streets and tunnels that cut through granite hills to open up the beaches to apartment high-rises. Now dominated by residential neighborhoods that hug the shoreline between Glória and São Conrado, the Zona Sul also encompasses upscale neighborhoods that abut the Floresta da Tijuca, including Laranjeiras, Cosme Velho, Humaitá, and Botafogo as well as Lagoa, Jardim Botânico, and Gávea. The Zona Sul is intimately associated with the Carioca middle and upper classes, yet the region has many pockets of working-class and popular-class housing including favelas, some with startling vistas onto the beaches of Leme, Copacabana, and Vidigal.

The ZONA NORTE—located to the north and west of the Centro—was once an intermediate zone between the urban core that grew near the port and the agropastoral hinterland that stretched into the upper reaches of Guanabara Bay. Tramways, constructed in the late nineteenth century, enabled urban expansion into middle-class suburbs, including Tijuca and Vila Isabel. Railways and later highways accelerated the spread of industrial enterprises that, in turn, attracted working-class migrants from southern Europe, the interior of Rio de Janeiro state, and the Brazilian northeast.

Industrial activities were especially prominent around São Cristóvão, site of a major gas works complex that operated from 1911 until 2005. The working poor filled humble homes and public housing constructed throughout the region from Penha to Madureira. Although Zona Norte neighborhoods cover a wide spectrum of human development indices, the high concentration of irregular settlements contributes to the zone's close association with favelas, a deceptively simple term used to describe a heterogeneity of popular construction and land usage in precarious areas (e.g., hillsides, swamps, underpasses, wastelands).

A rough natural topography, dominated by three forbidding massifs (*maciços*), the Atlantic Ocean, and brackish lagoons isolated the ZONA OESTE from the historic core and the Zona Norte until the second half of the twentieth century. In the colonial period, parts of the region were turned over to agricultural estates, including the Fazenda Santa Cruz. In the nineteenth century, the forested hillsides leading toward the Serra do Mendanha were laboratories for the coffee cultivation that transformed agrarian life in Rio and São Paulo provinces. Over the last century, the farms of the Zona Oeste have supplied local markets for oranges, bananas, chayote (*chuchu*), and ornamental plants. As rail spurs expanded in the latter nineteenth century, followed by the major highways Avenida Brasil and the Rodovia Presidente Dutra in the twentieth, industry spread from Bangu toward Campo Grande. Over the past fifty years, the region has been transformed by massive urbanization largely driven by the demands—and social distortions—of private automobiles, civil engineering, and consumerism. The Zona Oeste, like the rest of the city, is a district of great socioeconomic contrasts, exemplified in the glittering oceanside condominiums and shopping centers of Barra da Tijuca and the rough-and-tumble sprawl of Cidade de Deus, in the lowlands of Jacarepaguá.

The Atlantic Ocean crashes down upon a spectacular coastline that extends across the mile-wide entrance to GUANABARA BAY. Oceanic tides pulse throughout a great natural harbor covering more than four thousand square kilometers, but steep mountain ranges flanking the oceanic canal shield coves, islands, marshes, and mangrove forests along the bay's inner shores. Landfills and bridges now link many islands of the bay to the mainland, and urbanization has despoiled much of the original wetlands. Nonetheless, various islands featured in maps that date from the colonial period remain recognizable features of Rio city: Cobras, Enxadas, Fiscal, Fundão, Governador, Paquetá, and Villegagnon. These islands are blessed with unobstructed views of inland mountain ranges (*serras*) of varying heights and shapes, including the Serra dos Órgãos, where the peaks evoke the form of organ pipes. Aside from the city of Rio de Janeiro, the other municipalities that surround Guanabara Bay are (clockwise) Duque de Caxias, Magé, Guapimirim, Itaboraí, São Gonçalo, and Niterói (linked to Rio city by bridge since 1974). In addition to forming the watershed for the bay, these municipalities of Rio de Janeiro State are the core of the Metropolitan Region of Rio de Janeiro, popularly known as Grande Rio (Greater Rio).

Acknowledgments

The editors gratefully acknowledge the numerous individuals who made *The Rio de Janeiro Reader* possible by offering us their time, their expertise, and the fruits of their own scholarly research. Flávio Di Cola, Benjamin Cowan, James N. Green, Monica Grin, Henrique Espada Lima, Bryan McCann, Stuart Schwartz, and Lise Sedrez provided collegial advice, intellectual support, and paleographic insight. We are especially grateful to fellow researchers who were willing to share some gems from their own excursions into the archives and the streets of Rio de Janeiro: Alessandro Angelini, Leandro Benmergui, Paulo Fontes, Ben Penglase, Paula Ribeiro, and Cassia Roth.

We are immensely lucky to have benefited from the historical acuity, linguistic skills, and professionalism of research assistants Andre Pagliarini and Shawn Moura, without whom it is difficult to imagine having completed this book project. We also thank Araceli Centanino, Nathan Dize, Daniel Richter, Raissa Dornelas, Jerry Metz, and Luciana Pinheiro for their research and translation assistance at various stages in this project.

The staffs of numerous libraries, archives, and museums in Rio provided invaluable assistance in locating sometimes evasive materials and in supporting our efforts to publish them. We thank Rosane Coutinho (Arquivo Nacional, Rio de Janeiro), Beatriz Kushnir (Arquivo Geral da Cidade do Rio de Janeiro), Daniella Gomes (Museu Histórico Nacional), and Vera Saboya (Biblioteca Parque de Manguinhos), as well as the staffs of the Arquivo Público do Estado do Rio de Janeiro and the Museus Castro Maya. The staffs of the National Archives in the United Kingdom and the New York Public Library also provided assistance that made possible the research we carried out at each location.

We would like to thank Catalina Toala and Paula Barriga-Sánchez at the University of Maryland for mobilizing the financial and administrative resources needed to complete this project.

Cassia Roth, Chacal and Fernanda Abreu, Claudia Ferreira, Kelly Hayes, and Henrique Tanure generously allowed us to reproduce in this book material for which they hold copyright.

Over the numerous years during which this project was conceived, carried out, and brought to its conclusion, we would also like to acknowledge the work that the amazing editorial team at Duke University Press did at every step of the way; we thank editors Valerie Millholland and Gisela Fosado, project editor Liz Smith, and assistant editors Lorien Olive and Casey Stegman for everything they have done to bring *The Rio de Janeiro Reader* into existence.

Introduction: The Marvelous City

Cidade maravilhosa, cheia de encantos mil
Cidade maravilhosa, coração do meu Brasil

[Marvelous City, full of a thousand charms
Marvelous City, heart of my Brazil]

—André Filho, "Cidade Maravilhosa" (1934)

The opening lines of "Cidade Maravilhosa" gracefully capture the enchantment of Rio de Janeiro. Composed by Rio native André Filho (1906–1974) for the 1935 Carnaval season, the memorable phrasings "Cidade maravilhosa" (Marvelous City) and "encantos mil" (a thousand charms) have acquired the aura of foundational myth. In 1960, municipal leaders designated Filho's march as the official anthem of a city originally founded on March 1, 1565. The song has been covered by samba schools, North American jazz greats, the titans of Brazilian Popular Music, and countless amateurs. The Brazilian *axé* musician Daniela Mercury belted out a spirited version of "Cidade maravilhosa" at the opening ceremonies of the 2007 Pan-American Games, held in the great Maracanã stadium. The nickname "Marvelous City" and variants such as "Wonder City" and "A Marvel of a City" have served as shorthand for all that is extraordinary about The Very Loyal and Heroic City of Saint Sebastian of Rio de Janeiro (A Muito Leal e Heróica Cidade de São Sebastião do Rio de Janeiro), as the city is known in its fullest glory. Cariocas, the modern demonym for Rio's native-born, are the beneficiaries and proponents of such beguiling formulations of pride, awe, and amazement.

Yet Filho was hardly the first to rhapsodize on his hometown. His now-famous Carnaval ditty took its inspiration from idioms dating back to the late nineteenth century.[1] Even before Rio was officially established in 1565, European travelers and early modern humanists marveled at a place of natural beauty and abundance inhabited by a theretofore unfamiliar people of preternatural goodness. In 1765, a colonial governor wrote to the reform-minded Portuguese prime minister Sebastião José de Carvalho e Melo about a port city of such great richness and potential that it would be a "fundamental stone" of the empire and "a key to Brazil."[2] In the 1820s, the heir

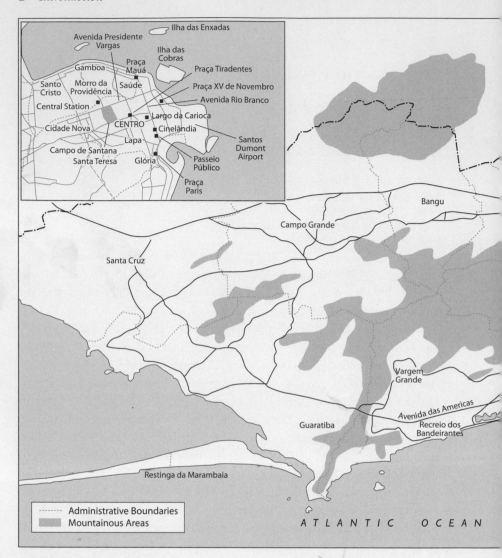

Map of Rio de Janeiro, Brazil.

to the throne of the United Kingdom of Brazil, Portugal, and the Algarve recognized Rio as "very loyal and heroic" to underscore the city's place as the heart and brawn of an emergent American nation.

A familiar trope of the nineteenth-century travel narrative was the maritime entrance into Guanabara Bay and a detailed description of a passage

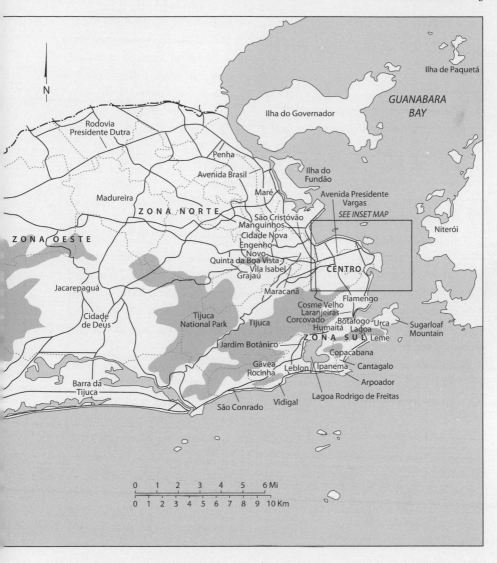

through an urban idyll in the tropics. This framing device lasted well into the twentieth century. For example, the 1936 Metro-Goldwyn-Mayer newsreel "A City of Splendour" opens with deckside visuals of the bay, Sugarloaf, and Corcovado.[3] Three decades later, Tom Jobim's musical valentine "Samba do Avião" (1963) enumerated the breathtaking sights to be taken in on approach to Galeão, Rio's international airport. The successful bid to include the Carioca landscape in the UNESCO World Heritage List included the justifications that Rio is "one of the most beautiful settings in Brazil and the world" and "of outstanding universal value."[4] Even "Vagalume," a memorable samba march released for the 1954 Carnaval season, denounces the lack of reliable water and electric service in the burgeoning city only after opening with the alluring expression "Rio de Janeiro / City that seduces us."[5]

The Rio de Janeiro Reader explores the many facets of a world metropolis that has inspired such descriptors expressing admiration, fascination, and affectionate satire. This book affirms, contextualizes, and disrupts many of the expectations (and quite profitable business operations) that have made Rio de Janeiro, its people, and its spaces exceptional, wondrous, singular, and world marvels. We look at some of the most compelling proponents of Rio's enchantment: travelers, municipal leaders, songwriters, and The Girl from Ipanema. We follow a city's self-presentation of its unparalleled great beauty, cultural innovation, and social conviviality. *The Rio de Janeiro Reader* simultaneously looks at everyday people and their daily routines lived amid a natural and human landscape of shared delights.

This book also listens attentively to the voices of disenchantment, pain, fear, and loathing. There are many, as Cariocas are the heirs, interlocutors, and perpetrators of the brutal dynamics of colonial domination, social inequality, and environmental degradation. In a variety of documents ranging from police investigations to Facebook pages, we accompany the experiences of exclusion and disappointment in the Marvelous City over the course of its history. In listening to such voices, we might ask ourselves: Is perhaps the cruel irony of Rio that its mythological wonder is out of reach for so many? Or is it that the Marvelous City is a mere mirage? Perhaps the city's magical nature is merely a *fantasia*—that wonderful Portuguese word that can refer to a dream, to make-believe, or to a fanciful costume worn for Carnaval.

Opening the pathways to explore these and other questions, *The Rio de Janeiro Reader* covers the broad chronological scope of a storied city that celebrates its 450th anniversary on the eve of hosting the Games of the XXXI Olympiad. We start with a handful of sixteenth-century documents drawn from the early years of European expansionism into the South Atlantic when "Rio de Janeiro" (River of January) earned its somewhat curious name in the misidentification of Guanabara Bay as the mouth of a river that flowed from green mountains into the Atlantic Ocean. The selections that follow illuminate a city's evolution from a small outpost on the remote

Marvelous: "Rocinha Rio de Janeiro Panorama 2010." Photograph by Chensiyuan.
Licensed under Creative Commons Attribution-Share Alike 3.0, http://commons
.wikimedia.org/wiki/File:Rocinha_rio_de_janeiro_panorama_2010.jpg.

edge of the Portuguese empire into the bustling capital of Brazil, Land of
the Future.

Perhaps the more suitable honorific should be "capitals of the Brazils." A
onetime hardscrabble town in a remote colonial captaincy catapulted into
the upper tiers of Portuguese port cities during an eighteenth-century gold
boom in the adjacent captaincy called, appropriately enough, Minas Gerais
(General Mines). The outward flow of precious metals through the port of
Rio was matched by the inward flow of Portuguese immigrants, African
slaves, the reformist ideas of the Enlightenment, and terrifying news of
revolutions in France and Saint-Domingue. The 1763 transfer of the administrative seat of the Brazilian viceroyalty from Salvador da Bahia to Rio de
Janeiro advanced Rio's claim to be the premier city of the Portuguese realm.
In the two and a half centuries that followed, Rio has held the honors and
privileges of the seat of the Brazilian viceroyalty (1763–1815) and the Luso-
Brazilian Co-Kingdom (1815–1822), the court of the independent Brazilian
empire (1822–1889), the capital of the Brazilian Republic (1889–1960), the administrative center of the State of Guanabara (1960–1975), and the capital
city of the state of Rio de Janeiro (1975–present).

In its multiform lives as the political capital of a vast colony-into-empire,
an empire-into-republic, an ephemeral "state-city" named Guanabara, and
an autonomous state of the Brazilian federation, the city of Rio de Janeiro
has been built, razed, and rebuilt to match the aspirations and responsibili-

ties of national primacy. Cariocas proudly think of their city as the cultural capital of the nation. In the international imaginary, Rio is synonymous with Brazil itself. The iconic landmarks Sugarloaf Mountain, Christ the Redeemer, and Copacabana Beach are mandatory elements in locating Brazil. The light-skinned Afro-Carioca dancers who lead Rio's samba school processions, dressed in feathers and sequins, are archetypes of Brazilian female beauty. The hillside favela of Rocinha is a stand-in for all forms of irregular housing anywhere in Brazil. The Carioca samba is the rhythm of a people. No other city, no landmark, no regional "type," no form of built environment, and no competing expressive form defines "Brazil" with the same power and immediacy as those associated with Rio. We are compelled to read the Marvelous City as a singular place of Brazil and as a metonym for all Brazil, that proverbial "sleeping giant" that has now awakened.

No doubt the aspirations and projections of primacy have been repeatedly frustrated by the limitations of mountains, water, and pestilence. Ideological partisanship, cynicism, and racism have constrained human potential. A genuine democratic inclusiveness has been incomplete and marred by institutional torpor and corruption. Economic cycles have limited the fruits of wealth creation tethered to uneven global flows of commodities, labor, and credit. Rio faces the constant challenge of other regions of Brazil that seek primacy in economic, cultural, and political decision making. An unnerving history of violence—of so many dimensions—is the dark underside of the laurels of preeminence. Such violence looms large in the local, national, and international imaginaries of the Marvelous City, and by extension of all Brazil. Yet the aspirations and the trappings of Rio's stature endure, fueled by a resilient combination of human capital, political institutions, markets, and mythmaking. The success of such a powerful combination in Rio de Janeiro echoes the larger, often confounding, success of the Brazilian nation.

The daunting challenge for *The Rio de Janeiro Reader* and its readers is how to grapple with the scope of a city that originated nearly half a millennium ago, to grow from a small fortification at the base of Sugarloaf into a municipal jurisdiction that extends almost five hundred square miles. We are tested to make sense of the whole when the component parts are so numerous, so infinitely diverse, and so often in tension. Today's Rio de Janeiro counts nearly 6 million inhabitants; it is located in a metropolitan region of 11 million that is part of a larger megalopolis of 45 million. Is it possible to think of so many in the singular? Can Cariocas share a coherent history and culture? *The Rio de Janeiro Reader* provides us with the cardinal directions, if not precisely a GIS map, to explore such conundrums.

The early chapters of *The Rio de Janeiro Reader* paint a multidimensional portrait of a Portuguese colonial city initially built with indigenous labor that was the site of a frustrated French enterprise in the sixteenth century, was later sacked by corsairs in 1711, and went on to shelter the Portuguese royals seeking refuge from the French occupation of Lisbon. Traveler accounts, maps, and engravings, among other texts, follow the itinerant Portuguese mariners, colonial administrators, military engineers, clergy, and royals who projected a fortified Ibero-Catholic city onto the verdant lands surrounding Guanabara Bay. Documents related to the Cachaça Revolt of 1660 give voice to the ascendance of a local landowning and commercial class in search of self-rule and profit. Other chapters reveal the presence of English-speakers who set down roots in Guanabara, among the city's Luso-Brazilian ruling classes.

Throughout, *The Rio de Janeiro Reader* follows the long and deep contours of a great *cidade negra* (black city) whose rhythms, customs, and social fissures developed among the tight connections that drew Guanabara Bay close to the slaving ports and hinterlands of West Central and southeastern Africa. The lives of enslaved Africans and their descendants are a constant theme among documents that date from the rise of black chattel bondage through final slave emancipation, joyously acclaimed in front of the Paço Imperial on May 13, 1888. The transitions from slavery to freedom and the aspirations and vexations of Afro-Cariocas in the postemancipation order are manifest in a variety of selections drawn from the twentieth and twenty-first centuries. Such aspirations and frustrations offer clues to Rio's peculiar place in the rise and fall of a curious Brazilian ideology of racial harmony.

The multiform outlines of contemporary Rio sharpen, and then blur, in documents authored after the Proclamation of the Republic (1889), in the period when the former slave city evolved into a multiethnic, cosmopolitan metropolis. Coverage of the republican period includes ample documentation of rapid modernization and infrastructural reforms. Rio's role as a laboratory for experiments in authoritarianism and participatory democracy, the Brazilian welfare state, and tropical modernism are detailed in chapters that cover the years that followed the Revolution of 1930. We consider the half century of dislocations, decline, and resurgence that accompanied the transfer of the federal capital to Brasília, when Cariocas were left to rearticulate a political compact and economic system no longer grounded in the privileges and bragging rights of national capital status. The concluding chapters about recent Rio present the unevenness of human and physical development in a global city bursting with a genuine optimism for its starring role on the world stage of sporting competitions yet deeply troubled by the outrages of violence, corruption, crumbling infrastructure, and environmental spoliation.

Documents have been selected from a wide variety of archival, published, visual, and internet sources, including archival manuscript materials, government and legal documents, speeches, travelers' accounts, ephemera, the visual arts, works of literature, musical compositions, the print and illustrated press, photographs and film stills, and online social media. Documents are authored by a diversity of actors and social types, from the evolving city elite to everyday men and women of numerous ethnic, religious, and racial backgrounds. There is an admixture of local voices with the words, images, and lyrics produced by the many outsiders who share with Cariocas a fascination with (and sometimes a repulsion to) the city.

The Rio de Janeiro Reader may ultimately reaffirm much that is spectacular about the Marvelous City, but its core intent is to equip the English-language reader with the tools to embark on multiple and intersecting, sometimes troubling excursions through a city of ever-changing space and time, of pleasure and disgust, and wonder and puzzlement.

Shall we begin?

Notes

1. Although a radio program, *Crônicas da Cidade Maravilhosa*, was the immediate inspiration for Filho, the phrase "Cidade Maravilhosa" has been attributed to a short piece of writing authored by Brazilian writer Henrique Maximiano Coelho Neto (1864–1934) that appeared in the November 29, 1908, edition of *A Noticia*. Often overlooked is evidence that the phrase circulated earlier, with the couplet "Cidade Maravilhosa / Salve Rio de Janeiro" (Marvelous City / Hail Rio de Janeiro) appearing in the daily *O Paíz*'s coverage of the 1904 Carnaval season on February 16. The phrase even made sporadic appearances in the late nineteenth-century Rio press, in reference to Paris, France.

2. Maria Fernanda Bicalho, "O Rio de Janeiro no século XVIII: A transferência da capital e a construção do território centro-sul da América portuguesa," *Urbana* 1, no. 1 (2006), http://www.ifch.unicamp.br/ojs/index.php/urbana/article/view/1046.

3. "Rio de Janeiro: A City of Splendour," MGM *Traveltalks* (1936).

4. "Rio de Janeiro: Carioca Landscapes between the Mountain and the Sea," Nomination File (2011), UNESCO World Heritage Centre, World Heritage List, http://whc.unesco.org/en/list/1100/documents/.

5. "Rio de Janeiro / Cidade que me seduz / de dia falta água / de noite falta luz." (Rio de Janeiro / City that seduces me / during the day there is no water / at night there is no power.) Vítor Simon and Fernando Martins, "Vagalume" (1954).

I

Colonial Rio

The history of Rio de Janeiro as a European colonial city begins in the sixteenth century. A human history of the region, however, begins earlier. A variety of allied Tupi-speaking clans, living in small villages situated among subtropical forests and wetlands, settled the region of southeastern Brazil that would give rise to a world metropolis that the Portuguese named São Sebastião do Rio de Janeiro (Saint Sebastian of Rio de Janeiro). Numbering more than fifteen thousand at the turn of the sixteenth century, the Tamoios lived on the shores and islands of Guanabara Bay. These native peoples hunted, fished, and cultivated manioc, beans, and peanuts in cleared woodlands. Their human footprint produced substantial secondary-growth forests.

Although indigenous Rio was not physically or spiritually "conquered" along the lines of Aztec Tenochtitlán and Inca Cuzco, Portuguese mariners and clerics, alongside other Europeans, aspired to dominate and Christianize the natives and their lands. The outsiders' demands for brazilwood exacted a heavy toll on the landscape and its indigenous peoples. War and epidemic disease caused substantial disruption to Tamoio lifeways. In the hinterlands, thousands of Indian or other ethnic groups were forcibly settled in villages (*aldeamentos*), where they could be more easily overseen and converted to Catholicism. Many were periodically drafted into Rio's early colonial labor market.

The large bay that Europeans initially mistook for the mouth of a great river gave the future city its curious name, Rio de Janeiro (River of January). That name stuck as an artifact of the misapprehension typical of the colonial enterprise in the Americas. Significantly, a variant of Tupian terms for "sea" also stuck, and the European settlers adopted the word "Guanabara" for a bay surrounded by impressive topographic features, many named after Catholic saints. A river that ran from the Tijuca forests into the bay acquired the toponym "Carioca," understood by many linguists to be Tupi for "white man's house." Rio's spectacular "natural" landscape was born from this combination of indigenous local knowledge, the aspirations of early modern Europeans, and the expansion of the Christian faith.

Portuguese sailors are believed to have first entered Guanabara Bay in 1502, two years after the first contact with Amerindians residing near present-day Porto Seguro, Bahia. Although precious metals were not found anywhere near the bay, the width and depth of the body of water, its multitude of small islands and inlets, and the bounty of nearby forested lands made it attractive for colonial enterprise. In the early decades of the sixteenth century, the Portuguese experimented with various largely unsuccessful modes of indirect dominion over lands between the Atlantic Ocean and the line of demarcation drawn in 1494 between Castile and Portugal. In 1549 the Portuguese Crown assumed direct control of all Brazil under a form of royal administration that paralleled measures taken by Castilian rivals elsewhere in the New World. Throughout Portuguese America, the Crown confronted the immense challenge of establishing stable, orderly settlements, principally near the Atlantic coastline. Indeed, the first governor-general prohibited settlers from venturing into *terra firme* without formal permission. The population of colonial Brazil remained largely coastal until the eighteenth century, when a mining boom summoned waves of settlers and slaves to the interior of the southeast, bolstering Rio's wealth and prestige as the coastal city closest to the mining district.

Portugal's European rivals also sought a foothold in Guanabara Bay. Ships of many flags sailed along the Brazilian coast, stopping in the bay to rest and restock. Brazilwood, the source of a prized dyestuff, was especially important for French trading expeditions. The French Crown actively opposed having been overlooked in the division of the New World between the Iberian powers, and French interlopers forged alliances with the Tamoios. Together, the two groups prevented Portuguese governor Tomé de Souza from disembarking at Guanabara Bay in 1552. In the absence of secure Portuguese dominion, the bay became the site of France's short-lived South American colony, known as France Antarctique. The French enterprise, commanded by Vice Admiral Nicolas Durand de Villegagnon, included Huguenots seeking refuge from the religious strife of the Counter-Reformation. The presence of Protestants in the midst of a nominally Catholic realm gave the Portuguese justification to mount a successful campaign to expel the Villegagnon colony. On March 1, 1565, the city of Rio was officially established by Portuguese commander Estácio de Sá, who had been sent to put the definitive brake on French pretensions in southeastern Brazil.

The Crown of Portugal administered its vast American colony from

Salvador da Bahia, the seat of the viceroyalty. Yet much of Brazil played a marginal role in the larger global empire ruled from Lisbon. In its first half century of formal existence, the city of Rio was a forsaken place. The first settlement at the base of Sugarloaf Mountain was little more than a provisional fort. Once permanent occupation moved to the Morro do Castelo, a true colonial city took root around the church dedicated to Saint Sebastian, patron saint of the city. Upon nearby hills named São Bento, Santo Antônio, and Conceição sprouted homes and churches. As the risk of another French incursion abated, colonists came down from the hills and settled the lands with better access to water. With the labor of Indians, enslaved Africans, and Portuguese exiles, among others, dirt streets, rudimentary squares, convents, churches, and storehouses grew up. Dwellings for Rio's poorer residents were humble houses with beaten earth floors. Those who were better off constructed multistory buildings, called *sobrados*, whose upper floors were used for the family's dwelling and the ground floor for a shop, storehouse, or slave quarters. Small rural plots, called *chácaras*, grew the foodstuffs that fed the city and built the local economy.

The three main religious orders to take on the Christianization of Rio—the Benedictines, Franciscans, and Jesuits—were instrumental to colonial urbanism. The Jesuits were especially prominent land- and slaveholders in and around the colonial city. In the construction of places of worship and seclusion, the patronage of the arts, and learning, the Society of Jesus and other orders exerted great influence over the aesthetic and intellectual development of urban life. By the late seventeenth century, an ornate Baroque style helped transform the first improvised chapels into resplendent temples, including the Igreja da Ordem Terceira de São Francisco da Penitência, located atop the Morro de Santo Antonio and the Benedictine monastery that sat atop Morro de São Bento, right above the bay. Church influence extended to much more than the built environment and sacred art. The Christian faith formed a fundamental part of daily life for Rio's residents. Private lives were devoted to prayer, devotional work, and Catholic moral codes. Public life revolved around the annual cycle of feast days and the observance of the Sabbath. Many ostensibly Christian events often assumed profane dimensions, especially when participants incorporated traditions of popular religiosity and festivity originating in Iberia, Africa, and Amerindian America.

Colonial Rio was a city of waters. Rainfall was generally abundant, and residents lived off the bounty of the saltwater bay, brackish swamps, and freshwater streams and rivers. Nevertheless, early colonial administrators confronted the challenges of regulating common access to potable water, especially in an urbanizing core surrounding the early hillside settlements. As demand outstripped the availability of resources suitable for domestic life, the landscape was altered by public works to channel the Carioca River and other waterways toward areas dedicated to residential, religious, military, and commercial land uses. By the end of the eighteenth century, a huge Roman-style aqueduct delivered waters from the Carioca to the base of Morro de Santo Antonio. Now known as the Arcos da Lapa, the aqueduct is an enduring feat of colonial civil engineering.

Most people got around the city on foot, but the privileged few traveled by sedan chairs, often borne on the backs of the enslaved Africans who built, fixed, and serviced the city. Rio's peculiar geography—many forested hills and mountains, limited navigable rivers—made long-range travel beyond the shores of Guanabara Bay difficult. Connections to the hinterland were precarious, along short and narrow dirt trails largely run by muleteers. Yet colonial Rio emerged as a global city, linked to Europe, Asia, and Africa though the circulation of people, goods, and ideas that traveled by ship. The city served as entrepôt for a range of commodities—wines and cane brandies, commercialized foodstuffs, precious metals and gemstones, valuable spices, and enslaved laborers—coveted in regional and global markets.

Labor scarcity was a perennial problem, leading Portuguese settlers and authorities in Rio to adopt a range of recruitment strategies rehearsed in southern Iberia, the Atlantic Islands, and the Brazilian northeast. Such arrangements ranged from convict labor to outright chattel bondage. The labors of enslaved Indians and Africans were essential to the guarantee of basic provisioning and the construction of the rudiments of Christian civilization. The success of the Portuguese colonial enterprise in Rio was always dependent on strategic alliances with multicultural male brokers, often born from sexual relations between European men and indigenous women in the Americas and African women across the Atlantic. Such figures gave rise to the large class of mixed-blood, multicultural colonial subjects called a wide variety of terms, including *mestiço, mulato, cabra,* and *caboclo.*

Despite Portugal's relative disinterest in its American colony and the greater importance of agrarian over urban life, New World cities like Rio were instruments of royal absolutism. The colonial cityscape contained many symbols of imperial authority, including the whipping post, the pillory, and the royal coat of arms. The supreme representative of the reigning monarch was the governor-general and, after 1763, the viceroy. Yet the city and its residents also enjoyed a certain level of local self-regulation. A municipal council (the Câmara Municipal) exercised powers of fiscal autonomy. The locally born served in militias and staffed Church offices. The built and visual environments were largely made by the hands of the Brazilian-born. When local prerogative might be threatened—by tax reform, predatory corsairs, or perceived violations of customary rights—the residents of Rio were known to raise their voices (and sometimes their weapons) in the defense of their self-interest.

The agro-commercial production that developed in Rio's immediate hinterlands was a source of everyday violence punctuated by episodes of upheaval. Order was largely maintained by private means; there was no effective royal police force or constabulary until the nineteenth century. Bush captains plied the forests in search of fugitive slaves. The labor regime and colonial legal distinctions in this highly stratified society were maintained through a mixture of private discipline, religious devotion, and racial and gendered bars on participation in various aspects of public life. The prevalence of everyday violence in all registers of urban life, including production, cannot be underestimated. Public punishment, from executions in the street to whippings at the pillory, were common. The wanton cruelties of the slave market established at Valongo in 1779 exemplified the brutality of a wider slave society entering a phase of expansion in the late eighteenth century. Yet recent archeological evidence of human remains excavated at Valongo reveal that enslaved West and West Central Africans brought with them sacred objects and other manifestations of culture that survived the Middle Passage. Thus we must consider the rising profile of slave imports through the lens of a city's evolution into a polyglot, multiethnic extension of Africa and African cultures in the Americas.

Animated by a zeal for reform, spectacle, and prosperity, the Portuguese Crown and colonial governors oversaw many changes to the economic and social order of the city over the course of the eighteenth century. Rio's rise as one of the principal whaling stations of the South Atlantic reflected wider shifts afoot in economic relations that accompanied the intensification of transatlantic trade in precious metals and enslaved bodies. In recognition of the shifting political and economic geography of Brazil, the viceregal capital was transferred from Salvador to Rio in 1763. The changing intellectual and cultural milieu that came to Rio along with the viceroy, high judges, and clerics could be disquieting, especially as royal agents grew suspicious of the influences of radical ideas circulating throughout the Atlantic, including the aspirations of republicanism, personal liberties, and antislavery that flowed from British North America, Saint-Domingue, and France. The residents of late colonial Rio witnessed the censorship, interrogation, and punishment of lettered men and even artisans who were drawn to such "dangerous" ideas imported from overseas.

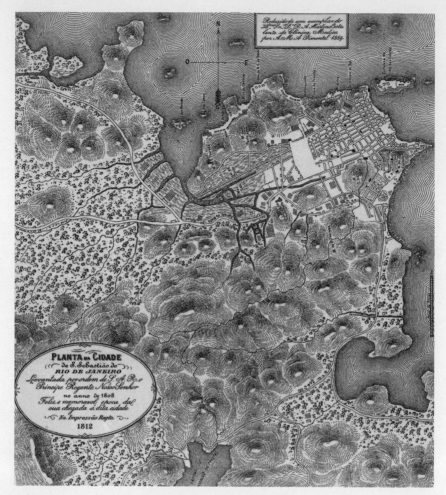

Planta da cidade de S. Sebastião do Rio de Janeiro levantada por ordem de S. A. R o Principe Regente Nosso Senhor no anno de 1808, feliz e memoravel epoca da sua chegada à dita cidade. Engraving by Lespinasse after Paulo dos Santos Ferreira Souto and Ignacio Antonio dos Reis (1812). From *Almanaque Brasileiro Garnier* (Rio de Janeiro: Livraria Garnier do Brasil, 1911), 9.

By the late eighteenth century, Brazil had experienced a dramatic ascent within the Portuguese imperial system, becoming wealthier than the metropole. European powers excluded from direct trade with Portuguese America clamored for access to Brazilian commodities and strategic ports like Rio. When Napoleon's armies invaded the Iberian Peninsula in late 1807, the Portuguese royal family took flight to Brazilian shores. The event opened up Brazilian ports to foreign trade and ended colonial-era restrictions on local manufacturing, printing, and mapmaking. The news that Prince Regent João and his entourage were headed to Rio precipitated enormous excitement among colonials who had never seen the monarch. In March 1808, the principals of the House of Bragança began their prolonged residence in Rio, making the city the main stage for Portuguese America's peculiar path toward independence. A former colonial backwater assumed its place of privilege as the once and future capital of the independent Brazilian nation-state.

A Navigator's Diary

Pero Lopes de Sousa

*On December 3, 1530, the Portuguese nobleman Martim Afonso de Sousa (c. 1500–1571)
set out from Lisbon to extend his sovereign's dominion into southern Brazil. Eventually traveling as far south as the River Plate, the expedition stopped at various
points along the Atlantic coast, including Guanabara Bay, where Sousa founded the
first permanent European settlement in the region. Pero Lopes de Sousa (1497–1539),
the commander's brother, registered the expedition's three-month stay on lands that
would become part of the city of Rio.*

*The precise location of the Sousa settlement remains a matter of some contro-
versy. Gaspar de Lemos, an earlier Portuguese navigator who entered Guanabara
Bay at the start of 1502, originated the confusion of the "River of January," but his
stay was brief, and the expedition had left no permanent way-finder. Lopes de
Sousa, who also used the term "river," may have been familiar with a disputed
account of the Brazilian coastline by Italian explorer Amerigo Vespucci (1454–1512).
In any case, Lopes de Sousa's diary of the 1531 expedition, excerpted here, registered
the construction of a fortified structure on the bay shore. He noted the abundance
of provisions and the easy access to shipbuilding materials. The traveler's account
also contained observations about the geography of the islands and mountains that
surround the bay as well as the Portuguese mariners' contacts with local Indians,
described as a "gentle people" (gentil gente) who engaged in a friendly exchange of
products and gifts. Although the diary takes note of an unnamed Indian noble who
informed the Portuguese about gold and silver near the far-off Paraguay River, the
account seems questionable, as precious metals were rare in Rio until late in the
seventeenth century, when gold was discovered in an inland region that came to be
known as the captaincy of Minas Gerais (General Mines). Nevertheless, Lopes de
Sousa associated Guanabara Bay with the potential for economic profit in one of the
earliest written records of a European presence in Rio and its environs.*

Saturday, 30 April, early morning we arrived at the mouth of the River of
January, and as the winds died down, sailing at a depth of fifteen lengths
of clean sand, we came alongside an island situated at the entrance to the

said river. At noon, the breeze rose up from the ocean and we entered with our ships. The river is very large, and it has within it eight islands, and a number of small anchorages. We came in from north to south, tacking from the northeast to the southeast. To our southeast lie two islands, and another two to the south, and three more to the southwest; and among them one can navigate large merchant ships [*carracas*]. The river is clean, with a depth of twenty-two lengths at its deepest point, lacking in shoals and with a clear bottom. Outside the mouth there are two more islands to the east, and another band to the west with four small islets. The mouth is no more than a type of a bow; it has in its middle a flat rock island, right at sea level; alongside it there is open sand about eighteen arms in length. It is situated at twenty-three degrees and a quarter.

As we entered, the captain ordered that a fortified house be built, with a fence all around. He ordered that we take leave on shore, and that a forge be set up such that we could make things of which we had need. From there, the captain ordered that four men set out into the interior; they were gone for two months, walking the land some 115 leagues, of which 65 were across very large mountains and the other 50 through wide open plains; they walked until they came upon a great king, lord of all these lands, who paid them great honors and accompanied them back to the captain; the lord brought much crystal, and gave news that, as in the Paraguay River, there was much gold and silver. The captain paid the king great honors, and gave him gifts and bid him leave to return to his lands. The people of this river are like those in the Bay of All Saints [Bahia]; that is, they are an even more gentle people. All the land of this river is made up of mountains and hills of great heights. The best of waters that might exist are to be found on this river. Here, we remained for three months, gathering provisions to last for one year for the four hundred men whom we brought with us; and we made two brigantines and fifteen rowers' benches.

Tuesday, the first of August 1531, we left this Rio de Janeiro, with a northeastern wind. We made a route to the west, tacking a quarter to the southeast.

Translated by Daryle Williams

On "Brazilian Savages"

Jean de Léry

In 1555, a group of settlers from France founded a settlement in Guanabara Bay on an island now known as the Ilha de Villegagnon. Internal rifts led some of the colonists to move to the mainland to live among Tupinambá Indians. Portuguese forces, working in alliance with rival Indian groups (notably Temiminós led by chief Araribóia), managed to expel the French by 1560. The famous chronicles of Jean de Léry (1536–1613), a seminarian who joined a second wave of French-speaking Protestants to settle in Guanabara Bay, recounted the experiences of the short-lived French colonial enterprise known as France Antarctique (Antarctic France).

Léry's History of a Voyage to the Land of Brazil, published in Geneva in 1578, has been read as a New World extension of Old World sectarian strife between Protestants and Catholics. Yet Léry's description of disputes between French commander Nicolas Durand de Villegagnon (1510–1571) and French Huguenots (members of a sect of French Protestants) from Geneva may not have had any direct correspondence with events in Europe. The Léry narrative, nonetheless, presents several compelling descriptions of the native peoples of Guanabara and their interactions with Europeans. His accounts helped construct in the European mind the image of a "noble savage" taken up by early modern humanists such as Michel de Montaigne (1533–1592). Moreover, from Léry's descriptions of the French encampments, we learn how much the early colonists depended on local Indians for sustenance. The Léry narrative illuminates certain dynamics of collaboration between the French and locals.

Léry's observations were shaped by a strain of respect for the cultural practices of the Tupinambá. However, one should take into account the way Léry drew implicit, somewhat misleading contrasts between a peaceful New World and a Europe mired in religious warfare. The favorable image of the healthful, morally pure American "savages"—acts of cannibalism notwithstanding—turned on a critique of the dire circumstances in Europe. As such, the passages here must be read with a certain degree of skepticism toward the accuracy of claims about Indians' "natural qualities" and disposition prior to the definitive establishment of Portuguese colonial dominion.

Thus far I have recounted both what we saw on the sea and on our way to the land of Brazil, and what took place on the Island and Fort of Coligny, where Villegagnon was staying while we were there; I have also described the bay called *Guanabara*. Since I have gone so far into these matters, before reembarking for France I also want to discuss what I have observed concerning the savages' way of life, as well as other singular things, unknown over here, that I have seen in their country.

In the first place then (so that I begin with the chief subject, and take things in order), the savages of America who live in Brazil, called *Tupinamba*, whom I lived among and came to know for about a year, are not taller, fatter, or smaller in stature than we Europeans are; their bodies are neither monstrous nor prodigious with respect to ours. In fact, they are stronger, more robust and well filled-out, more nimble, less subject to disease; there are almost none among them who are lame, one-eyed, deformed, or disfigured.

Furthermore, although some of them reach the age of a hundred or a hundred and twenty years (for they know how to keep track of their ages and count them by moons), few of the elderly among them have white or gray hair. Now this clearly shows not only the benign air and temperature of their country (in which, as I have said elsewhere, there are no frosts or great cold, and the woods, plants, and fields are always greening), but also—for they all truly drink at the Fountain of Youth—the little care or worry that they have for the things of this world. And indeed, as I will later show in more detail, since they do not in any way drink of those murky, pestilent springs, from which flow so many streams of mistrust, avarice, litigation, and squabbles, of envy and ambition, which eat away our bones, suck our marrow, waste our bodies, and consume our spirits—in short, poison us and kill us off before our due time—nothing of all that torments them, much less dominates or obsesses them.

As for their natural color, considering the hot region where they live, they are not particularly dark, but merely of a tawny shade, like the Spanish or Provençals.

Now this next thing is no less strange than difficult to believe for those who have not seen it: the men, women, and children do not hide any parts of their bodies; what is more, without any signs of bashfulness or shame, they habitually live and go about their affairs as naked as they come out of their mother's wombs. And yet, contrary to what some people think, and what others would have one believe, they are by no means covered with hair; in fact, they are not by nature any hairier than we are over here in this country. Furthermore, as soon as the hair begins to grow on any part of the body, even the beard and eyelashes and eyebrows, it is plucked out, either with the fingernails, or, since the arrival of the Christians, with tweezers that the latter have given them—which makes their gaze seem wall-eyed, wandering, and wild. It has been written that the inhabitants of the island of Cumana in Peru do the same. As for our Tupinamba, they make an exception only of the hair on their head, which on all the males, from their youth forward, is shaved very close from the forehead to the crown, like the tonsure of a monk; behind, in the style of our forefathers or of those who let their hair grow, they have it trimmed on the neck.

To leave nothing out (if that is possible), I will also add this. There are certain grasses in that land with leaves about two fingers wide, which grow slightly curved both around and lengthwise, something like the sheath that covers the ear of the grain that we call "Saracen wheat." I have seen old men (but not all of them, and none of the young men or children) take two leaves of these grasses and arrange them together and bind them with cotton threads around their virile member; sometimes they wrapped it with handkerchiefs and other small pieces of cloth that we gave them. It would seem, on the face of it, that there remains in them some spark of natural shame, if indeed they did this on account of modesty, but, although I have not made closer inquiry, I am still of the opinion that it is rather to hide some infirmity that their old age may cause in that member.

To go on, they have the custom, which begins in the childhood of all the boys, of piercing the lower lip just above the chin; each of them usually wears in the hole a certain well-polished bone, as white as ivory, shaped like one of those little pegs that we play over here, that we use as tops to spin on a table. The pointed end sticks out about an inch, or two fingers' width, and is held in place by a stop between the gums and the lip; they can remove it and put it back whenever they please. But they only wear this bodkin of white bone during their adolescence; when they are grown, and are called *conomi-ouassou* (that is, big or tall boy), they replace it by mounting in the lip-hole a green stone (a kind of false emerald), also held in place inside by a stop, which appears on the outside to be of the roundness and width of a testoon, with twice its thickness. There are some who wear a stone as long and round as a finger (I brought one such stone back to France). Sometimes when these stones are removed, our Tupinamba amuse themselves by sticking their tongues through the slit in the lip, giving the impression to the onlooker that they have two mouths; I leave you to judge whether it is pleasant to see them do that, and whether that deforms them or not. What is more, I have seen men who, not content with merely wearing those green stones in their lips, also wore them in both cheeks, which they had likewise had pierced for the purpose.

DE L'AMERIQVE.   121

"Of the natural qualities, strength, stature, nudity, disposition, and ornamentation of the body of the Brazilian savages, both men and women, who live in America, and whom I frequented for about a year." Woodcut by Jean de Léry. From Jean de Léry, *Histoire d'un voyage fait en la terre du Brésil*, 5th ed. (Geneva, 1611).

As for the nose: our midwives over here pull on the noses of newborn babies to make them longer and more handsome; however our Americans, for whom the beauty of their children lies in their being pug-nosed, have the noses of their children pushed in and crushed with the thumb as soon as they come out of their mothers' wombs (just as they do in France with spaniels and other puppies). Someone else has said that there is a certain part of Peru where the Indians have such outlandishly long noses that they set in them emeralds, turquoises, and other white and red stones with gold thread.

Our Brazilians often paint their bodies in motley hues; but it is especially their custom to blacken their thighs and legs so thoroughly with the juice of a certain fruit, which they call *genipap*, that seeing them from a distance, you might think they had donned the hose of a priest; and this black dye is so indelibly fixed on their skin that even if they go into the water, or wash as much as they please, they cannot remove it for ten or twelve days.

They also have crescent shaped pendants, more than half a foot long, made of very even-textured bone, white as alabaster, which they name *y-aci*, from their name for the moon; they wear them hung from the neck by a little cord made of cotton thread, swinging flat against the chest.

Similarly they take innumerable little pieces of a seashell called *vignol*, and polish them for a long time on a piece of sandstone, until they are thin, round, and smooth as a penny; these they pierce through the center and string onto cotton threads to make necklaces that they call *boüre*, which they like to wear twisted around their necks, as we do over here with gold chains. I think this is what some people call "porcelain shell"; we see many women over here wearing belts of it. When I arrived back in France, I had more than fifteen feet of it, as fine as you might ever see. The savages also make these *boüre* of a certain kind of black wood, which is very well suited to this since it is almost as heavy and shiny as jet. . . .

Now that I have fully treated what can be said concerning the exterior of the bodies of the American men and of the male children, if you would picture to yourself a savage according to this description, you may imagine in the first place a naked man, well formed and proportioned in his limbs, with all the hair on his body plucked out; his hair shaved in a fashion I have described; the lips and cheeks slit, with pointed bones or green stones set in them; his ears pierced, with pendants in the holes; his body painted; his thighs and legs blackened with the dye that they make from the *genipap* fruit that I mentioned; and with necklaces made up of innumerable little pieces of the big seashell that they call *vignol*. Thus you see him as he usually is in his country, and, as far as his natural condition is concerned, such as you will see him portrayed in the following illustration, wearing only his crescent of polished bone on his breast, his stone in the hole in the lip, and, to show his general bearing, his unbent bow and his arrows in his hands. To fill out this plate, we have put near this Tupinamba one of his women, who, in their customary way, is holding her child in a cotton scarf, with the child holding on to her side with both legs. Next to the three is a cotton bed, made like a fishing net, hung in the air, which is how they sleep in their country. There is also the figure of the fruit they call *ananas*, which, as I shall describe hereafter, is one of the best produced in this land of Brazil.

Channeling the Carioca River

Municipal Chamber

Seventeenth-century local authorities considered the costs of channeling the Carioca River toward Rio's central parishes. The undertaking required significant earthworks and civil engineering to divert the river from its natural course, which began high in the Floresta da Tijuca. Eventually, some of the diverted waters flowed across a grand aqueduct built atop Roman arches that spanned the Morro do Desterro (today's Santa Teresa) and the Morro de Santo Antonio (largely demolished in the 1950s). The works, completed in various stages over the colonial period, supplied a number of public fountains in the central city, the most famous being the Chafariz da Carioca, located near what is now the Largo da Carioca metro station. The availability of fresh water would remain an ongoing challenge for local authorities, as the demands placed on the Carioca and other waterways exceeded supply. Runaway slave encampments in the forest, known as quilombos, sometimes diverted waters destined for the city. Downstream, the Carioca, as well as the Catete River, was fouled by animal and household waste. Successive town councillors turned to local policing agents and chartered companies to remedy these problems, making water rights an active part of public policy and economic activity in colonial Rio.

In 1648, municipal councillors adopted a measure to grant a concession to a figure named Franco to bring the waters of the Carioca closer to the residents of the growing city. The resolution appears in the oldest surviving registry of local administration, the Accordãos e Vereanças do Senado da Câmara. *This resolution represents an early record of the public concession of basic services to private interests that has remained fundamental in areas of public administration and urban infrastructure.*

The Carioca

On the twenty-fifth day of April, sixteen hundred and forty-eight in the city of São Sebastião do Rio de Janeiro, before the Council appeared the magistrate Dr. Franco who stated to the undersigned officials that since he arrived in this city he has found that it would be of great utility for the people and the residents to have the Carioca River brought to the city as there is a great need for its use among the residents. Upon making inquiries as to whether or not it would be of great expense to do this, it appeared that it would not cost much and that it would be of great service for his majesty to take on a feat of such great importance. Finding agreement, it shall be ordered by public announcement the construction of wooden culverts and supports to the parts where arches shall subsequently be built. The aforementioned officials found it sound to work with that said individual and made publicly known that the matter be handled by his agent who shall take up the matter and as such they agreed I wrote in this registry all those who signed, I, Jorge de Sousa, scrivener of the Council, who wrote it down.

Translated by Daryle Williams

The Cachaça Revolt

Salvador Correia de Sá e Benevides and Others

A violent tax revolt, alternatively known as the Revolta da Cachaça (The Cachaça Revolt) and the Revolta do Barbalho (Barbalho's Revolt), rocked Rio and its environs in late 1660. The two period documents here offer contrasting perspectives on these notable events that took their name from cachaça, a cane brandy consumed in everyday life in colonial Rio and central to slaveholding on both sides of the Atlantic.

The first document, dated November 8, 1660, announces an insurrection. The declaration describes how "the people" were rebelling in a broad movement that incorporated protests lodged by a representative group from São Gonçalo, a region that produced the most sugarcane and cachaça in greater Guanabara, against colonial authority. More than one hundred signatures accompanied the manifesto, suggestive of an alliance of local aldermen, military officers, and slaveholding landowners seeking greater representation in municipal administration. Calling for the removal of Governor-General Salvador Correia de Sá e Benevides (1602–1688) and his interim substitute, Thomé Correia de Alvarenga, the rebels hoped to see Agostinho Barbalho Bezerra, a nobleman from São Gonçalo who had fought in the war to end Dutch occupation of the Brazilian northeast, take on governance. Barbalho's brother, Jeronimo, ended up as the rebellion's choice. The second document is a proclamation from the governor issued from the captaincy of São Paulo on January 1, 1661. Characterizing the insurgency as armed and dangerous, and condemning its leaders as traitors, the governor-general nonetheless accepted the demands that he be replaced.

On April 6, 1661, Crown troops arrived from São Paulo and Bahia to retake Rio. The rebels were imprisoned and Jeronimo Barbalho hanged. His decapitated head was placed on the pillory (pelourinho, popularly known as the polé) that stood as symbol of royal authority and public punishment in the square now known as Praça XV de Novembro. Upon learning of the tumultuous events in Rio, colonial councillors in Lisbon found some legitimacy in the rebels' motivations. Correia de Sá e Benevides was dismissed, bringing an end to the preeminence of a family who had been part of Rio's governing class since the founding of the city. The Overseas Council also decided to open municipal political representation to less historically prestigious families as well as rural plantation owners.

Extracts from the Announcement of the Election and Acclamation of
Governor Agostinho Barbalho Bezerra, Rio de Janeiro, November 8, 1660

In the 1660th year of the Birth of Our Lord Jesus Christ, on the eighth day of this very month, in the city of São Sebastião do Rio de Janeiro, the people of the city and its district gathered at the town hall at five in the morning. The crowd, filling the chamber and overflowing into the street, summoned the current officials of the Council. First the people hailed the King our lord D. Affonso, and affirmed themselves to be his loyal servants, and reported that acting as such, on the thirtieth day of October past, they had gone to another region of this city known as Ponta do Brabo [today's Gradim, São Gonçalo], to recount there the wrongs, injustices, and oppressions that stemmed from the vexatious tyrannies, taxes, penalties, outrageous demands, and ruination of estates that General Salvador Correia de Sá e Benevides had visited upon them. They claimed that General Salvador Correia de Sá e Benevides, the former governor of this area, acted only in his own convenience in disregard for the common good and well-being of the aforementioned people, insulting them as well as the officials of the town council with injurious, scornful aspersions, leaving everyone agitated, galled, and depressed. Because of this they appealed to Thomé Correia de Alvarenga, who was presently acting as governor due to the absence of the aforementioned Governor-General, who had traveled to the mining fields in the captaincies south of here. But seeing that the four agents they sent to the aforementioned Thomé Correia de Alvarenga brought back no result, they themselves went in person for the above-noted reasons to exclude and remove General Salvador Correia de Sá e Benevides from the office of Governor of this region, and they hope that Your Majesty, who has the goodness to act in the utility and preservation of these city residents and vassals of the aforementioned King, would help them and not oppress them. . . . And soon the people pledged their reverence and homage to Agostinho Barbalho Bezerra, whom they had elected again, which was the reason for celebrating anew, and indeed they brought a missal in which appear the Saints of the Gospel, upon which Agostinho Barbalho Bezerra swore with both hands that he promised His Majesty King D. Affonso as your loyal servant to secure and maintain this region and defend it with care but without duplicity, assuring above all his service to the King even at the cost of his own life; that he would hand control of the region to no one outside the order of our beloved King, and then he accepted the praise of the people. It was furthermore stated by the people that there was an uprising, based on popular allegiance, to displace the aforementioned Governor Thomé Correia de

Alvarenga, and that this document serves notice that he has been removed from regional government, and also that the events detailed here transpired exactly as they were recorded.

I, Antonio Francisco da Silva, judicial notary public, prepared this account by mandate of the aforementioned people, and of the notary publics Sebastião Serrão Freire and Antonio de Andrade, and of additional city councilmen present, and of numerous noblemen, many of whom signed it; and because the common folk were there in such prodigious numbers it was impossible for all of them to sign it as well. I the aforementioned Notary swear that they called for Captain Jeronimo Barbalho Bezerra to sign it for them. . . .

*Extracts from the Proclamation by Governor Salvador Correia
de Sá e Benevides, São Paulo, January 1, 1661*

I am informed that, in the early days of December last month, the residents of São Gonçalo in Rio de Janeiro breached the limits of obedience by arming themselves and forcing the town ministers, with great alarm and agitation, to seek refuge in the São Bento monastery; and continuing their tumultuous campaign they beat on doors and rang the bell of the town hall, demanding that one and all heed their voice. Then they declared as their leader Agostinho Barbalho Bezerra, an act defying their fealty to Thomé Correia de Alvarenga, whom I through an official ordinance left to govern that region. They captured Thomé Correia de Alvarenga, along with the administrator of the treasury, and deeply unsettled the special magistrate by forcing him to craft various illegal documents giving powers to other residents, four of them from noble families: Jeronimo Barbalho, Jorge Ferreira, Pedro Pinheiro, and Matheus Pacheco; and another four officials, Mathias Gonsalves, Manoel Borges, Antonio Dias, and Antonio Fernandes Vallongo. All elected themselves royal ministers, among other excesses perpetrated against legitimate royal jurisdiction. I am further informed that these actions were precipitated by a few crude individuals, rooted in problems with the distribution of subsidies and taxes, an issue that the people had previously spoken on, and registered by town officials, and people elected to administer the matter. But some residents, in response to the increased tariff on cachaça, and enabled by a poorly sustained local military, have attacked and overturned ships, according to two judicial inquiries and a significant number of letters from notable people of the region (notwithstanding the many assurances of diligent care of vessels engaged in maritime trade). As I find disagreeable the notion of abandoning the services to Your Majesty that I currently hold, namely discovering mines in these southern captaincies and preparing them for exploration, I have resolved to have it publicly advertised throughout the small towns of these captaincies, starting here in São Paulo, that the aforementioned eight agents of disruption—solicitors, a sergeant, officers and ministers of the fort—are traitors to the Crown. To correct them, as they are presently unfit for the privilege and obligation of royal service, I condemn them for life to participation in the conquest of Benguela [Angola], and to whatever additional punishments Your Majesty would care to lay on them. These eight should be punished for the rest of their lives, including the loss of their property, as heads of the insurrection, and I order it in the name of Your Majesty. The common residents who simply followed their lead into mutiny should remain free from the worries of punishment. I also mandate that, as I am much occupied away from that region in royal service, it should be governed by Agostinho Barbalho Bezerra, of whose person and quality I am satisfied, notwithstanding that he has been elected by the traitors. . . .

Translated by Jerry D. Metz

French Corsairs Attack

René Duguay-Trouin and Jonas Finck

In August 1710, against the backdrop of the War of the Spanish Succession (1701–1714), the residents of Rio valiantly fought back an attack by French pirates. The captain of the thwarted raid, Jean-François Duclerc, later died in Portuguese custody. Fortunes would be reversed the following year. In the early hours of September 12, 1711, a squadron of seventeen heavily armed French ships sailed into Guanabara Bay under the command of René Duguay-Trouin (1673–1736). Around five thousand soldiers disembarked and laid siege to the city. The French corsairs encountered feeble resistance to the second attack, as much of the local population had panicked and joined the Portuguese militias in fleeing the city. A pillage ensued. Once the raiders had secured control of Rio, Duguay-Trouin opened negotiations over a ransom to free the city. Demands included stocks of gold and coinage held in local reserves as well as boxes of sugar and livestock. Ultimately, nearly all the city's wealth was depleted. To add insult, the French offered the city's merchants the opportunity to buy back the ransacked merchandise.

On October 13, 1711, Duguay-Trouin's squadron set sail for France, where he and his forces were received in triumph. The capture of Rio won Duguay-Trouin both notoriety and the post of lieutenant-general of the French navy. Meanwhile, the Portuguese governor of Rio, Francisco de Castro Morais (known by locals as "O Vaca," or "The Cow"), was roundly condemned for the heavy losses suffered on his watch. The unfortunate governor was exiled to India.

Duguay-Trouin's raid entered the historical record as one of the most lucrative hauls ever taken by corsairs, and the 1711 attack was the largest and costliest defeat of the Portuguese military in the Americas. The French commander's memoirs recounted his private and military careers, including the events of 1711 in Brazil. A letter from Duguay-Trouin to Governor Castro Morais, published in a 1732 English translation of those memoirs, appears here.

Jonas Finck, a German Protestant printmaker who happened to be aboard an English vessel anchored in Guanabara Bay during the French attack, also registered his impressions of the corsairs' sacking of Rio. An excerpt from Finck's eyewitness account, published in English translation in 1718, also appears here.

Sir,

The king my master requiring satisfaction for the cruelties exercised towards his subjects, whom you made prisoners the last year, and his majesty being informed, that after having caused the surgeons to be massacred, whom you had permitted to come on shore to dress the wounded, you have starved to death, and otherwise destroyed, those in your custody, detaining them prisoners, contrary to the cartel settled between the crowns of France and Portugal; I am ordered to make the best use of his majesty's ships and troops, to force you to submit yourself to his discretion, to give me up all the French prisoners, and to raise such a contribution upon the inhabitants of this colony, as may be sufficient to indemnify his majesty from the charges of so considerable an armament.

I have deferred this summons till I saw myself in a condition of forcing you to surrender, and of laying your City and country in ashes, if you do not yield to his majesty's discretion, who has commanded me to spare all those who shall readily submit, and repent their having offended him thro' his officers. In the meantime I hear that M. du Clerc, their commander in chief, has been assassinated: I have not as yet made any reprisal upon the Portuguese who have fallen under my power, it not being his majesty's design to carry on the war, in a manner so unworthy a most christian king: I am ready to believe you a man of too much honor to have had any concern in so shameful a deed, but that is not enough: his majesty requires you to name the authors, that they may be brought to exemplary punishment; so that if you refuse to obey his will, neither all your artillery nor all your numerous multitude shall prevent me from executing his orders, or from laying your whole country waste with fire and sword. I expect your answer; let it be speedy and decisive; or you shall know, that, if I have forewarned you hitherto, it has only been to spare myself the fearful horror of involving the innocent with the guilty.

I am, &c.

We were anchoring in Rio de Janeiro, when on the 24th of August, intelligence was brought to the Portuguese governor here that a fleet of about 15 or 16 sails was set to approach the Coast of Brazil. Some would not believe it and others were afraid that if the French should once get footing in these parts, they would then revenge to the purpose the hard usage their countrymen met with here a year ago. Where I must mention by the way, that in the action, which happened last year, the Portuguese took eight hundred prisoners from the French, together with the general that commanded them. They massacred afterwards the general in cold blood, and about half of the officers and soldiers miserably perished under the cruelty of the Portuguese. The remainder of these men we saw here in a starving condition: They expressed a great satisfaction at the arrival of an English ship, in hopes they would commiserate their hard and deplorable circumstances.

And now the Portuguese began to prepare for a defense, being afraid of a siege, which also fell out accordingly the first of September following. It was then the governor of Santa Cruz fired some guns, to give notice to the other forts of the approach of the enemy. This was attended with the French fleet itself, consisting of fifteen sails, which in an hour's time entered the mouth of the river, and two hours after, cast anchor in the best and safest place of the harbor.

The next day Admiral Trouin landed three thousand five hundred men, partly in a small island lying on one side of the town, and partly on the firm land on the other side, to fire from these two places upon the Portuguese forts, whereof there are eight in number. What relates to our ship in particular, we had no time to weigh anchor; wherefore Captain Austin ordered to cut the cables and to remove with all speed out of the reach of the enemy's cannon. This was done accordingly, and the ship was now four English miles off of the French fleet. And it was then I returned on board with Governor Collet with whom I had been in town. The day following, the governor went ashore again and retired farther up into the country, to get some intelligence of the siege the French had laid to the town. But I declined attending him again, being resolved to stay in the post which I thought Providence had assigned me, and there patiently to wait the issue of our deplorable circumstances.

Mapping the City's Defenses

João Massé

A year after the 1711 occupation of Rio by French corsairs, Portuguese king João V appointed João Massé, a French military engineer and infantry brigadier with field experience in the War of the Spanish Succession, to chart an improved defense of Portuguese America. Massé's map of a fortified Rio, completed in 1713 (reproduced here and as a color plate), has proven to be the finest visual representation of the city's layout in the early eighteenth century. It was the first map of Rio to be drawn to scale.

The primary objective of Massé's map was to lay plans for a strengthened network of military defenses. The principal security innovation for Rio was to be an urban wall, marked on the map with the letter S. Work on that wall, begun in 1718, followed a course extending from the Morro da Conceição to the Morro do Castelo. The map also projected the fortification of other key points around the city outside the wall. Undoubtedly, the most controversial proposal was the construction of a fort atop the Morro do Castelo, in the area around the chapel dedicated to Saint Sebastian, the patron saint of the city. That fort never came to be. The map includes other proposed works, such as a small fort on the Morro de Santo Antonio (T) and renovations to preexisting works on the Ilha das Cobras (V), including a footbridge linking the island to the continent. Such ambitious projects of military engineering had their drawbacks. The Campo da Ajuda (near today's Cinelândia), which received water from canals leading from the Morro do Desterro (today's Santa Teresa), was left outside the security perimeter. Another problem was that the plans projected a strip of empty land outside the wall, limiting the city government's ability to levy taxes on close-in lots. Urban development eventually spread in ways not envisioned in the original project, altering the nature of Massé's original concept. Indeed, the city quickly spread outside the walled defenses. Ironically, the defensive capabilities of the wall envisioned by Massé were never tested.

The 1713 map depicts numerous nondefensive features of the city, some realized and others merely imagined. The four waterfront warehouses and a pier that runs

Massé: *Planta da cidade de São Sebastião do Rio de Janeiro com suas fortificações.* Illustrated map by João Massé, 1713. Courtesy of Arquivo Histórico Ultramarino, Lisbon.

between the São Tiago fort and the Morro de São Bento signal the dynamics of maritime economic activities and transport in a colonial port. Also shown are the first governor's house (L), the royal storehouses (G), and the mint (H). In the nineteenth century, the mint was repurposed into the viceregal palace and then the Paço Imperial, the administrative palace of the Bragança monarchs.

The Wages of Indigenous Labor

Municipal Chamber

The administrators of colonial Rio repeatedly returned to the ambitious project of diverting the Carioca River—a waterway that flows from the Floresta da Tijuca into Guanabara Bay—toward population centers. Under Aires de Saldanha de Albuquerque Coutinho Matos e Noronha, governor of Rio captaincy between 1719 and 1725, work on an aqueduct began in earnest. By 1723, water from the river flowed into the Chafariz da Carioca, a public fountain built on the Campo de Santo Antonio (today's Largo da Carioca). The undated document here speaks to labor needs associated with bringing the Carioca to the city center. Its principal concern is not with the aqueduct proper but rather the labor of indigenous workers needed to build it.

Colonial regulations dating back to the sixteenth century restricted many types of indigenous labor, but Portuguese royal officials and private actors in Rio still managed to recruit native laborers to carry out forest-clearing, transportation, construction, food production, and defense. Indigenous men and women of working age were subject to a periodic tribute labor draft at the service of the Crown. These native laborers often worked under violent, compulsory regimes. Following a practice common for tribute laborers, the Indians recruited for the Carioca works received in-kind compensation. Around 1720, the Jesuit rector hoped instead to pay them in cash. The arrangement apparently met with resistance from the Municipal Chamber, even though the combination of food, clothing, and money was hardly unusual for productive activities administered by the Society of Jesus, an important landholder in Rio until its expulsion in 1759.

Although the document gives us a glimpse of the importance of native peoples in the workings of colonial Rio, it is difficult to discern from the missive to the king what life was like for these laborers. They are simply labeled "Indios," but the laborers' ethnic affiliation and kinship ties go unspecified. However, other evidence shows that groups of Tamoio and Tupinambá, among others, were pressed into service as paid laborers during the project to make water available to the colonial city.

The officials of the Municipal Chamber of the City of São Sebastião do Rio de Janeiro say that they are currently continuing work on bringing water from the Carioca River to the City as Your Majesty ordered that it be ascertained. This work could not be carried out without the assistance of Indians, who are the workers who usually work in those areas, and it was always customary to give them food as their daily payment, such as in the work projects of the aforementioned Municipal Chamber as well as private farms, and at the end of the month to give them so many *varas* of cotton; and because now the Reverend Father Rector of the Company [of Jesus] of the aforementioned City wishes to alter this ancient custom by giving the said Indians four *vintens* each day, about which we make this plea to Your Majesty and to the aforementioned Father Rector that Your Majesty not agree. Otherwise all of the income of the small subsidy budgeted for this said work project will not be sufficient for these aforementioned Indians' wages, because there are many of them who work on this said project, and the food alone that would be given to them comes at a considerable expense, and for this reason we request that Your Majesty not alter the form of payment of the said Indians heretofore observed.

Begging for your mercy.

André Soares de Souza

Translated by Amy Chazkel

The Customary Rights of Market Women

Quitandeiras of Rio de Janeiro and Carlos Julião

The socioeconomic power of female street vendors called quitandeiras *signaled the importance of the food trade in the urban economy of colonial Rio. The persistent threat of food shortages focused a great deal of official attention on these figures who provisioned hungry city households. Street vending, moreover, was especially important to black women who found steady employment and political status in supplying daily necessities.*

*As the Portuguese Crown attempted to impose greater order on the colonies in the second half of the eighteenth century, the urban food trade fell under new regulations. The documents here register the reaction of a group of quitandeiras to new rules on the sale of food near the municipal chambers, located beside the Arcos do Teles (on today's Praça XV de Novembro). Facing a move to force vendors out of spots where they had long sold basic foodstuffs to consumers, the market women appeal to the municipal council, called the Senado da Câmara, to restore their customary rights of vending. A public attorney (*procurador*) writing on their behalf added the language of "public good," fairness, and consistency of rule. The petition and the reaction from municipal officials give us a view onto the provision of basic foodstuffs, the regulation and welfare of the laboring poor, and the perpetual contest over the use of the city's public spaces.*

The image here offers a different perspective on the market women of colonial Rio. Executed by Carlos Julião (c. 1740–1811), an Italian-born military engineer who made a series of drawings and watercolors during a long residence in Portuguese America (including travels through the captaincy of Rio de Janeiro), the watercolor presents two black women in the middle of their work day. Both are peddlers; one also works as a caregiver to a young white charge. The absence of footwear in one figure makes the strong association with enslavement. The image provides clues to certain dimensions of quitandeiras' lives above and beyond their labors; small pouches, called bolsas de mandinga, *dangling from a sash contain substances used for protection, pointing to the world of these women's spirituality. Typical of eighteenth-century genre scenes of the colonial Americas, Julião's images displayed ordinary and exotic aspects of quotidian life: sugarcane, local styles of dress, body markings, guinea fowl, and slaves. Such images of African-descended vendors form part of a long tradition of representing the "uses and customs" of Rio for local and global audiences.*

The Senado da Câmara Lets It Be Known
Hearing the Attorney General of the same Chamber
Rio de Janeiro
May 29, 1776

Most Illustrious and Excellent Sir:
     The quitandeiras say that they have always enjoyed the practice of occupying the area in front of the Chamber facing the Sea for selling their goods, and also in the area of the stalls where they sell fish, without causing any problems for access to the streets; and that they usually get an annual license from the municipal chamber and duly pay the fee, as the same recording clerk and Treasurer of the municipal chamber can attest; however, the Most Honorable Sir Circuit Judge summarily sent them away from their customary places, whose order the Chamber President is now contemplating, the members of the Chamber affirmed, prosecuting those who do not comply: and as the Supplicants, confirmed as stated, have already paid the fee to use this land [*afforamento do chão*] for them to sell on the aforementioned site, and this expulsion has brought them grave harm, which will become even greater from now on because they do not have another place more suitable, according to what the same Municipal Chamber has also affirmed.

     Therefore

     Your Excellency is requested to order that they not be barred from selling in that area from which they are being expelled owing to the great inconvenience to buyers, and the very notable harm to the Supplicants.

     May You Receive Mercy

In light of the information that the Attorney General of this Municipal Chamber to which Your Honors refer, I must say to you that I feel that Your Honors have to make a decision about the order to evict the

Vendedoras. Painting by Carlos Julião. Watercolor on paper. From *Riscos illuminados de figurinhos de brancos e negros dos uzos do Rio de Janeiro e Serro do Frio* (Rio de Janeiro: Biblioteca Nacional, 1960), plate 31. Courtesy of Fundação Biblioteca Nacional, Rio de Janeiro.

Quitandeiras from the place where the said Chamber placed them to sell their goods, and for which they pay the annual fee, for which Your Honor referred this case to me, without having indicated why; along the lines that the case should not be allowed to advance in the absence of instructions from a higher authority, it would be indecorous for the same Chamber [illegible] to alter what it had been willing to do before; because everything is determined for the benefit of the common good, that private utility must prevail; in conforming with this, Your Mercy should allow the Quitandeiras to return right away to their place from which they have been evicted. . . .

Rio de Janeiro
June 11, 1776

Honorable Judge, President, and the other officers of the Chamber of
this City

Antonio Nascentes Pinto
Ignasio da Fonseca Lima
João Antonio M. Lima

Translated by Amy Chazkel

Valongo, a Notorious Slave Market

Bráz Hermenegildo do Amaral and Jean-Baptiste Debret

Physician, educator, and politician Bráz Hermenegildo do Amaral (1861–1949) was an accomplished intellectual whose best-known writings dealt with the political history of his home state, Bahia. An avid practitioner of archival research, Amaral also pioneered ethnography and the anthropology of race, two fields of inquiry that tied closely together the intelligentsia of Salvador and Rio at the turn of the twentieth century. In 1922, Amaral presented findings on "tribus importadas," that is, African ethnic groups imported into Brazil during the slave trade. The research into African life in Portuguese America looked at slave markets, those dreadful places where enslaved Africans were sold into Brazilian society. In the excerpts here, Amaral described the dismal state of health among freshly landed Africans in Salvador and Rio, Brazil's two largest slave ports. Through the use of direct quotations from a 1779 viceregal report authored by the Marquês do Lavradio, Amaral also outlined measures taken by colonial authorities to regulate the treatment of slaves, largely on the grounds of protecting the health and social order of nonslaves.

Under orders from Lavradio (Luís de Almeida Portugal Soares, 1729–1790), the housing and sale of newly arrived slaves in Rio was moved from Rua Direita (today's Rua Primeiro de Março) to Valongo, a semirural area between Conceição and Saúde hills. Slave burials were also relocated from the Largo de Santa Rita to Valongo. The subsequent construction of wharves at Valongo facilitated disembarkations and transfers to the various slave markets that surrounded the Largo do Depósito, a square now known as Praça dos Estivadores. French history painter Jean-Baptiste Debret was one of numerous foreigners to register the grim conditions at Valongo, a place synonymous with slave trafficking until the early 1830s, when disembarkations of new arrivals from Africa were outlawed.

Although the Valongo region has been reurbanized on several occasions, its history of human trafficking is strongly felt in the archaeological remains of an abandoned cemetery located off Rua Pedro Ernesto (formerly the Rua do Cemitério), where slaves who died before sale were unceremoniously buried along with household waste and other debris. Estimates on the number of human remains range between six thousand and twenty thousand, mainly West Central Africans. The

number of bones from children and adolescents is disproportionately high relative to
overall slave imports, suggesting the steep mortality of the young in the odious trade.

The business of slave trafficking concentrated in the capital cities of Pernambuco and Bahia, as well as Rio de Janeiro. Some slaves arrived based upon prior orders. Others were sent there to be sold in lots. Still others were sold one by one.

According to the information now available to us, as well as in the documentary record, we learn the following: according to a letter from the Conde da Cunha and a petition submitted by José Maria dos Santos Lopes, Africans were unloaded at the wharves and led to storehouses, where they remained for the inspection of buyers.

During the day the slaves were made to go outside these storehouses to be exhibited for sale, as is done today with cattle.

Interested buyers could browse at their leisure through that human herd.

Yet is it curious to observe that no special locale or structure had been set aside for the market of human flesh. Nor do we find evidence that slaves were sorted by categories, as the ancients of Greece, Rome, and Asia did.

In the eighteenth century the slave cargoes, once unloaded, were thought to be the cause of the transmission of highly contagious disease.

In Rio de Janeiro, the Marquês do Lavradio, viceroy, wrote in 1779:

> There was in this city the terrible custom that every negro who arrived at the ports from the Coast of Africa, immediately after disembarking, come into the city, through the public streets and main thoroughfares, not only full of infinite maladies, but naked, and with that quality of folks who have no learning, the same that any other brute savage in the middle of the street sitting on some planks there laid out doing whatever nature impelled, causing not only the greatest stench in the said streets and its surroundings, but being also the most horrible spectacle the eyes could see. . . . This unruliness, which was known to all, was assiduously avoided and it demanded constant resolve on my part for it to be properly regulated.
>
> It was determined by my resolution that every slave arriving in these disembarkations immediately after clearing customs should be sent in the direction of the ranch called Valongo, in the city's suburbs, removed from all communication; that there they would make use of the many homes and storehouses that are there to be used; and that those ranches

Loge [sic] na Rua do Valongo. Painting by Jean-Baptiste Debret, c. 1820–1830. Watercolor on paper, 17.5 × 26.2 cm. Courtesy of Museus Castro Maya, Rio de Janeiro.

belong to interested buyers, and that the buyers could never enter the city between four and five at which time the slaves were to be dressed; that until the slaves were led to the mining district, or to the country farms after being purchased, they be kept at the Campo de São Domingos, where there are to be appropriate accommodations, freeing the city of the nuisance and damage which for so many years it has suffered due to the aforementioned unruliness. I watched very closely the execution of this working order and, though not without considerable work, was able to see it fulfilled.

Some years later, in Bahia, Luiz Vilhena, author of *Notícias Soteropolitanas e Brasílicas* wrote, in 1800:

"Another blight on health in Bahia are the more than twenty embarkations which every year enter this Port, coming from the Coast of Africa, carrying negroes infected with scurvy, smallpox, measles, yaws, syphilis, scabies, etc. and, finally, with Plague, which is to be believed."

And José Maria dos Santos Lopes, businessman from Bahia, in a petition made in 1806, exposes the need for a house reserved for the collection of slaves (which he proposed and offered), where each head would pay 600 réis, "in order to stop the spread of diseases that these people brought, as they were traded, deposited in storehouses or in other houses, always in the same manner, at night while during the day they remained exposed for sale."

There is little doubt to the veracity of Lavradio's comments on the slaves' dress. They were far from lavish, as the masters opted to economize.

Translated by Andre Pagliarini

Fire and Reconstruction of
an Asylum for Women

João Francisco Muzzi

Antônio do Desterro (1693–1773), sixth bishop of colonial Rio, inaugurated an asylum for women, called the Recolhimento do Parto, in 1759. The construction phase of the austere three-story structure that stood alongside the Nossa Senhora do Parto church (f. 1653) had taken nearly seventeen years. For a half century after the bishop's inaugural blessings, the building housed women without male protectors. Unmarried mothers, adulterous wives, and rebellious daughters were well represented in an institution for women committed to a life of penance and modesty. While some residents, such as widows, came to the Recolhimento by choice, others were compelled by husbands and fathers to live in a regime of forced seclusion. Nineteenth-century memorialist Joaquim Manuel de Macedo (1820–1882) characterized the institution as a women's detention facility whose name could be invoked by the irascible husband seeking to discipline a disobedient wife.

On the night of August 23, 1789, the Recolhimento was severely damaged by fire. The dramatic efforts to rescue the women residing in the asylum, as well as furnishings and religious objects, were captured in an oil painting by João Francisco Muzzi (?–1802), an Italian-born artist who had settled in the capital of Portuguese America. Four months after the fire, Muzzi painted a companion piece to celebrate the building's reconstruction. The two canvases follow the language of the ex-voto, a Catholic devotional object offered in thanks for heavenly intervention that often depicts the person, body part, or possession that is the beneficiary of divine grace. The Muzzi paintings also capture the masculinist logic that animated the Recolhimento itself. That is, in the first painting, men bravely rally to put down the flames, whereas the terrorized female penitents and their black servants flee. In the second painting, as the asylum is in the midst of rapid reconstruction, the women are entirely absent as Viceroy Luis de Vasconcellos (center right, in red frock) receives architectural drawings from the mulatto architect Mestre Valentim (c. 1745–1813), who bows before various dignitaries.

Both the Recolhimento and the adjoining Nossa Senhora do Parto church were

Fatal e rápido incêndio que reduziu a cinzas em 23 de agosto de 1789 a igreja, suas imagens e todo o antigo Recolhimento de Nossa Senhora do Parto, salvando-se unicamente ilesa dentre as chamas a milagrosa imagem de Nossa Senhora. Painting by João Francisco Muzzi, 1789. Oil on canvas, 113 × 138 cm. Courtesy of Museus Castro Maya-Chácara do Céu, Rio de Janeiro.

Feliz e pronta reedificação da igreja do antigo Recolhimento de Nossa Senhora do Parto, começada no dia 25 de agosto de 1789 e concluída em 8 de dezembro do mesmo ano. Painting by João Francisco Muzzi, 1789. Oil on canvas, 113 × 138 cm. Courtesy of Museus Castro Maya-Chácara do Céu, Rio de Janeiro.

demolished in various urban reforms of the nineteenth and twentieth centuries, but the memory of these adjoining structures, so closely associated with spiritual lives and social strictures for women in colonial Rio, remains in the modern-day Igreja de Nossa Senhora do Parto, a downtown church located near the intersection of Rua Rodrigo Silva and Rua da Assembléia.

Whaling in Guanabara Bay

Leandro Joaquim

From the seventeenth century, royal contracts regulated whaling on the northern coastline of Portuguese America. As whale hunting became one of the colony's important commercial ventures in the eighteenth century, the system of royal monopolies extended southward to include Guanabara Bay. The bay was an excellent site for the whaling industry, as its waters afforded ample room for the processing of the captured sea mammals. Moreover, local demand for whale products was high. The spermaceti extracted from the whale's head went into the candles, detergents, amalgam, emollient, and cosmetics used by the residents of Rio and their trading partners in the hinterland. Whale by-products found their way into the mortar used in building construction. Above all, whales yielded the "fish oil" (azeite de baleia) used in public illumination, first installed in the late eighteenth century.

Around the time that whale-oil lamps first appeared in Rio, Viceroy Luis de Vasconcellos e Souza (1779–1790) commissioned local artist Leandro Joaquim (c. 1738–c. 1798) to paint a series of canvases to adorn the pavilions at the Passeio Público, a pleasure garden. One such scene painted by Joaquim was a whale hunt in Guanabara Bay. The action centers on the various phases of the hunt from the chase to the kill and the work of dragging the harpooned animal to shore for processing. The sails of the whaling vessels, curved and full of wind, imply vigor as the hunters hurry in pursuit of their prey. The artist may have exaggerated the density of whales and boats in the bay by collapsing sequential actions into one frame, but the vivid depiction of whaling activities would have been familiar to residents of late colonial Rio.

The Joaquim seascape also depicts the built environment of a thriving port. In the foreground appears the fort on the Ilha de Villegagnon. The cluster of buildings at the top left is an armação (whaling station) named São Domingos, located in what is today's Niterói. Like others built along the coast of Brazil, from Bahia to Santa Catarina, the armação at São Domingos was an engine for urbanization and protocapitalism in colonial Rio.

Pesca da Baleia na Baia de Guanabara. Painting by Leandro Joaquim, 1790. Oil on canvas, 83 × 113 cm.

Lettered Men under Investigation

Conde de Resende and José Bernardo da Silveira Frade

Viceregal Rio was located far from the Portuguese empire's official institutions of learning and printmaking, but a certain level of royal support and institutional protections was extended to lettered men who took an interest in the study of the natural sciences, religion, and political philosophy. Such relations soured in 1794, when Viceroy José Luiz de Castro (the Conde de Resende) reacted sharply to accusations leveled against Manoel Inácio Silva Alvarenga (1749–1814), a mulatto poet originally from Minas Gerais and educated in canon law at Coimbra who taught rhetoric. According to his accusers, Silva Alvarenga played host to the suspicious activities of a learned society that met at his residence on the Rua do Cano (today's Sete de Setembro).

José Bernardo da Silveira Frade, a lawyer who had disputed with Silva Alvarenga, and Raimundo Penafiel, a priest motivated by a defense of the Catholic Church, implicated Silva Alvarenga in trading in tracts critical of the Crown, the Church, and social hierarchy. Suspicions circulated that Silva Alvarenga and associates of the Sociedade Literária do Rio de Janeiro (an association of lettered men founded in June 1786 as a continuation of the Academia Científica do Rio de Janeiro formed seven years prior) had fallen under the influence of revolutionary France. The viceroy ordered detentions and an investigation. The imprisoned men were held in the Forte da Conceição. Of the ten accused, four belonged to the Sociedade Literária. Silva Alvarenga was interrogated on numerous occasions, but in sharp contrast to the death sentence given to Joaquim José da Silva Xavier (1746–1782), the figure better known as Tiradentes who had been executed for organizing an antiregalist sedition in Minas Gerais in 1791, no harsh punishments were meted out when the inquest in Rio concluded.

The first document here communicates the viceroy's instructions to High Judge Antônio Diniz da Cruz e Silva to initiate an inquest (devassa) that included the seizure of various papers and books owned by Silva Alvarenga and his associates. The second document registers Silveira Frade's accusations against the Society. Elsewhere in the investigation records, one finds rich documentation about a world of ideas and print in a colonial city, as well as the social interactions of master trades-

men (e.g., a shoemaker, a cabinetmaker, goldsmiths) with the accused. Historians of
the so-called Inconfidência do Rio de Janeiro (Conspiracy of Rio de Janeiro) catch a
captivating glimpse of the lettered social milieu of the late-colonial city.

Conde de Resende to Antônio Diniz da Cruz e Silva

It has come to my attention that a number of people in a city characterized
by love and loyalty for our most fair and just sovereigns dare to dispute
matters related to the governments of the states not just in private homes
but also in the city's public spaces. Given the current turmoil in Europe,
these figures take leave of their senses and dishonor their good Portuguese
names. Some have even scandalously averred that kings may be unnecessary; that men are free and can, at any time, demand their liberty; that the
laws that now govern the nation of the French are just, and that the same
laws might be brought to this continent; that the French should come to
conquer this city; that the Holy Scripture, just as it grants kings the right to
punish their vassals, also grants the right of vassals to punish their kings.
These propositions, and others of similar nature involving religion, do not
merely reveal the lack of faith of those who utter them; they also deceive
and seduce the crude and unlearned people, pushing them away from the
love and fealty they owe their natural and legitimate sovereign. Even if the
utterance of these ideas leads not to the damned results they seek, at all
times, and especially at present, they can produce very dangerous consequences and should be cut short. It seemed appropriate for me to recommend to Your Excellency, as I do in this report, to proceed immediately to
an exact accounting or inquest that will serve as the *corpus delicti*, adjudi-
cating through interviews with any number of appropriate witnesses, matters related to the above infractions. I shall receive a detailed report of its
findings so that I may take measures in accordance with my service to Her
Highness [Maria I of Portugal], to whom I remit a copy of this resolution. I
nominate as scrivener for the account or inquest the civil court judge João
Manoel Guerreiro de Amorim Pereira, trusting that in such a delicate and
weighty matter he will act with the care and zeal incumbent upon him in
the position that he occupies.

May God protect Your Excellency

Conde de Resende

Rio, June 11, 1794

Statement by José Bernardo da Silveira Frade

On December eighteenth in the year seventeen ninety-four in this city of São Sebastião do Rio de Janeiro, at the residence of judge Antônio Diniz da Cruz e Silva, I, the scrivener charged with registering this deposition, record the testimony of the witnesses named herein, summoned by the judge to testify in this hearing. I, João Manoel Guerreiro de Amorim Pereira, scribe, named to prepare this deposition, note as follows:

José Bernardo da Silveira Frade, between thirty-six and thirty-seven years of age, originally from Arraial de Raposos in the township of Sabará [Minas Gerais], now residing in Rio, is an occasional lawyer in this city, married, making his living from litigating cases now and then.

The magistrate officiated the oath on the Holy Bible upon which the witness swore to tell the truth as he knew it and as questioned. Asked about the subject of this inquest and related matters, he stated that the home of Manoel Ignacio da Silva Alvarenga, Professor of Rhetoric, functioned as a kind of academy, and that, despite this being proscribed by the Most Illustrious and Most Excellent Viceroy of Brazil, the said Manoel Ignacio de Silva Alvarenga continued to organize private seminars in his home. They were attended by a *bacharel* [degree holder] named Mariano, last name unknown, the physician Jacinto, and a professor of Greek named João Marques. Other times the seminars also included Estolano so-and-so, a primary school teacher named Manoel Ferreira, and a doctor named Vicente Gomes.

The witness testified that the participants often discussed France and its revolution in laudatory terms, attacking Religion and claiming the Bible was untruthful when it said Moses melted the Golden Calf and forced his followers to drink it upon descending from the mountain. To the latter, the witness responded that Moses did not melt the Calf but instead ground it into powder, in keeping with the words of Scripture—*cum trivit usque ad pulverem.* On that same occasion, they mocked God's justice, questioning His slaughter of thousands of men for worshiping the Golden Calf. João Marques, the professor of Greek, had ironically exclaimed "behold, such justice." They denounced the Scripture as false, claiming that the dynasties of China, reaching their height well before the time of Creation as stated in Scripture, belied the Bible's veracity.

The witness also testified that various papers were read at one such secret meeting, and while he could not say if they were merely gazettes, he could attest that they were written on loose sheets of paper in French and dealt with the French Revolution and its liberty, inspiring the same speakers to make tendentious and hateful remarks about Monarchy, revealing a great passion against that form of government and strong support for republicanism, praising the happiness enjoyed by people living under that form of government. To this the witness retorted that the liberty enjoyed under republican governments does not align with the customs of our nation, habituated to obedience to a single sovereign who is the father of the nation, loving his subjects like his own children. Manoel Ignacio responded ironically: "Your Grace speaks in maxims. There is much prudence in speaking thusly." The witness assured his listeners that he spoke only the truth, at which point they attacked him, to then praise liberty, reading articles of rights and the newly established laws in France, and criticizing the government and actions of Our Lord the Prince Regent. They said that in the absence of a Frenchman the Prince had been at the mercy of a friar's direction, and so full of fanaticism that he ordered water from the River Jordan brought to her Highness the Princess and asked the Archbishop of Braga to report on his actions to a friar whose name escaped the witness but who might have been called Friar Gaspar.

The preceding statements against the august personage of His Highness, the Prince, according to the witness, were made by João Marques, the professor of Greek, but the other attendees supported him and even added that the Prince had banished a few young men to India only because some friars had complained about them. João Marques then exclaimed that a king could do as he saw fit with no objections which should not be the case since He ought to be held accountable for unjust actions.

Gregorio José Bitancur elsewhere revealed that one night on the wharf the aforementioned João Marques began expounding on and praising liberty, which Bento Sanches (who today is in São Paulo) opposes. Bitancur silenced Sanches by convincing him—in the same way that the previously named Manoel Ignacio, João Marques, and Mariano, had, as Gregorio José told the witness—that the culprits in the Minas uprising were condemned as insurrectionists because they failed, whereas if they had succeeded they would be called heroes.

He also attested that he had heard it said to Domingos Gomes Rodrigues that the physician Jacinto and the bacharel José de França had publicly spoken against religion at the door of the Igreja do Hospício, purporting that there are no such things as miracles and that saints have no power to perform them. The day after the arrest of Manoel Ignacio, João Marques, Manoel, and the doctor Jacinto various people came to the witness's house, including Manoel Antonio Salgado, Domingos Gomes Rodrigues, and the aforementioned Gregorio José Bitancur, all of whom spoke against the defendants. They pointed out the impunity with which the culprits had spoken at their gatherings, giving thanks to God and praise to the Most

Illustrious and Most Excellent Viceroy of this State for having them jailed since they would otherwise delude a great number of people and would bring about much suffering. Others said that if the French Armada were to descend upon this city the defendants would be against us and would rush to deliver us all to the invaders. Gregorio José Bitancur said that a certain person he would not name told him a few of the culprits claimed that in the coming years there would be no more heads with crowns upon them.

A retired lieutenant named Jacinto Martins Pamplona also told the witness that the professor of Greek João Marques had spoken out against our illustrious Monarchs such that he thought the defendant deluded with an excessively loose tongue and that on another occasion he had heard vague rumors that the culprits had been meeting to discuss French matters at the home of the lawyer José de França and at an apothecary shop on Rua Direita where a balding man named José lives along with a man named Antonio Joaquim, a scrivener for the lawyer Silvestre de Carvalho. In these conversations José Teixeira, commonly called the bailiff of the church, would counter the opinions of the defendants.

Despite all he has already recounted, however, the witness does not know of any insurrectionist plans formulated by the defendants or their adherents to incite a rebellion. Furthermore, neither the doctor Vicente Gomes, Estolano, nor the primary teacher Manoel Ferreira were present at those meetings even though some of them held the same beliefs and attended the same seminars as the defendants. The retired lieutenant Jacinto Martins Pamplona added that on the day after the arrests, an apothecary named Luiz José who lives in the countryside told him that he had heard the defendants state publicly that the arrival of the French naval fleet in this city would be just as well since the people here are so foolish as to subject themselves to the rule of a single man, in marked contrast to the superior arrangement in France. He recalled Gregorio José Bitancur being told that João Martins, who owned a warehouse on Rua do Rosário, had once remarked to José Carvalho on a certain occasion at the Igreja do Hospicio when they found themselves in the midst of the culprits currently under arrest: "Let us remove ourselves from here since these men speak too openly and are sure to be penalized somehow."

The witness had no more to add and signed his name after having his testimony read back to him and finding it in agreement with his statement. I, João Manoel Guerreiro de Amorim Pereira, with the aforementioned judge, the scribe nominated to write this inquest, made this note.

Silva

Translated by Andre Pagliarini

Cultivating Cinnamon in Late Colonial Rio

Bernardino António Gomes

*In 1798, Portuguese botanist Bernardino António Gomes (1768–1823) wrote a memória (treatise) on the cultivation of cinnamon in Rio. Drafted during the viceregal tenure of Luís de Vasconcelos e Sousa (1742–1809), a colonial administrator who took an interest in the natural history of Portuguese America, Gomes's treatise identified the location and qualities of a number of mature cinnamon trees that grew in the environs of Guanabara Bay. Animated by the prospects of stimulating the local propagation and improvement of a spice that had brought great wealth to French, Dutch, and British traders, Gomes described the topographic, hydrologic, and climatic conditions most favorable to cinnamon cultivation. Gomes's chief point of comparison was Ceylon (contemporary Sri Lanka), an early Portuguese colony where true cinnamon (*Cinnamomum verum*) trees flourished. Mapping local and global spaces of cultivated aromatics, medicinals, and culinary spices, the Gomes treatise also describes the social uses of the exotic tree, including its incorporation into a raucous pre-Lenten festival known as* entrudo.*

In the excerpts here, we see the deepening relationships between natural history and commercial enterprise in Rio at the turn of the nineteenth century. We also see Rio's place on a global spice road that wended through a city rapidly transitioning from a print-poor colonial place with tightly regulated trade into a bustling Atlantic port marked by expanding relations of production and exchange, commercial and scientific innovation, and the printed word. Finally, we have access to a text that circulated in print at the same time Prince Regent João put into action the establishment of a royal botanical garden in Rio.

On the Existence of the Indian Cinnamon Tree in Rio de Janeiro

In Bahia, I came upon a handful of cinnamon trees, and I was assured that there were others; around Rio, there are many, perhaps in excess of one hundred within a distance of three leagues from this City. That is, even before accounting for the newest and wise measures that the viceroy has taken to stimulate the production of the valuable tree.

Judging from the thickness of the trunks and the number and size of the branches, almost all of the mature trees—apparently planted without much forethought, and subsequently neglected—appear to be quite old. Many without doubt date from the time of the Jesuits [prior to 1759], who popular opinion believes to have introduced the tree in Brazil. Be that as it may, it is certain that cinnamon is an exotic introduction to Rio, as one finds it solely in cultivated areas.

On the Usefulness of the Rio Cinnamon Tree

In this fortunate land where, like so many other places, the locals lack knowledge of Nature's liberal bounties, only the leaves of the cinnamon tree have any use; they are prepared as an aromatic water, without much utility other than for throwing wax balls during entrudo.

On the Climate of Rio de Janeiro with Respect to Cinnamon Cultivation

The discussion of this topic demands some comparison between the climate of Ceylon, where the tree is well known, and the climate of Rio. . . . The Cinnamon Fields [of western Ceylon] is where one finds the types most valuable in Commerce, and I will make my comparisons to that region, extending from the southern Coast and the western side of the island from Negombo to Gallieres. . . . Aside from the proximity to the Equator, it is noted that the entire island is mountainous, offering some protection to Cinnamon Fields. These circumstances lead us to believe that the Climate where the trees produce the best cinnamon in the world is quite hot.

If we note that Rio de Janeiro is situated at a latitude of twenty-three degrees south, we are forced to acknowledge that a plant native to Negombo, located just seven degrees from the Equatorial Line, shall degenerate should it be planted sixteen degrees closer to the Pole, as has been the case for trees transplanted in Rio. Nevertheless, the apparent great difference in climate resulting from the difference in latitude has been mitigated by the configuration of the local lands. Anyone who casts his eyes toward the horizon will note the hilly ranges that rise above the clouds; the resulting lowlands are formed by an immense bay serving as the port of the City; other low-lying areas are punctuated by hills of varying heights. Protected from the wind, a land of this type should be hot, much more than to be expected for the latitude, perhaps even exceeding some parts of Ceylon. . . .

Thus we have an average air temperature that is more equilibrated and uniform than most anywhere else on the globe, especially in the season called winter, or April to September, a time of little rain, when the thermometer rarely varies more than three degrees on the Réaumur scale, hovering at an average of sixteen degrees [68°F or 20°C]. In the summer, there is often no breeze; the resulting heat is intense; the regular evening thunderstorms come with much force, clearing away the stagnation and bringing rains that cool and cleanse the air. . . .

In a climate such as this, the cinnamon tree should flourish, as one observes; yet it is my belief that achieving a cinnamon of the quality of Ceylon might require an even hotter climate, as I believe it to be on that Island. When the heat works to the benefit of the essential oils in aromatic plants we come to understand the recent discoveries in Chemistry and Botanical Physiology, and we know such benefits in our daily lives.

Just observe how the most fragrant trees, such as cinnamon, India cloves, *pau-cravo* [a clove substitute also known as *cravo-do-Maranhão*], nutmeg, etc., are native to the hottest lands; in Europe, aromatic plants, including thyme, rosemary, and lavender are all native to the southern climes. . . . All this leads us to consider that one of the measures to benefit cinnamon cultivation here is to open up planting in the warmest regions and well-protected places, such as valleys that are neither overly wet nor shady; this way, the harvests will be so fruitful that better results are solely to be had in lands closest to the Equator, such as [the Portuguese colonies of] Maranhão, the islands of Principe and São Tomé, etc. . . .

On the Soil of Rio de Janeiro with Respect to Cinnamon Cultivation

We dwell on the comparisons to be made between local soils and Ceylon, or better put, the Cinnamon Fields where, we are told, sandy soils run along the southern and western Coasts of the Island. Here in Rio, the soil contains much clay. The hills are nearly all clay: a quality that makes them inferior for cinnamon cultivation. This may help explain the generally declined state of the older trees. . . .

All aromatic plants, especially those in lands with hot climates, require soils of moderate moisture, with sun exposure necessary to develop coloring and aromatic agents. In shade, or with abundant moisture, the plants grow larger, as they are swollen with sap, but it is a watery liquid that impedes the secretion of aromatic oils, for which rays of the sun are required. It should not be strange then that the flavor and scent of cinnamon found in Rio is weak, and dissipates easily upon extraction, as the essential oil in which such qualities reside and the conditions in which the cinnamon trees are to be found are imperfect, making the trees less fragrant and of fleeting aroma. Such assertions can be proven decisively when we observe the cinnamon trees found in wet places surrounded by trees, such as the small farm of Radamacker [Daniel Radmaker, a Dutch merchant] in Andarahy [modern-day Tijuca], when the trees are of a dark green color, and the cinnamon bark very pallid. In contrast, the plots owned by Dona Emerenci-anna [Emerencianna Isabel Dantas e Castro, widow of Antonio de Aguiar e Castro] in Campo Santa Anna [today's Praça da República], and the record-ing clerk of the Comarca de Carahy [Icaraí, in today's Niterói] where cin-namon trees grow in a drier soil, with greater sun exposure, whose leaves are of a lighter green and the bark more reddish; that flavor of the leaves collected in Andarahy grew weak in just three days, but the leaves collected in Carahy lasted eight. On the plots of the deceased João Opman [João Hop-man, a British transplant who pioneered coffee cultivation] in Mataporcos [today's Estácio], whose lands are sandy and exposed to the sun, I obtained two pieces of bark from a cultivated cinnamon tree that had been collected four years prior; the bark remained red in color, and had a sweet flavor, with a lingering fragrance, though much weaker, I shall confess, than any cin-namon from India.

Translated by Daryle Williams

Eagerly Awaiting the Royal Family

Padre Perereca

Luiz Gonçalves dos Santos (1767–1844), better known as Father Perereca, was born in Rio shortly after the city's elevation to the seat of viceregal authority. Son of a failed Portuguese silversmith who had married a Brazilian woman, Gonçalves dos Santos was educated in the classical subjects of eighteenth-century learning: philosophy, ancient languages, and the Catholic religion. He studied rhetoric, poetry, and geography under Manuel Inácio da Silva Alvarenga, a principal figure of the so-called Inconfidência do Rio de Janeiro. Ordained in 1794 and eventually taking on the posts of presbyter of the São Pedro brotherhood and canon of the Imperial Chapel, the short-statured Gonçalves dos Santos was devoted to a favorable reading of Brazil's progress from colony to united kingdom to independent empire. Rio played a starring role in that story of progress.

Perereca was eyewitness to and propagandist of many of the key moments that surrounded the transfer of the Bragança court from Lisbon to Rio, including the numerous social, political, and physical changes that took place in the royals' new Brazilian home. In 1825, the year prior to the death of João VI, Perereca published in Lisbon a three-volume patriotic memoir that doubled as a history of Brazil and a monument to João's enlightened rule. (This devotion to King João, then back in Portugal after his extended Brazilian residence, prompted charges that Perereca was suspect in his commitments to the Brazilian separatist cause.)

The excerpts here recount the two-month period of surprise, anxiety, and expectant joy as the residents of Rio learned of the French invasion of Portugal, the hurried escape of the royal family, and a chaotic transatlantic passage that separated João (prince regent until his mother's death in 1816) from some of the royals, including his aunt Maria Benedicta, the dowager princess of Brazil. Concluding with the arrival of the ship carrying João, the passages offer wonderful descriptive detail of the charged atmosphere of early March 1808, when public and private buildings were cleared out to accommodate the royals. The description of the extended nighttime illumination is especially evocative of the exceptional measures taken to receive the prince.

(1) When His Excellency the Conde dos Arcos, D. Marcos de Noronha e Britto, viceroy of Brazil, received orders from the royal court to take measures in this city of São Sebastião do Rio de Janeiro, capital of Portuguese America, to repel any enemy invasion, he acted with his customary zeal, courage, and prudence. Some assumed the invaders would be English and others believed they would be French, but everyone's spirits ran between fear and apprehension for the fate of an imperiled Portugal. The Emperor Napoleon demanded that His Highness the Prince Regent sever ties with the English, close ports to them, and expel them all from his dominion. We were no less fearful for our own safety, since it remained quite possible that one of the belligerents, subject to the Court's course of action, could declare itself an enemy of the Portuguese and attempt to invade some of the coastal provinces of Brazil, a place with an extensive coastline with many ports and easily accessible inlets to facilitate disembarkation. We feared the English the most, with their overwhelming naval superiority and knowledge of our waters and coasts. So it was that on January 14, 1808, the warship *Voador*, commanded by Frigate Captain Francisco Maximiliano de Sousa, arrived in the port of Rio de Janeiro with the foreboding news that the French had, along with the Spanish, crossed the border into the Kingdom of Portugal under the pretense of offering friendly protection against the English but in reality marching with hostile and perfidious intent against the venerable figure of His Highness the Prince Regent. Happily, having been sufficiently forewarned, His Highness had embarked the entire royal family, along with a large number of his court and many others of various orders who wished to join Him, and left from the port of Lisbon on November 29, 1807, with Rio de Janeiro as the final destination. The fleet that escorted the sovereign and the royal family to Brazil was to arrive quickly so that His Highness might establish his court in this city until peace has been restored.

(2) Never has any announcement brought such tragic yet flattering news! I cannot explain the fright, consternation, and emotion we have all felt for the travails of the Mother Country. Tears streamed from the eyes of everyone and many were unable to utter even a single word upon hearing of such an unfortunate development. Some thought of their parents, relatives, and friends; others thought of their children, their interests, their commerce, all of which they judged to be lost. In short, all lamented the distress that befell our nation and feared for a terrible future of strife. This general consternation, however, was

mitigated by the happiness everyone felt for the safety of His Highness and the royal family as well as for the stroke of luck by which we might soon lay eyes upon our beloved prince. We were further pleased that it should be our city, above any other in his dominions, that His Highness would choose as the seat of his court in Brazil. If the causes for sorrow and worry are great, so too are the causes of solace and joy. A new order of things was to begin in this part of the southern hemisphere. The Empire of Brazil was before us, and we waited with bated breath for His Highness the Prince Regent to cast the first stone of the new empire's future greatness, prosperity, and power.

(3) And so a more pleasant outlook came to replace the preceding one. Military preparations were exchanged for festive adornments, the fears and worries replaced by tranquility and joy, the horrors of war by the comforts of peace. In short, the spirits of everyone were concerned only with the merciful and venerated Prince of the Universe. He was the subject of every conversation; every mouth spoke eloquently in praise. Our hearts burned with desire to see Him. Hours felt like days to us, and the days like months. We thanked Divine Providence that, while trying us with so many misfortunes, dried our tears and filled our hearts with hope, which brought so much good out of so much adversity. The French occupation of Portugal was certainly a lamentable disaster, a public calamity. But His Highness's safe escape, His arrival in Brazil, and the emergence of a new Lusitanian Empire in America was a source of great happiness for Brazilians and all Portuguese subjects. The Prince Regent, Our Lord, delivered honor, glory, and the Portuguese monarchy. The transfer of the throne will make it even stronger, more powerful, and respected.

(4) Considering it necessary to prepare living quarters for such august guests and the attendant *fidalgos* with all due haste and celerity, His Excellency the Viceroy ordered the entire palace to be vacated, including not just his residence but also the High Court and the mint. In addition, he ordered the homeowners and tenants of a great number of houses, including some most excellent ones, to vacate the premises and deliver the keys to the viceroy by the time the royal fleet appeared in the bay, at the very latest. He immediately sent notices to the governors of Minas Gerais and São Paulo to share the wonderful news of His Highness's imminent arrival and to beseech them to supply this city with all the provisions they could spare. He ordered that the palace be immediately decorated and furnished with all of the grandeur and opulence that time permitted and that the state of the country

allowed. It was certainly a source of great satisfaction for those strolling along the wharf and palace square to see the zeal and indefatigable vigor with which His Excellency worked to assure that His Highness the Prince Regent and the royal family would find amenable accommodations. The same was true of the diligence and contentment evident among those working toward that end, even those of the lowest status and slaves themselves, whose happiness showed on their faces. In order to ensure that His Highness and the royal family, who had crossed the ocean in such a difficult journey, had all the things that might soften the discomforts they had endured, boats packed with refreshments and supplies were sent to meet the royal fleet. They were unaware of the extent of the defeat the fleet had suffered, as we shall see later on. In truth, we must confess that His Excellency the Conde dos Arcos gave a very public demonstration of his care and solicitude, tending to so many and so varied matters that had to be dealt with hastily in order to receive His Highness the Prince Regent, who was expected at any hour. For that reason, many matters went overlooked; others remained to be accomplished; and many, forgetting the present moment, left unfinished in the uncertainty of whether or not they would be completed before the arrival of the royal fleet.

(5) At daybreak the following Sunday, January 17, after all these preparations and due diligences were under way, there was a signal from the peak where the horizon is observable in every direction that the royal fleet had been sighted. There was general excitement and happiness throughout the city and in the streets all one could hear were voices saying: "His Highness has arrived!"; "The ships carrying the royal family are already in the bay!" A terrible storm had separated part of the fleet on the night of December 9 and on the next day, not seeing one another, the ships took different routes. The first ship to arrive in the bay did not have on board His Highness the Prince Regent, but it did carry precious cargo that was no less worthy of our esteem and veneration, namely the most serene ladies Dona Maria Francisca Benedicta, the widowed Princess of Brazil, and the infanta Dona Marianna, the sisters of Her Most Faithful Majesty the Queen, who carried with them the most serene infantas Dona Maria Francisca and Dona Isabel Maria, the daughters of His Highness the Prince Regent. All the people rushed to receive such illustrious figures. The troops and militiamen assumed their respective posts, awaiting the hour of disembarkation of Their Royal Highnesses. At four in the afternoon the ship of the Queen of Portugal entered the bay, with Por-

tuguese and English companion vessels, and by five o'clock the port at the front of the city was consumed with jubilee and the general satisfaction of all residents. As Their Highnesses chose not to disembark before the arrival of the rest of the fleet, they received on board anything they might have needed on that afternoon as well as in the days after. The most distinguished persons from every state also went aboard to honor the safe completion of this happy voyage, joyfully kissing the hands of Their Highnesses, the first members of the royal family that Brazil had ever seen up close, and to kneel submissively and reverentially before them.

(6) As per the time-honored and venerable tradition, this city of Rio de Janeiro was to be illuminated for three nights before the feast of its patron saint, the glorious martyr Saint Sebastian. That happy night of January 17 was set for the start of the lighting, which the Municipal Council decreed a two-day extension after the 20th to mark the joyous occasion of Their Highnesses' arrival. This in turn was marked by demonstrations of public joyfulness and tolling of the bells on the respective nights. Yet all this mirth was tempered by the fact that the remainder of the fleet, carrying our Sovereign the Prince Regent and other royal figures, had not yet arrived, and there was no word as to its whereabouts. For that reason, both the secular and regular clergy observed three days of solemn prayer to beseech the Almighty, through the intercession of the Holy Virgin Mother of God and the saints, to deliver swiftly the rest of the fleet, whose delayed arrival filled our hearts with agony. Everyone, desiring so ardently to see our August Prince and for the dangers and discomfort of His journey to come to an end, directed many fervent pleas toward the Heavens for the safe completion of His voyage. Meanwhile, Their Most Serene Highnesses and the infantas remained aboard the same ship on which they had traveled for over a month until, on February 19, a vessel arrived from Salvador da Bahia with the gratifying news that His Highness the Prince Regent had happily arrived at that port and sought to honor that city, the first capital of Brazil, with His royal presence. . . .

(12) As soon as word spread throughout this city of Rio de Janeiro that His Highness the Prince Regent was in Bahia, our anxieties caused by His delay were calmed and our fears allayed. Considering the danger to which Their Serene Highnesses, the Princesses and infantas, were still exposed by remaining aboard during a season of frequent treacherous thunderstorms; the discomforts experienced by the august Ladies, cloistered for so many days in the cabins of a single ship;

and the fact that His Highness the Prince Regent might linger for a while in Bahia while so much of the nobility and *fidalguia* [peerage] had already disembarked in this city, the most serene princesses decided to get off the ship and proceed directly to the royal palace. For Their Highnesses' arrival and reception, troops were stationed in the plaza facing the wharf alongside a great number of contented people, universally satisfied by the presence of such august figures. On February 2 at ten in the morning, to the sound of salutes from the ships and forts, Their Highnesses came ashore on the wharf facing the palace, accompanied by ladies-in-waiting, preceded by members of the nobility and fidalguia. They soon gathered themselves in the palace, where they graciously received the public who so understandably sought to kiss their hands. . . .

(16) On the joyous, and henceforth always memorable, day of March 7, the prearranged signals were sent from the bay's entrance announcing the arrival of the royal fleet. The entire city, assuming the greatest and most vivid contentment, immediately worked itself into a frenzied commotion, with much movement and confusion. Every task was put on hold, both public and private; almost every store and shop was closed; and a great number of houses emptied out as their occupants rushed to higher ground where they might better see the bay. Others raced to the beaches hoping to find vessels to take them out to sea to meet their lord and prince in accordance with the judicial edict that the Municipal Council had affixed in all public places. Still others hurried to vacate houses for the new arrivals; soldiers ran to their barracks, militiamen to the doors of their company. In short, on land as at sea, there were the most evident signs of an unexplainable joyfulness. As soon as the royal fleet appeared on the horizon, a few longboats from the ships docked at port were sent to meet His Highness. Very few from land managed to cross outside the bay from within it, and of those who attempted, José Caetano de Lima, his excellency the head of the fleet, navy quartermaster, stood as the first inhabitant of Rio de Janeiro to have the honor of kissing the august hand of His Highness the Prince Regent far outside the bay, for which he well deserved a benign reception from the royal sovereign.

(17) As the royal fleet drew near, every Portuguese and English warship anchored in this glorious bay was draped in banners, streamers, and flags of various colors (which made for an absolutely enchanting spectacle). Like the forts, they hoisted their banners, greeting the royal standard with twenty-one-gun salutes. With flags billowing amid as-

cending clouds of thick smoke, the rifle fire, one shot repeating after the other, echoed throughout this port's vast bay all the way into the high mountain ranges, announcing the Royal Presence of Our Sovereigns. The excitement that filled our hearts was greater even than the stimulation of our eyes and ears. This being the first public demonstration of merriment and reverence that Rio de Janeiro could offer to Her Highness, His Highness the Prince Regent, and the royal family, the city spoke as if with a single voice, from the most remote corners and through its entire population, to welcome its Sovereigns. The booming sounds of the cannon salutes, heard all around, and the merry chiming of the bells raised the spirits of everyone. Men, women, the elderly, and the young ran through the streets in a frenzy, anxious to witness the glorious entrance of the royal fleet and to offer their adulation to His Highness the Prince Regent by applauding the moment of His and His family's disembarkation.

(18) It was between two and three o'clock, the afternoon was fresh, beautiful, and quite pleasant on that eternally memorable March 7 that at daybreak had registered as the happiest for Brazil. Not a single cloud blotted out the radiance of the sun and the heat was mitigated by the coolness of a strong and steady breeze. It was as if that shining star had pushed aside every barrier impeding it from witnessing for itself the triumphant arrival of the first European monarch in the most fortunate city of the New World, wanting to take part in the jubilation and applause of a people so exhilarated by the most ardent joy. This was much different from when it had gone into mourning and hiding as it saw that same sovereign fleeing His capital, besieged Lisbon, so as not to have to witness such sadness and so many tears. With majestic pride, the royal prince's ship entered the bay and once again the air was filled with repeated joyful salutes from the forts and warships. The water was blanketed by smoke which the royal fleet speedily cut through to the immense pleasure of an enormous crowd of spectators who, on the hillsides and beaches, witnessed such a beautiful and enchanting scene and who could not stop cheering the safe arrival of the prince and the royal family in the port of Rio de Janeiro, honoring the city with His royal presence.

Translated by Andre Pagliarini

"Infectious Disorders" of the Port

W. Sidney Smith

William Sidney Smith (1764–1840) served the English Royal Navy in several pivotal events of the late eighteenth century, including the American and French revolutions. In 1807, Smith commanded the British naval blockade of Lisbon and played a central role in the Braganças' transatlantic escape to Brazil, just ahead of the French invasion. On June 4, 1808, the rear admiral entertained Prince Regent João of Portugal and his Spanish wife, Carlotta Joaquina, aboard the London, a Royal Navy ship anchored in the Rio harbor. The vessel was festooned in the colors of England, Portugal, and Spain. On the deck lay flags of France, to be trampled upon by Smith and his special guests.

Like its notable author, the document here is situated squarely within the turbulent currents of war, progress, and empire that remade the Atlantic world in the Age of Revolution. Writing to the Admiralty in London, Smith references conditions in a Brazilian port undergoing the rapid changes that followed the Napoleonic occupation of the Iberian Peninsula and the hurried transfer of the Bragança Court to "the Brazils." In other correspondence written at the same moment, Smith discussed the expansion of trade with nations friendly to Portugal and England and the ongoing threats of French incursions. Naval power was a major concern for Smith, whose letter to Admiral W. W. Pole references the Foudroyant, an eighty-gun British vessel once commanded by the hero of the Battle of Trafalgar, Admiral Horatio Nelson, which had been anchored in Rio since 1807.

Smith characterizes several pressing problems in a burgeoning New World city that he describes as burdened by its recent "state of barbarism." At the center of Smith's concerns are the dismal conditions of epidemic disease and poor sanitation that threatened the always precarious health of British crews who traveled the seas. With the support of José Caetano da Silva Coutinho (1768–1833), bishop of Rio and future legislator in the Brazilian parliament, Smith eyes the Ilha das Enxadas, an island in Guanabara Bay northeast of Gamboa, for a naval hospital that might protect British sailors and bring British naval medicine to the unhealthful city. (He makes no reference to existing public health facilities that served Brazilians, including the historic Santa Casa da Misericórdia.) An underlying theme of this document is the establishment of a permanent British naval station, on par with other outposts of England's expanding maritime reach, in the middle of a Portuguese American port that was opening to the world.

H. M. S. *London*
Rio de Janeiro, July 24, 1808

Sir,

Foreseeing the necessity of separating infectious disorders from the crews of His Majesty's ships to which this place has been subject and particularly exposed from its low, damp situation, the extreme filth of the inhabitants, the burial of the dead immediately under the wooden floors of the churches, which stand in a swamp, and its very defective bad police in other respects, I early cast my eye around for an insulated spot in good air for the establishment of a Naval Hospital. A very suitable building offered itself on an island in the port, so situated as to receive the sea breeze direct and earlier than the unhealthy town and I secured the preference to His Majesty's service in the hire of it the authority of Government obliging the owner so to dispose it the moment I should require it of him, which I did not immediately, as the squadron continued tolerably healthy, but the arrival of the convoy from England with dysentery and the increasing, sickly state of the town has induced me to establish a Hospital on this Island of Inchadas, and I have appointed Lieutenant Haydon Governor and Mr. Roddam Surgeon of the President at the head of the medical and surgical department thereon, the necessity of the case obliging me to part with him and not appoint him to the *Foudroyant* as intended.

The Bishop of Rio Janeiro and the judge of the town have seconded my endeavours to impress on this government the necessity of a better regulation for their own safety and ours while we have intercourse with them and it is but justice to say that the members of government with whom I have conversed on this subject acquiesce most readily to my suggestions, but improvements go on slowly in a country but just emerging from a state of barbarism.

I beg you will please to move their lordships to give directions for the confirmation of the appointments and for the establishment to be put on the same footing as it is in other stations where there is the same proportion of Naval force permanently kept. The necessary documents shall be sent to the Transport Board by the next conveyance they cannot be prepared to go by this.

I have the honor to be
Sir
Your most obedient humble servant

W. Sidney Smith

The Passeio Público

John Luccock

John Luccock, an English merchant who resided in Brazil between 1808 and 1818, registered his impressions of the Passeio Público, a colonial-era pleasure park at the edge of Lapa that had opened to the public during the viceregal tenure of Luís de Vasconcelos e Sousa. Arriving in Rio a few short months after the refugee Bragança Court, Luccock witnessed the human and territorial occupation of a city swelled by recent arrivals from Portugal, English merchants, and African slaves. Notwithstanding his dim view of the upkeep of the Passeio Público, Luccock found the pleasure gardens to be a special place of public amusement. Curiously, Luccock wrote little about the actual plants in the park, other than passiflora, a South American native. He neglected to mention the gardens' place of privilege in horticultural experimentation and the instruction of natural history. However, his recollections, published in an 1820 English-language travel narrative, provide rich detail of the artwork installed in two pavilions ("summer-houses"): the paintings of a distinguished freeborn mulatto artist named Leandro Joaquim (1738–c. 1798). The "considerable stream" observed by Luccock in one of the paintings was the Lagoa do Boqueirão da Ajuda, a pestilent lagoon progressively covered over by landfill to make way for the Passeio Público and other "public" land usages. The Englishman also connects the artificial views of a Joaquim canvas with the actual sights of Guanabara Bay, including nearby islands and maritime wrecks.

Once situated at the insalubrious margins of Rio's built environment, the Passeio Público has remained an urban oasis, within steps of downtown, for more than two centuries.

The Public Gardens, though small, perfectly level, laid out in a very formal style, and most negligently kept, claim the pre-eminence among the few places of amusement in Rio. The entrance to this favourite retreat is from the Rua das Marrecas, through a handsome gate, above which is a medallion of the Queen, and her late husband, Don Pedro. In front of this gate, the principal avenue extends to a terrace on the opposite side of the gardens, raised about ten feet above the natural ground. Before it is a mass of grotto work, covered with verdure, among which are entwined in each other's folds, two bronze alligators, about eight feet long. They discharge water from their mouths, and seem just about to plunge into a stone reservoir, in which it is received. From hence the water is conveyed into two other basins, level with the ground, one on each side of the avenue, behind which are long stone seats, overshadowed by very fine trees, and plants supported by lattice work, where, under the shelter of the Passion-flower, the sun-burnt Brazilian enjoys the luxury of fresh air. Just by, arise two slender pyramids of granite, of good proportions, well wrought, and bearing suitable inscriptions. At either end of the esplanade is a broad flight of steps; near the top of that on the left hand, is a small statue of a flying and laughing cupid, who holds by its foot a land tortoise, through the body of which, water is discharged into a granite bucket below, furnished with a ladle, and inviting the thirsty to drink. On a label, loosely twined round the right arm, is painted an allusive motto,—"Ainda brincando sou utile."—Though playing I am useful. [The actual inscription read: "Sou util inda brincando."] The quaintness of the sentence, the countenance of the figure, and the refreshment derived from his proffered beverage, universally please, and often excite a smile.

The Terrace is nearly a hundred yards long, and proportionally broad, paved with a coarse chequer work of different coloured granites, and accommodated with seats. Toward the sea it has a parapet, on which are pots holding plants and flowers; toward the garden a well-wrought stone balustrade. At each end is a small square summer house, highly ornamented with painting and gilding. Their internal form is octagonal, with four glazed windows, and a pair of folding doors. The principal furniture is an old-fashioned gilded chair in each division, the one farthest from the door being raised on a low platform, affording formerly a sort of throne for power and distinction. The dome is an octagonal pyramid, on the sides of which, as well as in the upper part of the compartments below, are pictures. Those in one of the buildings represent the produce and manufactures of the country; plantations of indigo, cotton, and sugar, of mandioca and milho, the harvests of each, and the various modes and machines, by which they are brought to a marketable state. In the other are pictures of Rio scenery, and of some great events in the history of the city; of the entrance of the harbour, as it appears from that spot; of the manner of catching whales in the harbour, before they deserted it; of the land view; and of the state of the place, previous to the formation of the gardens. In this picture, the most remarkable objects are the convent of St. Thereza, the old white house, whence the inhabitants of the city are nick-named Caraocas [*sic*], and the arches of the aqueduct, under which a considerable stream is flowing. An ox is represented as passing through the stream, and shows the channel to have been about knee-deep; such I have learned was the actual state of the place about the year 1750, then covered with water; now occupied by these gardens and several good streets. Another of the compartments represents a naval engagement as taking place in the bay, the scenery of which cannot be mistaken; it is certainly Rio de Janeiro, but the enemy's vessels carry Dutch colours, and I know of no fact in the history of the place, to which this circumstance can possibly apply. I suspect that, by a little tissue of falsehood and flattery, to which the Caraocas are by no means averse, they intended to appropriate to themselves the honours of Bahia. The last division of the dome represents the burning of a large Dutch vessel; boats are towing her off from the rest of the shipping, which are placed behind the Ilha das Cobras; she is coming round the Eastern part of that island, and must be near the Ilha dos Ratos. On the Western side of this latter rock lie, at this day, the keel, stem and stern-posts, and some of the futtocks of a ship, which are said to be the remains of the identical vessel. The wreck, covered with barnacles, may be approached in still weather without danger, though almost surrounded by rocks.

II

Imperial Rio

Portugal's João of Bragança was among the fifteen thousand people who abandoned Lisbon ahead of a French invasion in late 1807. With the aid of the British navy, the Portuguese fled to Brazil. The prince regent—the first European royal to rule from the Americas—lived in Rio de Janeiro between March 1808 and 1821. João's prolonged residence included Brazil's elevation to Co-Kingdom (1815) and the prince's acclamation as king (1816). In this period, the population of Rio nearly doubled, to reach 112,000.

Although the inhabitants of greater Guanabara, then known as Fluminenses, generally favored their proximity to the Crown, the unplanned influx of royals and refugees strained resources and nerves. The residents of Rio were nonetheless impressed by a rising cosmopolitanism, marked by a public culture of pageantry that surrounded the monarchy. A favorite innovation was the ceremonial audience with the royal, known as the *beijamão* (hand-kissing). Housing shortages and disruptions of local provisioning were the downside to courtly life. The Crown commandeered the viceregal palace, an old prison, a Carmelite convent, and the municipal chamber. Some Fluminenses lost their homes and customary privileges. A city confronted new demands for infrastructure, defense, labor, services, and food.

The opening of Brazilian ports rapidly increased the circulation of peoples and goods. The impact on the city of Rio was immediate. New arrivals from Portuguese Africa and Asia joined compatriots who had escaped Lisbon. British merchants set up commercial houses. Planters displaced by the Haitian Revolution tried to reconstitute their slaveholding enterprises. A team of French artists arrived in 1816 to open a royal school of fine arts. These newcomers often found Rio to be uncultured, lacking the habits of life associated with the European public sphere. Some envisioned updating the aesthetic styles and social practices inherited from the colonial period. They looked to diversify a diet heavily influenced by slave cuisine. Alongside the staples of manioc, salt-cured meats, beans, and palm oil, city residents increased consumption of imported grains, wines, and sweets prepared in the French style. In hopes of bringing the airs of enlightenment closer, João authorized new initiatives for local institutions of medicine, military engineering, and the natural sciences. The end to colonial prohibitions on printing opened up a Brazilian press. Readers, writers, and printmakers engaged one another via maps, gazettes, pamphlets, sermons, broadsheets, almanacs, newspapers, books, and eventually illustrated periodicals. Piecemeal, the streetscape of the central city took on an orderly neoclassical appearance, especially in public buildings and fountains. Such changes often came at the expense of authority figures who had held sway prior to the Braganças' arrival. For example, the master craftsmen, draughtsman, and artisans (mainly men of color) who had elaborated an architectural and decorative style later known as the Fluminense School faced rising competition from new arrivals seeking royal and ecclesiastic patronage.

Latent conflicts between the native-born and outsiders, punctuated by incidents of interethnic violence, were a feature of urban living. Constitutionalist upheaval and crises of royal succession in Portugal added fuel to an underlying nativism that targeted non-natives, especially the Portuguese community. An ambivalence about the benefits of the political pacts of Co-Kingdom overlaid such tensions. Yet the independence movement, culminating in a formal declaration on September 7, 1822, avoided the bloodletting of patriot struggles elsewhere in the Americas. The independence process also avoided disruption to local slaveholding.

An enduring social peace was elusive. Portuguese merchants, English sailors, and Africans were frequent targets of xenophobic outbursts in the postindependence period. Rio also played stage to tensions between the central government and the provinces. The political tensions of the early decades of postcolonial rule involved conflicting interests of the administrative and commercial center in the capital and the immensely powerful landowning interests situated in the interior. In part to resolve tensions among the various roles that Rio played as national capital, royal court, and commercial port, the Parliament designated the city a Neutral Municipality (Município Neutro) in 1834. Although city and country remained closely tied to the slave economy, the political interests of a municipality commonly called "The Court" (A Corte) sometimes differed from the interests of the province of Rio de Janeiro, and agrarian Brazil more generally.

In its extended life as a Município Neutro (1834–1889), Rio underwent successive projects to modernize urban services, enliven public life, and regulate economic activity. Some projects, such as public illumination, required significant interventions into the urban soil. Other undertakings, such as the restrictions on the disposal of human waste, required the strengthening of the city's disciplinary powers over urban residents and their habits. A new police force was established in 1831; construction on a House of Correction began a short time later. Amid yellow fever and cholera outbreaks, the power and reach of sanitarians grew. Throughout such changes, the port of Rio expanded as the nexus of exchange for commodities, manufactures, foodstuffs, and luxury goods. Large swaths of the natural landscape were turned over to commodity production, including the forests of Tijuca, cleared for coffee plantations. One of the chief commodities to flow through the port was bonded laborers from Africa, whose legal importation lasted until 1831. The coastline of Rio province, including the shores on either side of the entrance to Guanabara Bay, received a large portion of the 750,000 Africans *illegally* imported into Brazil between 1831 and 1856. Foreign visitors of this period remarked on the violence employed in the commerce of slaves, and horrific acts of brutality were common beyond the dismal confines of the slave markets at Valongo and the holding pens at Jurujuba, in today's Niterói.

Paradoxically, bondage in nineteenth-century Rio endured without an analog to the slave revolt that rocked Salvador da Bahia in January 1835. A peculiar social compact was sealed by surveillance and punishment as well as shared understandings of slavery as one of the many forms of hierarchy, dependency, and property that were pillars of nineteenth-century Fluminense society. Extremes of exploitation might be moderated by the protections of priests, government officials, and the emancipationist leagues formed in the 1870s and 1880s. The permeable boundaries of bondage allowed many slaves to seek freedom for themselves or their kin. Finally, urban slaves carved out spaces of autonomy not possible on rural plantations. Enslaved day laborers circulated throughout the city, selling small consumer goods—baskets, charcoal, fruits, milk, and sweets—as well as their labor. Returning to their masters' homes in the evening, they might keep part of the day's earnings. Such monies might later be used to broker self-purchase or to make a contribution to a religious festival organized by one of the many holy brotherhoods that extended religiosity well beyond the rituals of the Catholic Mass.

Acts of outright resistance to bondage were always part of the story, and the city was surrounded by maroon communities. To the irritation of figures like police chief Eusébio de Quieroz, residents of the city colluded with these *quilombos*, bringing them goods and hiding urban fugitives. As one of the largest slave cities in the Americas, where black skin often meant a presumption of bondage, Rio curiously encompassed innumerable spaces and places for men and women of color to live as free persons, be that freedom status de facto or de jure, through manumission or birthright. In fact, well before Princess Isabel signed the summary abolition decree of May 13, 1888, most Fluminenses of African descent were already free.

The Constitution of 1824, imposed by Emperor Pedro I (Isabel's grand-father), made few legal distinctions among the Brazilian citizenry, yet social hierarchy was inscribed onto urban geography, work, and daily practice. Patriarchal values and male sexual prerogative unequally gendered domestic and public space. An out-of-wedlock birth could be an obstacle to an honorable life. Orphans, Free Africans, and the children of the poor confronted the dismal work of apprenticeships. Penal institutions and forts were among the many spaces of compulsory labor. Nonslave immigrants navigated axes of ethnic, religious, and legal difference. Contract laborers from Portugal were forced into commercial or domestic apprenticeships. Women were trafficked from Europe and the Ottoman empire for the purposes of commercial sex. Life conditions were undoubtedly hard, yet these immigrants added cultural and linguistic texture to social hierarchy and urban culture.

Prospering on the fortunes of an agrarian boom, titled nobles lived in urban mansions, called *solares* and *palacetes*, or on estates built in the hills of the Floresta da Tijuca and the rural parishes. With transportation improvements, especially railways into the interior and steam service throughout greater Guanabara, the urban elite drew closer to the fortunes of the coffee-growing regions of Rio and São Paulo provinces. Toward the end of the empire, the powerful estate owners of the Paraíba River Valley—many having acquired titles of nobility—lived much of their lives in the city. The thrill of banking and joint stock companies chartered in Rio drew financial power out of the countryside and toward a city tied to global capital markets.

The cultural implications of both urban and capitalistic growth were multifold. Readers voraciously consumed serialized novels and the *crônica*, a short-form serialized genre that combined journalism, humor, and social commentary. Theatergoing and musical salons became fashionable. Audience tastes were varied, including stage dramas of the Romantic tradition, Italianate opera, and the light theater that delighted audiences at the Alcázar Lyrique (est. 1859). At the Cassino Fluminense, the well-heeled danced to the French gavotte or the quintessentially Brazilian *lundu*. Portuguese *modinhas* were popular, as were waltzes and mazurkas. Admission prices and social prejudice denied the lower classes direct access to urban high culture, but the influences of commercial theater, the Imperial Conservatory, and the fine arts academy seeped into popular culture (and popular culture, conversely, informed the dramatic and musical sensibilities of all Fluminenses, including the Imperial Family).

Personal freedoms were often circumscribed by the interventionist police

Estudo para Questão Christie. Painting by Vitor Meireles de Lima, 1864. Oil on canvas, 47.2 × 69.3 cm. Courtesy of Museu Nacional de Belas Artes / IBRAM / MinC.

force and the expanding network of prisons and jails. Circulating about the streets after dark was technically against the law until 1878, an interdiction that only applied in practice to slaves and those who might be mistaken for bondsmen or bondswomen. Informal surveillance—through block captains and moral approbation—also limited social transit and personal freedoms. Yet the perambulations of daily life in the markets or at the public fountains turned household provisioning into the opportunity for gossip, romance, and politicking, notably for people of color. The walk to the parish church or the annual pre-Lenten revelry might allow working poor to make their voice heard in the hubbub of city life. Finally, the large ceremonial events organized by the Imperial Government, in celebration of a life passage for a royal or to mark the bitter victory in the Paraguayan War (1864–1870) or to put slavery to its symbolic death, were moments of communion in a city whose residents gradually embraced a sense of uniqueness informed by the status of national capital, as well as by local experience.

By the end of the Brazilian empire, technological and social shifts, and the administrative needs of business and state, brought the middle sectors out into the streets. (The poor were always there.) Gaslights eroded social interdictions against walking around at night. Tramways extended the range of a day's travel. The city center evolved into a place not just for government, commerce, and churchgoing but also for *footing, flirt,* and other practices of public performance that took foreign names. Though dirty and narrow, the fashionable Rua do Ouvidor in the city center attracted elite strollers wanting to see and be seen. Paraphrasing the Carioca novelist and chronicler Machado de Assis, Ouvidor was the main event and the shop windows the mere pretext.

In the last quarter of the nineteenth century, immigrants arrived from Portugal, Spain, Italy, and the Levant. The destruction of slavery prompted the inflow of blacks from the provinces of Rio de Janeiro and Minas Gerais. The droughts that punished the interior of the northeast pushed poor migrants toward Rio in search of relief. Parts of the city, in particular the zone to the west of Campo de Santana known as Cidade Nova (New City), urbanized quickly. The region came to be known as "Little Africa" for its place of privilege as a transregional hub of Afro-Brazilian culture.

From 1840, Pedro II ruled a vast American empire from Rio. Unlike his grandfather and father, who had abandoned the Americas to return to Lisbon, Brazil's last emperor cultivated an enduring relationship with Rio, the city of his birth. The emperor and Empress Teresa Cristina oversaw their children's upbringing at royal palaces in São Cristóvão, Santa Cruz, and Petrópolis. Pedro built an international reputation as a learned monarch who resided in a refined, bourgeois tropical city. Fealty and devotion to the monarch informed elite and popular culture in the Court. Nonetheless, the inhabitants of Rio did not rise up in rebellion when Pedro was deposed in November 1889. The city squares that had been the stages for the acclamation of a king and two emperors were quiet. The Largo do Paço, where a large multiracial crowd had gathered in 1863, to rally around Pedro in a showdown with the British navy, went silent. The silence was all the more remarkable as that same square was filled with song and dance in the days following final slave emancipation. Permanent exile was a painful experience for a Luso-Brazilian royal house that had become enamored of the sweeping vistas of Guanabara Bay and the Serra dos Órgãos. Monarchism remained important in certain sectors of post-1889 Rio, including the navy and some quarters of the popular sectors who chafed at the republicanization of ancient symbols of royal and religious authority. But the Republic soon conditioned the physical space and social experience of a place that was about to be nicknamed "The Marvelous City."

The Feast of the Holy Spirit

Henry Chamberlain and G. Hunt

Celebrated fifty days after Easter Sunday, the Festa do Divino Espírito Santo (Feast of the Holy Spirit), also known as Whitsunday or the Pentecost, commemorates the biblical narrative of the descent of the Holy Spirit upon the disciples of Jesus Christ. The celebration of this traditional holy day arrived in colonial Brazil by way of Portuguese immigrants from the Azores. With firm footing in orthodox Catholic religiosity as well as in secular popular traditions, the Festa do Divino was one of the most important popular traditions in nineteenth-century Rio. Folias, groups of devotees of the Espirito Santo, traditionally gathered to celebrate, carrying red flags with white doves symbolizing the Holy Spirit. The folia from the Santana church (demolished in the mid-nineteenth century) emerged as Rio's most important. The nearby Campo de Santana became the center of an annual multiday event, with public banquets, music, and games continuing into the night, culminating in the designation of a young boy or teenager as "emperor." This traditional symbolic act took on an additional layer of meaning in the context of independence-era Rio as Brazil transitioned from colony to Co-Kingdom to seat of an independent empire.

The coronation of emperors, actual and fictive, was a common theme in nineteenth-century travel narratives, including the sketches of Brazilian life collected by Henry Chamberlain (1796–1844), a Royal Artillery officer and amateur artist who resided in Rio, where his father served as a British consul general, for two years. While the elder Chamberlain carried out official duties, including posting regular dispatches on the events leading up to Brazil's independence from Portugal, his eldest son circulated about town, observing scenes of quotidian urban life, including the Festa do Divino. An engraving completed with the aid of British illustrator G. Hunt adds visual depth to Chamberlain's textual description of a view of a group of joyful celebrants moving along the Rua da Lapa toward Glória. That engraving, shown here, features a distinctively white woman who sits behind a latticework window dressing—called a gelosia, typical of late colonial architecture—observing the action in the street and the picturesque entrance to Guanabara Bay. This female spectator signals the truly public nature of this celebration. Perhaps she also stands for Chamberlain's commentary on the cloistered lives of Rio's elite women.

Unlabeled watercolor engraving by Henry Chamberlain and G. Hunt, 1822. From
Views and Costumes of the City and Neighbourhood of Rio de Janeiro, Brazil (London, 1822),
plate 27.

*Curiously, neither the image nor Chamberlain's travel narrative registers people of
African descent, though the Festa do Divino in nineteenth-century Rio was characterized by its processions of black barbers and skilled musicians, many of whom
were enslaved, who took an active part in the celebrations.*

The Feast of Espirito Santo,—Whitsuntide,—is celebrated in a particularly
splendid manner at the Largo da Lapa.

Some time previous to these Holidays, a Youth, from 14 to 18 Years of
age, is chosen Imperador, in commemoration of the Emperor Constantine,
and being decked out in full Court Dress, with a Chapeau bras, and a Star
on his Breast, perambulates the Streets, preceded by a party of Young Musicians, gaily habited, with Feathers in their Hats, and attended by two Men,
one on each side, bearing red Flags, in whose centres are richly embroidered
the Emblem of the Holy Ghost.

The Emperor takes no part in the Pageant beyond that of displaying his
finery and mock dignity. He merely walks in the Procession; but his two
Attendants industriously exert themselves to persuade those who pass to
contribute something towards the celebration of the Espirito Santo; and

the Salver and Bag they carry are for the reception of the trifles thus daily collected.

The charitable contributors are rewarded by being allowed to kiss the Holy Emblem on the Flag.

A large sum is thus obtained, and laid out in richly ornamenting the Interior of a Wooden Building, nearly opposite the Lapa Church, built for the purpose of this Feast, wherein the Emperor sits enthroned in great State, during the three Holidays; and on the Night of Whit-Monday, a great display of Fireworks takes place on the Green immediately opposite.

The View represents the Party on its way from the Lapa towards the Gloria, at the opening where the Entrance of the Harbour presents itself in an advantageous point of view.

The Emperor Dissolves the
Constitutional Assembly

Henry Chamberlain and Dom Pedro I

Sir Henry Chamberlain (1773–1829) served as the English consul general to the Crown of Portugal in the first decades of the nineteenth century. Like the Bragança royals, the Briton spent a considerable amount of time in Rio de Janeiro. Chamberlain witnessed the 1821 street rallies that called on João VI to return to Portugal to swear allegiance to a constitutional movement that had begun in Oporto. Chamberlain also observed the local experience of Brazilian independence—a transition that transpired with little violence in Rio—and the rising polarization that developed from the consolidation of a new nation and the contested definition of who and what an independent Brazil would be. Such polarization grew acute in November 1823, when Emperor Pedro I took unilateral action and proclaimed to the Brazilian people that the constitutional assembly meeting in Rio had been shuttered. Making the promise to issue a constitutional charter that would be "twice as liberal" as provisions passionately debated since March, the emperor put troops in the streets and ordered the detention of several radical voices.

The constitution issued under Pedro's royal authority in March 1824 contained many of the hallmarks of liberal rule. It provided for separation of powers, representative government, constitutional monarchy, the rights of a citizenry, liberal property rights, and equality before the law. Each was an innovation in the Luso-Brazilian political tradition. However, the charter also included provisions that protected monarchical prerogative. Radicals considered the document absolutist. Simmering ethnic suspicions between Brazilians and Portuguese ("Europeans" in Chamberlain's dispatch to English foreign secretary George Canning, excerpted here) would play into partisan political struggles throughout the 1820s and 1830s. As home to a considerable Portuguese immigrant community, including the Portuguese-born emperor whose father remained the king of Portugal, Rio was an especially active arena for the construction of a Brazilian national identity—descended from the mother country and its sovereign, yet uniquely American by birth and sentiment, and to be defended in blood if necessary.

The events that transpired in November 1823—the dissolution of an elected assembly, the imposition of martial law, the arrest of dissidents, and vague promises for a new and improved constitutional order—would be repeated numerous times in Rio's history, including 1889, 1930, 1937, and 1968. In this regard, Chamberlain documents a key incident in a long urban history of authoritarianism.

Rio de Janeiro 15th November 1823
To The Right Honorable George Canning

Sir,

The Crisis which my late Dispatches have announced to be approaching has taken place; but in a manner not at all expected, I believe, by either of the contending parties, and with Results generally as unforeseen, as they are alarming for the peace and Union of Brasil. Such I know is the persuasion of the Brazilians and I see but too many Reasons to concur in this opinion.

The Emperor, taking advantage of the State of Irritation produced amongst the officers of the Army by the attacks made upon them in the newspapers, and by one or two violent speeches in the Assembly, in reality intended against the Ministry (whilst the House had under consideration the petition of a Brazilian shopkeeper beaten in his own House by two European officers), signed a decree on the 12th Instant declaring the Assembly at an end; and putting Himself at the Head of the Army, which he had the day before collected at the St. Christovão, marched to the Outskirts of the City, and thence sent on a considerable detachment to enforce obedience. The House was surrounded, and the Assembly dissolved without the smallest Resistance, either on the part of the People, or of the Deputies; who were allowed to retire peaceably to their homes; with the exception of seven, *viz.* the three Andradas, Belchior, Rocha, Montezuma, and Vergueiro, who were arrested and sent Prisoners to Fort Lage, where they still remain.

His Majesty then rode through the principal streets, being everywhere received with great applause, and finally returned to St. Christovão whither the Army followed early in the Evening.

I am happy to be able to say that the day lapsed over without bloodshed, and even without the smallest popular disturbance; and that Tranquillity has continued ever since, no doubt principally in consequence of the precautionary measure of calling out the Militia and of causing the Streets to be patrolled night and day by strong parties of soldiers.

What effect this proceeding may have upon the Provinces remains to be seen. The Portuguese Party in the Capital consider it a victory, and themselves secure. The Brazilians as a violent wrong to be avenged, and very dismal prognostics are in circulation with respect to its Consequences.

The Inhabitants of the Provinces, who happen to be here for the moment, are anxious to depart, but no one is allowed to quit the City. They are almost unanimous in their predictions that the News of the violent dissolution of the Assembly, by an Imperial Decree carried into execution by an armed Force, and immediately followed up by the arrest of every member whose name is connected with the first struggles for Independence; will be the signal of General Discontent. The immediate forerunner of the Separation of the Provinces from the Imperial Rule; and of all the lamentable consequences that must follow such a Change.

The Decree of Dissolution, no doubt, also contains the Convocation of a new Assembly; but it is a question whether a second Assembly can be got together. Even supposing that none but the usual difficulties of distance, and a wide spread Population, oppose themselves to the Elections, and the meeting of the new Deputies in the Capital, this cannot reasonably be expected to take place under a period of nearly Twelve Months; and in the present, and probable, State of this Country, who can count upon what is likely to happen during that term! . . .

I have the honour to be with the greatest Respect.
Your most obedient humble Servant,

H Chamberlain
Consul General

PROCLAMATION
Brazilians.
One single will unites us. Let us continue to save our Country. Your Emperor, Your Perpetual Defender will aid you, as he did yesterday, and as he has always done, although he should expose his life. The Indiscretions of Men led away by Pride and Ambition were about to precipitate us into the most horrible abyss. It is needful, now that we are saved, to be vigilant as Argus. The Bases which are ought to follow, and sustain for our Happiness are: the Independence of the Empire, Its Integrity, and the Constitutional System. If we sustain these three bases without rivalry, always odious on which side soever regared [*sic*] and the lever (as you have just seen) that might have shaken this colossal Empire, we have nothing more to fear. These Truths

are undeniable, you well know them by your own sense, and unfortunately were about to know them better through anarchy. If the Assembly were not dissolved our Holy Religion would have been destroyed, and our garments would have been dyed in Blood. A new Assembly is convoked. They will meet as soon as possible to labour on the Project of a Constitution which I shall shortly present to you. If it were possible I should be glad that it should so far conform with your opinions that it might rule us (although only provisionally) as a Constitution. Be certain, that your Emperor's sole ambition is to continue to acquire more and more glory, not only for himself, but for you, and for this grand Empire, which will be respected by the whole world. The arrests now made will be considered by the Enemies of the Empire as despotic. They are not. You must see they are measures of Policy [a poor translation of the original: "police measures"], proper to prevent anarchy, and preserve the lives of these Unfortunate Persons, in order that they may yet tranquility enjoy them and ourselves Quiet. Their Families shall be protected by the Government. The Salvation of our Country which is confided to Me as Perpetual Defender of Brasil, and which is the Supreme Law, so requires it. Have confidence in Me, as I have in you, and you will see our Enemies internal and external, supplicate our Indulgence. Union and more Union, Brazilians, whoever adhered to our Sacred Cause, whoever swore to the Independence of the Empire, is a Brazilian.

THE EMPEROR.

Views of the Palace Square

Jean-Baptiste Debret

Throughout his residence in Rio (1816–1830), French history painter Jean-Baptiste Debret (1768–1848) filled his sketchbooks with watercolors and pen-on-paper works that captured the vast variety of social types, domestic and work relations, and customs of Rio and its hinterlands. Back in France in 1831, Debret used the images executed in situ to write an illustrated account of his "picturesque and historical voyage" in Portuguese America. The lithographed plates found in Debret's monumental travel narrative came to be one of the most frequently reproduced image banks of nineteenth-century Rio society.

The first two plates appearing in the third volume, alongside their corresponding explanatory texts, appear here. Both plates privilege the Largo do Paço (Palace Square), the political, commercial, and ceremonial epicenter of independence-era Rio. The first of the two vistas moves from the edge of the built city across an open square enclosed by colonial-era structures whose functions are described by Debret. The tower of the Carmelite convent (today's Faculdade Candido Mendes) rises toward the cloudless sky. At the edges of the scene, notably around the royal palace, private citizens and uniformed military go about their daily lives. Carriages assemble at the palace entrance, perhaps for an audience with the royals. On the steps leading to the water, porters carry goods to small embarkations. At the fountain and along the seawall, a variety of figures at leisure take in refreshments.

The second vista is from the bay. Passengers on the modern-day ferry service from Niterói may find it hard to recognize the Rio skyline. The verticalization of downtown, land reclamation, and highway construction along the shoreline and the destruction of natural hills have disfigured the landscape rendered by Debret. However, a close examination reveals the enduring topography, from the hill behind the Santa Casa da Misericórdia (the last remnant of the Morro do Castelo) on the viewer's left to the Morro de São Bento on the right. Appearing slightly to the left of center, the Palace Square—today's Praça XV de Novembro—is still recognizable.

View from the Largo do Paço in Rio de Janeiro

Upon taking refuge in Rio de Janeiro, Prince Regent João lived in the tiny viceregal palace that once housed the Casa da Moeda, located near the city center. Eager to indulge his appetites, the prince quickly availed himself of a farm in São Cristóvão, situated three-quarters of a league from the capital, to make his daily residence. The once-busy viceregal palace was reduced to little more than a ceremonial building occasionally used by the Court, especially on Sundays and on the days of the royal audience, known in Portuguese as the *beija-mão*.

The regent's wife, Princess Carlota, charged with the education of her daughters, remained in the central city. She took up residence in the apartments situated on the side of the palace that faces the great square. Following her example, the young prince Dom Pedro and his tutor occupied the rooms along the façade next to the royal chapel.

The Throne Room, situated on the corner that faces the bay, is illuminated by the last two windows to the right of the viewer as well as by four more that look out over the great square. The apartments of honor take up the rest of the principal façade.

During the reign of João VI, the last window on the left illuminated the king's private chapel. This room was later annexed to the apartments for the Empress Leopoldina [wife of Pedro I], situated alongside the Throne Room. The emperor's rooms took up all the windows at the center of the building; from the center balcony, the emperor would make an appearance. From this spot D. Pedro publicly announced that Brazilian independence had been recognized by Portugal, as well as the ratification of the suspension of the slave trade. . . . It was again on this same balcony that Prince Pedro, acting as regent, announced to the people that he accepted the title of Perpetual Defender of Brazil, accepting the obligation to reside in the country.

On celebration days, citizens and foreigners could count on seeing the imperial family appear at these windows, as processions circulated in the square before entering the Imperial Chapel.

In the days of the viceroy, a covered passage supported by an archway, at the same height as the first floor of the palace, connected to a theater constructed in the interior of the building. . . . This small theater, quite modest by all accounts, was the only one of its kind in the city of Rio de Janeiro. It was shuttered in 1809, to be replaced by a very large space that still exists today on the Largo do Rocio, called the Teatro Real de São João.

The rear of the square, including the former Carmelite convent and its cloistered chapel, was used as an annex to the king's palace for the arrival of

João VI. The perspective of this image hides from the viewer a passageway supported by two archways, but the structure was constructed at the same height as the first floor and used to cross the distance that separated the chapel from the main building, in which there was a hallway reserved for the prince and his entourage in the royal chapel. The second floor, reserved for the royal officers of the palace, was divided into small lodgings for the men in service of the court. On the ground floor, the vast court included the pantries, the kitchens, and the lodgings of the kitchen staff.

The main façade of the Carmelite chapel was still incomplete in 1808, so temporary tarpaulins were installed when the portico of the new royal chapel was provisionally installed. In 1823, this false front was replaced by a grand pediment that featured the imperial insignia cast in bronze. The restoration of the front steps of the Imperial Chapel included a new, much more presentable staircase bordered by ironwork that replaced an old, tasteless wooden railing.

Toward the end of 1818, they added a tenor bell to the Royal Chapel; its deep timbre could be heard as far as the palace at São Cristóvão. This beautiful bell, cast in Rio, was solemnly christened at the chapel, with the great pomp demanded of the king, an illustrious patron. The two smaller arches of the tower were torn down, to make way for a single arcade, built in proportion to the new bell.

The entire left side of the plaza, formed by a line of uniform and solidly constructed houses, was once occupied by the Portuguese merchants who supplied the Court and the employees in direct service of the king. By 1818, as the affluence of foreigners grew, the owners converted the entryways into stores, and rented them quickly to French café owners, who little by little took over the ground floor and turned it into a billiards hall. Later, they took possession of the rest of the structure, to turn it into a boardinghouse. Beautifully painted store names and front windows of marble columns imported from Paris now enrich establishments frequented by foreigners seeking to spend a moment in the city or to sleep near their ships. You can see on this same side of the plaza an archway [the Arco do Teles], a heavily used passageway, that leads to the oldest streets, where you find a French-owned inn that contrasts with the primitive Portuguese inn, recognizable by the enormous iron lantern on the balcony and a floral design artfully painted in pink and green. . . .

The entire ground floor of the buildings—on the side that faces the bay—is occupied by storage rooms for wet and dry goods; while the other extremity of the façade forms the beginning of Rua Direita (a spitting image of the Parisian rue Saint-Honoré), where we find stores owned by the rich merchants of Rio de Janeiro.

The luxurious fountain that decorates the docks of Palace Square provides water for the neighborhood as well as for any ships anchored in the bay. The pair of stairs was carved out of land that jutted out allowing one to access the base, offering two points of disembarkation that were, however, seldom used. While toward the left, the prettiest part of the wharf juts out; the palace façade can be seen from the stairs to the right. The stairs to the left, hidden here, are not much more than a small gradient, a point of departure known as the boat ramp of the palace, it was also where canoes were not allowed to dock. . . .

View Number Two from the First Plate

Here, I have re-created a view of Rio de Janeiro, on a much larger scale, amid the haze of Guanabara Bay.

Taken from the Ilha dos Ratos, very close to the Ilha das Cobras, it was easy for me to define the exact position and shape of its details such as they existed in 1831.

This old quarter of the city is situated upon a cove, which features two equally prominent dockyards and the Largo do Paço in the center. The background that borders the horizon to the left is composed of a mountain chain dominated by Corcovado, which extends to the right uniting it with the Tijuca mountains capped off by the peak called the parrot's beak, known as the Bico do Papagaio. On this end of the painting appear the two mountains closest to the viewer, which serve as the limits for the most densely populated portion of the city. The mountains to the left are the Morro do Sinal, also known as the Morro do Castelo, on top of which exists a fortress with large signal poles. During the reign of João VI, the main body of the fort served as the barracks for the captain of the army in Rio. Today, a part of this building is used as a prison and house of correction for fugitive slaves.

By looking at the mountain on the right side of the same plane, parallel to Castelo, one can see the bishop's house that overlooks its chapel. Finally, the Fortaleza da Conceição caps off the left extremity of the plateau, and the main body of the fortress is currently a well-respected arms factory.

Still on the same side, the slope of the Morro da Conceição continues to the base of Morro de São Bento, on top of which sits a convent of the same name. This Roman-style building, with its opulent interior décor, majestically borders one end of Rua Direita, and at the same time it towers over the

Vue de la Place du Palais, à Rio de Janeiro and *Vue Généralle de la Ville, du Côté de la Mer.*
Illustrations by Jean-Baptiste Debret. From *Voyage pittoresque et historique au Brésil, ou Séjour d'un artiste français au Brésil, depuis 1816 jusqu'en 1831 inclusivement*, vol. 3 (Paris: F. Didot, 1839), plates 1–2.

Naval Fleet, which is the forward-most point toward the right of the cove that surrounds the city. The Army's Fleet occupies and defends the opposite side of the city, or the parts closer to the mouth of the bay. The main body of the building overlooking these fortifications is a sort of museum where a small arts and trade school holds its classes for disadvantaged youth under the protection of the government. These young students receive a modest salary for their study of the fine arts and the application of industrial skills related to foundry work or arms manufacture, so that by the time they graduate they can be gainfully employed in the city or at the Navy dockyards. The first bell tower to the right belongs to the Hospital da Misericórdia; following the edge of the beach one can see a long series of infantry barracks forming the Largo do Quartel. This was one of the points of Duguay-Trouin's departure and here begins the beach named Praia D. Manoel, a point of departure and a beautiful market that continues until the lumberyard that neighbors the Largo do Paço. Immediately beyond the wharf, one can begin to see the numerous stalls that constitute the fish market, which lends the beach its name, until you reach the dockside warehouses of the customshouse, where the merchant ships discharge their cargo. Four piers are attached to the principal building of the customshouse, formerly the exchange, and after which begins the Praia dos Mineiros, a market of grains, pottery, bananas, and firewood. Candelária, a beautiful modern church, rises above the commercial beach below.

Finally, the foreground shows the foot of a rock named Ilha das Cobras whose beaches closest to the city are occupied by stores. At the summit of this rock is a fortress used as a state prison that covers the entire plateau. The foreground hides the naval shipyard to the right, the place from which the first empress, Archduchess Leopoldina, departed Brazil.

Translated by Nathan H. Dize

The Night of the Bottle-Whippings

O Republico

The Noite das Garrafadas (roughly: Night of the Bottle-Whippings) capped a week of tumult that rocked the streets of central Rio in March 1831. Since independence, insults and fisticuffs had been regularly exchanged between Brazilians and Portuguese men in everyday urban life. The widespread rioting of 1831 was precipitated by the local Portuguese community's resolve to demonstrate its public support for Emperor Pedro I. A radicalized Brazilian community—embracing a mantle of nativism, Lusophobia, and liberal constitutionalism—chafed at a brazen display of affinity toward a constitutional monarch maligned as an absolutist tyrant. Street clashes between Brazilians, known in Portuguese circles as cabras *(goats), and Portuguese, called by the Brazilians* pés-de-chumbo *(lead-foots) or* marinheiros *(mariners), led to several fatalities.*

The radical newspaper O Republico *was a leading voice of antiabsolutist and anti-Portuguese sentiment edited by Antônio Borges da Fonseca (1808–1872), a fiery lawyer and pamphleteer originally from the northeastern province of Paraíba. Fonseca adopted the eponymous nickname "Republico," and his paper played an important role in stoking nativist hostilities toward Portuguese merchants and sailors as well as the emperor, who was labeled a traitor. In the vivid language of first-person reportage (almost certainly written by Fonseca),* O Republico *detailed the attacks on Brazilian citizens that followed Pedro's entrance into Rio following a trip to the province of Minas. Excerpted here, the article "Pertubassões" (Disturbances) helps capture the extremist discursive landscape that pushed Pedro I toward his April 7, 1831, decision to abdicate and return to Portugal, leaving the Brazilian throne to a young son born in Rio, the future Pedro II. The piece casts rich color on the cultures and spaces of political factionalism. The wider context encompasses currents of hypernationalist, xenophobic sentiment in the Brazilian capital, as well as the appeals of constitutionalism and sovereignty that brought down the First Reign and ushered in a period of radical reformism and reaction that lasted until the 1840s, when the boy-emperor Pedro II was declared to be of age and was crowned in the Igreja de Nossa Senhora do Monte do Carmo.*

Now that I find myself somewhat unburdened, I turn to the attacks on Brazilians committed by the marinheiros (the so-called pés-de-chumbo). For some time now, we have watched as the Brazilian people have been insulted merely for being Brazilian, but the audacity of these cowards, aided by a treasonous government and the *great traitor [traidor mór]* who has brought on such ill-tidings to Brazil, have made things even worse with his proclamation to the people of Minas Gerais. With the arrival of the emperor, whose words inflame the spirits of these vandals, the gang of rascals at Quitanda, Direita, Pescadores, and Rosario streets, led by the *great traitor*, and sustained by malevolent merchants, now believe that the time has come to do away with all Brazilians, whom they brand with the nickname "cabras." They are exclusively known as marinheiros; because no Brazilian with any sense of shame gave the satisfaction of making an appearance at the arrival of the chief of government, when the state of things is found to be in such a put-upon and oppressed condition.

The hour was set, and the cabal already had decreed death to all cabras (Brazilians). Thursday and Friday, March 10–11, the marinheiros stirred up a tumult attacking the houses of Brazilian citizens and of the foreigners who failed to light their lamps. They shouted *Long Live the Absolutist Emperor of the Portuguese!* Groups of Brazilians, taking note of such attacks, set out in the streets on Saturday the 12th, and yelled *vivas* to the Constitution, to the Sovereignty of the Nation, to Article 174, to the Federation, and to a Constitutional Emperor. The moment that His Majesty shows himself to be absolutist, he will come to know the enmity of the Brazilian people. You can rest assured that they will unite in declaring war, as the Brazilians know that the emperor comes from the family of João VI and is the brother of Miguel. Nothing happened that day; yet that night and into the following day, Sunday the 13th, the marinheiros continued to ready themselves with arms, brandishing broken bottles. And when we passed unnoticed along the Rua da Quitanda, between São Pedro and Violas streets, the criminal and impious Father Malheiros backed by a police escort on patrol shouted right before our eyes *"Long Live the Absolutist Emperor!"* The people grew agitated, taking up positions against the police patrol, and compelling the officers to give their *vivas* to the Constitutional Emperor, to which they complied, and walking in the direction of the house of João Domingues d'Araujo Viana, THE FIRST AMONG THE IRREDEEMABLE ENEMIES OF BRAZIL, let fire a pistol, wounding two Brazilians, and shortly thereafter the vandals, acting as if they were ravenous wolves, threw themselves upon us and spilt our blood, not allowing us the ability to retreat, as we were unarmed and even with the confusion that came about during the unexpected attack. The entire police brigade set forth and, joined by the marinheiros, began to abuse us. Throughout the night the city was rocked by disturbances; the marinheiros respected no one, and accompanied by the police, walked about with grenadiers, swords, and clubs, landing blows here, inflicting mortal wounds there. Throughout the attack, they continued to pledge their faith in the *Absolutist* Emperor, and all that one could hear was a call for the death of the editor of *O Republico*; and even though I was in a tumult when I heard these cursed cannibals scream out: *Take Republico prisoner so that we can roast him in the bonfire!* On Monday, [the 14th], throughout the day the marinheiros continued to assault and stab any Brazilian who wore a ribbon on his hat; at night, numbering six hundred, they stalked about the streets of the city in the company of the police who provided reinforcements, insulting, slapping about and cutting any Brazilian whom they encountered; at that time I was to be found in the [Largo do] Rocio, along with twelve companions, and we barely escaped, and still not yet fully hidden, he heard the wicked gang scream out *Kill, He Who Is Republico!* and a poor Brazilian suffered a series of blows for the fact that he wore a straw hat, just as I had been wearing that day. And the miscreants walked about, day and night, spreading insult and injury, all with the support of the police. Over these two days (Sunday and Monday), copious amounts of Brazilian blood flowed, and there was no support for us from the government, traitorous that it is, nor from the marinheiros, who are backed by a government that betrays.

Tuesday the 15th was designated as the day that the emperor would receive visitors in the Palace [*dar beijamão*]. I had never seen such a sorry-state encampment in my entire life. There would be nothing more outrageous than the appearance of the emperor of the marinheiros. Surely four hundred or five hundred marinheiros approached the emperor's coach, some wearing jackets, others overcoats, still others waistcoats, and nearly everyone wearing sandals, and many wretchedly dressed. Beyond the troops, who were obligated to come along, not a single Brazilian approached, as a crowd of marinheiros and children made all sorts of loud *vivas* in a manner that should have embarrassed the emperor. Upon the stationing of the Brazilian troops (who want solely the Constitution, Independence or Death) in the Largo do Paço, where many Brazilians were already present prepared to join their brothers-in-arms in the fight for liberty (as the rumors had spread throughout the city that the day was to include an acclamation of the emperor's absolutist powers), stood this pitiful-guy named Soares, better known as a *punching bag*, who works in the customshouse, [and he] attacked the editor of the *Tribuno*; yet the non-uniformed Brazilians as well as the soldiers set upon him with blows of their batons, scaring away the supposed courageousness of the marinheiros, who see themselves as sustainers of the imperial throne, but who are in fact in such a state only as long as the Brazilians wish it to be so. As the function concluded, it seemed as if we were witnesses to a Festival of the Blacks of Rosário, as the people dispersed in every which direction, and the marinheiros, infamous as much as they are cowards, walked around Quitanda, Rosario, Ouvires, and Direita streets, attacking as many Brazilians as they might casually happen upon. . . .

On Wednesday the 16th, we saw not only a repeat of the attacks that had so wounded the nation's pride, as unsatisfied with their attacks upon congressional deputy Evaristo Ferreira da Veiga, they also attacked deputy Baptista Caetano de Almeida for wearing a ribbon around his hat. . . .

What are you waiting for Brazilians! Aren't such outrages enough? Can you not see that the traitorous government seeks to enslave you? Ah! If you wish to stand by as a lifeless spectator to such crimes, such betrayals, perhaps it be better that you seek out life in hell, as that is where you will find the best protections. We have been assaulted; resistance to oppression is a natural right, and the Criminal Code grants its authorization, and Title IV, Cap. 7, Art. 145 of the Constitution of the Empire says "All Brazilians are obligated to take up arms in support of the independence and integrity of the Empire, defending it against enemies foreign and domestic."

Let there be no doubt that independence is under attack. . . .

There is treason all about: the marinheiros are scheming up their plan of attack. The principal points of their actions are the War Arsenal, São Bento, and Banco, and they should be stocking up at Castelo, to be able to fire down upon the city. Yet they, the cowards, are also spreading rumors that the garrisons of the French and English navies are readied to attack Brazilians in order to enslave them. This is a great insult to the French and English who love liberty. Besides, how could it be that the admirals of these nations would interfere in the internal affairs of Brazil, given that their nations have repeatedly pledged not to intervene in other nations' domestic matters. You can believe this without supposing that the French and English governments might assist in the cause of recolonization. . . .

People of Minas Gerais and São Paulo: can you not hear the laments of your brothers from Rio de Janeiro? Prepare yourselves, and set yourselves at the ready to help them. People of Rio Grande do Sul, you who love liberty so much, you cannot be indifferent to our plight; prepare yourselves, lest tyranny come to you as well, and it's necessary that we find ourselves ready for defense. War to the death to the marinheiros (who are also called pés-de-chumbo, *luzos*, *marotos* [Lusos, tricksters], etc.) because they are our irreconcilable enemies who operate under the cover of the Great Traitor. And you people from Bahia and Pernambuco, and all other Brazilians: We have been provoked into a war, and war is necessary as the marinheiros go about every day assassinating Brazilians one by one. . . . LIBERTY OR DEATH! Arm yourselves and resist.

Translated by Daryle Williams

Mapping the Capital of Imperial Brazil

E. de la Michellerie

As the postindependence political classes developed the symbolic language of Brazilian nationhood, they reimagined Rio as a space of new civic functions and commemorative possibilities. The powerful found in the city fertile ground to invent the iconography of an American constitutional monarchy. And the populace found the spaces to enact fealty to the sovereign. For example, the old Largo do Rocio—originally named after an important square in Lisbon—was renamed Praça da Constituição (Constitution Square) to commemorate the site where Emperor Pedro I swore his allegiance to constitutional rule. The nearby parade grounds now known as the Campo de Santana took the name Campo da Aclamação (Acclamation Field) to mark the locale where Pedro was acclaimed monarch.

The citywide scope of symbolic reconfiguration can be seen in the map here, published in 1831. Credited to Eugène de la Michellerie (1802–1875), a French watercolorist who lived in Rio between 1826 and 1831, the map reversed the orientation of Paulo dos Santos Ferreira Souto's and Ignacio Antonio dos Reis's highly detailed Planta da cidade de S. Sebastião do Rio de Janeiro levantada por ordem de S. A. R. o Principe Regente *(Map of the City of St. Sebastian of Rio de Janeiro, printed upon the order of His Royal Highness the Prince Regent; 1812), the first map printed in Rio.*

To the lower right of Michellerie's map appears a muscular Indian man, an allegorical symbol of nativism common in nineteenth-century fine arts. Together with the renderings of verdant mountains and a ship-filled bay, the stately Indian and the palm that stands above him are intended to evoke the robust nature of an American capital on the rise. The map is equally notable for its accurate rendition of a living city, marked out by urban streets, built structures, and the internal boundaries of city administration. Each colored section (see color plate) delimits a central parish: yellow denotes Candelária; pink, São José; blue, Sacramento; green, Santana; peach, Santa Rita. The peculiarity of mapping imperial Rio in this fashion is that the municipal jurisdictions of the independence era rested on an older colonial-era ecclesiastical partitioning of space. Other important elements of the map include Matacavalos and Mataporcos, the two most important roads leading out of the city. We also see the contours of the suburbs. To the left, at the end of the Rua do Aterrado

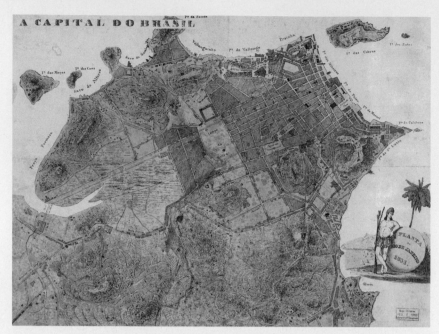

A Capital do Brasil. Map by E. de la Michellerie (S.I., 1831). Scale not given. 1 map: hand col.; 36 × 47 cm. G5404.R6 1831.M5 TIL. Courtesy of the Library of Congress Geography and Map Division, Washington, D.C.

opposite the wetlands of Mangue, a bridge connects the lightly populated regions near Praia Formosa with São Cristóvão, site of the emperor's residence, and beyond. The uncolored lower registers of the map demonstrate how the cartographer's urbanist imaginary left rural and mountainous areas to look like uncharted wilderness.

The Slave Dance Called Candomblé

Eusébio de Queiroz

The Constitution of 1824 was silent on slavery, and the central government of the young empire largely refrained from intervening in the relations between masters and slaves. However, the word escravo *(slave) and the problems of slaveholding appear throughout Rio's municipal ordinances of the postindependence years. Local authorities often fretted over slaves who walked about the streets. The unruliness of petty commercial activities often controlled by bondsmen, bondswomen, and freed peoples prompted measures to regulate the large and multifarious enslaved population. Notwithstanding such municipal controls, Rio's ethnically diverse population of enslaved men and women found time to engage in communal and leisure activities, however fleeting or furtive. Foodways, religious practice, associative life, and music and dance styles coalesced into a heterogeneous, hybrid Afro-Brazilian culture. Percussion instruments like the* tambor, *to which the document here refers, could be made from found objects, and such musical implements were an important means through which West and West Central Africans maintained drumming traditions.*

The "slave dance called candomblé" mentioned in this letter from Chief of Police Eusébio de Queiroz (1812–1868) to the Municipal Chamber appears to refer to body movements, perhaps made during a syncretic Afro-Brazilian religious ritual, accompanied by drumming. This document leaves ambiguous just what the gatherings were, and it is not clear what the authorities would have understood candomblé to be. We cannot say how closely Queiroz's views on candomblé matched the practitioners' actual experience of ritual, music, and social encounter. Nonetheless, it is clear that Queiroz found candomblé to be an affront to public order. Queiroz would go on to have an important relationship with the transatlantic institution of slavery, including the enforcement of laws that ended the transatlantic trade to Brazil after 1850. One wonders what effect his earlier experience heading Rio's police force, with its constant concern about regulating a city of captives and containing their culture, had on his later career.

For the good of public security, I judge it convenient to entreat Your Lordship to tell the Municipal Chamber of the necessity of a Regulation that would prohibit the use of the tambor in the slave dance called candomblé, which can be heard a league's distance away and attracts slaves from neighboring farms; such meetings might give rise to the evils to which Your Lord is no stranger.

God Save Your Lordship
June 1, 1833
Illustrious Sir Dr. Eusébio de Queiroz Coutinho Mattoso da Camara, Judge and Chief of Police

Translated by Amy Chazkel

From the Dungeon to the House of Correction

Eusébio de Queiroz

In 1837, Chief of Police Eusébio de Queiroz (1812–1868) registered a sequence of events that involved three of the most important penal institutions in postindependence Rio: the Calabouço, the Aljube, and the House of Correction. The first institution, whose name meant "dungeon," was located at the foot of the Morro do Castelo. It was reserved for the punishment and detention of slaves. The Aljube, originally built in the eighteenth century as an ecclesiastical prison at the foot of the Morro da Conceição, was used for the incarceration of all sorts of common criminals, many of whom were simply awaiting judicial proceedings. Because of its deplorable, crowded conditions, that facility would finally be shuttered in 1856, when the House of Detention took over its function. The third and newest institution, the Casa de Correção, was still under construction. Built according to reformist models taking root throughout the Americas and in Europe, the corrections house was meant to leave behind the arbitrariness and purely punitive nature of colonial-era penal justice, instituting a new form of punishment—"prison with work"—that would teach a work ethic to wrongdoers. A part of this new building would be dedicated to the incarceration of slaves who had committed crimes, and it would house enslaved inmates removed from the Calabouço in 1837, as shown here.

This document gives a glimpse of the process through which Queiroz and other authorities established the operational norms of slave discipline in urban penal institutions. Prisoners were bound by a libambo, a set of iron restraints commonly used to join together a line of slaves by their hands and necks. The routine duties of the guards at the House of Correction included whippings, and the lash was a potent symbol of the inhumanity and humiliation that was transferred with enslaved people to the city's modern penal institution. In a curious passage, the authorities arrange for incarcerated runaways to be exhibited before the public at three specified times of day.

On May 30, 1837, the Administrator of the Calabouço prison registered the following:

Sir Administrator of the Calabouço, in fulfillment of the Order issued on December 28 of last year, please be advised that the runaway slaves that are found in the Calabouço must be transferred this coming June 3 to the House of Correction, the prison to which they are to be consigned, as the Administrator of the House of Correction must be aware. There, the slaves will be put to work, following the orders of the Administrator of the afore-mentioned House, and in accordance with his order to establish a certain time of day in the morning, and another at midday, and another at the end of the day at sunset for the slaves to be seen by ordinary people [*pessoas do povo*] who may wish to examine them. After such an understanding in this respect is reached with the Administrator of the House of Correction, an announcement will be made in all the newspapers not only of the transfer of the slaves to that Establishment but also of the times of day when the slaves will be put on public view. Likewise, according to the aforementioned Ad-ministrator, he will see whether he might find comfortable lodgings inside the aforementioned Administration building.

Likewise, a place will be chosen on the grounds where punishment by whipping can be conveniently applied, and all this will be reported to me on the first of June for my knowledge and governance, so that I can request the necessary forces to effect the removal. Sustenance and other expenses related to the aforementioned slaves provided by the current Calabouço ad-ministration will be provided by the House of Correction administration, the responsibility thus becoming simply the daily sustenance of what had been the job of the Calabouço, as well as the administration of the slaves with respect to everything that is not related to the chains and other parts of the libambo to be delivered to the Jailor of the Aljube, from whom we will require a receipt. And any queries concerning the execution of these orders must be presented to me with the necessary haste, so that they can be carried out without disrupting the removal on the day on which it has been planned.

Queiroz

Translated by Amy Chazkel

"Rocinha Rio de Janeiro Panorama 2010." Photograph by Chensiyuan. Licensed under Creative Commons Attribution-Share Alike 3.0. http://commons.wikimedia.org/wiki/File:Rocinha_rio_de_janeiro_panorama_2010.jpg.

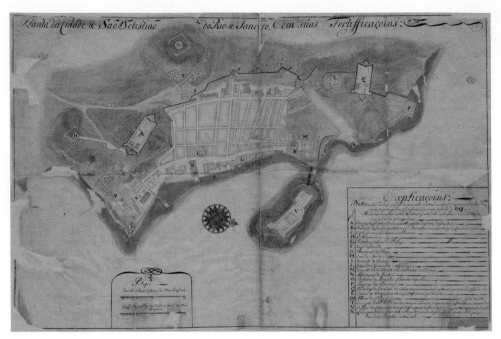

Planta da cidade de São Sebastião do Rio de Janeiro com suas fortificações. Illustrated map by João Massé, 1713. Courtesy of Arquivo Histórico Ultramarino, Lisbon.

Loge [sic] *na Rua do Valongo*. Painting by Jean-Baptiste Debret, c. 1820–1830. Watercolor on paper, 17.5 × 26.2 cm. Courtesy of Museus Castro Maya, Rio de Janeiro.

Unlabeled watercolor engraving by Henry Chamberlain and G. Hunt, 1822. From *Views and Costumes of the City and Neighbourhood of Rio de Janeiro, Brazil* (London, 1822), plate 27.

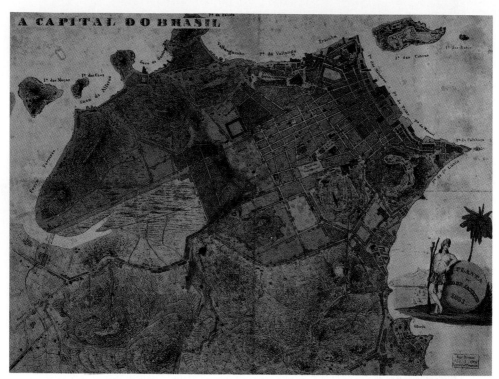

A Capital do Brasil. Map by E. de la Michellerie (s.i., 1831). Scale not given. 1 map: hand col.; 36 × 47 cm. G5404.R6 1831.M5 TIL. Courtesy of the Library of Congress Geography and Map Division, Washington, D.C.

A Carioca. Painting by Pedro Américo de Figueiredo e Melo, 1882. Oil on canvas, 205 × 135 cm. Courtesy of Museu Nacional de Belas Artes / IBRAM / MinC.

Rio, 40 Graus. Poster. Film directed by Nelson Pereira dos Santos. Rio de Janeiro: Equipe Moacyr Fenelon, 1955.

"Marina da Glória 4." Photograph by Rodrigo Soldon, 2009. Licensed under Creative Commons Attribution 2.0 Generic license.

"Santuário Anastacia." Photograph by Kelly E. Hayes, 2006. Vicente de Carvalho, Rio de Janeiro. Used by permission of Kelly E. Hayes.

UM LUGAR TÃO MARAVILHOSO COMO O RIO NÃO COMBINA COM HOMOFOBIA.
RESPEITE LÉSBICAS, GAYS, BISSEXUAIS, TRAVESTIS E TRANSEXUAIS.

RIO SEM HOMOFOBIA É UMA INICIATIVA DO GOVERNO DO RIO DE JANEIRO. MAS PODE SER A SUA TAMBÉM.
Como qualquer forma de preconceito, a homofobia deve ser combatida em todos os lugares e, por isso, o Governo do Rio está lançando o Rio sem Homofobia. Uma iniciativa inédita que vai contar com vários setores do governo e promover a cidadania e a conscientização da sociedade. Afinal, respeitar a diversidade é um dever de todos. Faça parte do Rio sem Homofobia. A População LGBT merece seu respeito.

"Rio Sem Homofobia." Campaign by Governo do Estado do Rio de Janeiro, Secretaria de Assistência Social e Direitos Humanos / Superintendência de Direitos Individuais, Coletivos e Difusos. Licensed under Creative Commons Attribuio 2.0 Brasil license, http://www.riosemhomofobia.rj.gov.br/campanha/ver/8_rio-sem-homofobia.

"Sem camisinha não dá!" Poster by Ministério da Saúde, Departamento de DST, Aids, e Hepatites Virais.

Photography Arrives in Rio

Louis Compte and Jornal do Commercio

Shortly after the French artist Louis-Jacques Daguerre (1787–1851) introduced pho-
tography to the Parisian public in 1839, Daguerre's friend Louis Compte arrived in
Rio with a camera. The pioneering process of daguerreotypy was introduced to Bra-
zil on January 17, 1840, when Compte took three perspectives of the capital's Largo
do Paço (today's Praça XV de Novembro). The novelty attracted the attention of the
local press, including the daily newspaper Jornal do Commercio.

   One of the first photographs of Rio, shown here, presents a splendid visual docu-
mentation of the city's central square on a sunny summer day at the dawn of the
Second Empire. The large number of people, including uniformed soldiers, grouped
at the formal entrance to the royal palace indicates the building's place of privilege
in everyday street life as well as ceremonial occasions associated with the comings
and goings of the imperial government. The horses, standing on what appears to be
unpaved ground, signal one means by which people and goods moved about the city.
In addition to the towers of the Imperial Chapel and the Carmelite convent, we note
the façade of the Hôtel de France, a rooming house especially popular with travelers
who arrived at the bayside docks located just outside the frame of the photograph.

   Compte's daguerreotype registered several architectural and urbanistic changes
that had transpired over the first four decades of the nineteenth century. The roof
of the Paço Imperial is capped by balustrades and terraces that were not part of
the original viceregal palace, once notable for its slanted roofline. Such additions,
neoclassical in form, hid the architectural outlines of the Portuguese colonial past.
The perspective of the image, taken at some elevation from street level, also conveyed
a new, modern way to see the city. The numerous hills that dominate the natural
landscape beyond the Largo do Paço are largely obscured by buildings. Such images
of built Rio would form a popular subgenre of the photographic market that quickly
captured the imagination of the young emperor Pedro II, local elites, and foreign
visitors in imperial Rio.

"Largo do Paço." Photograph by Louis Compte, 1840. From *De Volta a Luz: Fotografias Nunca Vistas do Imperador* (São Paulo: Banco Santos, 2003). Courtesy of Fundação Biblioteca Nacional, Rio de Janeiro.

"NOTICIAS SCIENTIFICAS. PHOTOGRAPHIA"

The daguerreotype has finally come across the seas, and photography, previously only known as a theoretical concept in Rio de Janeiro, can now be known by the facts that surpass everything ever read in the papers, about real or painted life.

This morning at the Hotel Pharoux there was a photography demonstration of the most interesting sort, being that it was the first time that the new marvel was revealed to Brazilian eyes. It was the abbot Combes [Compte] who conducted the trial: he is one of the travelers to be found aboard the French corvette *L'Orientale*, who brought with him Daguerre's ingenious instrument, because of the ease with which one obtains a representation of the objects that one desires to preserve in an image.

One must see such a thing with one's own eyes to have a sense of the speed and the outcome. In less than nine minutes the fountain at the Largo do Paço, the Praça do Peixe, the São Bento monastery, and all the other surrounding elements are reproduced with a fidelity, precision, and fineness of detail. One might think that the thing had been made by the very hand of nature, without the intervention of the artist. It would be futile to overstate the importance of the discovery for which our readers have worried themselves so: the simple exposition of the fact says more than all the superlatives.

Translated by Daryle Williams

Transient Laborers of the Fazenda Santa Cruz

Paulo Barboza da Silva

In 1834, a group of forty slaves owned by the Brazilian government were lent by the Fazenda Imperial de Santa Cruz, a state-owned estate on the rural outskirts of western Rio, to a foundry located in the town of Sorocaba, São Paulo, 330 miles from the Brazilian capital. Ten years later, the director of the São João de Ypanema ironworks alluded to the difficult experiences of those slaves from Santa Cruz: premature death, flight, continual threats to family stability. It is a poignant record of the precariousness of slave life in nineteenth-century Brazil.

A former Jesuit estate that had been expropriated by the Portuguese Crown in 1759, the Fazenda Imperial depended on a complex network of diverse, transient labor arrangements. Through the 1860s, slaves were central to the estate's core agro-pastoral operations. At the margins, displaced Indians, fishermen, muleteers, and small farmers were also active. Foreign laborers—silkworm workers and tea farmers from China; Spanish and Portuguese agriculturalists—were found at Santa Cruz during the slow transition to nonslave labor. The São João de Ypanema ironworks also housed a varied and mobile labor. Like the Fábrica de Pólvora, a gunpowder plant located in what is today's Jardim Botânico in Rio's Zona Sul, the factory in Sorocaba was born out of a small manufacturing boom that accompanied post-1808 measures revoking colonial-era mercantilist bans on local production. In the interior of São Paulo, slaves labored alongside free workers, including some recruited from northern Europe.

The Fazenda Santa Cruz and the São João de Ypanema ironworks operated in tandem. The rural estate in Rio served as a labor depot, where the ministry of war and other government authorities administered a supply of coerced laborers across various institutions located throughout the empire. Reading this document, one can see how Brazilian-born slaves moved in and out of Rio, at the convenience of the government and its labor needs. Yet the narrative was not purely one of victimhood. In their forced movements and the related hardships, workers from Santa Cruz found opportunities to build ties of work and affection with laborers from the distant reaches of the Brazilian empire, including enslaved workers from the northern province of Piauí.

Most Illustrious and Excellent Sir
February 5, 1844

Being that the Most Excellent former Tutor of His Imperial Majesty, in the name of the same August Sir, lent to the Fábrica São João de Ypanema forty slaves from the Fazenda Imperial de Santa Cruz in 1834 until they were no longer needed, and because ten years have gone by since this loan was granted, during this period several have died, others have deserted, and finally it should be included here that their numbers have been reduced to twenty-something, and that some have gotten married to slaves from the Fábrica, and vice versa, making the separation of those from Santa Cruz difficult without destroying matrimonial bonds and occasioning the separation of parents from children, and other inconveniences, that are within the reach of all, and for this reason it occurs to me to propose to Your Excellency that those slaves from Piauí who are at the Gunpowder Factory could be used in exchange, with Your Excellency sending to me the same sexes and ages, all Brazilian-born, filling out registries for this exchange, without the onus of transferring ownership, and the only thing that to be changed is the type of service.

May God Protect Your Excellency

Office of the Chief of Staff of the Imperial Household,
January 27, 1844
Most Illustrious and Excellent Dr. Salvador José Maciel

Paulo Barboza da Sylva

Translated by Amy Chazkel

Recollections of Nineteenth-Century Women

Adèle Toussaint-Samson

Adèle Toussaint-Samson (1826–1878?) was a cultured Parisian who took up residence in Rio, along with her merchant husband and their children, in late 1849 or early 1850. Administering a household that was connected to Rio's French commercial and diplomatic community, Toussaint-Samson published occasional short pieces in the Courrier du Brésil *as well as general-interest periodicals published in Paris. She taught French language classes on the Rua das Bellas Artes and in Glória. A self-styled liberated woman, Toussaint-Samson traveled the streets of the Brazilian capital, presumably unchaperoned, to take in the hustle-bustle of Rua Direita and the dizzying heights of Corcovado. Her transit through public and private spaces involved intimate contact with the women of color whose labors supplied the city's daily needs and helped sustain urban households founded on agrarian wealth.*

Sometime after 1862, Toussaint-Samson returned to France and began to systematize her recollections of her sojourn in Brazil. In 1883, a photo-illustrated edition of her memoirs appeared in France, quickly followed by a Brazilian translation published in Rio. Framed in the style of a travel narrative—beginning and ending with a ship voyage—the publication recounted a deadly yellow fever epidemic in 1850 and the triumphs of stage actor João Caetano (1808–1863). Toussaint-Samson offered sketches of an educated woman's circulation among urban homes and country estates where wealth rested on slave-based agriculture and the rising availability of risk capital. She described the cultured life of the Brazilian Court, highlighting the refined tastes of the polyglot emperor and the gendered conventions of elite Brazilian homes.

In 1890, an American edition of Une Parisienne au Brésil, *prepared by Adèle's daughter Emma, was published in Boston. The excerpts here conveyed to an English-language reading public, along with counterparts in the French- and Portuguese-speaking worlds, the cosmopolitan woman's thoughts on the women of Rio, notably the boisterous market women known as bahianas and the ascendant ladies of elite households. In these passages, one notes how Toussaint-Samson projects onto the women of Rio a color line of purported morality—black female debauchery and violence on the one side and ever-improving white womanliness on the other. White women best their African and Afro-descended counterparts in intelligence. How-ever, one might discern a certain respect for the wily resourcefulness and bearing with which the women of Rio, black and white, navigated surroundings not of their making, where patriarchy, male sexual prerogative, and the brutality of the lash shaped women's lives.*

The Bahianas

When you enter the city of Rio Janeiro by the Largo do Paço, the first street which presents itself to you is Dircita Street [Rua Direita]. It is one of the most beautiful streets of the city; it is quite wide, and bordered on each side by houses of one or two stories, painted in different colors, having, in the majority, their balconies decorated with red and white blinds. The majority of houses are of ancient construction; many even have kept the verandas around the residences. This street is very lively, for it is here the stock exchange is held. Three or four beautiful churches, among others Santa Cruz [dos Militares] and the church dos Carmos, are remarkable.

The whole length of the street, on the steps of the churches, or at the doors of the shops, are squatted the large Minas negresses (the Minas originally came from the province of Mina, in occidental Africa), adorned in their most beautiful things: a fine chemise, and a skirt of white muslin with ruffles, worn over another skirt of some bright color, form all their costume; they have their feet bare in a sort of slipper with high heel, called *tamancas*, where only the point of the foot can enter; their neck and their arms are loaded with gold chains, strings of pearl, and all sorts of pieces of ivory and of teeth, sort of manitous, which, according to them, must conjure evil fortune; a large piece of muslin is rolled three or four times around their head, turban shape, and another piece of striped cloth is thrown over their shoulders, to cover themselves with when they are cold, or to encircle their hips when they carry a child.

Many men find these negresses handsome; as for me, I acknowledge that the curled wool, which does duty for hair, their low and debased forehead, their blood-shot eyes, their enormous mouth with bestial lips, their disjointed teeth, like those of deer, as well as their flattened nose, had never appeared to me to constitute but a very ugly type. What is the least vulgar is their carriage. They walk with head held high, chest prominent, hips raised, arms akimbo, holding their load of fruits always placed on the head. Their feet and their hands are small, their waists are firm and curving, and their walk, of easy gait, is always accompanied by a movement of the hips quite suggestive, and yet filled with a certain dignity, like that of the Spanish woman. Their bosom is hardly veiled by their fine chemise, and sometimes even one breast is seen; but few among them have fine necks. It is only in the very young mulattresses that this beauty is sometimes found.

As regards the negresses, nothing has been exaggerated in saying that they easily nursed their children placed on their backs. I have seen it done by some of my servants, only that it is really not from the middle of the back that the child nurses, but from under the arm. There is nothing more debauched than these Minas negresses; they are the ones who deprave and corrupt the young people of Rio Janeiro; it is not rare to see foreigners, especially Englishmen, maintain them and ruin themselves for them.

It is not rare either to hear of the *facadas* (knife-cuts) given to whites by the jealous blacks.

When one desires these creatures, one has only to make them a sign, and they follow one. I have had some in my house, who, their work being finished, would disappear to give themselves to this fine trade, and found it very singular I should reprimand them on the subject. They'd reply very simply, "I must go and earn something with which to buy a piece of lace. Our Brazilian ladies are not like madam, and allow us several hours each evening for that."

Brazilian Ladies

As for the Brazilian ladies, penned up as they are by their husbands in the enclosure of their houses, in the midst of their children and their slaves, never going out unaccompanied to either mass or processions, one must not imagine, on that account, that they are more virtuous than others, only they have the art of appearing so.

Everything is done mysteriously in these impenetrable abodes, where the lash has made the slave as silent as the tomb. Under the cloak of the family even, many things are hidden. All this is, or at least was (for since several years the Brazilian ladies go out alone),—all this is the fruit of the sequestration imposed upon women. Besides, the appearances are so well guarded that one must live years in the land to begin to know the inner life of these homes, of such patriarchal customs and habits, at first sight, where frequently three generations live together under the same roof in the most perfect concord; for one must say, in this regard, that the Brazilians are much our superiors. They have found the secret of uniting in the same house son-in-law, mother-in-law, daughter-in-law, without there ever being conflict. That ferocious hatred for the mother-in-law, which is at present professed in France, is unknown over there. One does not believe that, by the simple fact of marrying her daughter or her son, a mother who has been good and devoted all her life can suddenly become a monster. One has the greatest respect for the father and the mother.

When the Brazilian comes home he finds in his house a dutiful wife, whom he treats as a spoilt child, bringing her dresses, jewels, and ornaments of all kinds; but this woman is not associated to him, neither in his business, his preoccupations, nor his thoughts. It is a doll whom he dresses for an occasion, and who, in reality, is but the first slave of the house; although the Brazilian of Rio Janeiro is never brutal, and exercises his despotism in a manner almost gentle. All this besides, as I have already said, is undergoing complete changes.

The Brazilian ladies of today, educated in French or English boarding schools, have little by little taken our habits and our manner of seeing; so that very gradually they acquire their liberty. Then, as their intelligence is very quick, I think that in a short time they will have surpassed their teachers.

It is in the interior of the country, whose roads are impassable but on donkey-back, and which render communication with the capital very difficult, that one can still study all these customs of Portuguese or Spanish origin. Likewise, when you arrive in a *fazenda*, do you never perceive the senhora, while she always has the means of seeing the stranger without their ever being aware of it.

Workers, for Sale or Rent

Diário do Rio de Janeiro

Brazil's first daily newspaper, the Diário do Rio de Janeiro *(1821–1878), was known for keeping a distance from the turmoil of formal politics. Journalistic content favored ostensibly nonpartisan facets of urban daily life. In keeping with its role in disseminating quotidian information, the* Diário *published numerous classified advertisements. Anyone interested in placing a classified could submit the text via boxes placed throughout the city. The resulting ads were, in effect, the medium through which the literate reached beyond their intimate family circles to talk to each other in an increasingly large and impersonal city. In reading through these classifieds, we can eavesdrop on such conversations.*

As we see in this page taken from an ordinary date in 1850, most ads placed in the Diário *concerned small-scale commercial transactions—matters of employment and the private sale of material and consumer goods. Such ads also point our attention to the commonplace nature of slavery in Rio's daily life. (More than 70 percent of Rio's middling classes at midcentury held at least one slave, usually engaged in domestic service.) A "comely black woman" could be purchased for 260 milréis. Another female, perhaps healthier or of higher skill, was offered at the asking price of 450 milréis. Yet the ads also illustrate the great diversity of laborers and labor arrangements in and out of legal bondage. The ad for the sale of a young male porter who could yield a daily wage of 800 réis (the price equivalent of seven pounds of refined sugar, or one-fourth the price of a hundredweight of imported potatoes) demonstrates the common practice of purchasing a slave who would then be hired out to others. The "white senhora" who is offered "for rent" in another ad may have been party to a service rental contract, a legal arrangement of rising importance in the gradual transition to a wage labor economy.*

The individuals represented in these ads ostensibly appear as dehumanized factors of production (and reproduction, when we consider the four advertisements about wet-nurses, who themselves were mothers) to be bought, sold, and rented. Yet readers can sometimes glean valuable information about the names, lives, and experiences of the working poor. The Africans Caetano and Antonio, for example, each had visual impairments, attesting perhaps to accidents that they sustained or to inflammatory eye diseases that spread on slave ships during the Middle Passage. The fugitive Caetano's habit of changing his name lets us glimpse at a possible strategy employed by those trying to escape bondage and remake their lives as free people in the city.

FOR SALE an excellent adolescent boy, coffee porter, will earn 800 rs. a day; Rua do Piolho, 20.

ON Rua do Senhor dos Passos, n. 21, a beautiful and elegant open carriage with two wheels, new, for a fair price.

FOR SALE on the Largo da Sé, n. 5, a very good black woman, irons with great perfection, a perfect sweets-maker, launders with soap and washboard.

FOR SALE on the Largo da Sé, n. 5, a comely black woman, knowing how to cook, clean, and shop, for 260$ rs.

FOR SALE a black woman eighteen years of age, kept in the house, in which she knows how to iron and starch, clean, sew, and knows how to take care of children, free of vices and illness; anyone interested should go to Rua das Violas, n. 77.

IN the sugar refinery on Rua dos Barbonos, n. 54, extra fine refined sugar for sale at 4$ rs. per *arroba* [approximately thirty-two pounds] and by the pound at 130 rs., refined sugar at 3$400 and at 110 rs. per pound, refined turbinado sugar at 2$600 and by the pound at 90 rs., from two to eight pounds: there are likewise other foodstuffs available, everything at a very good price.

FOR SALE wooden furniture, with a sofa, a round table, two dressers, twelve chairs, two with arms; on Rua do Silva Manuel in the house between numbers 24 and 28.

FOR SALE a small farm on the lands of Dr. Freitas, in Niterói, at Fonseca, with plenty of trees, with water, good cottage, oven, and water wheel, etc.; to discuss go to the street behind Rua da Lapa, n. 24.

FOR SALE a business, with two very faithful black women, without vices, twenty years of age, perfect laundresses, iron women, they cook, and they sew, too; on Rua Velha de S. Francisco da Prainha, n. 81. The reason for this sale is that the owner would like to move away to take care of his health.

POTATOES. At Rua do Sabão, n. 9, excellent quality potatoes for sale from Hamburg, at 3$ rs. per hundredweight [*quintal*].

FOR SALE on the Largo da Sé, n. 5, a black woman who knows how to cook, clean, iron, and embroider well: her price 450$ rs.

FOR SALE a black man in good shape, perfect craftsman upholsterer; on the Largo da Sé, n. 5.

FOR RENT a robust, young black man, who even carries boxes, for 14$ rs.; at Rua do Piolho, n. 20.

FOR RENT a black man who is a very good cook and shopper, for all kinds of work in the house, is very faithful; on Rocio Pequeno, n. 6.

FOR RENT a good housemaid, for 12$ rs., for all kinds of service inside; at Rua do Piolho, n. 20.

FOR RENT a black man for all types of service; at Rua do Rosário, n. 67.

FOR RENT the townhouse at Rua da Ajuda, n. 97, good rooms for a family; those interested go to that address.

FOR RENT black woman who knows how to cook and wash well, iron, launder clothes, treat children well, is very faithful and without vices; Rua de Santa Anna the house next to number 47 B.

FOR RENT a white lady [*uma Sra. branca*], who knows well how to sew and iron, for the appropriate household; Rua de Santo Antonio, n. 7.

ON the Rua do Principe dos Cajueiros, n. 80, seeking to rent a housemaid, who knows well how to wash and iron.

FOR RENT a house with very good rooms, good well water for washing clothes, garden plot, with lots of land and forest, located on Praia Vermelha, n. 2, a very healthy place close to the embarkation point for steamships and omnibus, and has a fountain with good water very close by; it could be rented for three or more years for a very low rent.

WET NURSES.

WILL RECEIVE a freeborn child, to be nursed with tenderness and vigilance; on the rua da Ajuda n. 97.

A brown-skinned lady [*uma Sra. parda*], for rent as wet nurse; in the Bêco do Cotovello, n. 54.

FOR RENT a great nursemaid from her first birth, secluded at home, seventeen years old, with abundant milk; on the Largo do Rocio, n. 28.

FOR RENT a black woman [*preta*] as a nursemaid with very good milk; at Rua do Ouvidor, n. 21.

FOUND.

WHOEVER is missing a little black girl [*negrinha*] that appears to be twelve years of age, who was found yesterday in the woods nearby this city, and does not want to say to whom she belongs; please by means of this *Diário* tell the national origin, dress and any distinguishing sign, so I can send her to you.

FUGITIVE SLAVES.

RAN AWAY on January 20, a black man [*preto*] named Caetano, from the Angola nation, blind in his left eye, he is short and dusky-colored, and he has the habit of changing his name; whoever brings him to Rua do Carmo, n. 15, will be rewarded with 20$ rs.

DEAR PEDESTRIANS. Ran away on the 23rd of this month, the Brazilian-born black [*crioulo*] Sérgio, carpenter craftsman, regular stature, talks a lot, from 22 to 24 years of age, is missing a front tooth, beard beginning to grow, he is kind of knock-kneed in his legs, and a toenail is growing on his big toe; whoever turns him in at Rua do Sabão, n. 195, or at Praia de São Cristóvão, between numbers 39 and 41, will be rewarded.

RAN AWAY on February 25, a black man named Antonio Mozambique, regular stature, about 30 years old, more or less, has some pockmarks, and the right eye is crossed; whoever apprehends him and brings him to Travessa Quindaste, n. 6, will be paid for his effort.

Translated by Amy Chazkel

Maria Angola Denounces
Illegal Enslavement

Maria Angola and Miguel Paes Pimenta

Many residents of nineteenth-century Rio engaged in a variety of shady maneuvers as well as acts of outright violence to reduce to slavery freed and freeborn blacks. Free Africans (also known as africanos livres or emancipados), a small subgroup of the illegally imported Africans who had been declared to be free under various treaties and laws, were especially vulnerable to the predations of Brazilian citizens, Portuguese immigrants, and public authorities who sought to circumvent the law and humanitarian appeals that developed around the suppression of the transatlantic trade.

One of the many Free Africans to confront the precariousness of freedom in imperial Rio was Maria, a West Central African mother who had been rescued from slavery sometime around 1840. Presumably liberated by the antislavery Anglo-Brazilian Mixed Commission, which operated in Rio between 1831 and 1844, Maria had been consigned to the care of Miguel Paes Pimenta, a Portuguese-born, naturalized Brazilian cobbler and slave master who resided in Sacramento parish. The details of Maria's life as a Free African in Rio are fragmentary, but we can piece together that she bore three children. Her twins had died sometime before 1853, the year she denounced Paes Pimenta for the enslavement of her surviving son, three-and-a-half-year-old Eugenio.

In response to changes leveled by Maria, Paes Pimenta presented a curious story involving a mistaken baptism ordered by his sister-in-law. Other protagonists of the episode include the top British diplomat in Rio, Henry Howard, the superintendent (curador) of Free Africans, Carlos Honorio de Figueiredo, and Paulo Manoel Hoz de la Sierra, a Spaniard who served as legal representative (procurador) for Maria and other Free African women petitioners. The final outcome of this case is unknown, but it appears that Paes Pimenta and his sister-in-law departed for Europe on January 5, 1855. The fates of Maria and Eugenio are lost to history, but Maria's complaints, registered here, give us a glimpse of the scourge of reenslavement. The stories of Free African mothers who denounced the illegal enslavement of children *born in Rio (who were, by Brazilian law, citizens of the Brazilian empire) are espe-cially gripping.*

Petition "to Alleviate and Soften the Situation of this Unhappy Mother and Child"

Your Excellency Mr. Minister of Her Britannic Majesty in the Court

Paulo Manoel Hoz de la Sierra, resident of Rua dos Barbonos, number 11A, in this City, so moved by the call of piety and philanthropy has taken it upon his shoulders the arduous and painful burden of lodging a denunciation in favor of the unfortunate Free African woman who currently finds herself taken to the city's House of Correction, being that she had been reduced to slavery, just as her children had been as well. She goes by the name Maria, of the Angola nation, taken by the cruiser that pursued traffickers of human flesh. This black woman, Your Excellency, was consigned to the care of a private citizen, in conformity with the respective Instructions and Regulations, who goes by the name Miguel Paes Pimenta, residing at Rua do Cano, 62 of this Court, where he has heaped great burdens upon these unhappy people. Notwithstanding the constant protection of the Wise Government of Her Britannic Majesty, Paes Pimenta baptized her as a slave of a woman, going by the name Maria Bella d'Avellar, who claims to be his sister-in-law. But this was not the totality of the outrages of those individuals: to wit, upon the birth of Maria's children, Paes Pimenta baptized them as the slaves of that most atrocious woman. All this was communicated to the Curador of the Free Africans, and he made inquiries into the truth of the facts, by means of documents that were placed before him, including a certificate of baptism, admissible evidence in the Laws of this Country. The Curador interviewed the black woman, and came to recognize the existence of a crime. Yet, the fate of the unfortunate *preta* [black woman] and the son who survives has not improved, it in fact worsened even more, as she was taken to the House of Correction where she finds herself burdened with the most violent labors, and with even less liberty than that which she had as a slave of the author of the Crime. Thus, the Supplicant confides in the active and solid protection of Your Excellency who must commit to provide aid, to alleviate and soften the situation of this unhappy mother and child; making it such that punishment is meted out to those who would traffic in their flesh, and that the tutelage that this wicked Man has held be denied him. The Supplicant awaits the opportunity to deliver into the honorable hands of Your Excellency those documents that are to be found readied, and hope that the guardian-ship of these two poor souls be turned over to him, and that they might be protected by Your Excellency, being certain that you will find them ready and humble in following through on this accusation.

Your most respectful servant,

Paulo Manoel Hoz de la Sierra

A Reply from Miguel Paes Pimenta

Sir

So says Miguel Paes Pimenta that having under his power a Free African [*huma Africana livre*] woman, whose services had been confided to him, who goes by the name Maria, of the Rebola nation, and being that she has been employed to serve his sister-in-law who goes by the name Maria Bella do Amaral [*sic*], who lives with the petitioner; that said African gave birth to a son, who was in a grave state of health and ran the risk of life, was sent to the parish to be baptized, and there he was declared to be the son of a slave of the said Maria Bella, without the Petitioner having received notice, and without granting his consent for such a declaration; only upon finding this out did he take action to correct the baptismal registry of the African woman's child, declaring him to be free, as the accompanying document proves. In response to the denunciation, the Curador of Free Africans, to whom the Petitioner submitted a copy of the registry, sent to the House of Correction the said African and her son, accompanied by a certification of the first baptism. . . . Now the Petitioner humbly submits himself before His Im-perial Majesty seeking the favor of declaring to the said Curador of Free Africans that the Petitioner has already declared to His Imperial Majesty the case of the child's baptism, and that there has been no crime on his part, and because of this that said African woman and her child should be restored to him.

Be that His Imperial Majesty deign to effect His Unimpeachable Jus-tice to grant the Petitioner his request

May You Receive Mercy

Miguel Paes Pimenta

Translated by Daryle Williams

The Capoeira Gangs of Rio

João Jacintho de Mello

The martial arts and dance form known the world over as capoeira flourished in the streets of nineteenth-century Rio, growing out of acrobatic, sometimes violent body maneuvers that originated in West and West Central African combat games. The term "capoeira" also applied to the black men—male street vendors, domestics, and other laborers—who used such maneuvers to negotiate daily life and interpersonal conflict in a slave city. Organized gangs of capoeiras, known to Rio authorities as maltas, carved up the city along lines of ethnicity, occupation, and kinship.

The following complaint gives us a glimpse into the activities of capoeiras at mid-century. The petitioner, João Jacintho de Mello, administrator of the Free Africans (africanos livres) consigned to the municipal government, writes to the president of the city council to report an assault on Demiciano, a Free African out on errands. The denunciation reveals a complicated relationship between Mello and a black male ward whose "good conduct" is contrasted with the unruliness of two capoeiras, at least one of whom is enslaved. The site of the assault, Rua São Pedro, was close to Rua das Violas (today's Rua Teófilo Otoni), where one of the alleged assailants resided. One wonders if the perpetrators were defending turf from an inadvertent incursion into their territory. Ironically, the timing of the assault may have been grounds for the police to arrest the victim and his attackers, as the residents of imperial Rio lived under a highly selective and unevenly enforced curfew. People of African descent were formally prohibited from walking the streets after the evening church bells. With the approaching dusk, Demiciano may have been in technical violation of curfew, though Mello's permission to set out for the cigars might have provided the necessary protection to avoid arrest.

In the face of police persecution, capoeira and its practitioners remained popular and widespread. The cultural significance of the form was strong and the persecution of maltas largely ineffectual. Moreover, capoeira gangs could prove useful to the ruling classes, as capoeiras were sometimes used as hired thugs in political and personal disputes. Capoeira would not be formally criminalized until the republican penal code of 1890. Yet by the mid-twentieth century it had evolved into a celebrated feature of Brazilian urban popular culture with worldwide resonance.

With friendship to the Illustrious Sir Chief of Police
Rio de Janeiro
November 25, 1858

Dear Mr. Fausto,

I have the honor of reporting to you that yesterday at around
7 o'clock at night I asked the African named Demiciano to go to the
store to buy cigars, when on his return home he came upon two Capoeiras on the corner of Rua São Pedro, who surrounded Demiciano and injured him with two blows, neither of which being insignificant, one on
the left side of his chest and the other on the left arm. I was notified that
this had taken place and went immediately to the gathering of the aforementioned Capoeiras, and going after them, I was only able to grab the
hat of one of them, and he declared himself to be a slave belonging to
Senhor Dr. Pena, who lives on the Rua das Violas. I would like to bring
to your attention that these cases have occurred with frequency around
these neighborhoods, what with all the Africans. I must note that the
paucity of efforts to prevent such occurrences has been brought to your
attention and to the attention of the public on numerous occasions. I am
greatly interested in requesting that measures be taken to punish the
perpetrators of this crime, and I would also like to make sure that the
injured African, who is very well behaved [*é de muito boa conduta*] and is
incapable of provoking anybody, and whose condition might worsen, is
taken quickly to the apothecary to be given the necessary medical treatment, in his living quarters if necessary.

May God Protect you

Rio, November 23, 1858
The Most Illustrious Sr. Dr. João de Oliveira Fausto
President of the Most Illustrious Municipal Chamber

João Jacintho de Mello
Administrator

Translated by Amy Chazkel

French-Language Classifieds

Courrier du Brésil

French immigrants were pioneers in Rio's world of print, notably the burgeoning market for nongovernment periodicals, lithography, and almanacs. As French printers adapted to the local Portuguese-language readership, some printing houses also launched newspapers for a French-reading public. Titles included L'Indépendent (1827), Revue Brésilienne (1830), L'Écho Français (1838–1839), L'Écho du Brésil (1859–1860), France et Brésil (1875), and Le Messager du Brésil (1878–1884). Maritime traffic between Rio and French ports, principally Le Havre and Marseille, also expanded the availability of French-language serials and illustrated magazines. The classified advertisements in Courrier du Brésil *(1854–1862) shown here demonstrate the wide variety of commercial and cultural transactions conducted in the French language at a moment when steamship service and the evolving tastes of the Fluminense elite drew Rio closer to the French-speaking world.*

Courrier du Brésil was an eight-page Sunday weekly published under a banner of "Politics, Theater Reviews, Science and Arts, Industry, Commerce." As for most general-interest titles of the period, column space was divided between current events summarized from the government press, public notices, and other newspapers, intermixed with original editorials, arts reviews, serialized literature, poetry, letters submitted by readers, and voluminous ads.

The paper's classifieds shared much with the advertisements found in Portuguese-language periodicals. For example, the pitch for the purported therapeutic properties of Holloway's Pills and Ointment (a globalized patent medicine that was a concoction of aloe, myrrh, and saffron) was a staple of print ads directed at local readers. In some instances, advertisements placed in the Courrier *drew in Brazilian readers with an appeal to the level of refinement associated with imported goods, Francophone culture, and commercial establishments modeled on French standards. Notably absent in the* Courrier *were paid advertisements for the purchase, sale, or rental of chattel slaves. This would have been consistent with the political leanings of editor-in-chief Antoine Adolphe Hubert, a French transplant who resided in Rio for at least twelve years before returning to France and later participating in the Paris Commune.*

CAFÉ DES ARTISTES

Rua do Rosario N. 127 suite 1

This establishment, completely renovated, stands out in its extreme elegance and refined taste made evident by its décor and layout. Here you will find all the amenities of Parisian cafés: billiards, salons, private rooms, etc.

–The staff will attend with the greatest care, the most extreme politeness and unbounded promptness.
–Customers may arrive at any point in time and there will always be members of staff to welcome them.

EUGÈNE LAVOGADE

Attention Merchants:

Has transferred his business from Rua dos Ourives, 155 to Rua do Sabão, 251 and that he continues as in the past to gild chains, watches, etc., without the slightest delay. Repairs any jewelry.

"LA GRENOUILLE AUX CAMELIAS"

(TWO SINNERS)

Quadrille for Piano by Alfred Claudel

CHANGE OF ADDRESS

Henri Lemale

Dental surgeon of the Imperial Household

Has transferred his consultation office to suite 5 at Rua Direita, 29.

ONE AND ONLY LEGAL FRENCH MIRROR DEPOT

BROT ET FILS

Rua de S. José, 75

Deals with everything having to do with the mirror trade and always has the most gorgeous assortment of mirrors with gold-plated frames, direct from Paris.

HOTEL RAVOT

Rua do Ouvidor, 163

Restaurant.—Baths.—Furnished rooms and apartments.

The Hotel Ravot whose reputation once left its public wanting, has just been newly restored. The new owner has stopped at nothing to maintain the comfort and all of the luxuries sought out by his clientele. The entrance to this establishment is noticeable for its simple décor and refined taste. Being situated in the center of commerce and in close proximity to theaters, the Hotel Ravot offers travelers all the possible conveniences. The food is prepared with extreme care, providing a large variety of dishes, do not forget the food is unlike any other private establishments.

FROM THE VIEWS OF PARIS

Rua do São José, 28
Merchants, be advised that we have just received new and beneficial goods at very moderate prices.

BOOKKEEPER

Didier Roiffé is looking for bookkeeping work in French or in Portuguese; he also teaches bookkeeping lessons. He can be found at Rua Ouvidor, 110, or Rua dos Ouvires, 73.

HÔTEL PHAROUX

New owners have just acquired the delightfully situated Hôtel Pharoux, overlooking the Rio harbor.
The commodious and well-furnished apartments offer all the desirable features. The restaurant, whose windows overlook the bay and the Largo do Paço, features one of the foremost Parisian chefs.

ROCHER, DENTIST-SURGEON

Dr. Dupont's successor, Rua do Ouvidor, 13, entrance located at Rua da Valla, 71.

NOUVEAU CAFÉ PARISIEN

Mademoiselle Pauline Lyon has the honor of informing the respectable public of this capital of the opening of a café on the Rua dos Pescadores, 49, named the Grand Café Parisien: with 5 billiards tables. Mademoiselle Pauline will do all in her power to please the people who honor her establishment. Seven days a week the clientele will have at its disposal refreshments and beverages of the highest and most refined quality.

A COMPLETE TREATISE

ON THE CONJUGATION OF REGULAR AND IRREGULAR FRENCH VERBS, BY CASIMIRO LIETAUD

Professor licensed by the Executive Council for Public Instruction of Rio de Janeiro. On sale for the price of 2$000 in the Pinto, Garnier, and Laemmert bookshops, and in the French College run by the author, Rua do Cano, 52.

SPECIAL: HATS FOR LADIES

Made of silk, straw, and novelties starting at 8$000, 10$000, 14$000, 16$000, 18$000

AT THE BELLA UNIÃO

This shop distinguishes itself based on the great quality of its merchandise and low prices.

HEALTH AND WELL-BEING!!

Holloway Pills
Awarded prizes by every government.
Known and respected in every country in the world.
Prescribed by the most famous doctors.
No blood cleansing remedy to date enjoys a reputation like Holloway Pills.
Many doctors and distinguished members of major practices recommend to their clients or to hospital directors the use of this beneficial medicine that restores the strength of even the weakest complexion, and one that has given life to the best of people who were already tired of the uselessness of other prescriptions. These famous pills have been available to us for a long time, and each one of us will know by asking those who use them each and every day that their properties are real and their effectiveness is trusted.
Holloway Pills, formulated under the direction of their inventor, can be found in these general establishments: in London, no. 244, Strand, and in New York, 80 Maiden Lane.
Stores in Brazil: In Rio de Janeiro, at Messrs. dos Santos Mesquita, Rua Direita, 26; H. Prins, Rua do Hospicio. In Pernambuco, Messrs. Soum & Co. In Porto Alegre, Mr. A. Cornell. In Bahia, Messrs. Von Bergen & Co. In Maranhão, Messrs. J. J. de Azevedo Almeida & Co.

A French woman looking to take care of children ages 2 to 6. She will take care of them from 8 in the morning until 5 o'clock in the evening, and the children will be treated as well as they are at home. She can be found at Rua da Carioca, 91.

VOICE COACH

A distinguished artist has just arrived in Rio de Janeiro; Mr. Lollio, a bass singer, wishes to teach singing lessons.

Mr. Lollio is one of the best students to come out of the Bergame school, he has always held positions as first bass in major theaters throughout Italy and beyond with companies featuring the most famous artists such as: Messrs. Mines, Bosio, Cinti, Damoreau, Ruleini, Caizoloti, etc., etc. Even if the city of Rio de Janeiro already possesses great piano teachers, it does not have the same level of vocal coaches. M. Lollio understands perfectly the art of voice projection, having done a study of this particular subject, in very little time, he puts himself to the task of fixing one's voice to render it soft and supple for the vocalist. He has given undeniable proof of his abilities in Paris.

Mr. Lollio remains available to families and beginners at his residence, Hôtel Ravot, Rua do Ouvidor.

Translated by Nathan H. Dize

Public Entertainment in Imperial Rio

Joaquim Manoel de Macedo

As entertainment options multiplied over the second half of the nineteenth century, almanacs listed Rio's wide variety of venues for dramatic and comedic performance, operas and operettas, and ballets. The well-heeled public frequented exhibitions of painting and sculpture as well as musical recitals. The thrills of dioramas, curiosities, and grotesqueries could be had for modest prices. This cultural efflorescence was fed by local productions as well as imports from Europe and the United States. The growth in leisure activities fueled the popularity of the crônica, a type of serialized newspaper column characterized by humorous, sometimes polemical takes on daily life and urban pastimes.

Born in the interior of Rio province, Joaquim Manuel de Macedo (1820–1882) became a master of the crônica about Rio city. Educated as a physician, Macedo made a name for himself as a Liberal Party legislator and favorite of the Bragança monarchy. Local politics and quotidian life were common themes in "Labirinto" (Labyrinth), a short-lived crônica serialized in the Jornal do Commercio *between April and December 1860. Other crônicas appeared in Macedo's books* Um Passeio pela Cidade do Rio de Janeiro *(A stroll around the City of Rio de Janeiro, 1862–1863) and* Memórias da Rua do Ouvidor *(Memories of Rua do Ouvidor, 1878).*

The November 19, 1860, installment of "Labirinto" offered up the author's wry observations on the limits of recreation and leisure in Rio. Macedo describes the pleasures of horse racing, sailing regattas, and musical bands. Yet he also characterizes entertainment as a field of social exclusion. Only elites had the means to enjoy the city's sumptuous balls and expensive theaters. Poor people were left the mundane pursuits of working, drinking, small-time gambling, and the vote. Such observations offer an ironic perspective on the lives of the free poor in a slave city. As Macedo explores the harsh social truths revealed in popular entertainment activities, he criticizes religion when tithing practices associated with small devotional altars degenerate into a form of extortion. Typical of the genre and Macedo's skill, this somewhat playful assessment of urban public diversions ends up containing a broad, secularist indictment of religion and the unwanted influence of the clergy in urban life.

Rio is a city without mirth: a capital that holds two hundred thousand inhabitants, where there are few festivals and even fewer public amusements.

This is not a function of some strict enforcement of the laws of labor, as vagrants and the idle sort are as common as dirt; nor should one conclude that the cult of philosophy and political economy is observed religiously. Philosophers and economists may indeed be counted at a rate of a dozen a street corner, but everything is so confused on matters of mind and money such that what we have is a modern Tower of Babel where innumerable languages stumble upon one another.

But the fact of the matter is that the people of the capital have no festivals, no public amusements, and no innocent distractions.

The life of the common people is shrill prose: work hard, eat and sleep as you can, wear a uniform of the National Guard, vote in elections, and *bon soir la compagnie*! . . . [1]

Balls are amusing distractions exclusive to the rich. The man in the street can go to the theater but once in a great while, buying his measly general admission ticket, but a poor chap who's married cannot take his Eve to a dramatic show because the price of a theater box costs the equivalent of four days' salary.

And besides the theaters what else is there? . . .

The breweries;

The battalion parading by, led by some tune;

The musical band of this or that corps, playing for two hours on some afternoon at the Passeio Público;

The food stalls set up at the Campo da Aclamação during the month of June;

And nothing else! . . .

This really is so much fun! . . .

[. . .]

There are, of course, a multitude of public spectacles and entertainment options attainable to all. Many such activities might be of use to the nation.

We shall note some, pointing out those that are already among us.

The horse races are cherished by our people, and are recommended for their known usefulness. It is a form of entertainment that awakens and entices the desire to breed the finest stock of horses. It is well known that racehorses are not the most useful, but interest develops with these shows, enthusiasm surges, and breeders never limit themselves to preparing horses only for races. [. . .] The regattas are to the sea what the horse races are to the land, and the former perhaps exceed the latter in charm and beauty when they are well ordered and directed.

We lack the Romanesque canals to host the style of excitement-filled, graceful boat races run in Venice, the Princess of the Adriatic. Nevertheless, what could be more beautiful and romantic than our own Botafogo Bay, so serene and charming, so remote and yet so near the city, so gorgeous as to be most inviting. Might one host a party there? . . . [. . .]

Besides these and other diversions, we believe that the incentives created to encourage and develop certain gymnastic exercises would be quite fruitful as they could lay the groundwork for marvelous spectacles. The added benefit is such activities are so beneficial to health and the development of physical strength.

[. . .] We address now a little business that has been more than a slight bother of late.

We refer to the predilection that children have for treating the *oratório* as some plaything. It appears as though such children take in too little from their altars set up indoors. Thus, they turn the street into a stage for this religious pastime, the expense of which is ultimately left to the respectable public.

Six or eight boys gather in the street and near the windows of the houses in which they live to set up a devotional oratory with the image of some saint, before which burn four or six slender candles.

Up to this point we have before us two inconveniences: the first is the ridiculous display of an image worshiped by the Church; the second is the havoc these farces wreak on public transit.

But we have not yet touched on the business of the matter: here it comes now.

One of the frolicking boys stands with a cup in hand, like a sentinel, and, flinging himself at each and every person who passes by, asks for a donation to the honored saint. If he receives alms after the first request, he clears the way; but if he is denied his two copper pennies, he and the entire pack of devotees so cruelly chase down the passerby that the latter is forced to pay forty réis just for the right to carry on in peace.

Sometimes the stubborn man who can withstand the yelling of the boys and not offer his tribute to the donation cup is subject to insults hurled from behind a fence or from a window. Yet it is neither child nor boy that launches such fusillades.

After a few hours the donation cup fills up; the boys have had their fun; half of their collection has paid for the candles and the lead candleholders, and one or two gambling tickets; and the other half . . .

The other half belongs to the donation cup business.

Now, we protest against the donation cup business for all the evident reasons and also, especially, for the care owed to children.

Even raised and educated in the donation cup business, what will become of them in the future? . . . Perhaps, and the fewer the better, they will become brothers of alms with true habits. But we already have so many of this type that we can well dispense with their multiplication.

Translated by Andre Pagliarini

Note

1. In this selection, ellipsis points enclosed in square brackets indicate omitted material; those not enclosed in square brackets are original to the document.

Sex Trafficking in the Imperial Capital

759 Citizens

In the latter half of the nineteenth century, the Brazilian ruling classes settled on a juridical and political consensus that prostitution was a necessary evil to be tolerated in the national capital. Such a consensus recognized the fact that commercial sex was geographically segregated by class and race: cheap street prostitution, chiefly offered by women of color, was concentrated in Sacramento parish, north and west of the docks. On the other end of the social spectrum, the multiracial prostitutes who serviced an elite clientele enjoyed certain freedoms of movement among the city's bordellos, cabarets, and private homes. The city police episodically harassed women who sold sex, especially the poor, applying laws against vaguely defined infractions including vagrancy and "offenses against morality."

Foreign sex workers were objects of special social and moral consternation, as concern over the supposed influx of foreign prostitutes blended with a tendency to blame immigrants for social problems. Although the passionate controversies over the so-called white slave trade would only reach a fever pitch in the early twentieth century, the issue of foreign prostitutes already attracted public concern in the 1870s.

European prostitutes were the object of worry for the numerous signatories of the following petition sent to the lower house of parliament in 1879. The signature page has been lost, but the petition indicates that "759 citizens resident in this capital, both Brazilian and foreigners," signed the document. Presenting themselves as "heads of families" and representatives of retail commerce, the signatories asserted a class and gender legitimacy to speak on behalf of the two institutions at the core of petit bourgeois propriety: the patriarchal family and property rights. Argument turns on an assumption central to the juridical thought of the age: that the proper family must be protected from people of loose morals. Yet this document is more than a denunciation against prostitution. In an interesting twist, the petitioners express concern that prostitutes' big-spending agents tended to force up rents, pricing those who practiced "honest commerce" out of Rio's central neighborhoods. The lower chamber shared the petitioners' ire over the impact of sex work and human trafficking on the central business district. The deputies, nonetheless, resolved that new laws to curb prostitution were unnecessary. Monitoring public morality, they insisted, was already the role of the police and was a local public health matter to be resolved by municipal ordinances and not national law. All the while, property rents remained subject to the vagaries of the market.

Most August and Dignified Deputies, Representatives of the Nation:
The signatories below come respectfully before this august chamber to present our stance against the most reproachable scandal that is now flagrantly going on, shamelessly and unbridled, in the capital of the Empire to the detriment of public modesty and social dignity. It was three years ago that certain individuals established, as a means of livelihood, the shameful traffic in licentious women. These individuals go themselves or hire people to go to Europe in order to establish prostitution among us, with the intent of attracting more clients and, thus, gaining income that guarantees them the leisure to live in luxury and to set up shop in the busiest squares and streets in our capital city, offending families and causing harm to many businesses. Such activity is prejudicial to many businesses because they have been forced to relocate their establishments, since they are unable to pay the fabulous rents that agents of the infamous traffic offer to building proprietors in order to get the preferential locations, and thus the center of honest work is replaced by immoral commerce. Such activities offend families because these women, in order to satisfy the greed of their bosses and their own pecuniary ambitions, seek out customers by exposing themselves seminude in the windows, proffering obscene words and going down into the street to make themselves known to solicit passersby. And thus it is, august and most dignified representatives of the nation, that Rio de Janeiro, formerly so peaceful and with its austere customs, today offers the indecorous spectacle of a dissolute Babylonia. Under these circumstances, those signing below seek recourse with the Brazilian Parliament, appealing to its patriotism, to its morality, and [to its] ability to remedy an evil that discredits us before the moralized foreigner and that profoundly affects our social education. August and Dignified Sirs, the people of Rio, commerce, and in particular the heads of families would give you the greatest acclaim, august sirs, if you might free us from this scourge.

May you receive Mercy
Rio de Janeiro, July 2, 1879.

Translated by Amy Chazkel

Visualizing "A Carioca"

Pedro Américo de Figueiredo e Melo

Born in the northeastern province of Paraíba, Pedro Américo de Figueiredo e Melo (1843–1905) was a celebrated student and teacher at the Imperial Academy of Fine Arts (f. 1826), the precursor to today's fine arts school at the Universidade Federal do Rio de Janeiro. A classically trained painter, he won acclaim and celebrity for his dramatic treatment of themes taken from the Bible as well as from Brazilian national history. Since the nineteenth century, Américo's large-scale paintings of the Paraguayan War—now hanging at the Museu Nacional de Belas Artes and the Museu Imperial in Petrópolis—have been crowd-pleasers. A Carioca (The Carioca) (1865) wonderfully demonstrates the special place of Rio in the fine arts repertoire perfected by Américo and his contemporaries.

Américo painted two versions: the Imperial Household rejected a gift offer of the first, citing the painting's sensual subject matter; the second (shown here), painted in 1882, was incorporated into the national art collection. Exemplifying nineteenth-century academic treatments of allegory, landscape, and the human form, the canvas presents an exuberant, feminized, and sensual setting of natural and human splendor. Américo's contemporaries—who often referred to the residents of Rio as Fluminenses, rather than today's familiar demonym Cariocas—might have heard in the title a reference to the Chafariz da Carioca, a public fountain that supplied fresh water to the city center. The image itself makes the obvious connection to the Carioca River, which begins near Paineiras, high in the Floresta da Tijuca, and flows toward Guanabara Bay, largely following today's Rua Cosme Velho and Rua das Laranjeiras.

The essential qualities of a "true" Carioca woman would provoke controversy, but Américo's aesthetic choices of female body type—luminous white skin and indeterminately southern European or indigenous hair color and facial features—presented his viewers with a compelling point of view of the gender, race, and color of an "authentic" native of nineteenth-century Rio de Janeiro.

A Carioca. Painting by Pedro Américo de Figueiredo e Melo, 1882. Oil on canvas, 205 × 135 cm. Courtesy of Museu Nacional de Belas Artes / IBRAM / MinC.

A City Celebrates Slave Emancipation

A. Luiz Ferreira and Machado de Assis

With the news of the final slave emancipation, decreed Sunday, May 13, 1888, the streets of Rio filled with a multitude of happy people—the newly freed, former runaways, children, aged blacks, and the ex-slaves' allies who had organized the abolitionist leagues and emancipation clubs that had turned the city's courts of justice, theaters, and press into contested terrains of freedom. Mass rallies broke out in front of the Paço Imperial, and celebratory parades wended throughout imperial Rio. On May 17, thousands joined the ailing emperor's daughter Isabel (1846–1921) at the Praça D. Pedro I (site of today's Centro de Tradições Nordestinas Luiz Gonzaga) to mark the destruction of bondage in all of Brazil. Already known for her abolitionist convictions, Isabel ascended a makeshift altar and secured her public image as the pious "Redeemer" (A Redentora) who had delivered freedom and restored humanity.

Photographer A. Luiz Ferreira captured the thanksgiving Mass of May 17: Isabel (left, under the embroidered canopy) and her husband, Gaston d'Orléans, better known as the Conde d'Eu, join thousands of onlookers who turn somewhat awkwardly toward the photographer. Closest to the royals are representatives of the governing elite and military as well as leading abolitionists. Chief among the latter is José do Patrocínio (1854–1905), an Afro-Brazilian pharmacist, journalist, and Rio city councilman born to a slave mother in the north of Rio province who had become an ardent advocate of emancipation and a staunch defender of the Bragança monarchy.

Although his photograph was staged, Ferreira still managed to capture the unscripted pageantry of the occasion. Attendees hoist banners with images of saints. The national flag (far right) flies among hundreds of smaller flags typical of market fairs. A bust (center left) pays homage to José Maria da Silva Paranhos, the Baron of Rio Branco, a statesman closely associated with the Law of the Free Womb (September 28, 1871). The sartorial distinction of the crowd—notably the sea of hats—conveys a mood of restraint and orderly rectitude consistent with the tone of thanksgiving.

This photo contrasts with the jubilant mood remembered five years later in a crônica penned by the famed Carioca writer Machado de Assis (1839–1908). In his *unique style, Machado's recollection weaves together practices of remembrance in nineteenth-century Europe with a variety of horticultural and floral references to comment on the nature of memory itself.*

Yesterday morning, as I entered the garden, the grass, flowers, and foliage were cold and dripping wet. It had rained all through the night; the ground was wet; the sky, ugly and sad; Corcovado had donned a somber *coroza*. It was six o'clock. The forts and ships launched into their commemorations of the fifth anniversary of the Thirteenth of May. There appeared to be no chance for sunshine and I asked myself if we truly would not have any on this great anniversary. It is so nice to be able to exclaim: "Soldiers, it is the Sun of Austerlitz!" [Napoleon's words as the sun chased away the morning mist at the Battle of Austerlitz, December 5, 1805.] Indeed, sunshine is the natural partner of public jubilations; even private ones seem muted without it.

There was sun, and much of it, on that Sunday in 1888 when the Senate ratified the law, approved by the Princess Regent, and we all took to the streets. Yes, I, the most withdrawn hermit, also went into the street, joining the procession in an open carriage at the pleasure of a fat absent friend of mine. Everyone breathed happiness, everything was ecstasy. Truly, it was the only day of public euphoria that I recall ever witnessing. Those memories washed over me, as the bards meanwhile recounted the names of the great reformers and champions who received their much-deserved accolades yesterday in this very column. Amid it all, however, a faint sadness. Did the meager sunshine reflect the popular mood? Would the public ebullience give way to the awareness of the everyday?

The newspapers were delivered to me. In them I read that a delegation from the association named for Rio Branco would deliver a wreath of laurels and pansies to the headstone of that esteemed statesman. I could see the logic behind the act: it was in recognition of the first shot across the bow of slavery. It did not assuage my melancholy. I imagined the delegation entering modestly into the cemetery, sidestepping an anonymous burial, and proceeding in all piety to lay the wreath at the grave of the victor of 1871. One delegation, one garland. And then my mind turned to other flowers. When the Senate concluded its voting on the law of September 28, flowers by the fistful rained down from the galleries and balconies above the head of the victor and his peers. And then my mind turned to still other flowers. . . .

These were from distant climes. *Primrose Day* [anniversary of the death of British prime minister Benjamin Disraeli]! O! If we could only have our own day of primroses! That hallowed spring day is dedicated by idealistic and poetic England to the memory of Disraeli. It is the day of his death,

"Missa campal em Ação de Graças em 22 de maio de 1888, para comemorar a Lei Áurea." Photograph by Antônio Luís Ferreira, May 17, 1888. Albumen, 28.7 × 51.5 cm. Courtesy of Instituto Histórico e Geográfico Brasileiro, Rio de Janeiro.

thirteen years ago. Every year on that day, the pedestal of the statue to that statesman is lined with silk and covered by countless wreaths and garlands. It is said that primroses were his favorite flower. Hence the day's designation. Here are the newspapers that recount the celebration on the nineteenth day of last month. *Primrose Day*! O! If only we had a primrose day! We could begin, no doubt, by having the pedestals.

One of our old authors—I believe it was João de Barros; I cannot confirm it at present so let's just say it was João de Barros. That old author once mentioned a proverb that stated: "os italianos governam-se pelo passado, os espanhóis pelo presente e os franceses pelo que há de vir" [The Italians govern themselves by the past, the Spanish by the present, and the French by what is yet to come]. Next he added "an empathetic rebuke to our Spain," considering that Spain is the entire peninsula but only Castile is Castile. Our own people, originally from Spain, deserve the same empathetic rebuke, governing ourselves by the present, barely accounting for the future, and not considering the past or, at best, hardly at all. I believe the English encapsulate the other three nations.

I fear our joy is slowly dying, and the memory of the past along with it, and that everything will end up as described in the hackneyed phrasing the press employed in the days of my youth. What, after all, were the celebrations of independence? A parade, a procession, a gala spectacle. All of that took up two lines, and the following took up two more: the forts and warships in the harbor, both foreign and domestic, issued their respective cannon salutes [*salvas de estilo*]. These meager gestures alone marked the great act that was our separation from the metropole.

As a boy I knew Major Valadares by sight; he lived on Rua Sete de Setembro, which was not yet called that, known then as Rua do Cano. Every year on September 7 he would decorate the door of his home with green and yellow satin, strewing it about the sidewalk and *folhas da Independência* [variegated croton, also known as *folha-imperial*, favored by the partisans of independence for its green and yellow coloring] in the corridors of his house, gathering friends, maybe playing music. That is how he would celebrate independence day. He was the last of that sort. After him, all that remains are the remnants of that style.

All these melancholic thoughts of mine fluttered away at the sight of the sun, which finally broke through the clouds and by three o'clock reigned over the open skies, except for a few patches where the clouds insisted on lingering behind. Corcovado removed its coroza, but with such listlessness that it seemed a vassal's duty, not a gesture of love, much less one of personal friendship or admiration. When I returned to the garden I found the flowers to be dry and mirthful. Long live flowers! Gladstone does not speak in the House of Commons without bringing one in his overcoat. His great rival had the same fixation. Imagine the effect it would have on us to see Rio Branco or Itaboraí sporting a rose on his chest, discussing the budget, and then tell me we are not a sad people.

No, no. I am the sad one. Probably indigestion. I ate fava beans and fava beans do not sit well with me. I will eat roses or primroses and ask you all for a statue and a party that will be observed with at least two anniversary commemorations. That is more than enough for a modest man.

Translated by Andre Pagliarini

III

Republican Rio

In the months that followed the Proclamation of the Republic (November 15, 1889), a new ruling coalition of military officers and liberal professionals tried to assemble a program to build a just, stable nation of equal and free citizens. The republican flag declared "Order and Progress." Rio de Janeiro was the political and symbolic center of a new regime, and the Phrygian cap—a classic symbol of the republican pursuit of liberty—was incorporated into a municipal coat of arms that amalgamated symbols of Portugal, Saint Sebastian, and the *botos* (dolphins) that frolicked in Guanabara Bay.

In practice, a wide spectrum of Brazilian society manifested discontent with the republican project, and the newly designated Federal District became a stage for social turmoil and armed insurrection. Dissident factions— monarchists, anarchists, positivists, among others—opposed key elements of the republican coalition. In 1893, naval officers mutinied against the provisional government, training heavy guns on central Rio. As the new century approached, a nascent urban labor movement agitated for rights and confronted hostility from private employers and the police. Racial theorists and social Darwinists took a dim view of making a citizenry out of former slaves. Amid such political and social ferment, the population of Rio swelled, surpassing 800,000 in 1906, a 54 percent increase over 1890.

To stem upheaval and disorder and to beautify and modernize the national capital, federal and municipal officials looked to urban infrastructure, sanitation, and public health. Working in concert, the administrations of President Francisco de Paula Rodrigues Alves and Mayor Francisco Pereira Passos, both in office between 1902 and 1906, initiated public works to transform the capital city's urban landscape. Inspired by Georges Hausmann's renewal of Paris, Pereira Passos oversaw widespread demolitions and street extensions. The port area underwent massive renovation and large cranes were installed to haul cargo from ship to shore. A grand Parisian-style boulevard, Avenida Central, opened in 1906. The accompanying campaign to sanitize Rio included sweeping hygienic interventions against tenements

"Brasão da Cidade de Rio de Janeiro (1896)." From Clovis Ribeiro, *Brazões e Bandeiras do Brasil* (São Paulo: São Paulo Editora, 1933), 193.

(*cortiços* or *estalagens*) such as one notorious structure popularly known as the Cabeça de Porco (The Pig's Head). Invoking extraordinary powers, chief of public health Oswaldo Cruz imposed aggressive measures to control contagious diseases and their vectors. Cruz's mandatory smallpox vaccination campaign provoked a five-day riot in November 1904. The ensuing repression of the rioters was brutal, especially in working-class neighborhoods and hillsides closest to the port.

Notwithstanding the public health gains from mandatory vaccinations, the scourges of tuberculosis, malaria, influenza, yellow fever, and malnutrition continued to ravage bodies and livelihoods, especially among the poor. As clinics, hospitals, and sanitation brigades became important points of contact between the municipality and city residents, medicine, nutrition, and cleanliness became primary functions of civic culture and state rule. Public health also shaped urban settlement, as residents displaced in slum removals and wetlands drainage were forced to relocate to hillsides or to the city outskirts, giving rise to the growth of the working-class suburbs.

The gains of urban beautification and sanitation and the benefits of bourgeois "civilization" were under continual pressure from immigrants who arrived from southern Europe, the Ottoman and Russian empires, and Japan. Although many of these immigrants were merely passing through Rio en route to the coffee fields of São Paulo, the residual population growth strained the supply of jobs, water, and housing. It stoked racial and ethnic

"Renewal of the Port of Rio de Janeiro." Photographer unknown, 1913. From *Álbum das Obras do Porto do Rio de Janeiro*. Courtesy of Arquivo Público do Estado do Rio de Janeiro, Rio de Janeiro.

hostilities between the native born and foreigners. The admixture of internal migrants from the interior, including many former slaves, depressed wages. Inflation further eroded poor people's ability to make a living. The city's most vulnerable confronted harsh vagrancy laws enforced by a muscular police. Yet the underclasses were not mere victims of urban growth, and they played instrumental roles in the articulation of the rules of work, a social order of respectability, and sexuality in the city.

By the turn of the twentieth century, population pressure pushed urbanization toward once-distant regions of forests and farms. Transportation innovation was a powerful force in urban expansion. Streetcars called *bondes*—so named because of the finance schemes used to pay for them—connected the city center with burgeoning suburbs. The Companhia Vila Isabel was one of three major bonde companies that annually carried millions of passengers throughout the city. The two main railway lines—Central do Brasil and Leopoldina—serviced suburbs farther afield. The Túnel Novo (today's Túnel do Leme) facilitated connections to oceanside Leme and Copacabana. Later, motorized buses expanded greatly the range and scope of daily transit. For the wealthy, the private automobile revolutionized personal mobility. Motorized transportation benefited from the demolition of the Senado, Castelo, and Santo Antônio hills, all razed between the 1890s and the 1950s. The landfill produced by these demolition projects extended the city boundaries several hundred meters into Guanabara Bay, creating land for automobile thoroughfares, Santos Dumont Airport, and the pleasure parks of Praça Paris. The shores of Urca, Copacabana, and Lagoa—where poor Cariocas had traditionally fished, bathed, and dumped waste—were turned over to speculative real estate, scenic vistas, and car parking.

Industrialization also drove urbanization. The smokestack came to tower over the church steeple in some neighborhoods. Financial and commercial institutions pushed the downtown skyline upward. Factories demanded electrification and infrastructure. The Companhia Progresso Industrial, a textile factory opened in the rural Zona Oeste suburb of Bangu in 1889, necessitated rail connections to central Rio. The housing built for the plant's workforce grew an industrial suburb with its own power and waste treatment facilities. Other factories manufactured shoes, ceramics, and foodstuffs destined for local consumption.

Laborers and tradesmen initially enjoyed few rights to organize; many suffered in dismal working and living conditions. Bouts of worker agitation culminated in a wave of general strikes in 1917. In response to mounting class tensions, a new generation of federal and local politicians tested out alliances with unions and the working poor. In 1931, physician Pedro Ernesto became the city's first elected mayor, taking his campaign into working-class neighborhoods to advocate for education and health. He cultivated ties with reformist organizations, including elite and middle-class feminists who agitated for women's voting rights and the protections of the welfare state. This conjuncture of political programs and alliances, often referred to as "populism," reached its fullest expression under Getúlio Vargas (1882–1954), a politician from Rio Grande do Sul who seized the presidency during the Revolution of 1930. Reforms passed during the two Vargas regimes (1930–1945 and 1951–1954) extended new social and economic rights to labor unions, civil servants, professional associations, and families. The common people, whom Vargas invoked as *Trabalhadores do Brasil!* (Workers of Brazil!), became heroes of populist rhetoric, endlessly disseminated through the Carioca mass media. Rio was a privileged stage for the cult of personality built by Vargas, notably in the extremely emotional responses from Cariocas of all stripes at the news, circulated by radio on the morning of August 24, 1954, that the scandal-ridden president had committed suicide at Catete Palace rather than face the indignity of being removed from office in

"Milhares de pessoas acompanham o cortejo fúnebre." Photograph by Campanella Neto, August 24, 1954. Arquivo André Carrazzoni (AnC), Foto 038_21. Courtesy of Centro de Pesquisa e Documentação da História Contemporânea do Brasil / Fundação Getúlio Vargas, Rio de Janeiro.

a military coup. The funeral cortege from the presidential palace to Santos Dumont Airport was a singular event in Rio's history.

An expanding federal government made a direct impact on the city's built environment. Under Vargas, the federal government underwrote monumental headquarters for the ministries of labor and finance as well as hospitals for public servants. New public memorials, museums, and historical landmarks embedded memory in the urban landscape. Mayor Henrique Dodsworth (1937–1945) enlisted planners and engineers to modernize (once again) the Federal District. Some of their projects drew from the sweeping plans proposed by guest architect-urbanists Alfred Agache and Le Corbusier. Others were developed by an increasingly professional, and powerful, coalition of Brazilian urbanists and engineers.

As intellectuals challenged the Europhilia that had dominated the Carioca aesthetic in the age of Pereira Passos, a new generation of architects argued that the built environment must suit local climates and traditions. The Ministry of Education and Health, inaugurated in 1943, became an iconic symbol of the ascendant tropical modernist style. At the helm of the ministry, Gustavo Capanema embraced writers, visual artists, musicians, composers, and designers who gravitated to Rio in search of inspiration and proximity to patrons and critics. Together with the faculty and students of the Universidade do Brasil, these figures formed the core of the modern Carioca intelligentsia.

Unplanned and popular Rio were equally part of the city's republican history. The city's first squatter settlements, or favelas, began as ad hoc solutions to the housing shortages and urban reforms of the 1890s. Although the legality of such unlicensed land occupation was questionable, favelas became a permanent feature of the landscape, especially as waves of migrants from Rio's hinterlands and the drought-stricken northeast arrived in search of opportunity. A building code passed in 1937 ordered that all favelas be demolished, but actual public policies vacillated between eradication, protection, and tolerance. Meanwhile, emergent neighborhood associations defended community rights, forming the basis for modern public policies of negotiation over favela eradication. The architectural styles and materials used in favelas became a central part of Rio's urban landscape, and a communal strategy of home construction for the poor called a *mutirão* (collective effort) became a central part of urban culture.

Shifting cultural mores and electrification brought Cariocas into the streets after dark. By the 1940s, nightlife flourished in downtown cafés and the theater district surrounding Praça Tiradentes. Lapa buzzed with bohemian cabarets and brothels. The mansions of Santa Teresa hosted literary salons and occasional masked balls. The cinema palaces of Praça Floriano (better known as Cinelândia) and Praça Saenz Peña in Tijuca dazzled moviegoers. Daytime leisure activities brought wealthier Cariocas out to the horse races, swank cafés, and the automobile rally. The middle classes turned to public squares, shopping arcades, and the beach for recreation, status, and romantic adventures. The working classes, who continued to make a calendar of Catholic feast days into an endless cycle of popular merriment, also took their seats at popular theaters, the circus, musical and dance competitions, and organized sporting events. On the waters of Guanabara Bay and Lagoa Rodrigo de Freitas, rowing and sailing attracted athletes and spectators who coalesced into sports associations that gave rise to the soccer clubs that would come to hold such importance in Carioca associational life and tribal identities.

Over the republican period, Rio cemented its place as the epicenter of Brazil's culture industries. Cinema blossomed after World War I; the first local film companies appeared in the 1920s. Recorded music drove interest in popular music and live entertainment. Radio programming brought recorded and live music into everyday and associational life, including the celebrity-obsessed fan clubs that took off in the 1930s. Until federal law outlawed gambling in 1946, entertainers like Carmen Miranda performed in refined ballrooms and swanky lounges that opened onto grand gaming salons. Rio's stunning natural setting, the growing attraction of its Zona Sul beaches, and the range of entertainment options called Hollywood celebrities, pleasure-seekers, and tourists to a sophisticated nightlife even after legalized gambling ceased. In 1951, the shuttered Cassino da Urca was repurposed into broadcast studios for TV Tupi, a pioneer in Brazilian television. Shortly thereafter, the cultural and economic juggernaut of the Brazilian *telenovela* took off and Rio played a starring role in televised soap operas.

The culture industries that developed around Carnaval and neighborhood-based Carnaval organizations called "samba schools" (*escolas de samba*) first formed in the late 1920s and brought together musicians, intellectuals, and culture consumers from across racial and class lines. Notions of white superiority never went away, but the ideals of racial democracy took hold in Carnaval culture and urban society. The Carnaval samba—originating among favelas, at festivals, and in salons, to be popularized in recording and radio studios—took its place as a national rhythm that was quintessentially Carioca. (In fact, samba and its related musical forms shared deep roots in northeastern Brazilian music as well as international musical forms of the jazz age.) As Carnaval and samba consolidated their place as the markers of Rio-ness, journalists and folklorists put out dictionaries of Carioca slang or wrote newspaper *crônicas* celebrating the colorful hucksters, scoundrels, and carousers associated with the Carnaval season. Everyday Cariocas made their own sense of annual revelry, through the playful perversions of excessive drinking, costuming, cross-dressing, and sexual escapades.

Outside the moments of merriment, the hardships of world wars and global economic cycles were unmistakable. Nonetheless, the period from the 1920s to the early 1960s was a time of hope and promise for Brazil, and Rio was capital city of the Land of the Future. Commercial aviation increased the circulation of culture, ideas, and people across the continents. The 1933 motion picture *Flying Down to Rio* was an early gesture toward a globalization of the image of a stunning, romantic, and promising tropical city that was gateway to all Brazil. The optimism and excitement culminated in the 1950s, fueled by Brazilian industrial and economic growth, the boom of Brazilian modernism, and the global aspiration that Rio be an exemplar of harmonious multiracialism.

This Golden Age had its many dark sides. Urban development was uneven, often uncontrolled. The 1954 Carnaval season—the so-called Carnaval of Denunciations—included the release of several tunes filled with playful complaints about frequent electrical outages and water shortages. Inflation produced financial insecurities. Meanwhile, conservative Catholics and middle-class patriarchs inveighed against moral decay and juvenile delinquency. The ambitious Carioca journalist Carlos Lacerda (1914–1977) exposed deep corruption in President Vargas's inner circle. Throughout the period, institutional authoritarianism curtailed personal and political freedoms. Political policing intensified in the 1930s. Alongside the common criminals thrown into Rio's courts and prisons, opponents of the Vargas regime filled jail cells and penal colonies. Torture seeped into police interrogations. After World War II, political policing expanded its scope as early anticommunism morphed into Cold War paranoia of hidden threats, foreign subversion, and domestic class hatred. By the late 1950s, key elements of the national security state had taken firm root in Rio.

Juscelino Kubitscheck, a charismatic politician from Minas Gerais, assumed the presidency in 1956 promising to bring about "fifty years of progress in five." The program of infrastructure, industry, and social reform associated with "JK" nurtured a climate of cool optimism that gave birth to the bossa nova "wave" soon to captivate the world. Kubitscheck also committed himself to fulfilling the constitutional mandate to transfer the nation's capital to the distant central highlands. The specter of the loss of national capital status hung over Rio de Janeiro in the late 1950s. With a certain sense of dread and nostalgia, the Marvelous City's rights to political primacy ended on April 21, 1960, when Kubitscheck joyously inaugurated hypermodernist Brasília.

Making the Federal District

Constituent Assembly

The 1891 constitution proscribed an important change in Rio's jurisdictional status, designating the former Neutral Municipality (Município Neutro) as the Federal District of the Republic of the United States of Brazil. Rio continued to hold a place of privilege in the Brazilian national political body. Nonetheless, the leaders of the young republic established the legal basis for the city's eventual demotion, once the seat of the federal government could be moved to the Brazilian Plateau in the country's interior.

The following articles from the Constitution of 1891 highlight republican Rio's triple life as the seat of the national government, as an autonomous urban polity, and as a placeholder for a new faraway capital. The constitution provided that Rio be administered locally, in recognition of its own interests. Local political and fiscal needs fell to municipal authority. Yet federal policymakers and power brokers also knew local politics in Rio to be unruly. The republicans ardently debated how best to make the nation's capital serve as a unifying and stabilizing force in a diverse, large country experiencing an influx of foreign immigrants and the transition from slavery. Out of these debates, an old idea arose: moving the federal capital away from the old centers of power.

In reaffirming Rio's right to continue to serve as the seat of national rule and in extending certain powers of self-governance, the framers of the 1891 constitution placed Rio in a state of political impermanence. The old Neutral Municipality could remain the center of the nation until the capital could be transferred to an expansive area somewhere in the hinterlands. The first republican constitution thus codified an idea that had been afloat since the early years of the empire, when the "Patriarch of Independence," José Bonifácio de Andrada e Silva (1763–1838), had proposed the transfer of the capital out of Rio. By the mid-1950s, long-distance trucking, commercial aviation, and the historic desire to develop the interior of the country created the technological possibilities and the political will to make this important geopolitical shift a reality. The nation's new capital city, Brasília, was inaugurated in April 1960, taking away the status of Federal District that Rio had enjoyed since the foundation of the republic.

Preamble

We, the representatives of the Brazilian people, gathered in the Constituent Congress to organize a free and democratic regime, establish, decree, and promulgate the following:

Title I: On Federal Organization, Preliminary Provisions

Article 1—The Brazilian Nation adopts as its form of Government, under a representative regime, a Federative Republic, proclaimed on November 15, 1889, and which shall be constituted by a perpetual and indissoluble union of its old Provinces, into the United States of Brazil.

Article 2—Each one of its old Provinces shall form a State and the former Neutral Municipality shall constitute the Federal District, continuing to be the Capital of the Union, for as long as the following article is not executed.

Article 3—A zone of 14,400 square kilometers in the central plateau of the Republic shall remain the property of the Union, which will at an opportune moment demarcate the establishment there of the future federal Capital.

Title II: On the States

Article 67—With the exception of the restrictions specified in the Constitution and in federal laws, the Federal District is administered by municipal authorities.

Translated by Amy Chazkel

The Legendary Festival of Our Lady of Penha

Alexandre José de Mello Moraes Filho

Rio's famed cult of Nossa Senhora da Penha (Our Lady of the Cliff) originated in the legend of a seventeenth-century Portuguese hunter walking about the rural out-skirts of the colonial city. Terrorized by a giant snake that crossed his path, the man prayed to Nossa Senhora da Penha da França, a popular figure in Iberian Catholi-cism, for deliverance from danger. A lizard suddenly appeared and chased away the snake. On that elevated spot, the man built a chapel dedicated to the Virgin Mary.

In time, the simple chapel grew into a stately white church visible from all around Irajá parish. An annual festival to honor Nossa Senhora da Penha took hold, reach-ing the height of popularity in the late nineteenth century as improved transporta-tion links to Rio's northern suburbs facilitated the arrival of pilgrims, bohemians, musicians, and revelers. Each October, thousands of faithful ascended a long stair-way leading to the sanctuary, some on their knees, to make a promise to the Virgin or to leave behind an ex-voto in thanks for an act of divine grace. Closely associated with the ritual life of Rio's Portuguese immigrant community, the multiday festi-val fused some of the most prominent aspects of Iberian Catholicism—the focus on miracles and the worship of Our Lady in her various manifestations—with local music, poetry, and foodways.

By the time Bahian doctor, poet, journalist, and folklorist Alexandre José Mello Moraes Filho (1844–1919) completed a compendium on Brazil's popular traditions, the annual festival to honor Nossa Senhora da Penha had entered its third century. Mello Moraes Filho's dignified portrayal of the festival and its participants, ex-cerpted here, stood out at a time in the early Brazilian republic when Portuguese immigrants faced persistent ridicule for being uncultured, backward outsiders. The 1895 ethnography of the festivities at Penha also registered the presence of trova-dores, the mixed-race bards from the backlands of the Brazilian northeast who re-cited poetic verses that invoked the last days of the Moors in Granada, Spain. Mello Moraes Filho's keen sense of ethnic, linguistic, and regional diversity deftly captures the ascent of Afro-Brazilian influences on a traditionally Portuguese event of Chris-tian piety and popular-class gaiety.

Another transplant from Bahia, Tia (Aunt) Ciata (Hilária Batista de Almeida,

1854–1924), a confectioner and patron of Afro-Brazilian culture, shared the attrac-
tion to the festivities at Penha, where she ran a food stand. Musicians associated
with Tia Ciata's circle later released "Pelo telefone" (1917), the legendary first re-
corded samba. Here, we glimpse some of the music making that surrounded Afro-
Brazilians in early republican Rio.

In the deepest recesses of colonial times, the primitive hermitage of Nossa
Senhora da Penha, built atop the 365 steps hewn in granite, stood tall over
the bay of Rio de Janeiro, the city, and the suburbs. . . .

Historically, the Portuguese predominated in the religious processions
at Penha. From the colonial period until the present day, their traditions
have been maintained in remembrance of similar festivals in the old metropole. One should note, however, that the celebrants here were generally
the offspring of the Continent. In these annual pilgrimages we would find
a certain class of uncultured Portuguese people, men and women destined
to do brute labor. This did not prevent the event from being among the
most notable and opulent popular festivals among our immigrant communities. Brazilians from Rio and places farther afield joined the celebrants.
They too made their contributions to the observances, often forming separate groupings. On one side of the village, the Portuguese gathered among
themselves; Brazilians on the other. What is important to emphasize here is
that the initiative, the accouterments, the enthusiasm, and the festival's true
quality cannot be claimed as ours. For this reason, it has endured.

The procession at Penha was raucous and joyful. Profanities and mis-
behaviors could not mar the event's unassailable religious nature. Amid the
wanderings and the commemorations practiced as part of this festival, simi-
larities and some exciting differences from our own festivals developed.

With the ringing of the ritual prayers, preparations were announced.
Woodcutters came through the forest, by order of the festival organizers,
to harvest long branches and to strip the leaves from them. These branches
were turned into tents and stalls, flagpoles, and the banners used by the
celebrants.

Nine days prior, everything had to be readied with the requisite urgency
and care demanded by such an elaborate, ornate procession whose storied
fame preceded itself. As if by enchantment the picturesque hamlet of Penha
was transformed; the comely temple, decorated with splendor, was cleansed
throughout in anticipation of the promises to be made; to the left of the
stone stairway, shacks were rented out to pilgrims for the safekeeping of the
devotional objects necessary for their important works.

In the vestry of the gorgeous church, the sacristan went about in circles.

He ran here and there, attending to the pilgrims bearing promises, putting the wax, gold, and silver miracles in their place, as well as the candles and votive panels that people from the area would bring on the eve of that solemn day.

In the village, from sunrise to sunset, they worked without rest. Food and drink stalls sprouted from the earth, one after another, beneath the canopy of the mango trees lining the churchyard as well as along the road. Everything was adorned with drapes, covered with burlap, decorated in greenery. From the rooftops dangled selected samples of foodstuffs for sale. Banners stretched out across the entrance, serving as beacons to the common people. From time to time, some ruffian or an old black man leading an ox-cart would appear along the road, to supply the stalls with wines, snacks, and magnificent fruits. The tasty watermelons that grew so plentifully in the locale were especially prized. In great profusion, flags, medals, pennants, shields of painted cardboard, pinwheels, candleholders, and little colored lanterns were threaded among the trees. The spectacle was without equal among us.

At the Sunday Mass that preceded the pilgrimage, men, women, and children—filled with faith—dropped to their knees to ascend the narrow steps up to Penha, keeping those promises of devotion made to the miraculous Virgin in times of suffering, danger, and misfortune. Such piety was a beautiful sight, and one might be brought to tears to see the procession of slaves and masters, the crippled and the miserable, each carrying an offering, occupying for days the long stone stairway that led up to the House of God, where they might pay homage to the Lady of Penha who had brought them serenity in their sufferings and relief to their ailments. So many left behind a material remembrance of her extraordinary power! . . . Think of the countless images deposited in gratitude for miraculous cures, for ships saved from destruction. The registries of hundreds of other extraordinary acts left there are a testament to the fact that the human sciences are overshadowed by the faith to be placed in divine mercy.

The church remained open for days, as the preparations for the pilgrimage played out in the city and surrounding areas, near and far. United by a spirit of great religiosity, members of the popular classes burst onto the scene by the multitude. They came from Inhaúma and Pavuna, from Irajá and São João de Meriti, from Campo Grande and the Ilha do Governador. The great landholders and their families, the small-scale farmers and their slaves lived for the occasion. Fishermen prepared their canoes and skiffs; larger launches and steamboats stood in reserve; and the beautiful saddled horses, shod and groomed, awaited their moment to make the voyage to

Penha. With a truss of new belts, the steer-drawn carts were primed, crop and yoke at the ready. The footmen and boys rehearsed their places for the forthcoming journey.

In the city, worker villas and tenements carried on in quite a state. The Marias and the Manoels of Portugal busied themselves in the laundering of garments and the washing of carriages; they retrieved gilt earrings from jewelry boxes. Everything scrubbed clean. White uniforms stretched out across chairs or hung on a clothesline to air out.

At dusk, a great movement ensued as the countryfolk arrived at Penha. The stalls filled up and fireworks burst incessantly. By nightfall the small church could be found covered in flags and banners. The illumination cast upon the façade and the iron gates of the circular lookout could be seen from a great distance, in the flutter of light reflected upon barren rocky patches.

At sunrise, multitudes of cityfolk disembarked at the bayside ports of Maria Angú and Fazenda Grande. They came to make their promises, to have some fun. From the airy veranda in front of the temple the most beautiful panorama unfolded, a marvelous sight for the variety of scenes, each one more extraordinary than the last.

In the bay, canoes and light watercraft carried forth through calm waters; oars caught the light of the sun. The sounds of *vivas* and fireworks filled the air. White kerchiefs moved about, as one group signaled to another, to the clamor of the pilgrims who had already touched on land. On the network of roadways and trails, cattle-drawn carts brought along families. Shining convoys of horses cut a wide path. Weary roadmen too many to count marched along, sweaty and dust-covered.

At Pedregulho and along the streets closest to Penha, spectators stood to watch the procession of the pilgrims, especially that festive Portuguese contingent that came from the central city in richly adorned carriages, in large carts, in two-wheeled buggies, and upon emaciated horses-for-hire.

Viva Penha! Viva Penha! These were the voices that filled city streets from nine in the morning, sometimes to the disharmony of the ongoing music, other times to the cadence of small fiddles [*rabecas*], violas, and tambourines [*pandeiros*] that accompanied the sounds of popular poetry.

And then in the middle of the tumult appears a buggy pulled along at full gallop, all decked out in colorful clothworks and greenery. The animals wore roses made of cloth on their heads. The car brought forth celebrants of both sexes, all dressed in white, who wore straw hats festooned in ribbons.

Slung around the necks of men were giant wine-filled horns gilt in silver. Around their arms hung the classic delicacies of the pilgrimage. They raised their hands to their mouths and cried out "Long live Penha!" And the celebrants on foot, waving their arms, responded with the same passion "Long live Penha!" . . .

By two in the afternoon, the festival had reached its prime; a sea of religious groupings [*ranchos*] were camped out under the shade of the mango trees. Alongside the vendors' stalls, the celebrants who walked alongside the numerous buggies went about with their songs, their national dances, jumping as they made their way along the route. Here the *canna-verde*. There the *chamarrita* and the *fadinho*. The *vai-de-roda* was all footwork. And lest we forget the ingratiating challenge dances.

The women danced, clapping their hands while moving about. They pirouetted with their partners, some of whom, a bit tipsy, strummed out a few chords on the viola or the *violino*. The *cavaquinho* carried a tune, and songs and dances were repeated, making the circle whole. . . .

Carriages moved by pairs of steer brought forth festive countrymen. The Bahian women danced [*sambavam*] under the aromatic mango trees whose branches were decorated with African clothwork. And conveyances of all types set out along trails, carrying the tireless and enthusiastic devotees of Penha.

Once the morning's religious ceremony had ended, the celebrants began to disband. Gradually the encampments packed up. By afternoon, the saints borne high on their litters, the decorated cars, and the masked horsemen all made their way into the city. Among the "Vivas!" the ebullience was incredible. Each pilgrim registered his devotion to Our Lady of Penha, sporting a ritual cloth in the style of the Veil of Veronica pinned to the chest of a white jacket. In the village of Penha, on the occasion of the recitation of the Te Deum prayer, our people sang as they went about their tasks.

Troubadours from the backlands of the north are found in those places, many of them mulattos and black slaves. Here, there was a four-lined poem to be improvised on the guitar, leavened with a touch of jealousy:

> I hope to meet up,
> With Manny Little Bird! . . .[1]
> Whose wings I want to clip,
> And set the nest on fire . . .

> [E tomára que *encontrá*
> Com *Manué* Passarinho . . .
> Que quero cortar-lhe as asas
> Tocar-lhe fogo no ninho . . .]

Further along, a farewell, a nostalgic spirit, a plaintive and dolorous verse:

> I'm going away, I'm going away,
> As the whale has gone,
> It's a shame to leave
> Marocas in a faraway land.

> [Vou-me embora, vou-me embora
> Como se foi a baleia,
> Levo penas de *dexá*
> Marocas na terra *aeia*.]

And over there in the direction of São Cristóvão, mounting a tired, lame horse, pounding his heels into its belly, disappearing into the darkness, stood the last of the Abencerrage caliphs. He forces out one more "Viva Penha!" In distraction, he chews on a simple and expressive quatrain:

> You say long live Lamego [Douro Valley, Portugal],
> Also long live Lameguinho,
> And long live the land of Oporto
> Where one drinks good wine . . .

> [Dizes que viva Lamego
> Viva tambem Lameguinho,
> E viva a terra do Porto
> Onde se bebe o bom vinho . . .]

Like the fire-spitting locomotive, the classic procession at Penha has been losing some of its devotional character and its former influence. Yet there are still many pilgrims who endure the long distances on foot, risking the dangers of the road, faithful to tradition.

As a popular procession, this is the only one that is still preserved in Rio de Janeiro. It represents, as an ideal type, certain colonial customs, which were modified in the provinces, in the past, when nativism was a virtue in Brazil.

Translated by Amy Chazkel and Daryle Williams

Note

1. The ellipsis points in the lyrics are original.

The Animal Game

Francisco José Viveiros de Castro

In the early 1890s, a privately owned zoo located in the outlying neighborhood of Vila Isabel obtained a license from the municipal government to run a raffle designed to attract visitors. The scheme thought up by zoo owner João Batista Viana Drummond (1825–1897) adapted practices already popular in the capital of the young republic. Drummond's idea was a hit, and in short order bookmakers began to accept off-site bets on the zoo raffle, subverting the terms of the original concession. Municipal police subsequently took action against the increasingly popular game that allowed players throughout the city to wager small amounts of money on combinations of numbers or animals. That proscribed lottery is still known as the jogo do bicho, the animal game.

　This document, an appellate case involving the jogo do bicho, shows how the animal game had already passed from a legal activity to a crime by 1899. José Roberto da Cunha Salles (1840–1903), a successful businessman originally from Pernambuco, had obtained a patent to operate a projection machine ostensibly intended to display announcements and advertisements. The police claimed that this "magic lantern," operating in a public theater in Lapa, was actually used to display images of animals associated with the clandestine lottery. Cunha Salles protested innocence and was eventually exonerated, a typical outcome in such cases. The case was later summarized in Jurisprudência Criminal (1900), a seminal text on criminal law authored by jurist Francisco José Viveiros de Castro (1862–1906).

　Viveiros de Castro provides a fascinating glimpse into the commercialization of entertainment at the turn of the twentieth century. Appellants Cunha Salles and Paschoal Segreto (1868–1920) were famous entertainment entrepreneurs of their day. The two former associates had opened Brazil's first cinema in 1897 on Rua do Ouvidor. Cunha Salles was backer of the Pantheon Ceroplástico, a museum featuring wax castings of Brazilian notables that was—unsurprisingly—also implicated in illicit games of chance. The appellants mentioned in the Viveiros de Castro text were among the many impresarios who opened other entertainment venues, such as sporting clubs, where visitors paid admission to watch or wager bets. Like the Cariocas who played the illegal animal game, their clients enthusiastically embraced *the commercialization of mass entertainment, even in the face of the regulation and criminalization of certain types of gaming and spectatorship.*

The following documents have been seen, reported, and argued:

Dr. José Roberto da Cunha Salles appeals the sentence of the Judge of the Sixth District, who on November 18, 1899, condemned him to the maximum penalty under Article 369 of the Penal Code [three months' imprisonment, surrender to the public treasury of all instruments and apparatuses used in the game, and a fine], because in April, in the Theatro Eldorado, on the Beco do Imperio, in a place frequented by the public, he established the jogo do bicho, which is a game of chance.

The appellant alleges: 1. That it was not he who committed the infraction, but in fact it was Paschoal Segreto, to whom the appellant had transferred the government's commercial license to operate the game; 2. That, being that the appellant had been legally making use of a privilege obtained in observance of the necessary legal formalities, no criminal action can be attempted for this licit act, and indeed it falls to the Government to approach the Federal Judiciary to propose that they annul the license. The nullification of the patent was a prior condition for the existence of a crime; 3. That the game established in the Theatro Eldorado was not a game of chance, because it depended only on the selection of an advertisement.

The ruling judges opined as follows:

That everything examined, the allegations duly considered in fact and in law:

Considering that the appellant did not produce any proof of having transferred the license to Paschoal Segreto: that the arrest records demonstrate that it was the appellant who actually operated the jogo do bicho in the Theatro Eldorado; that before the police authorities the appellant confessed to have committed the crime, although denying its criminal character;

Considering that the Government of the Republic granted a patent for the appellant's invention of a new system of announcements and advertisements by means of a magic lantern; that the appellant twisted the intentions of the patent granted to him, converting the invention into a new form of the jogo do bicho; that this Chamber had already decided that his defense is inadmissible;

Considering that games can be divided into three categories: 1. Intellectual games, or scientific games, that is, those in which experiments, or talent, or the calm reflection of the player are more important than the vagaries of chance, where even when unlucky, the player can win the game by ably taking advantage of the errors of his opponents, those games that require learning, such as checkers or chess. 2. Sporting games, those that depend on strength, agility, expertise, and dexterity of the players, including hygienic exercises, for example, swimming, wrestling, billiards, sailing, foot races. . . . 3. Games of chance, where success depending solely on the vagaries of luck, where the knowledge of the player does not matter, for example, roulette, dice, raffles, lotteries . . . ;

Considering that the game established by the appellant in the Theatro Eldorado, in a place frequented by the public, was a game of chance, because winning or losing depended not on the knowledge or on the agility of the players, but solely on luck;

But

Considering that the appellant setting up his magic lantern in various sites in this city, establishing games of chance in places that are frequented by the public under the pretext of this patent, did not commit a series of infractions but in fact only one continuous infraction . . . ;

Considering that the appellant was already tried and found guilty by the fact of having twisted the aims of the patent for his invention, and under the pretext of this privilege having established the jogo do bicho in a place frequented by the public;

Considering that the appellant cannot be condemned twice for the same fact.

The Judges of the Criminal Chamber of the Civil and Criminal Tribunal approve the appeal and, reversing the sentence, acquit Dr. José Roberto da Cunha Salles of the accusation that was made against him. Thus judged, the appellant should be immediately released.

Rio de Janeiro, December 20, 1899
(approved by Judges Muniz Barreto and Viveiros de Castro)

Translated by Amy Chazkel

An Allegation of Infanticide

Margarida Rosa da Assumpção and Others

This set of documents concerns an accusation of infanticide lodged in mid-1904. Accuser Margarida Rosa da Assumpção, a working-class woman living in a humble multifamily dwelling in Cidade Nova, approached the police to denounce neighbors for collaborating in a newborn's mysterious death. The accusations involved Antonia "China" Mendes Bezerra, an unwed minor who tried to hide the fruits of a sexual relationship with an older man named Saturnino Alves de Oliveira, a semiliterate stonemason. Assumpção also implicated Escalartina "Lina" Teixeira, an unlicensed midwife who had allegedly strangled China's infant son.

The intentional killing of a fetus or newborn was undoubtedly a crime. Both China and Lina might be subject to prosecution. However, Brazilian legal codes proscribed differential punishment for those involved in infanticide. The law implicitly considered a birth mother to be in an altered physiological state during the days just after giving birth. Infanticide committed by a new mother was treated differently from an act carried out by a third party. If proven guilty, the "sorceress" (feiticeira) Lina—a female entrepreneur allegedly engaged in a range of illicit services including the administration of abortifacients—might face a stiffer penalty than China. Moreover, the 1890 Penal Code proscribed lighter sentences for a distressed mother trying "to hide her dishonor." The documents reveal some of these complex, gendered codes of virtue and transgression in early republican Rio, when law and popular morality placed great value on female virginity. Women who were sexually active outside wedlock confronted the challenges of managing their reproductive lives and defending their social status in the face of harsh double standards of sexual comportment. Although China denied the accusation of infanticide, she did not disavow a premarital sexual relationship with Saturnino, based on the young man's promise of a future marriage. Apparently separated at the time of Assumpção's allegations, China and Saturnino present a familiar tale of consensual sexual relations that the police characterize as an act of deflowerment.

The police inquest did not determine whether China actually collaborated in carrying out the desperate act of killing her son. Yet these documents reveal certain conditions facing poor women and men in Rio at the turn of the twentieth century. Liv-

ing in the tight quarters of an estalagem *(tenement)* located on a crowded travessa *(mews)*, China and her neighbors acted out a complex mixture of deep solidarity and mutual assistance on the one hand and community censure and surveillance on the other.

> *Dr. Police Chief,*
> I am going to tell you something that happened in the Travessa 11 de Maio, n. 16, house n. 1 that everyone has surmised. In this house there is a great sorceress [feiticeira] by the name of Lina who does all sorts of spell-casting, procures men for women, and gives luck to those that don't have fortune and also rents rooms to young men at 500 réis per hour. I am going to tell about the case.
> There is in this house 2 young women, one is named Rita and the other China, who got involved with a boy by the name of Saturnino. Some time ago, this boy ruined [*fez mal*] China and she became pregnant she said to everyone that it was an illness. She went to consult Doctor Mourão, and he said that she was already 7 or 8 months pregnant and then the sorceress began to make medicine and magic in order to cast out [*bota fora*] the child but it was so that the child was born beautiful and smart and the sorceress squeezed the neck of the little innocent child and buried it in the basement of the same house. The father of these 2 young women is a machinist on the steamship *Brazil*. He is José Bezerra, and everything happened when he was on a long journey.
> The sorceress has a very old fetus in a bottle that she says was China's, but that is a lie, everyone in the boardinghouse knows that. It was Albertina who told me, she saw the incident. Lina got that fetus a long time ago.
> *Your Servant Margarida Assumpção*

> *Dr. Police Chief,*
> In the Travessa Onze de Maio number 16 a young woman had a child and that child was killed by a certain person, Aunt Lina, so that the fruit of a crime would not appear. This young woman goes by the nickname "China" and her father is the machinist of the steamship *Brazil*. This tricky scheme was done while the father was away for five months. So, if you want a witness, look on the same mews number 19, for the midwife Rosa who is a witness and Albertina who came to know [the situation] and the examining physician Doctor Mourão and said to somebody that

she was in a very advanced stage [of pregnancy], finally everyone from the tenement knows about this case. The child was buried in the basement of the house.

Margarida Rosa da Assumpção

Record of declarations made by Escalartina Lina Teixeira—Hereupon is presented Escalartina Lina Teixeira, fifty years old, single, native of the city of Rio, not knowing how to write, resident of ~~Rua~~ Travessa Onze de Maio number 16, house 1, who declared the following: That, she does not know if the underage China was or was not pregnant, not even of [the] service of midwife for the same [China]; that that minor and the sister are in her [Lina's] company for seven or more months, and that she, China, was brought by her father whom she [Lina] knows, and that the aforementioned minor dated . . . Saturnino, who sometimes goes to her house, not knowing in the meanwhile whether the aforesaid Saturnino did harm to the underage China. Lina further declares that she knows that the aforementioned minor had been in a sick state with her feet swollen and belly grown, which she attributed to an inflammation, and that the minor China had been subject to treatment under the care of Dr. Mourão. When questioned about whether she knows what medicine was taken and if she had in her possession the medication prescriptions, Lina responded that she ripped them up. She said further that, in the tenement where she lives, the underage China was said to have given birth to a child. She demanded that those people who said that come to her to give proof. She said nothing further nor was questioned, being in agreement with this statement, the Chief Antonio Gomez Pinto signs at her request.

I, Henrique Pereira de Mello, recording clerk *ad hoc*, wrote down the document.

Henrique Pereira de Mello, Raul de
Magalhães, Antonio Gomes Pinto

Record of declarations made by Antonia Mendes Bezerra—Herein is presented Antonia Mendez Bezerra, daughter of Manoel Martinez Bezerra, almost 19 years of age, single, resident of the Travessa Onze de Maio 16, house 1, knowing how to read and write, who questioned by the Chief of Police said that it is true that she had been the girlfriend of Saturnino Alves de Oliveira during the space of two years and one month, not being his girlfriend anymore. She also said that it is true that she had been deflowered by the same during the month of December of the year before last, when she, the deponent, made a visit to the house of the aforementioned Saturnino, who lived on the Rua Saldanha Marinho, 8. This fact occurred at night in the aforementioned building, being that the same Saturnino made her continual promises of marriage. She said also she was sick and suspicious of being pregnant, she took . . . medicine, in order to hide the crime from her father's eyes; that that supposition became a reality, whereby she the deponent gave birth to a child of the male sex on January 31st of this year, in the house of her Aunt Lina, where she currently resides, being that the child was stillborn, she the deponent put the aforesaid child inside a cardboard box, in the hands of Saturnino whose son it was, to perform the burial. [Saturnino] departed taking the cadaver of the child, his son, in order to perform that task, saying further that who assisted the declarant during her delivery was her Aunt Lina, who declared the child to be dead, having verified this to be true, she said nothing further nor was further questioned [and] agreeing with this statement she signs this document.

I, Henrique Pereira de Mello, recording clerk *ad hoc*, wrote down the document.

Henrique Pereira de Mello, Raul de
Magalhães, Antonia Mendez Bezerra

Record of declarations made by Saturnino Alves de Oliveira—On the twenty-ninth day of the month of August of 1904 in this Capital and Office of the Tenth Urban Police Precinct, where was presented the citizen Chief Raul de Magalhães with me, recording clerk ad hoc for this act named, sworn and below signed, here presents Saturnino Alves de Oliveira, thirty-two years old, single, native of Rio state, stonemason, resident of the Rua Pinto de Azevedo, 16, not knowing how to read or write, I mean to write knowing only how to sign his name. Who, questioned by the Police Chief, said the following: That it is true to have been and to be the boyfriend of the minor Antonia China, being also true to have been he who had deflowered her during the month of December of 1902, in the house on the Rua Saldanha Marinha, 8; saying also to be true [that] the aforementioned minor became pregnant and had given birth to a child of the male sex on January 31st of this year, being that this child was stillborn and was given to him in order to take care of the burial, declaring to be him who took the child to the Central Police Station and after to the Morgue, being convinced of being the father of the aforementioned child, that knowing more to have been Aunt Lina, who assisted the delivery of the aforementioned minor China; that he in the Central Police Station where he went to take the cadaver of the child in question, the deponent presented it as his natural child, declaring a made-up name for the mother of the child and not that of the minor China, giving nevertheless his residence as the dwelling of the same [the mother] at the Rua Pinto Figueiredo number sixteen and furthermore said nothing nor questioning, being in agreement, he signs this document.

I, Henrique Pereira de Mello, recording clerk *ad hoc*, wrote down the document.

Raul de Magalhães,
Saturnino Alves de Oliveira

Translated by Cassia Roth

The Hotel Avenida

Brasil-Moderno

This article captures the excitement that accompanied the inauguration of the Hotel Avenida, a landmark establishment on the grand boulevard named Avenida Central (today's Avenida Rio Branco). Occupying a place of honor in the city center, the hotel immediately became a point of reference for Cariocas and city visitors. Built in the eclectic architectural style of the thoroughfare, the building's broad façade stood as an imposing symbol of the ambition of the urban reforms associated with Rio's Belle Époque.

Prior to the opening of the Hotel Avenida, the selection of fine accommodations was thin. The Hôtel Pharoux (est. 1838) operated near the port at the Largo do Paço (today's Praça XV de Novembro), and the Hotel dos Estrangeiros (est. 1849) received guests in Catete. Accommodations in private homes, inns, and pensions were precarious at best. The Hotel Avenida changed the dynamic of the city's hotel sector, far surpassing its predecessors in size and a self-conscious aim to accommodate guests in modern, urbane style. The hotel suites had telephones decades before most private homes. The establishment boasted the novelty of electrical lights at a time when gas lamps, oil lanterns, and old-fashioned candles remained the main source of artificial illumination. The establishment's electric elevator was a marvel of engineering that presaged the verticalization of central Rio. As a luxury hotel that also served as the terminus for streetcar service between downtown and the Zona Sul, the Hotel Avenida stood at a nexus of urban transportation, public culture, and high society. The daily Gazeta de Notícias *regularly listed the names of prominent guests. Inside, well-dressed elites circulated among expansive salons, parlors, and banquet halls. Outside, the adjacent Galeria Cruzeiro was a popular meeting spot for intellectuals, tram commuters, and Carnaval revelers.*

This unsigned article gushes with praise for the hotel's owners, José Ignácio de Souza and Francisco Cabral Peixoto, lauding their fine taste and audacity in dreaming up a development project that would elevate Rio to the standard of a world-class capital. Yet such standards were always in flux, and some of the beaux arts buildings built near the Avenida Central had already been demolished by the 1920s. In spite of calls to protect the architectural heritage of the First Republic, the Hotel

Avenida itself would be pulled down in 1957. In its place stands the Edifício Central, a landmark high-rise tower whose lower levels house an indoor shopping mall that now specializes in electronics.

With a fine crowd in attendance, so numerous and well-heeled, one of the most important centers of hospitality in South America opened a few days ago. The proprietors, Messrs. Souza, Cabral and Company, gave the name that appears as the title of this news story.

At the lovely opening party the most illustrious elements of our noble classes, members of the daily and periodical press, commercial agents, and a great wave of curious people were represented.

Although we are looking at a specifically private undertaking and initiative, the extreme enthusiasm with which the flood of people accompanied the debut of the important, recently inaugurated center was intuitive and understandable.

Others may attribute this strong current of sympathy for the noisy opening that, according to local journalists of this trusted Company, proposes to bring about an establishment whose aims will astonish in their boldness and the quality and energy that drive this endeavor.

But what, above all, attracted the sympathy of the masses was the importance of the building in which the important hotel is installed, the majesty and solidity of the construction and the combined architectural effect of the hotel and its surroundings.

It is a colossal building. Solid and grand in its dimensions—it suggests to us a piece of New York transplanted in Brazil! At the same time, it evokes the beauty and harmony of the external lines of the famous palaces of Vienna, Austria.

Before its formal opening, we visited the entire admirable establishment, and it was during this visit that we really came to understand the kindness and the tenderness of Mr. Francisco Cabral, one of the proprietors. . . .

The man upon whom the dynamic responsibilities of heading such an establishment fall must have these qualities: kindness and scrupulousness, honesty and foresight. The owners of the grand Hotel Avenida are the incarnation of everything that one could expect in this regard. From their prodigious economic astuteness, equipped with the highest commercial spirit, they were dedicated to the idea of founding this hotel-colossus that represents an enormous act of courage, such were the capital used and the responsibilities undertaken for the public.

The establishment is the last word in hotels. Distributed among four ample floors, which are nothing more than extensions of one another, the

"Hotel Avenida e Galeria Cruzeiro." Photographer unknown. Courtesy of Arquivo
Geral da Cidade do Rio de Janeiro, Rio de Janeiro.

hotel is connected through a system of stairs, firm and easy to access, and
with splendid electric elevators installed under all modern precepts by way
of the latest triumphs of mechanics and electricity.

The visitors' lounge is ample like the vast rooms of Louis XIV; it evokes
the fine taste of the fashionable salons in Paris, Lisbon, and Buenos Aires.
The dining room is immense and airy. We saw two great banquet halls that
were empty but shall naturally come into their own, although the owners
were not yet able to inform us of these rooms' eventual use. The pantries
are models of general cleanliness and for all the fixtures that have been
installed. The kitchen takes up a generous space, where they rigorously observe a regime of hygiene, comfort, and speed.

There are several different ovens, in a variety of systems, one of them
colossal, all adhering to the standards of what is modern and the most comfortable. The bar is functioning in a true salon that is perfectly suited to
meet any demand or necessity. The whole building is illuminated by electric
light and gas. The various rooms and sleeping chambers are excellent.

Each of the 220 guest accommodations boasts light, air, and a strict regime of hygiene.

And, in addition to all this, the most far-flung parts of this great building are connected by impressive spaces, especially on the first floor, where the bar, kitchen, and pantries function. One finds gracious installations throughout the dining areas and the visitors' rooms. On this last subject, it is worthwhile to highlight the good taste that reigns here: in the furniture, details, décor, and so on. The floors are lustrously varnished and decorated with multicolored rugs, and the ceilings are a work of high-relief art.

Never has there been more cause to applaud the construction and the dedication of a Company of such high ambition.

Translated by Amy Chazkel

Rio's Kiosks

Augusto Malta

Shortly after Francisco Pereira Passos (1836–1913), a Parisian-trained engineer with grand plans for the Federal District, was appointed mayor in December 1902, he was introduced to Augusto Malta (1864–1957), a self-made man of many trades, including photography. Malta was at the right place at the right time, as Pereira Passos was looking for someone to create a visual record of the urban reforms that would define the era. Vast swaths of Rio's urban terrain were slated for demolition, and the project required expropriations of residential and commercial properties. The mayor needed documentation of the homes and shops about to be reduced to rubble, in part to manage indemnifications. The mayor hired Malta, initiating the then-amateur photographer's nearly half-century career as documentarian of daily life in Rio. Malta worked as the official photographer of the mayor's office between 1903 and 1936. Taking upward of sixty thousand prints, he documented factories, circuses, horse racing tracks, dry goods stores, urban folk festivals, Carnaval balls, and ribbon-cutting ceremonies. He shot images of a city responding to dramatic changes in the urban fabric.

Malta's tenure as the photographic chronicler of Rio's everyday life intersected with the short life of a characteristic feature of Rio's commercial landscape: the kiosk. These establishments sold refreshments, cigarettes, and other small conveniences throughout the city. In the 1870s, Brazilian and European businessmen began to solicit concession contracts to erect these small commercial structures with pointed roofs. By 1888, there were about 150 of them on street corners around the city, including the growing suburbs. By the turn of the twentieth century, the kiosks of Rio drew public controversy, as some claimed that they attracted unsavory crowds and fomented disturbances in public areas. When the concession contract with Companhia Kiosque expired in 1911, the municipal government opted not to renew. In November of that year the city closed down and demolished all kiosks. Malta photographed these structures on the eve of their destruction.

As both photojournalist and city employee, Malta was interested in urban archi-

"Rua da América." Photograph by Augusto Cesar Malta de Campos. Coleção Augusto Cesar Malta de Campos, IMAGE 1: MT 7 (031.596), Augusto Malta, 1911, black-and-white photograph, 18 × 24 cm. Used by permission of Museu Histórico Nacional, IBRAM, MinC autorização no. 015/2014.

tecture and urban residents. These three photographs show kiosks and their social uses in the port neighborhoods of Santo Cristo, in Cidade Nova (just west of the Campo de Santana), and on the Ladeira da Santa Teresa against the iconic backdrop of the Arcos da Lapa. Together, the images immortalize vernacular architecture and everyday life at the turn of the twentieth century.

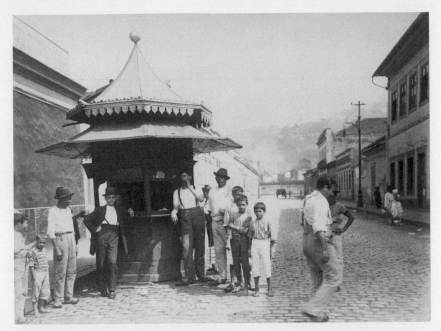

"Rua M. de Pombal." Photograph by Augusto Cesar Malta de Campos. Coleção Augusto Cesar Malta de Campos, IMAGE 2: MT 2 (031.590) Augusto Malta [1911], black-and-white photograph, 18 × 24 cm. Used by permission of Museu Histórico Nacional, IBRAM, MinC autorização no. 015/2014.

"O Kiosque da ladeira de Santa Teresa." Photograph by Augusto Cesar Malta de Campos. MT 1 (031.589), Augusto Malta, 1911, black-and-white photograph, 18 × 24 cm. Used by permission of Museu Histórico Nacional, IBRAM, MinC autorização no. 015/2014.

The Cult of Nostalgia

João do Norte

Between 1896 and 1914, a powerful convergence of civil engineering, public health, criminal justice, and capital investment leveled large swaths of historic Rio (later known as "O Rio Antigo," or Old Rio) and its habits. The chaotic dockyards surrounding the port, as well as the colonial-era streets and alleys between São Bento and Castelo, were rebuilt as efficient, orderly, cultured, and healthful urban spaces. Artificial illumination and formal landscaping along Guanabara Bay inaugurated the bourgeois pastime of ambling about the waterfront.

Surely a period of wonder and marvel, this beautiful age was characterized by widespread disruption and injury to traditional lifeways. Hundreds of structures dating from the colonial and imperial eras were torn down and thousands of residents displaced. The refinement of the Teatro Municipal (inaugurated 1909) and the National Library (1910)—structures that borrowed heavily from the cultural cachet of Paris—contrasted with the squalid favelas on hillsides ironically named Providência (Providence) and Saúde (Health) that rose up in the wake of demolition and displacement.

In late 1912, Gustavo Dodt Barroso (1888–1957), writing under the pseudonym "João do Norte" (João of the North), lamented the losses that came along with the civilizing process. Barroso, a twenty-four-year-old transplant from the northeastern state of Ceará, had not yet developed the rabid anti-Semitism and fascist sympathies that framed his political activities in the 1930s. In 1912, his perspective was a longing look backward, to physical structures and traditions facing extinction. In this overview of the cultures of the past in Brazil, France, and Germany, Barroso directs special attention to the destruction of the oldest parts of Old Rio. (Ironically, much of the "New Rio" that Barroso despised would also be pulled down after World War II.) Despite João do Norte's pessimism about his fellow citizens' capacity for a "cult of nostalgia," Barroso would go on to a successful career as the founding director of the Museu Histórico Nacional, inaugurated during the grand centennial exposition held in 1922, during yet another round of sweeping urban reform, dislocation, and "modernization." At the museum, Barroso oversaw a collection that included vestiges of the religious art, material culture, and civil architecture that had been taken down in the name of progress.

The undoing of our traditions has become an unpardonable crime. Case in point: the old gate to the Quinta da Boa Vista was a gift from the royal House of Hapsburg or, perhaps, Windsor. The gate is blessed with an austere beauty in its overall design and splendid structural elements. After being moved on numerous occasions, the gate now has recently been scandalously relocated to the recesses of the grounds, in front of the old cavalry barracks.

Never have we seen such scorn [*desamor*]. What is happening to historical objects can be equally seen with the traditions and customs that are representative of our regions, cities, and neighborhoods. Only one thing remains perpetual and untouched: Carnaval. And *that* is not even native to our land. The rest dies bit by bit. Even the *cordões* [festive street processions dating from the colonial era] have disappeared.

Here we are in December, the month of the birth of Christ, the time of the *usanças* [traditional Christmastime celebrations], the era of the festivals that our forefathers willed to us. What do we see? Nothing. We are left with shoes placed on the window sill—a perverse imitation of the shoes that used to be placed in front of the fireplace. One has never seen the city in such a state, one in which the bustle of the great transportation arteries and avenues kills the traditional look of the season's festivities. Rio de Janeiro has lost its traditions, and in this regard, it stands alone among the cities of the world.

Paris, with all its splendor and beauty, has never lost its old habits. In the markets at Les Halles, the women create a festive climate, giddy with wine and song, where a quartet of ladies appear dressed as queens, with one chosen as the reigning sovereign of the market for the coming year. The press provides ample coverage and large photographs of the festivities which are not unlike what we once saw here in Brazil in the times of slavery when the Reis do Congo [colonial-era festivals, also known as *congadas*, featuring the ceremonial coronation of an African "king"] were common.

There is not a single European city in which dates of historical importance fail to be celebrated. Carnival in Nice has its own traditions where the celebrants sweep into the streets in a triumphal manner, high atop oversized and imposing floats, decked out in gold. They take the city by storm, plunging everyone into three days of wild delirium.

In Nuremberg—a city that breathes the very air of the Middle Ages—

cornices and statues tucked away in obscure niches serve as small reminders of feudal times. The city is the reigning queen of historical pageants. And on those precious dates of historical remembrance, the streets fill with long lines of lancers, helmets and armor on their heads, protective body armaments at the elbows and nape, wearing breastplates made of burnished steel, dulled steel, as well as intricately worked Toledan steel.

In Westphalia, a wealth of reminders can be found in the city's public squares and back alleys. The golden sun shines and sparkles on the refurbished helmets and worked metals. Amid knights and lower nobles come the princes and barons, serfs and caretakers, humble peasants and the proud townspeople dressed up as rabble. One sees long flowing robes and short waistcoats, the wooden staff of the shepherd here, pikes and javelins there. And all around, the air is filled with the melody of old songs swirling about as wisps of nostalgia for days gone by.

The evocation of the past in those streets, where the house locks are engraved with the Tree of Jesse and warlike insignia all in a golden patina, is most complete and magnificent. And watching it all . . . the blonde, disciplined German people dream of a traditional life along the legendary Rhine, where ruins of castles are preserved as national monuments. It is a story of the motherland parading before their eyes, retold in the iron of the soldier, on the velvet of the nobles, on the holsters of the cavaliers, and in the weathered staffs of the shepherds. The procession captures a saga of war, politics, and feudalism that was once common to Swabia, Franconia, Thuringia, and Bavaria. And all the while the respectful crowd watches as the past streams before its eyes.

Orléans, in its own historical pageant, celebrates the historic entrance of Joan of Arc. With clanging sounds, the armies of the King of Bourges appear at the corner. Behind the crossbow carriers march the dejected English prisoners, dressed in their woolens torn upon the heaths. Upon a fine white steed adorned with gold and red, Joan of Arc raises a triumphal standard. In the same manner, Calais commemorates the surrender of the English. Other cities celebrate other great events. All the history of France is replayed within these festivals, in the colors, in the costumes, in all of the detail. Every year, the cadets of the military academy of Saint-Cyr reenact the bloody Battle of Borodino [September 7, 1812]. The Cossack farmers of the Volga cower in a wooden fortification which has been set up in the center of the school's patio. Napoleon and his marshals direct the maneuvers. The imperial guard marches to the assault with white baldricks crossed over blue tunics. A band plays "Veillons au salut de l'Empire." The retelling of the Battle of La Moskowa is perfect.

Yet here in Brazil, we have nothing of this sort. Ouro Preto [Minas Gerais], that cradle of tradition and glory, is bit by bit defeated, crushed. No one shores up the crossbeams hewed from brute stone, nor the crumbling walls. Almost no one came to the festival held there to commemorate the Inconfidência Mineira [a frustrated 1789 antiregal conspiracy that resulted in the death sentence for Joaquim José da Silva Xavier, better known as Tiradentes]. Olinda [Pernambuco] is overtaken by weeds. Nothing has been saved in the reurbanization of Salvador da Bahia. And here in Rio, all tradition is wiped away. The past goes abandoned.

I challenge anyone to try to reverse this lamentable state of things. Go ahead and dedicate yourself to the preposterous task of organizing some event. Put on a historical pageant or organize a mounted procession to remind us of the founding of the city by Mem de Sá, replete with Indians with crowns-of-feathers and helmeted soldiers. Try to reenact the procession that led Tiradentes to the gallows of Lampadosa. You will quickly see that everyone will laugh at your charade. Ridicule will forever be heaped upon you.

The Cult of Nostalgia is still not for us.

Translated by Daryle Williams

Anarchists under Arrest

Corpo de Investigação e Segurança

Pública do Distrito Federal

Anarchist groups seeking radical alternatives to bourgeois capitalism and the government of the Republic exerted a strong influence on the early decades of urban labor activism in Brazilian cities, especially the major ports. Anarchism initially took root in workers' disenchantment with the republican regime's failure to implement real democratic reform. Some embraced labor actions, including strikes. Others turned to violence against state officials and industrialists. In Rio, where anarchism was especially popular among immigrant men from the Spanish-speaking world, federal and municipal authorities reacted with repressive measures that reinforced the anarchist idea that the nation-state was a dangerous antagonist to the interests of the proletariat.

The following document, sent by the Corpo de Investigação e Segurança Pública do Distrito Federal (Public Security and Investigation Bureau of the Federal District) to Rio police chief Aurelino Leal (1877–1924), lists seventeen men arrested in 1918 on suspicion of anarchist activities. Eleven of the detained men were foreign-born, a reflection of an official mind-set that labor activists involved in anarchist networks were "outside agitators" and subject to a 1907 law stipulating the expulsion of foreign "militants." The report reveals that several of the detained men were associated with the working-class press. Rio's anarchists maintained intimate connections with the world of print, and anarchist newspapers were frequent targets of official surveillance and harassment. In the report, we glimpse the pathways through which the anarchist movement influenced the political consciousness of the laboring classes. We also see the state's definition of dangerous behavior and "subversive" activity.

Rio de Janeiro, September 27, 1918

Most Excellent Sir Dr. Aurelino Leal
His Most Dignified Chief of Police of the Federal District

With reference to the official letter from the Most Excellent Sir Minister of Justice and Interior Affairs, transmitting the request for information made by the Chamber of Deputies concerning the anarchists who were detained here, it is my duty to communicate to Your Excellency the following clarifications:

As a public security measure, motivated by the agitation that took place in the bosom of the working class and owing, in large part, to anarchist propaganda, the following confessed anarchists were detained by the Bureau:

RAYMUNDO DOMINGOS MARTINS, Spanish, confessed anarchist and agitator, inspires movements in reaction against bosses and public powers.

Spreads anarchist propaganda in the columns of *O Cosmopolita*, anarchist instrument, and in workers' centers.

For the above reason, he was detained by the Bureau: on August 3, 1917, for investigation; on April 16 of this year, by order of His Excellency, and on the 6th of last month, by virtue of the latest strikes, having been the last two times quickly released and, in the last time, released on the 31st of last month.

JOSÉ CAIAZZO—Italian—Confessed anarchist and agitator, supporter of the use of explosives.

Has been taking part in all proletarian movements in this Capital. He corresponds with anarchists from the interior [of Brazil] and abroad. Is a supporter of communism and of revolution.

For the above motive, he was detained on May 11, 1917, August 3, 1917, and the 8th of last month, having been released on the 31st.

RAPHAEL LOPES or RAPHAEL PEDRO LOPES—Spanish—Confessed anarchist and agitator, supporter of the use of dynamite bombs. Has been taking part in all workers' movements.

For this motive, he was arrested on April 14 of this year, by order of Your Excellency, released soon after, and on the 8th of last month, being released on the 31st.

ALBERTO ZAMORANO, also known as FRANCISCO BENITEZ, Uruguayan, expelled from Buenos Aires in July of 1910 for being a dangerous anarchist, fervent supporter of revolutionary action, having presented these statements at the workers' centers in this Capital city.

He was arrested on July 23, 1916, when, at 5 o'clock in the morning on the Praça da Republica, he distributed flyers, inviting workers to a rally against the foreigner expulsion law.

On July 18, 1917, he was detained to give explanations for the theft of consumer stamps [*sellos de consumo*] and, on the 8th of last month, because of the anarchist propaganda that he has been fomenting in the workers' centers, organizing strikes, having been released on the 31st. This anarchist, among others, maintains a correspondence with ALEXANDRE ALRA, who, in Rosario de Santa Fé, in the Republic of Argentina, heads the anarchist newspaper *La Rebellion*.

MANOEL GONÇALVES DE OLIVEIRA—Brazilian and confessed anarchist, detained, as a public security measure, on the 6th of last month, having been released on the 31st.

DJALMA NOGUEIRA LEITE—Brazilian, detained, as a public safety measure, on the 7th of last month, on the occasion of the strike of Cantareira [Niterói], when he carried a note from an anarchist from Niterói to the anarchist ASTROGILDO PEREIRA. He was released on the 1st of the current month.

ANTONIO JOSÉ DA CUNHA, commonly known as "MINEIRO," confessed anarchist and distributor of subversive flyers, detained, for that reason, on April 15, 1917, and on the 6th of last month, having been released on the 31st.

VALENTIM JOAQUIM DE BRITO—Portuguese, habitual agitator. His records include a legal case in the Seventh Police District, as an infraction against Article 204 of the Penal Code. He was arrested on May 11 of last year, for having taken part in the disturbance brought about by the workers in the Corcovado factory, on August 3rd of the same year for investigation, on the 12th of last month, for having fomented worker agitation, having been released on the 31st.

BENTO ALONSO or BENTO ALONSO ALVAREZ—Spanish, agitator, for which reason he was detained on August 11, 1917, and on the 19th of last month, having been released on the 31st.

ASTROGILDO PEREIRA—Brazilian—Anarchist and agitator, being the only editor of the anarchist weekly entitled *Cronica Subversiva*, in which the present social regime is fought.

FRANCISCO PERREIRA, also known by the names JOSÉ FERNANDES, JOSÉ MARIA FERREIRA and JOSÉ MARIA—Portuguese—Fervent anarchist, having entered the House of Detention for having been found guilty of an infraction of Article 330 of Section 1 of the Penal Code, a term in the Dois Rios Correctional Colony [Ilha Grande] and seven entries in this Inspector's office, the last of which having been on the 9th of last month, as a public security measure, being released on the 31st.

RAPHAEL SERRAT MUNHOZ—Brazilian—Among the most audacious agitators, feared even by the very leaders of the Coffee Porters' Association to which he belongs.

He systematically places himself in the leadership in all kinds of dissident acts and, acting as an anarchist, he calls himself a socialist.

He has been brought twice to the Inspector's office and appears in the General Registry of the Office of Identification and Statistics under number 1942, having had two detentions at the House of Detention for having been tried for Article 1 of Law 1.162 of December 12, 1890 [prohibiting the use of threats or violence in work stoppages and agitation for salary adjustments] and for Article 399 of the Penal Code, having been found not guilty.

Detained, as a public security measure, on the 8th of last month, and he left on the 31st.

JOÃO DA COSTA PIMENTA—Brazilian—Confessed anarchist, editor of *O Cosmopolita*, whose columns propagate his ideas. He has taken a significant part in all incidents of worker agitation.

For this reason, he has been brought four times to this Inspector's office, the last of which was on the 9th of last month, being released on the 31st.

ANTONIO RODRIGUES MAÇÃES—Portuguese—Self-confessed and audacious anarchist. For this reason, he has been brought three times to this Inspector's office, the last of which on the 6th of last month, having been released on the 31st.

ANTONIO FERNANDES—Spanish—Habitual agitator and editor of seditious flyers, in which the constitutional authorities of the Republic are attacked. Detained, for this reason, on the 19th of last month, and released on the 31st.

ABILIO MOREIRA LOBO—Portuguese—Agitator. Detained, for this reason, on the 19th of last month, and released on the 31st.

DIAMANTINO LOPES MOREIRA—For the same reason, detained on the 19th of last month, and released on the 31st.

All of these individuals were detained in a room in this Inspector's office, without any contact with common prisoners, having been provided special meals according to each one's choice.

Translated by Amy Chazkel

Demolition of the Morro do Castelo

Carlos Sampaio

Before taking the reins of Rio's city hall in 1920, Carlos César de Oliveira Sampaio (1861–1930) pursued a lucrative career as an investor, engineer, and professor. President Epitácio Pessoa (1865–1942) appointed Sampaio mayor for his experience running engineering projects. Sampaio had already been involved in improvements to the city's dockworks and the leveling of the Morro do Senado (a project that created the Parisian-like traffic circle now known as the Praça da Cruz Vermelha). During his mayoral tenure, Sampaio introduced a citywide plan for modernizing the capital that improved on reforms undertaken under Pereira Passos. Sampaio envisioned major improvements to sanitation and flood controls as well as the enlargement of usable land area through reclamation. Under Sampaio, the sandy marshes surrounding Lagoa Rodrigo de Freitas were urbanized, creating conditions for a middle-class embrace of the good life in the Zona Sul neighborhoods of Lagoa and Jardim Botânico. The mayor's most famous act of urban planning was the decision to raze the Morro do Castelo.

In the run-up to a visit of the Belgian royals and the centennial of national independence, celebrated in grand fashion in 1922, Sampaio pushed ahead with the controversial project to level Castelo, a centrally located hilly neighborhood with a storied history dating back to the early colonial era. In 1921, the city council approved plans for a demolition project that would create a level surface area equaling fourteen city blocks. Hydraulic equipment subsequently blasted buildings and rocks downhill into Guanabara Bay. Sixteenth-century churches and 5 million cubic meters of earth were turned into landfill.

Rio's citizens voiced a myriad of opinions about the destruction. Some lauded Sampaio for his visionary leadership of a city striving to modernize and eradicate epidemic disease and substandard buildings; others lodged accusations of corruption against a municipal executive who had personally profited from prior public works concessions. Residents resisted removal from their homes and businesses. Some intellectuals lamented the loss of material and popular culture slated for rubble. Nonetheless, down came Castelo.

In the report on his administration presented to Pessoa excerpted here, Sampaio

"Morro do Castelo." Photographer unknown, 1921. Coleção Iconografia Avulsa, 543 K 038.691, first-generation black-and-white photograph, 14 × 18 cm. Used by permission of Museu Histórico Nacional, IBRAM, MinC autorização no. 015/2014.

highlighted the achievements of his term. Well aware of the furor that his projects generated, the mayor worked to protect his legacy and manage public opinion. The accompanying photograph shows the demolition work, as the shell of a colonial-era building stands precariously on the verge of obliteration. The iconic slopes of Sugarloaf can be seen in the distance, on the opposite shore of the bay.

I am here to present to Your Excellency a synthetic report on municipal administration during the two and a half years of my mayoral tenure.

At the beginning of June 1920, Your Excellency invited me to take the position of mayor of the Federal District. Your Excellency did this with the knowledge of the GRAVITY of the financial state of the Municipality, and in anticipation of the city's preparations to receive the Belgian King and the festivities for the Centennial. Circumstances dictated that we take certain fiscal measures that provoked accusations of the gravest nature lodged against a man like myself who was not a politician and who had never accepted a position in public administration. . . .

Prior to setting forth any particular program of governance, and having resolved to act in light of the circumstances that presented themselves to me, I sought, with the nearly exclusive goal of increasing the city's revenues, to undertake a series of public works that came to be judged productive. Measures included sanitation, public transit, and improvements in general circulation. If possible, such works would concomitantly enlarge the central area of the city, lessen the impact of flooding that afflicted other parts of the city, and contribute to general beautification.

It proved impossible, however, to overlook a program of tree-planting and the installation of gardens in this capital city, just as it was not possible to disregard street sweeping and food provisioning, much less to ignore public education and public assistance, which still need to be studied in a convenient manner, with a gravity similar to that shown toward our municipal finances, but without the corresponding proceeds.

Concerning how I carried out my plans, the facts known to the inhabitants of this city speak the best.

And here I highlight the principal accomplishments:

The leveling of the Morro do Castelo, with the goal of ventilating and sanitizing the center of the city, enlarging previously deficient areas of the great value to the City, and constructing a seawall to allow us to make use of the quays and the warehouses of the Customs House. . . .

We might ask, were these works productive?

Suffice it to remember that the urban lands made available in the public works on Castelo alone will probably provide about 80 thousand contos, and the works in Lagoa, another fifteen thousand. That is, ninety-five thousand contos of income (a calculation based on a very low value), a sum that does not include that totality of public works—and this, without even counting the growth of city properties and the increase in property tax income and other taxes and fees.

Translated by Amy Chazkel

Exhuming Estácio de Sá

Various Notables

In 1922, a group of Rio notables gathered at the venerable Igreja de São Sebastião, atop the Morro do Castelo, as described in this ceremonial resolution, to exhume the remains of Estácio de Sá (1520–1567). In paying homage to this historical figure whose family had played a foundational role in the city's colonial beginnings, these notables performed their roles in a network of social status that joined together the twentieth-century intelligentsia, the press, the technical elite, traditional religious associations, and immigrant mutual aid societies. In the solemn act of exhumation, these men also confronted pressing questions of local and national historical memory in the context of dramatic urban change.

The son of a noble Portuguese family, Sá had traveled to Brazil with the military aim of stopping French attempts to colonize Guanabara Bay. He first sailed to Salvador da Bahia and then further south, where with the help of the Jesuits and native allies he founded Rio on March 1, 1565. Two years later, he died of battle wounds. His uncle, Mem de Sá (1500–1572), assumed the governorship of Rio briefly before Estácio's brother, Salvador Corrêa de Sá (1540–1631), became the governor-general. In 1583, Estácio de Sá's remains—removed from their original burial place on the Morro Cara de Cão, near Sugarloaf—had been reinterred in the church dedicated to Rio's patron saint, built atop the Morro do Castelo.

By the early twentieth century, Castelo stood as a poor and working-class neighborhood that attracted the negative attention of politicians and public health agents. The neighborhood's insalubrious, precarious housing and rough popular traditions had no place a short distance from the Teatro Municipal, some argued. The hill occupied potentially valuable, centrally located real estate. Despite opposition, Mayor Carlos Sampaio planned for Castelo's demolition. The imminent razing posed a dilemma for the precious relics located inside the Igreja de São Sebastião, including Estácio de Sá's mortal remains. A tombstone and founding stone of the city were moved to the Igreja dos Capuchinos in Tijuca. Famed modernist architect Lúcio Costa later designed a monument to the city founder, inaugurated in 1973 in the

Parque do Flamengo. The journey of Sá's remains from a sixteenth-century church to a subterranean crypt beneath a stark stone obelisk suggests the power of the modernist approach to urban memory in twentieth-century Rio.

Decree granting the exhumation of the mortal remains of the founder of the City of São Sebastião do Rio de Janeiro and its first Capitão-mor, Estácio de Sá, carried out in the church of São Sebastião atop the Morro do Castelo:

On the fifteenth day of the month of January in the year nineteen twenty-two, gathered in this church of São Sebastião on the Morro do Castelo, the undersigned, along with members of the various commissions with whom the present decree has been affirmed, first went to the city's founding landmark, which until now has occupied a place outside the present temple on the northwest corner of its main façade. This, in fact, was on account of the commissions that represented in this decree the Sociedade Central dos Arquitetos and the Instituto Brazileiro dos Arquitetos recognizing this landmark as having existed at that location, planted on that mount when in 1567 Salvador Corrêa de Sá—"the Elder"—governor of the city, upon orders of Mem de Sá, Governor-General of Brazil, transferred to the Morro do Descanso, today's Castelo, the humble abode of the city founded by Estácio de Sá on the Morro de Cara de Cão, today's São João peninsula, at the northern base of Urca and Sugarloaf in fifteen sixty-five under the denomination "Village of São Sebastião do Rio de Janeiro" and later known as "Villa Velha."

This landmark was set at the present location upon a road in the jurisdiction of the former high chapel of the same temple. Afterward, the edge of the grave and the gravestone of the tomb containing the sepulcher were lifted, where, according to the decree issued in the year eighteen sixty-two, the mortal remains of the aforementioned Capitão-Mor were laid. This task was completed without incident, thus the stone lid was placed at the head of the platform above the open grave. A pit then emerged from the ground, formed by walls of masonry and split in half, crosswise, by a partition of bricks. In the largest of these two trenches, there was a granitic ashlar with a cobblestone lineament, measuring eighty-eight centimeters long by sixty-six centimeters wide, and of an undetermined depth. Inside the ashlar was found the urn made of Brazilwood that, according to the decree of eighteen sixty-two, contained the mortal remains of Estácio de Sá, a fact ascertained by the white Carrara marble tombstone that covered this trench made of granite which, extremely well preserved, in easily legible gold lettering read the following . . . . [1]

The Mortal Remains of Estácio de Sá / Exhumed from this sepulcher / on November 16, 1862 / Returned here to it on January 20, 1863.

Translated by Andre Pagliarini

Note

1. The ellipsis points here are original to the document.

Gaúchos Take the Obelisk

Anonymous

In 1930 an armed insurgency ousted Washington Luís (Pereira de Sousa, 1869–1957) from the presidential palace in Catete. The brief civil war included deadly clashes in the southern state of Paraná, fought between legalist troops who remained loyal to Luís and insurgent armies who rallied behind the frustrated presidential aspirant Getúlio Vargas (1882–1954). The bloodshed would have surely been greater if Luís, deposed October 24, 1930, had secured a more vigorous defense from troops stationed in the federal capital. Instead, the rebel troops faced little resistance in their march on the capital. A striking act of symbolic aggression that reinforced the fall of Luís and the First Republic (1889–1930) was the insurgents' aggressive embrace of the term "revolution" to describe what might otherwise have been deemed an unconstitutional coup d'état launched by one faction of regional kingpins dissatisfied with a competing faction that had controlled presidential succession since the late nineteenth century.

Rio became a privileged stage on which the insurgents elaborated on a drama of "revolutionary" change. An early example of the revolutionaries' aspirations for change, real and symbolic, is captured in this photograph. Flores da Cunha (1890–1959; with hat and mustache, center), an ambitious politician from the southern state of Rio Grande do Sul, stands amid a group of soldiers dressed in the neckerchiefs and heavy ponchos worn by the plainsmen of southern Brazil. His ensemble has hitched horses to the twenty-eight-meter granite obelisk standing at the end of Avenida Rio Branco, in central Rio. The shot includes the bronze plaque, dated 1906, that paid homage to president Rodrigues Alves, public works minister Lauro Müller, and Paulo de Frontin, the chief engineer in the construction of the showpiece thoroughfare originally known as Avenida Central. A group of onlookers—boys and men of varying ages, attire, and skin tones—join the rebels in peering at the photographer, who registers a moment in which one of the most iconic markers of the bourgeois city, erected amid the sweeping urban reforms of Rio's Belle Époque, has been taken over by outsiders, styled as rustic horsemen who exhibit a great social distance from the top-hat-and-waistcoated elite of the deposed republican regime.

Shortly after this photo was taken, Vargas became chief of the provisional gov-

"Luís Flores da Cunha e outros no obelisco da Avenida Central no Rio de Janeiro."
Photographer unknown, 1930. Arquivo Oswaldo Aranha [OA], foto 478, black-and-
white photograph, 17.5 × 23.5 cm. Courtesy of Centro de Pesquisa e Documentação da
História Contemporânea do Brasil / Fundação Getúlio Vargas, Rio de Janeiro.

*ernment. Using extraordinary powers, he named Flores da Cunha interventor
(governor) of Rio Grande do Sul, their shared home state. Vargas and a new group of
military and civilian allies quickly proceeded to construct a state apparatus that put
a strong federal imprint on agricultural production, health and education, culture,
and labor policy, among other fields of public administration. The obelisk at the
end of Rio Branco remained in place, but the Vargas regime's resignification of central Rio progressively relegated the monument to relative insignificance in the civic
imaginary—a process that began in the event photographed here.*

"Flying Down to Rio"

Louis Brock

American film producer Louis Brock (1892–1971) wrote the concept for Flying Down to Rio, *a hit RKO motion picture that premiered at New York City's Radio City Music Hall in December 1933. Brock's original film treatment, excerpted here, sets the action in the Brazilian capital and the mountain retreat of Teresópolis in the lead-up to the inauguration of a fabulous hotel on a "beautiful tropical beach in the suburbs." Screenwriters at RKO later fleshed out scenes in Miami and Haiti, but the final product remained true to Brock's imagination of Rio as the ideal setting for musical romance played out on the silver screen.*

Brock's hotel was modeled on the Copacabana Palace, opened in 1923 to attract global luxury travelers. The film's director, Thornton Freeland, made liberal use of aerial shots of the actual Copacabana Palace and the surrounding oceanfront neighborhood to add some authenticity to a production filmed on a soundstage located thousands of miles from Rio.

The film's most memorable number, "The Carioca," takes place in a cabaret fronting a grand bayside park that took inspiration from Rio's Praça Paris. Two American hoofers (Fred Astaire and Ginger Rogers) usher onto the screen Brock's dream of a dance craze primed to eclipse other Latin dances popularized during the repositioning of inter-American relations and U.S. empire in the 1930s. The number begins as the Turunos do Rio, a local band, strike up a popular tune. The audience jumps to its feet. The dancing is temporarily suspended as a group of light-skinned blacks dance with reckless abandon. Caught up in the excitement, the Astaire character, also named Fred, jumps to the dance floor to wow them all. The film adaptation presented variations in plot turns and characterizations from the original treatment, but "The Carioca" remained a grand number in which a multiracial cast playing Rio residents are impressed by the talents of their American guests. With lyrics by Gus Kahn and Edward Eliscu and music by Vincent Youmans, "The Carioca" was nominated for an Academy Award in 1934, the same year an eponymous dance craze swept the world, popularizing Brock's vision of a romantic city hospitable to outsiders, sexy and modern, with unmistakable undertones of the exotic.

"Flying Down to Rio" contemplates a modern, rhythmical, musical treatment of a story which, against the alluring background of Rio de Janeiro, one of the world's loveliest cities, is a romance filled with novelty, color, seductive music and a religious avoidance of these synthetic qualities which ordinarily characterize musical comedies and features based on South America.

Aside from the deference to authenticity and the avoidance of the artificial and illogical, it is well knit for a musical, in that each one of the principal musical numbers are so dramatized as to have the audience plugging for them. It will have at least six very exploitable novelties, such as: 1) the piano-plane; 2) a marriage performed by the pilot of a regular air liner; 3) a dance new to America—the "Carioca" which possesses a certain physical characteristic rendering it easy to the Americans to take up and dance, in contrast to the Rhumba and more intricate ballroom steps; 4) for the first time a seductive tango with real South American rhythm but good hot American lyrics which the public can remember and sing; 5) the most startling musical number yet attempted—namely, "Flying Down to Rio," which will be performed in the air; 6) a scenic background which will surpass anything ever presented on the screen before—including the Swiss scene in a recent English musical.

While this will provide an ideal book for a man like Youmans to give us a really important musical score, it will still have a sufficiently dramatic basis to give a competent director a chance to do some scenes which will touch the heart. While the general tone of the production is one of charm and enchantment, as well as impressive outstanding novelties, it will leave no synthetic taste in the mouths of either the American or the foreign audiences. This picture, if not cluttered up with unnecessary melodrama which is out of keeping with a musical comedy, and which by reason of the foreign background might involve unfavorably certain foreign characters, can gross us an additional hundred thousand dollars in the foreign fields. I cannot emphasize this too strongly, as I am qualified to speak on the foreign situation. [. . .][1]

The second evening of their arrival, Julio takes them [Fred's band, the Yankee Clippers] out to hear the "Turunos do Rio" orchestra at a local cabaret in a park facing the bay. It will be well for them to get some ideas of the local competition which they are expected to top. . . . The Turunos, anxious to impress, strike up a Brazilian number—the latest hit which has swept Brazil like a forest fire—it is the "Carioca" dance. The first strains of the music cause the boys to sit up—here is a tropic rhythm new to them . . . punctuated by weird instruments and swingingly danced to by the patrons who

Flying Down to Rio. Film still. Directed by Thornton Freeland, 1933. Los Angeles: RKO Studios.

arise from various tables on all sides. Here is something even more sensational than the first Rhumba which crashed New York when Don Azpiazus' "Havana Casino" orchestra introduced the "Peanut Vendor" to America!

Here is a dance that would easily catch on in the United States, as one of its characteristics is that most of the steps which are danced in the swinging manner finds the dancers with foreheads touching, instead of cheeks, as is the custom with the punks at home. This music would get anyone!

The patrons stop as a group of "High Yellows" in native costume come out on the platform and start hotter and more elaborate steps of this seductive dance. There is more abandon in two bars of this music than there was in a cycle in Pompeii.

While this is a ballroom dance for two people, it is performed by the present dancers in pairs, but in unison—as in a chorus. A singer introduces the lyrics (not yet written), which are to the effect that:

> We don't care for your foxtrot
> We dance the "Carioca"
> Brazilian girls will not get hot
> Except to the "Carioca"
> Don't waste your time with the waltz or gavotte,
> The local ladies will give all they've got
> If you give them the "Carioca."

This number is staged in such a way as to work up the entire crowd in the place who sing certain lines of the song alternately with the soloist. We go in for German effects of hands playing instruments familiar and strange; the cochalho, a long thin tube filled with fine pebbles, carrying the tempo in a swishing sound . . . . . . the pandero [sic], a large tambourine on which an expert can play solos. . . . the violão [guitar] . . . . . and many others.

The Yankee band is stopped——how the hell are they going to top such a performance. The local Latin band is much too hot for their northern music. [. . .]

In the meantime, Fred has arrived in Rio—flown up to the private landing field of his pal, Julio, and is informed there that Julio is down at the Beira-Mar Casino, and Fred proceeds there at once, arriving in time to witness part of the dance before Julio and the other boys see him. When they do, there is much excitement, and Fred is hailed out on the floor to try the "Carioca" and show the Brazilians how an American can dance. Grabbing a partner, Fred starts an interpretation of the "Carioca" that tops everything yet. The boys are again cheerful as they have confidence in Fred to help them sell the Yankee Clippers band to Rio.

Note

1. In this selection, ellipsis points enclosed in square brackets indicate omitted material; those not enclosed in square brackets are original to the document.

Bertha Lutz Goes to Congress

Bertha Lutz

In March 1934, the prominent women's rights advocate and accomplished botanist Bertha Lutz (1894–1976) joined adherents of the Partido Autonomista do Distrito Federal (Autonomist Party of the Federal District, f. March 1933) in a banquet held in honor of Federal District mayor Pedro Ernesto Baptista (1884–1942). Backed by the Liga Eleitoral Independente (Independent Electoral League, f. 1932), Lutz brought to Rio party politics the demands of a feminist agenda that had recently won the franchise for literate women. Lutz's alliance with this party also bolstered her campaign for a congressional seat. She advocated for expanded political representation for the residents of Rio, mayoral selection by popular election, improved access to public education and health services, and the extension of government protections to women and children. Lutz was keenly aware of the gender limitations on her political ambitions to represent a city that had grown to one and a half million residents. In the photograph reproduced here, Lutz (seated, fourth from left) is the only woman to appear, and once seated in congress, she would be one of just two female federal legislators.

Like many of the party leaders in attendance at the banquet, Lutz, who was born in São Paulo, was not a native Carioca. Nevertheless, her professional and political work in Rio helped build her party's growing popularity in various city neighborhoods. Lutz also helped lend the support of the middle-class feminist movement to Ernesto (born in Pernambuco) as the charismatic mayor built ties with organized labor, the progressive clergy, radio broadcasters, and popular associations, such as samba schools. Like Ernesto, Lutz cultivated close relations with high-placed federal politicians, including president Getúlio Vargas.

Lutz was elected an alternate (suplente) in the October 1934 congressional elections. Upon the death of the winning candidate, former Rio mayor Cândido Pessoa (1888–1936; born in Paraíba), Lutz assumed a seat in the Chamber of Deputies. Her inaugural address, excerpted here, set her political priorities in an international context of political tensions, welfare state reform, and the inclusion of women in the political arena. Mindful of the tense conditions in Europe, Lutz set her sights on political reform and social uplift, notably for Cariocas.

"Pedro Ernesto, por ocasião de banquete oferecido em sua homenagem, com a presença de membros do Partido Autonomista e outros." Unsigned, March 1934. Arquivo Pedro Ernesto Bastista (PEB), foto 095, 18 × 24 cm. Courtesy of Centro de Pesquisa e Documentção da História Contemporânea do Brasil / Fundação Getúlio Vargas, Rio de Janeiro.

The congressional seat that I now occupy has been passed on to me from the most generous hands of the Congressman who now rests in the Peace of the Lord. Covered by the mantle of struggle, this seat forever links the name Cândido Pessoa to the Brazilian feminist movement, like those other illustrious Brazilians, both alive and deceased, who have stood with us not in the easy moment of triumph, but in the bitter time of sacrifice that preceded it.

I have endeavored to follow the righteous path that Cândido Pessoa laid out, being a friend of his friends, trying to be judicious and fair to all and with my colleagues in the defense of the legitimate interests of the Federal District.

Mr. President, although I defend a cause and an idea, my presence here is almost superfluous. The causes that redeem and the ideas that march forth bring within themselves their own strength and their own impetus. No obstacle can contain them indefinitely; no person is indispensable to the banner of a cause often arduous, but always triumphant.

It was thus in generous, complete—near unanimous—fashion that the members of congress and the state officials present today defended the recommendation made in the run-up to the current Constitution that named me as the women's delegate to a project in which I, personally, would not have hesitated to leave the protection of women's rights to the men of Brazil. It is the woman of Brazil, however, who desires me present in the National Assembly.

We still have a ways to go before achieving a scientific government of the people; from that mode which already reigns in engineering and surgery, for example, and which, detaching them from the ambit of Power, will one day depersonalize public affairs. Our era presents government by the consent of the governed as the highest form of political expression.

Within a democracy all voices should be represented in political discourse.

Women make up half the population, the less favored half. Their labors in the home are unending and unrecognized; their professional work is poorly remunerated, and in most cases their talent is stifled in terms of opportunities for development and growth.

It is thus fair that women be included on the ballots of political parties and that women receive the right to vote.

We live in a time of tumult and dissonance. In this century—as perhaps in all others—civilization is under the daily attacks of barbarism. The noble impulses of the human heart live in eternal conflict with its interests, instincts, and passions.

If we tune our ears to the Old World, a place rich in lessons good and bad, we hear strange phenomena: sick vanities that manifest themselves in theatrical and puerile gestures; illicit ambitions that enslave the weak, within and across the borders of their country; the defeated who utter humiliating litanies of subservience and terror. Elsewhere, we hear of other, more fortunate countries, where peace, order and the law reign. If we observe them closely, we see that each time civilization is overtaken by barbarism, peace, justice and the law are taken down with it; public freedoms and individual rights diminish. Also lost is respect for the human person, especially the human person who does not possess arms, as is the case with women.

And every time, thanks to a superior political culture, civilization advances and sustains itself within the reign of peace, law and order grow stronger with it, as does respect for the inherent rights of all human beings, be they poor or rich, educated or ignorant, be they man or woman.

We see, furthermore, that every time women have their rights respected and their participation in public affairs guaranteed, they seek constructive collaboration with men. That is what the female electorate does in the United States and in New Zealand, inspiring among representatives of the

People laws that reduce infant and maternal mortality to the lowest possible rate; that is what the Scandinavian and British congresswomen do, defending housing for the poor, fighting for the interests of the laborer, and clamoring for women's justice.

The women elected by the Brazilian people proceed in the same fashion, like my noble colleague from São Paulo, Dr. Carlota de Queiroz, whose name I speak with pleasure and who has dedicated herself to the cause of abandoned minors [Queiroz thanks Lutz for her kind words] . . . the young state legislators, Maria Luiza Bittencourt, who studied public finance at the renowned Harvard University; Dr. Lili Lages, who breathes life back into defunct municipalities in Alagoas, securing enough budgetary commitments such that public health officials can carry out their mission; that is what Maria de Miranda Leão, the outstanding congresswoman from Amazonas, does, and many others, who take under their care every law related to women's work, maternity, childcare, and the home.

It is with this in mind that I make here, today, Messrs. Congressmen, my profession of faith. The home is the basis of society, and women will forever be linked to the home; but the home no longer fits within four walls—the home is also the school, the factory, the workshop. The home, Mr. President, is, above all else, the Congress, where the laws that govern the family and human society are voted.

Expanding her vision as her horizons broaden, the Brazilian woman, embodied in me, is among you, sir legislators, in your constructive task of creating the legislative mold for the Brazil of tomorrow.

And it is in that spirit, Congressmen, in that essentially feminine, and essentially human, spirit that I bring to you today, as a representative of the people of Rio, the modest collaboration, unpretentious but sincere and well intentioned, of women.

Translated by Shawn Moura

The Fount of the Queen

Armando Magalhães Corrêa

Armando Magalhães Corrêa (1889–1944), a Carioca sculptor and illustrator, saw beyond the densely urbanized central parishes dating from the colonial era and the close-in suburbs that developed along the shores of Guanabara Bay, tramways, and the central rail lines. After an early education at the Escola Militar, a military academy in the Zona Oeste suburb of Realengo, Magalhães Corrêa entered the National School of Fine Arts, where his talents landed him a prestigious prize that funded his study in Europe. Upon returning from Paris, Magalhães Correa took up a teaching post at the Museu Nacional and established himself as an important figure in the Rio fine arts scene. In the 1921 national salon, he entered a plaster female nude, A Carioca, representative of his fascination with Rio as subject.

Magalhães Corrêa resided in Jacarepaguá, a Zona Oeste suburb far from the city's fine arts circuits. He took advantage of this distance to document—in prose and in illustrations published in the Rio daily Correio da Manhã—the natural and human geography of the Sertão Carioca (Rio Backlands) and other areas that fell outside the orbit of cosmopolitanism. In 1935, two years after the publication of a collection of Magalhães Corrêa's articles on the Rio sertão, the Instituto Histórico e Geográfico Brasileiro published a series of illustrated articles about the many public fountains of Rio and the water-carriers, washerwomen, muleteers, and others who used them. Excerpted here is Magalhães Corrêa's treatment of the Bica da Rainha (Fount of the Queen), a nineteenth-century fountain located in Cosme Velho, about one hundred yards from the terminus of the Corcovado train station.

In his brief history of the fountain, Magalhães Corrêa covers 120 years of leisure, health, and provisioning in a verdant neighborhood that had remained semirural until streetcars, and later automobiles, provided fast connections to the city center. He describes the inventive ways Cariocas met basic household needs in the absence of municipal utilities. We also observe evidence of vernacular and formal activities to protect landmarks and the environment. We glimpse how a self-taught naturalist acted as a popularizer of the movement to marshal popular sentiment and state resources toward the protection of natural and cultural monuments. The federal government recognized the Bica da Rainha as national cultural patrimony in 1938.

On the slopes of Morro de Dona Marta exists a natural spring. From that source of natural mineral waters, the locale took its name. The only surviving registry of the fount's original siting on the right bank of the Carioca River (today's Rua das Laranjeiras) is an old lithograph.

That spring was a favorite among the Carioca elite, who took to going out for a jaunt at the locale, either in sedan chairs or on horseback. Thus, when Dona Maria I [the mentally incapacitated Portuguese queen who arrived in March 1808] would go for a walk, she would frequently show up at the spring, with her ladies-in-waiting in train. From this practice evolved the popular idiom "Maria vai com as outras" [Maria's out with the other ladies], a reference to the queen's mental delirium. This saying endures to this day to refer to those who know not how to govern themselves.

People grew so accustomed to seeing Dona Maria that the spring came to be dubbed the "Bica da Rainha." After the queen's death in 1815, the area continued to be favored by Carlota Joaquina, wife of Dom João VI, who would go there to douse her temperamental flare-ups.

Many people frequented the locale, particularly those suffering from anemia, on account of the salubrious properties of the ferrous waters. At the time, we might recall, the options for medical treatment were scarce, a situation quite unlike today where we find a market crammed with imported preparations.

The fount was simple, walled, with a staircase on its side that led up to the spout. Next to it was a walkway that led into the woods. Behind, there was a high wall with a platband at its center supported by two broad pillars and with two cone-shaped moldings at either extremity. In the middle and upper part of the fountain there was an irregular molding in the shape of an octagon. At its center was the inscription "Bica da Rainha." Below the described ornamentation stood an iron grate and a bronze spigot from which flowed the mineral waters.

Around 1905 the fountain was in a state of total abandonment. A merchant was denied permission from the city council to erect a small shop there. Later on, another private citizen restored the fountain, leaving it in a condition good enough to once again receive visitors.

And today, as before, the water vendor draws from the well to fill a large tank loaded onto a wagon that can carry 1,085 liters [287 gallons] of water. Pulled by a donkey, the wagon supplies the neighborhoods of Laranjeiras and Catete, distributing water in small 15-liter [four-gallon] barrels.

The wagon is owned by a female licensee who sells the barrels to private homes at the price of one milréis. Her business is thriving.

Nowadays, the Bica da Rainha is to be found on the odd-numbered side of Rua das Laranjeiras, number 107, in the neighborhood called Cosme Velho. It is located to the rear of a small lot situated below street level. The visitor must reach the fountain by descending nine steps. In the back there is a wall with an exterior of classical lines showing two columns—the bases of which, adjoined by an entablement at the top, support a platband with a notice bearing the date 1845 and a rosette on either side.

Under the entablement, between the pillars, reads "Bica da Rainha" in embossed letters separated from the fountain by filigree running the length of the construction. At the center of the fountain there is an opening of painted stone crowned by a small ornamental flourish: a conch shell with symmetrical spirals on its sides. This opening is enclosed by a beautifully designed iron fence with a gate through which neighborhood residents enter to fetch the much-valued water. Their journey is a veritable pilgrimage, just like old times.

On the upper registers of the fountain, on a painted and nearly illegible placard, there reads a warning to the public: "Please respect the public and private forests, conserving them with care, so that the headwaters of this age-old mineral-water spring might not suffer" [*Pede-se respeitar as matas da união e as particulares, conservando-as com carinho, para que não venham sofrer os mananciais desta lendária fonte de águas férreas*].

Translated by Andre Pagliarini

A Writer's Brazilian Diary

Stefan Zweig

Stefan Zweig (1881–1942) was an Austrian Jewish writer born into a life of consider-
able privilege who won global fame as a novelist, biographer, and playwright. In
his worldwide journeys, he sailed into Guanabara Bay on three occasions. The first
arrival, in August 1936, was en route to Buenos Aires, where Zweig was the dis-
tinguished guest at a gathering sponsored by the worldwide association of writers
known as PEN. During the Brazilian stopover, Zweig was fêted at a series of public
lectures in Rio and escorted tours in the states of Rio and São Paulo. Letters written
at the time reveal a man enchanted by the Brazilian landscape and people.

When Zweig returned to Brazil for the third time in 1941, he faced the grim reality
that the war in Europe had done irreparable damage to the refined café society that
he once knew. Dispirited by Old World racism and total war, Zweig and his second
wife, Lotte Altmann (1908–1942), took refuge in Petrópolis, a small city located in
the mountains above the Brazilian capital. In reclusion, the world-famous author
worked on an autobiography and other writings. However, a profound depression
brought him to take his life. It was a double suicide, as Lotte also ingested a fatal
overdose of barbiturates. A suicide note took stock of European self-destruction while
paying homage to Brazil.

"Brazilian Diary," excerpted here, was a travelogue written five years earlier,
at a time when Zweig was developing his laudatory vocabulary about Brazil and
the Brazilian people. The piece includes Zweig's first impressions of Rio, taking the
reader from the deckside views of the beaches of Copacabana to the passenger port
near Praça Mauá and on into the city streets of mansions and skyscrapers as well
as hillside shantytowns. The diary was originally published in Pester Lloyd, *a*
Budapest daily that circulated among a German-language readership witnessing
the elongating shadow of Nazism in Central Europe. The English-language transla-
tion, published in The Living Age, *a North American literary magazine that dated*
from the antebellum period, rehearsed themes later synthesized in Brasilien, ein
Land der Zukunft *(1941). Best known in English translation,* Brazil: Land of the
Future, *Zweig's book internationalized an image of Rio as the capital of a country*
of exceptional wonder, great promise, and racial harmony.

If I begin, dear European reader, with a little course of instruction, I do so because of my conviction that we know astonishingly little about Brazil. This, indeed, was my own first embarrassed feeling. For the most part we have forgotten what we learned in school, and what we remember is of little account, for figures and dates have long since become obsolete, overtaken by the rapid pace of events.

Moreover, it is high time that we became accustomed to abandoning our European way of looking at things, to recognizing that other continents are developing in quite different ways and that the world's center of gravity is shifting away from our "small Asiatic peninsula" (as Nietzsche called Europe) with alarming rapidity. It is a typical psychological shortcoming of parents that they are always the last to notice that their children have long ago grown into independent individuals. Thus many of us are still unable to get used to the idea that the one-time colonies of Europe became long ago organic States and even worlds of their own, spiritually as well as economically. . . .

Early in the morning all the passengers are already waiting impatiently on deck, armed with binoculars and cameras. None wishes to miss the famous entry into Rio de Janeiro, no matter how often he may have admired it before. The ocean still gleams blue and metallic, as it has for days, in calm but tiring monotony. Yet one feels that one is approaching land. One smells the nearby soil before beholding it; for all at once the air grows moist and sweet, playing softly round mouth and hands. A dark fragrance drifts slowly nearer—a fragrance brewed from plant breath and the moisture of flowers in the depths of the giant forests. It is the indescribably warm, sultry, fermenting breath of the tropics, which intoxicates and exhausts at one and the same time.

Now at last there are shadows in the distance. Uncertain, cloud-like, a mountain range looms into the empty sky, the outlines growing more distinct as the ship draws nearer. It is the range which protects, with its outstretched arms, the Bay of Guanabara, one of the largest in the world. Its great arch, with the many smaller bays and promontories, is large enough to harbor the ships of all the nations, and within this gigantic open shell innumerable islands lie scattered like pearls, each different in form and color. Some rise gray from the amethyst sea; at a distance they might be taken for whales, so bare and naked are their backs. Others are long, and rock-ribbed like crocodiles. Still others are covered with houses or guarded by fortresses.

Others again seem to be floating gardens, with palms and flower-beds, and while through the glass one is curiously admiring their unsuspected multiplicity of form, the background of the mountains like a huge relief, emerges, each one different, each with its own individual contour. One will be bare and the other clothed in a green robe of palm; this one will be rocky, the other encircled by a lustrous girdle of houses and gardens.

It is as though nature in her bold sculpture had tried to juxtapose all earthly forms, and indeed popular imagination has given earthly names to each one of these mountainous figures. The Widow [Morro da Viúva], The Hunchback [Corcovado], The Hound [Cara de Cão], The Finger of God [Dedo de Deus], and, above all, the Pao de Assucar [Pão de Açúcar], the Sugar Loaf, which rises right in front of the city in steep suddenness like the Statue of Liberty in New York—the ancient, immovable symbol of the city. Yet high above all these single monoliths and hills rises the chief of this giant tribe, the Corcovado, blessing Rio de Janeiro with a huge cross electrically illuminated at night—like a priest raising the monstrance above his kneeling flock.

Now at last, having threaded the labyrinth of islands, one beholds the city; but one does not see it all at once. Unlike Naples, Algiers, Marseilles, this panorama of buildings does not open out at one blow, like an arena with rising steps of stone; picture after picture, section after section, vista after vista, Rio unfolds like a fan; and it is this which makes the entry so dramatic, so perpetually surprising. For each of the separate bay communities, only the sum of which makes up the whole shore-line, is separated by mountain ranges—as though they were the ribs of a fan framing each picture, yet holding the whole together.

At last the arched beach comes into view, an enchanting spectacle: a wide promenade, above the foaming surf, with houses and villas and gardens. One can plainly distinguish the great hotel, and, rising up the hill, the villas in the woods. But no! It is only the beach of Copacabana, one of the most beautiful in the world, but only a suburb, not the city itself. The Pao de Assucar, the Sugar Loaf, still bars the view, and must be circumnavigated.

Not until then does one see the city, with its bay, looking out crowded and white on the beach, and scrambling confusedly up the green heights. One sees the newly laid-out beach parks and the flying field which has just been wrested from the sea. Now the wharf is near, and impatience will be satisfied. But no! Again we are wrong. This is only the Bay of Botafogo and Flamenco [Flamengo]. The ship moves on, and still another fold of this divine fan, shining polychrome, opens before us.

The Navy Islands must be passed, and that little one [Ilha Fiscal] with the Gothic palace where, two days before his abdication, Emperor Pedro gave his last ball, in blissful ignorance of what was to come. Now at last the towers greet us—a single, vertical mass. Now the quays come into view, the ship can moor, and one is in South America, in Brazil, in the most beautiful city in the world.

This hour-long entry into Rio is a unique experience, and makes a very deep impression comparable only to the arrival in New York. But New York's welcome is harsher, more energetic. It is like a fjord in the northland with its icy cubic piles. Manhattan's greeting is more masculine, more heroic, the steeply piled human will of America, a single explosion of concentrated force. Rio de Janeiro does not hurl itself at the visitor: it opens soft feminine arms, it receives, it draws one to its breast, it yields to view with a certain voluptuousness. Here all is harmony—the city, the sea, the green and the mountain. All flow, as it were, melodiously into each other. Even the sky-scrapers, the ships, the colorful illuminated signs do not clash.

And this harmony is repeated in ever new chords. The city's appearance seen from the hill is different than that from the sea; but everywhere there is harmony—loosely arrayed multiplicity that is forever a complete unity. Nature has become a city—a city which gives the effect of nature. And the city holds one with the same inexhaustible multiplicity, with the same grandiose magnanimity with which one is welcomed. From the moment of one's arrival one knows: the eye will not grow tired, nor the mind sated, of this unique city.

To be truly vital a city must contain within itself a number of strongly opposed forces. A merely modern city is monotonous; a backward one soon begins to grow irksome. A proletarian city is oppressive, while a center of luxury soon comes to exude a dreary boredom. A city is the more attractive, the more strata it possesses, the more colorful its range of contrasts—as is the case with Rio. Here the extremes are furthest removed, yet merge into each other with peculiar harmony. Here wealth does not provoke; the feu-dal mansions, furnished with astonishingly good taste, do not exhibit con-spicuous façades. They lie scattered in the greenery, with beautiful gardens and ponds, and with choice furniture, generally old-Brazilian. Because of the absence of urban showiness and their closeness to nature, they seem to have grown organically rather than to be arrogantly exhibited.

One must actually search before finding them, but when one has the pleasure of being a guest in one of these houses, one never tires of admir-ing them. For from every room here the view reaches through open doors into the landscape and even the most precious objects seem modest beside a natural background so perfect.

Strangely enough the poorest of the slums, the *favellas* [sic], have the same charm. Throughout the city there are rocky and wooded slopes, in part covered by beautiful villas. But wherever the ground is not built up, there the poor settle. They have no rights to the land where they build their houses and huts, the *favellas*. Tomorrow they may be driven out; but so long as no one claims the land they squat there. Thus there are hundreds upon hundreds of such shacks and shanties, rising from nothing: four walls of pressed clay, a roof of thatch or hemp or corrugated iron, a few rusty plates of tin gathered somewhere along the harbor—and there you have the entire family, mostly Negroes or half-breeds, and perhaps even a few pigs and chicks. Amid the metropolis here hundreds of thousands live in utter primitiveness, exactly as in the jungle or the bush. The astonishing thing is that these poor quarters seem neither tragic nor oppressive. For they lie in the open, among the green, with the most beautiful view in the world at exactly the same height and on the same streets as the luxurious villas.

It is understandable that the people in these adobe shacks feel happier than they would in a tenement. Here they are free, they may go about half-naked and do as they please. Should the land be taken from them, they simply settle a bit further on. No law keeps them from transporting their flimsy houses—one is almost tempted to say—on their backs. I have seen views across the bay from these *favellas* which are as beautiful as those from the finest villas. To preserve this multiplicity without regulating it, without violently organizing it—may that be the fate of the city, rather than the geometric insanity of straight avenues and sharp intersections, this fearful checkerboard ideal of the modern high-speed city which sacrifices to symmetry and monotony of form precisely that which is the incomparable heritage of every city: its surprises, its stubborn individuality, its nooks and crannies, and, above all, its contrasts—the contrasts of old and new, town and nature, of rich and poor, of work and leisure—which are here enjoyed in unique harmonious relaxation.

Rio and World War II

U.S. War Department and Walt Disney Studios

The devastation of World War II (1939–1945) unfolded far from Guanabara Bay, yet the conflict had a strong impact on Rio. When president-dictator Getúlio Vargas embraced a tactical shift away from domestic protofascism in 1937, Rio police chief Filinto Müller (1900–1973) used national security and looming war in Europe to intensify surveillance of suspected Axis sympathizers. Brazilian adherence to the Atlantic Charter, an August 1941 pact signed between the United States and Britain, sealed an official alignment with the Allies. When Brazilian merchant vessels were torpedoed in 1942, the Rio streets filled with anti-German protesters, and pro-Allies slogans accompanied an official war declaration. Rio was the base for the logistics of a sizeable expeditionary force sent to the European front. Wartime disruptions to trade and credit led to rationing and price controls. Meanwhile, the municipal secretariat of education intensified efforts to militarize school-age youth through scouting, physical education, and civic commemoration. Radio and film markets opened up to American mass media, promoted by private initiative and the Office of Inter-American Affairs, an agency of the United States government directed by Nelson A. Rockefeller. A memorable artistic outcome of this time of wartime "Good Neighbors" was Saludos Amigos (Hello Friends), a 1942 Walt Disney animated motion picture that introduced Donald Duck to Zé "Joe" Carioca, a green parrot. Zé Carioca's style of dress, demeanor, and playful wit telescoped the malandro, a stock character of Rio popular culture known for his street smarts. In the film's final segment, the two avatars of the American-Brazilian alliance tour the Marvelous City, including the famed undulating patterns in the cobblestone sidewalks of Copacabana (pictured here), to the musical accompaniment of "Watercolor of Brazil," a hypersentimental samba by composer Ary Barroso (1903–1964) first popularized in 1939.

Months before the Japanese attack on Pearl Harbor, the U.S. Department of War conducted a strategic survey of the Brazilian capital. The survey produced a contour map (also pictured here) that follows the arc of the shoreline from the Morro da Viúva to the port facilities separated from the Central do Brasil rail lines by various steep hillsides covered by favelas (a land usage not indicated on the map). Although the U.S. government map contains all the basics for a tourist excursion, its intent is geo-

Saludos Amigos [Hello Friends]. Film still. Directed by Wilfred Jackson, Jack Kinney, Hamilton Luske, and Bill Roberts, 1942. Los Angeles: Walt Disney Studios.

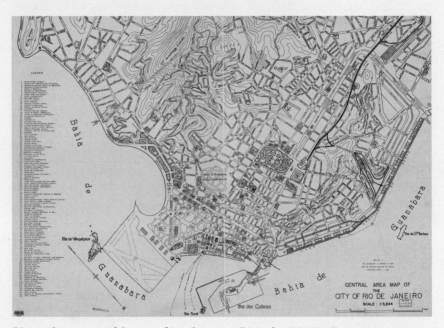

"Central area map of the city of Rio de Janeiro." Map by U.S. War Department, 1941. Typographia A. P. Rio de Janeiro. Courtesy of the Library of Congress Geography and Map Division, Washington, D.C.

strategic. "Confidential" appears twice on the copy held by the Library of Congress. A red-ink legend, superimposed on the original map, provides an English-language index to 119 sites, including dozens of points of military importance. The map plots strategic points in a city that might require defense in the event of an attack by Axis powers already feared to have their sights set on invading the Brazilian northeast.

Notwithstanding its military value, the map presents a wealth of information about major infrastructure projects that had transformed the city core. The intersection of Avenidas Rio Branco and Beira-mar map two major urban interventions, reconfiguring land and bay, completed prior to 1930. The prominent Santos Dumont airfields herald Rio's entrance into the age of commercial aviation. Finally, the map affords a view of Rio's future. The Morro de Santo Antonio, center, is labeled for arrassamento *(leveling).*

A Fond Farewell to Praça Onze

Herivelto Martins

Prince Regent João dubbed the lands between the Campo de Santana and São Cristóvão the "Cidade Nova" (New City), to differentiate the area from the "old" colonial city. As the region was urbanized through road construction and the use of landfill to reclaim swampy lowlands, immigrant communities of Jews, Portuguese, and Italians took root. A buzzing street commerce, inexpensive housing, and proximity to the port and the D. Pedro II train station (today's Central do Brasil) attracted poor, predominantly Afro-descended migrants. Accordingly, Cidade Nova and environs came to be nicknamed Pequena África (Little Africa). By the late nineteenth century, this polyglot, multicultural region was home to popular exuberant Carnaval celebrations, especially around a square named Praça Onze de Junho.

"Praça Onze" was a special place for samba, a music and dance form that descended from multiple cross-fertilizations between a Bantu-derived dance and song form called lundu, *the hybrid dance known as* maxixe, *and European dance and music styles including the polka and waltz, as well as the Portuguese* modinha. *The samba schools (escolas de samba) that developed in the 1920s out of older religious associations called* ranchos *often gathered at Praça Onze. The square was also famous for its relationship to municipally sanctioned Carnaval parade competitions, first organized in 1933. Yet the official imprimatur on Carnaval would not stop the urban reforms that resulted in the demolition of Praça Onze. When Avenida Presidente Vargas was completed in 1944, everything in its path had been razed except the Igreja da Candelária, too grand to be torn down. The original Praça Onze was reduced to rubble.*

Anticipating the square's demolition, two great personalities of the Rio music and performance scene, Afro-Brazilian actor and singer Grande Othelo (Sebastião Bernardes de Souza Prata, 1915–1993) and musician and composer Herivelto Martins (1912–1992) collaborated on a samba that became an anthem for the square and, by extension, other locales destroyed by city planning. The composition combined traditional elements of samba with the innovations of their time. The group Trio de Ouro's recording of the song was released for the 1942 Carnaval season to great success. The tune expresses a mixture of resignation, preemptive nostalgia, resilience, and celebration. Its lyrics make reference to the square as well as the poor hillside communities (morros), such as Mangueira, reachable by train. The destruction of a space of citywide sociability joined these diverse communities in lament.

They're going to do away with Praça Onze
There'll be no more Samba School
No, there won't
The *tamborim* weeps
The whole morro weeps
Favela, Salgueiro, Mangueira, First Station
Put away your *pandeiros*, put them away
Because the Samba School won't be taking part in Carnaval
Farewell, my Praça Onze, farewell
We already know that you are going to disappear
Take our memories with you
But you'll stay forever in our heart
And one day we will have a new square
And will sing of your past.

[Vão acabar com a Praça Onze
Não vai haver mais Escola de Samba,
não vai
Chora o tamborim
Chora o morro inteiro
Favela, Salgueiro, Mangueira, Estação Primeira
Guardai os vossos pandeiros, guardai
Porque a Escola de Samba não sai
Adeus, minha Praça Onze, adeus
Já sabemos que vais desaparecer
Leva contigo a nossa recordação
Mas ficarás eternamente em nosso coração
E algum dia nova praça nós teremos
E o teu passado cantaremos]

Translated by Amy Chazkel

Avenida Presidente Vargas

Hélio Alves de Brito

Extending more than two miles in length and nearly 325 feet wide, Avenida Presidente Vargas ranks among the world's largest urban thoroughfares. Inaugurated in 1944, the artery made a definitive statement that automobiles were to be the principal form of circulation between the city center, the residential and industrial neighborhoods of the Zona Norte, and the highway leading to Petrópolis with connections to São Paulo. Urban planners and engineers also considered stormwater management and flood control for a low-lying region that been built over swamplands and the Maracanã River floodplain. The street's history is closely tied to Getúlio Vargas, one of the chief figures in twentieth-century Brazilian politics, and his Estado Novo dictatorship (1937–1945). The president-dictator visited the thoroughfare on numerous occasions to oversee the progress of construction and to accompany patriotic and military parades staged there.

The avenue's size accentuated the towering grandeur of the war ministry (opened 1941) and the central railway station's art deco clock tower (opened 1943). High-rise commercial skyscrapers eventually rose at the avenue's intersection with Avenida Rio Branco, opened during the Pereira Passos reforms. Although the improvements to stormwater management offered respite from flooding, construction of Avenida Presidente Vargas exacted tremendous costs, as the demolition work that opened downtown to the automobile and private real estate development brought down historic churches and hundreds of humble residences and commercial establishments that housed working-class Cariocas. Their resistance had proven futile. The construction also truncated part of the historic Campo de Santana. Subsequent works on Avenida Presidente Vargas, and related disruptions, included access routes to the Santa Bárbara tunnel, opened in 1963; a new city hall in Cidade Nova; three of the five stations to inaugurate metro service in 1979; and the staging areas for Carnaval competitions held in the Sambódromo, inaugurated in 1984.

Hélio Alves de Brito, an engineer closely associated with public works in the Federal District, published a report on the massive project of civil engineering and displacement that was winding up in early 1944. The excerpt here privileges technical details, including the unrealized plan to link Avenida Presidente Vargas to the Zona

*Sul via a diagonal street between Lapa to the site of the old city hall. Brito ellipti-
cally references land seizures, the "disappearance" of old constructions, and the aes-
thetics of the new built environment. These provide clues to the authoritarian political undertones of a street now considered to be a necessary, if unloved, part of Rio.*

Avenida Presidente Vargas is an undertaking of great magnitude among the
accomplishments of Mayor Henrique Dodsworth's administration. Within
the Master Plan, it is the City's most important axis.

As the general aspects of the project's outlines are read against the precepts of urbanism, we see the avenue through the lenses of vehicular traffic,
sanitation, and building construction.

Given the general grid pattern of the streets of Rio de Janeiro, a weighty
legacy of the colonial and imperial eras, the development of the City—
driven by the reforms undertaken in the administrations of Pereira Passos,
Carlos Sampaio, and Prado Junior—contributed to the great increase in the
volume of motorized traffic. This left the need to open up a wide artery
through the city center whose principal function is to channel the intense
movement from the Zona Norte, and to connect that traffic to an overall
system of circulation that might solve problems of surface traffic.

Initiated as an extension of the old Avenida do Mangue, from Praça XI
de Junho to the dockworks located on the Visconde de Itaboraí, the Avenida
Presidente Vargas has absorbed the urbanized blocks between Ruas Visconde de Itaúna and General Câmara, in one direction, and Ruas Senador
Euzébio and São Pedro, in the other direction.

By way of the Avenida Diagonal—to be opened across the future Esplanada de Santo Antônio that begins in the Largo da Lapa, ending on the
site where the old Paço Municipal used to exist—the Avenida Presidente
Vargas will establish a linkage between the Zona Sul and Zona Norte that
bypasses the commercial center. We also consider the future confluence
where streets are extended toward the Avenida Almirante Barroso, diverting traffic away from the Esplanada do Castelo and environs.

Important improvements in vehicular flow are also to be realized as the
Avenida Presidente Vargas connects with Avenidas Rio Branco and Perim-
etral, the latter envisioned in the Master Plan to establish a link between
Santos Dumont Airport, Praça XV de Novembro, and Praça Mauá.

The region of the City that extends from Rua Santana to the area surrounding Praça Tiradentes and Rua Frei Caneca over to the foot of the
Morro da Providência makes up part of a storm drainage system characterized generally by modest sloping, in function of the region's low elevation relative to sea level. The brick-lined storm drains along the old Rua

Visconde de Inhaúma are inadequately sized and present the misfortune of dipping low near the Canal do Mangue, where they discharge by means of two iron pipes, eighty centimeters in diameter, dropping the waterline below the average tide level. Such conditions result in the frequent inundation of innumerable streets in the region, including a portion of Avenida Gomes Freire as well as Ruas Frei Caneca, Senado, Visconde de Rio Branco, Constituição, São Pedro, Bento Ribeiro, Barão de São Félix, among others.

Once the Avenida Presidente Vargas opens, it will be possible to construct a drainage system of reinforced concrete, projected to be able to handle the storm waters from all subsidiary drainage canals, thus making improvements to the flow-bearing capacities of the Canal do Mague, the principal drainage feature of the region, as well as local features. This should resolve in a satisfactory manner the region's flooding problem.

The Avenida Presidente Vargas also plays an important role in the transformations that will take place with the disappearance of old constructions in the urban center built on tiny lots with extremely inadequate frontages where one notes the poverty of the architectural elements of the façade and the near total absence of unbuilt space, exacerbating the structures' disagreeable aspects as well as the extremely precarious conditions of illumination and ventilation.

Adjoining corridors will be cleared and a new system of lot assignments will be brought to existing urban codes on setbacks, buildable areas, and mandatory construction elements. We thus achieve all the necessary conditions for new buildings to present a dignified appearance, contributing through the suitable architectural composition, to complete the realization of the great artery in all of its monumentality.

Translated by Daryle Williams

Introducing the "Civilized Indian"
João José Macedo

Cândido Mariano da Silva Rondon

Cândido Mariano da Silva Rondon (1865–1958) is best known for his work in the interior of northern and far western Brazil, where he supervised the installation of telegraph lines and the establishment of the nation's first indigenous reservations. A high-ranking army officer whose mother was of indigenous Terena and Bororo origin, Rondon is often considered the architect of Indian policy in modern Brazil.

The following document illustrates how Rondon's life work in Indian affairs resonated in urban Brazil. In 1949, Rondon writes to Rio mayor Ângelo Mendes de Moraes (1894–1990) to ask that João José Macedo, described as a "civilized Indian," be given a job as a driver for the mayor's office. This letter says little about Macedo; ethnic self-identification and place of birth go unstated. Nevertheless, the document reveals something of Rondon's mind-set about a native Brazilian who had adapted to mainstream urban life and the customs of a modern capital. Rondon's attempt to help Macedo land a public sector job is characteristic of patronage in public service positions. (We see that Rondon had been working for years to assist Macedo in moving up from his position at the Hospital Getúlio Vargas, a federal health care facility in Penha opened in 1938.) Rondon likely wrote this letter at the headquarters of the Indian Protection Service, located in an old mansion adjacent to the site where Maracanã stadium now stands. Between 1953 and 1977, that building housed the federal Museu do Índio (Museum of the Indian). Such connections to urban space suggest how post–World War II Rio—a rising megalopolis situated far from the regions where the majority of Brazil's indigenous people actually live—served as a privileged place for the protection and exhibition of indigenous life and culture.

Rondon's attention to Macedo's success as an automobile driver points toward a changing transportation infrastructure that refashioned cities and connected metropolitan centers. As private automobile ownership increased, urban life adapted to the needs of passenger cars and drivers. By 1949, autos had become ubiquitous features of Rio's landscape. The "civilized Indian" Macedo was a participant in transforming Rio into a car city.

From: Cândido Mariano da Silva Rondon, President of the National Council for the Protection of Indians (CNPI), Ministry of Agriculture

To: His Excellency General Ângelo Mendes de Moraes—His Most Dignified Mayor of this Federal District

Subject: Introduction of the Civilized Indian João José Macedo

I. The holder of this letter is the civilized Indian João José Macedo, Registry number 18496, driver classification type A.E., who already performed this service for the mayor's office eight years ago, having worked in various parts of the mayor's office and presently finding himself exercising the same occupation at the Hospital Getúlio Vargas.

II. For a long time, I have been interested in getting this Indian a promotion, because his more modern colleagues have already obtained the access that he seeks; I am thus making one more direct entreaty to my noble comrade, in order to better help this Indian who has already incorporated himself into our civilization and, because of his personal efforts, managed to obtain a driver's license.

III. I will take this opportunity to express my high esteem for Your Excellency, as an old comrade and a humble servant of humanity,

C. M. da S. Rondon, President of the
Conselho Nacional de Proteção aos Indios

Translated by Amy Chazkel

Madame Satã, a Grifter in Lapa

João Francisco dos Santos and Others

João Francisco dos Santos (1900–1976) was an Afro-Brazilian who won notoriety in the legendary underworld of bars, brothels, gambling dens, and run-down boarding-houses scattered throughout Lapa, a historic neighborhood adjacent to downtown Rio. In September 1949, Santos was among three suspects hauled into a police sta-tion on suspicion of robbing a public servant whom they had duped into a sex-for-pay scam. Earlier that same year, Sixth Precinct police had interrogated Santos about another robbery complaint. Born into poverty in the Brazilian northeast, er-ratically employed, illiterate, and living on street smarts, Santos was a frequent target of Rio's criminal justice system. Late in life, the grifter boasted of twenty-nine formal charges, for crimes ranging from immoral acts to street fighting to homicide. Ten cases, he claimed, had led to conviction.

As the charging records here indicate, Santos often went by "Madame Satã," a street name taken from the title of a racy MGM movie directed by Cecil B. DeMille. The Carioca alter ego of the fictional Madame Satan was a revered figure in the Lapa demimonde, well known for a long-standing association with the Caçadores de Veados ("Deer Hunters," a word play on "Faggot Hunters"), a street association known for the participation of cross-dressing homosexual men who organized elabo-rate Carnaval pageants.

In the early 1949 complaint, Santos readily admitted to a deceased wife and children, yet his numerous liaisons with men were a public fact. In an interview granted in 1971 to the editors of the irreverent Carioca satirical periodical O Pas-quim, Santos answered the question about his rumored homosexuality: "I always was, I am, and I will remain." He also discussed capoeira, which he often used for self-protection. In short, Santos was a transgressive figure known to be both hyper-masculine and unmasculine in his sexual appetites and public presentation. Cap-turing the voices of Santos and his antagonists, the following documents bring to light the urban experiences of the resourceful poor men of color who lived, played, brawled, and swindled in and around Lapa.

Complaint by Radajasis dos Santos Vianara against Aristoteles de Jesus and others, September 25, 1949

At 11:50 p.m. Mr. Radajasis dos Santos Vianara, Brazilian, unmarried, forty-five years old, public employee, resident of Rua Antonio Murtinho, number 438, came to this police station to file the following complaint: Having gone today at around 8:00 p.m. to Rua Conde de Lage, number 40, he was escorted by a passive pederast, who used the street name of "Eros Volusia," on the hope of procuring a woman. Upon entering a room in the house and removing his clothes he realized it was in fact the pederast who was offering himself for anal coitus which Vianara refused before dressing and leaving the house. Moments later on the street, placing his hand in his pocket, Vianara discovered that 1,400 cruzeiros in bills denominated two hundred had been stolen from him, after which he decided to come to this police station to register a complaint. Later, I ordered this station's surveillance team, headed by detective 442 and made up of investigators 1103 and 1258, with the assistance of investigator 968 from the Delegacia de Costumes e Diversões [a special unit of the municipal police, founded in the early 1930s, charged with combating vice and regulating public entertainment] to proceed with diligence to the scene in order to investigate. After a search, they found the money well hidden underneath a box in a backroom and retrieved it. It became clear that the above-mentioned "Eros," whose real name is Aristóteles de Jesus, Brazilian, unmarried, nineteen years of age, brown-skinned [*cor parda*], busboy, resident of Rua Benedito Hipólito, 131, after entering the room with the customer and having carnal relations with the same had left outside the individual João Francisco dos Santos or João Braz da Silva, also known as "Madame Satan," Brazilian, black, forty-three years old, unmarried, passive pederast, resident of Avenida Mem de Sá, 88. Left alone, he took advantage of the situation to enter the room and steal the money from the pants pocket, exited quietly and then handed off the cash for safekeeping to the individual Wantuir Gonçalves de Oliveira, also known as "Quiquita," Brazilian, brown-skinned [*pardo*], unmarried, twenty-six years old, passive pederast, residing at Rua Conde de Lage, 40, who hid the money in the aforementioned location to turn it over to the other pederast at a later time. He was spotted by the individual Waldemar de Queiroz Sardinha, Brazilian, unmarried, thirty-one years old, busboy, resident of Rua Conde Lage, 40, who went to the police to report the plot executed by the three pederasts to take the money of the injured party. The money was turned over for safekeeping.

Gilberto Paiva de Lacerda, Commissioner

Dispatch: An inquest is opened, delegated to the Chief of Thefts and Burglaries, to seek clarifications on this incident.

Eunapio Castelo Branco, Officer

Depositions by Walfrido Andrade and João Francisco dos Santos,
January 19, 1949

WALFRIDO ANDRADE DEPOSITION

On January 19, 1949, in the Federal District and in this station of the sixth police precinct the Doutor José Alberto Potier Junior, the police chief in charge, and I, his official recording clerk, along with Walfrido Andrade, forty-four years old, single, white from the state of Pernambuco, son of Cristóvão Paes de Andrade and Amélia Bandeira, a self-employed merchant, residing at Rua Riachuelo, 27, apartment 41, knowing how to read and write, and who, upon being questioned, responded the following way: the deponent, on the evening of December 4 last year, came across João Francisco dos Santos and another man known as Osvaldo at the Largo da Lapa. The deponent was unacquainted with the latter but he had known the former for many years. Both were born in Pernambuco. After speaking for a while, already at daybreak the next morning—last December 5—João Francisco dos Santos asked the deponent to take Osvaldo to the deponent's home at Rua Riachuelo, 27 apartment 41, so as to offer him something to eat. By this point the deponent was quite intoxicated and thus did not hesitate to take Osvaldo back to his home to give him some food. Once at his home and after giving said Osvaldo some food, the deponent fell asleep. Upon waking up at around seven o'clock, however, he noticed the following pieces of jewelry were missing: a gold Joch Lequit watch with a golden band worth five thousand cruzeiros; a white silk shirt worth two hundred and fifty cruzeiros; a regular brown leather wallet worth one hundred and fifty cruzeiros with one thousand and nine hundred cruzeiros inside; a gold tie pin with a large pearl; and a gold keychain with a diamond-studded *figa* amulet and an encrusted horn. The defendant recognized the aforementioned pair of cufflinks, the tie pin, and the chain with the figa and horn as his property when shown to him. Naturally, he was immediately suspicious of Osvaldo, who he later learned was known by the alias "Lerna Horne," and subsequently came to the police station to register a complaint. The deponent does not believe that Osvaldo carried out the robbery together with João Francisco dos Santos, who he later learned was known by the alias "Madame Satã." However, he knows that the latter received the stolen jewelry from the hands of the alleged perpetrator Osvaldo who is currently on the loose. The deponent's friend Manoel de Queiroz, owner of the Queiroz jewelry store on Rua Visconde do Rio Branco, 25, upon being made aware of the circumstances, recognized the tie pin and the pair of cufflinks shown to him by João Francisco dos Santos when dos Santos came into the aforementioned shop. Then the deponent said nothing else. He told the police officer to conclude his statement and, after reading the document and finding it agreeable, signed as a deponent.

I, [illegible], the recording clerk, have typed and signed this document.

José Alberto Potier Junior
Walfrido Andrade

JOÃO FRANCISCO DOS SANTOS DEPOSITION

On January 19, 1949 in the Federal District and in this station of the sixth police precinct the Doutor José Alberto Potier Junior, the police chief in charge, and I, his official recording clerk fulfilling the task declared herein, along with the accused João Francisco dos Santos—also known as "Madame Satã"—pardo, to whom the police chief made the following questions:

What is your name? João Francisco dos Santos, he replied.

Who are your parents? Manoel Francisco dos Santos and Firmina Felismina da Conceição, he replied.

What is your age? Forty-six, he replied.

What is your marital status? A widower with two children, he replied.

What is your occupation? A cook, working at Rua Pedro Rodrigues, 7, on the Praça da Bandeira, he replied.

What is your place of birth? Pernambuco, he replied.

What is your home address? Avenida Mem de Sá, 88, he replied.

Can you read and write? He can sign his name, he replied.

Since he said nothing else and was asked nothing else, the police chief ordered that the statement be concluded.

I, [illegible], the clerk, have typed and signed this document.

Next, with the accused present, the police chief proceeded to ask questions to which he responded that he was aware that his associate, Osvaldo, better known as "Lerna Horne," on an unknown December day last year had stolen jewels belonging to his other acquaintance, Walfrido Andrade, at the latter's residence, located at Rua Riachuelo, 27 apartment 41. The deponent was repeatedly sought after by the police in relation to the theft only because he personally knew the accused, Osvaldo of unknown surname. He then decided to look for the accused Osvaldo to tell him to return the stolen jewelry so that the deponent could be free of the police inquiries. At about one in the morning on the fourteenth of this month, on the train platform at Pedro II railway station, he met with the accused Osvaldo, taking him to the Campo de Santana where he interrogated the accused about the robbery in question, which the accused initially denied. However, when the deponent found the jewelry, the same shown here, on the person of the accused, the accused decided to tell the truth. The deponent then took the jewelry from Osvaldo, taking it home with him and the next day around six in the evening he went to the Queiroz jeweler on Rua Visconde do Rio Branco to appraise the tie pin with the pearl, which is a piece of the jewelry stolen by Osvaldo. The person who served the deponent at the aforementioned establishment asked if the tie pin was for sale, to which the deponent responded in the negative. At that moment a police investigator came into the store and escorted the deponent to the tenth police precinct, carrying with him the tie pin and a pair of cufflinks the deponent had on, both of which were shown here and which belong to the injured party, Walfrido Andrade, as was assumed. The deponent was then escorted to this police station and clarified the facts to investigator Coutinho, to whom he also made known that the rest of the stolen jewelry remained in his possession, including a gold chain, a diamond-studded figa of gold and coral, and an encrusted horn amulet, all of which are the same as were shown here collected by the aforementioned police officer. The deponent reaffirmed that he absolutely did not steal the injured party's jewelry but instead snatched them from the accused Osvaldo. Although he was being accused of theft, the deponent maintained that he was incapable of committing such an offense. Then the deponent said nothing else. He told the police officer to conclude his statement and, after reading the document and finding it agreeable, Jovenílio de Sousa Coutinho and Reinaldo Rosadas, both investigators in this police precinct who viewed the deposition, signed along with the deponent.

I, [illegible], recording clerk, have typed and signed this document.

José Alberto Potier Junior
João Francisco dos Santos

Translated by Andre Pagliarini

A City's Crushing Defeat at the World Cup

Jornal do Brasil *and* Correio da Manhã

Brazil hosted the fourth World Cup over June and July 1950. Nicknamed the Jules Ri-
met Cup, the event marked the triumphant return of a popular international sport-
ing competition that had been suspended since 1938. The tournament also marked
Rio's elevation on the post–World War II world stage. Host to several preliminary
matches and the final championship, the city had not held an event of this magni-
tude since the Universal Centennial Exposition of 1922.

The tournament's most important match was the final game between Brazil and
Uruguay, held July 16, 1950, at Maracanã Municipal Stadium (later renamed Está-
dio Jornalista Mário Filho), a massive facility that took its name from a neighbor-
hood surrounding an eponymous river in the Zona Norte. Two years earlier, Rio's
mayor, Ângelo Mendes de Morais (1894–1990), had participated in the placement
of the stadium's cornerstone on the site formerly occupied by the Derby Club horse
racing track. Opponents had criticized the massive scale of the construction project.
Standing incomplete at the opening of the tournament, Maracanã was still consid-
ered the largest sports venue in the world. It remains the preeminent site for soccer
matches, including the 2014 FIFA World Cup, as well as the stage for large interna-
tional music festivals.

The Brazilian team distinguished itself in the 1950 tournament, easily reaching
the final match after a round-robin final group stage. At worst, the home team only
needed a tie against opposing finalist Uruguay to win it all. Residents of Rio and
tourists mobilized in search of tickets to watch the grand finale. The cafés of the
Galeria Cruzeiro, a bustling commercial and transportation arcade on Avenida
Rio Branco, hummed with excitement. Newspaper coverage, like the excerpts here,
revealed the city's vibrancy on the day of the final match, attended by more than
199,000 spectators. Brazil held a one-goal lead through the sixty-sixth minute, but
Uruguay surged late in the second half. When referee George Reader blew the final
whistle, the Uruguayans had won 2–1. Sadness overtook the stadium. A bitter si-
lence and disappointment replaced expectations for a large Carnaval-like celebra-
tion. In the following days, the Brazilian players were the subject of moral condem-
nation, and the press exploited public criticisms of Mayor Mendes de Morais. The

Brazilian team would go on to win its first World Cup title eight years later, begin-ning a track record that would distinguish the country in the world of sports and give Rio residents a leading voice for a soccer-mad nation. Nonetheless, the upset of July 16, 1950, was an enduring, painful event for Cariocas, who still know the fateful day by its Spanish nickname, "Maracanazo" (The Blow at Maracanã).

The ghosts of the Maracanazo returned in July 2014 as the Brazilian national team was defeated twice in World Cup play. For Cariocas, perhaps there was some relief that the successive blows of 2014, including a historic semifinal drubbing by Germany, took place in Belo Horizonte and Brasília.

The City of Rio de Janeiro on the Eve of the Final Matches of the Jules Rimet Cup: Unsurpassable Interest Aroused in the Biggest Futebol Event in Recent Times

It has been a long time since the city last experienced moments of such anxiety and enthusiasm. The Jules Rimet Cup, under way this year in Bra-zil, inaugurates the great Maracanã Stadium—a monumental work of engi-neering that is the largest sporting arena in the world.

Yesterday—the eve of the contested final matches of the tournament, with the Spanish and Swedish teams playing in São Paulo, and Brazil and Uruguay in Rio de Janeiro, our Capital felt quite different from most any other day. There was an intense movement of tourists anxious to arrive on time for the great sporting spectacle where the adversaries of the day—the teams of two brother countries linked by indissoluble friendship across the years—will face each other on the open field.

Securing a spot to watch the most breathtaking combat of a world cham-pionship—because it is the final—has been disputed in every way and at any price. When there is an enormous group of people or even long lines at ticket sales locations, it is not uncommon to find someone offering up to one thousand cruzeiros for a seat that the Brazilian Sports Confederation provides to the people for forty cruzeiros.

There are even those who spend the night next to the official ticket win-dows so that as soon as the booths open, they are the first to acquire the tickets, making it possible, or better yet guaranteeing, that they will be able to enter the stadium. These examples, small as they may be, allow us to ap-preciate the common people's interest in and anxiety about this afternoon's game.

The city finds itself full of people from every part of Brazil. Automobiles with license plates from every state drive through the streets or park in spots never previously visited by other vehicles. The foreign tourists who find themselves in Rio de Janeiro are so numerous that the city's many hotels cannot adequately handle them all, instead lodging them in the most humble fashion—at times with five people in just one room! Just yesterday, the *Conte Grande*, a steamer from Montevideo, transported into port around two hundred passengers whose sole objective was to watch the final match of the Jules Rimet Cup. Without stop, airplanes originating in every part of the Americas and all the states of Brazil bring more and more aficionados of the world's biggest sport.

The Galeria Cruzeiro is in a constant buzz of people from north and south passing the entire night attending speeches, expressing their opinions, and making prognostications about the outcome of this afternoon's game at Maracanã.

Brazil is living one of the most vibrant moments in sports. This afternoon, fate will choose the team to be crowned champion of the world in 1950.

. . . *We Lost the Title That Was Already in Our Hands*

One final hope remained. Taking a corner, Friaça shot the ball across the goal tended by Maspoli. Just as the sphere, still hanging in the air, came dangerously close to a group of players inside the 6-yard box, Mr. Reader blew the whistle. And a sad silence abruptly took hold of the stadium. No one moved. Only tears fell.

And so ended the great spectacle that for days had united Brazil's attention and longing at Maracanã. The practically impossible had occurred: Brazil lost the Championship. After spectacular displays. After roundly slaying great adversaries. After convincing everyone that they were the greatest in the world. And precisely because they lacked grit. Exclusively because of it. The Carnaval that was planned would not take place. There was no glow of victory. Maracanã painfully emptied out. Sadness blocked our path and inhibited movement; it silenced every mouth. And when everyone left, it seemed that the "giant" also felt the failure. It does not help that its colossal size can shelter so many scores of players in its belly. The end would still have to be sad. . . .

The usual race to exit the stadium did not occur. The exhausted fans, covered in dust and sadness, departed in full-scale retreat. They hid away the ticker tape [*serpentinas*]. They discarded the confetti and consigned themselves to fatigue. It seemed like daybreak on Ash Wednesday. We tried to listen, to gauge the opinion of the fans. No one spoke. Only once on the streetcar, after the first moments passed, did the arguments start. They tried to justify it, but no one could. Release at last arrived: it was bad luck. What bad luck? Many kinds. "Didn't you see that for the first time we attacked toward Avenida Maracanã?" one argued. And soon another: "and also for the first time Ademir didn't score?" All that was bad luck. Only this was not. You saw the principal cause, argued a third. Mendes de Morais had the worst luck. He's the one who got blamed for it all. . . .

Translated by Shawn Moura

Carmen Miranda Shines in "Ca Room Pa Pa"

MGM *Studios*

Nancy Goes to Rio *(1950) was a moderately successful MGM musical built around a series of misunderstandings between aspiring teenage actress Nancy (Jane Powell), her mother (Ann Sothern), and their shared love interest (Barry Sullivan). Under the direction of the North American Robert Z. Leonard (1889–1968), the movie typified a Hollywood version of mid-twentieth-century Rio as a South American city of spacious mansions, moonlit landscapes, swank nightclubs, and lavish Carnaval parades. Romance and sex were everywhere.*

The film's second billing went to Portuguese-born and Rio-raised Carmen Miranda (1909–1955), a stage-and-screen entertainer who had launched her career in Rio before achieving wild success in the United States after 1939. In the role of cabaret singer and coffee agent Marina Sousa Lopes Castro Rodrigues, Miranda plays comedic foil to the principals' amorous misadventures. A standout of Miranda's performance was "Ca Room Pa Pa," a visually stunning song-and-dance number with extravagant choreography by North American Nick Castle and eye-popping costume design by Helen Rose. Miranda shows her trademark verve as she bounds forth from a giant tambourine.

The sequence takes place during Carnaval (shown in live footage) on a soundstage that evoked the sights and feel of actual nightclubs in Urca and Copacabana. A Hollywood version of the Maciço da Tijuca appears through the windows. The song lyrics that accompany the nonsensical title, written by American Ray Gilbert, pair the heat of the tropics with the hot musical beat. Midsong, Miranda is joined by an acrobatic dancer festooned in colorful umbrellas that echo the tiny parasols on her head. This interlude was a stylization of an earlier musical hit, "Baião," by Brazilian composer Humberto Teixeira (1915–1979; born in Ceará, arriving in Rio in 1930) and singer Luiz Gonzaga (1912–1989; born in Pernambuco, arriving in Rio in 1939), as well as the frevo, *a dance from Pernambuco characterized by the dancer's use of an umbrella. In luscious Technicolor, Miranda, her trusted Banda da Lua accompaniment, and numerous extras work up to a breathless finale, captured in the*

Nancy Goes to Rio. Film still. Directed by Robert Z. Leonard. Los Angeles: MGM Studios, 1950.

film still reproduced here. The scene is eminently Carioca in its ability to synthesize in a playful manner various strains of Brazilian regional culture. It is also transnational, forging linkages between the entertainment industries of Rio de Janeiro, New York, and Hollywood.

"Soldiers of Fire"

Getúlio Vargas

A new style of political leadership, known as populism, emerged throughout Latin America after World War I. The phenomenon was less about a fixed set of doctrines and more about new relationships between national leaders, the state, and citizens. Populism grew around an expanded political arena and the appeals of rule via the consent of the people. Most populist leaders spoke of bringing new benefits and rights to nonelites, especially the urban industrial classes, as well as public servants. In many cases, the populist leader's charisma helped forge a sense of emotional solidarity with these social sectors. This document, a speech by one of the most prominent of his generation of populist leaders, powerfully demonstrates this special connection between a populist and his constituents.

On July 2, 1952, President Getúlio Vargas (1883–1954) visited the central headquarters of the Rio de Janeiro firefighting corps to deliver a speech infused with classic elements of populist discourse. Recently returned to the presidential palace in open elections, this onetime dictator presented himself as the defender of Brazilian democracy and the welfare state. He advocated the expansion of rights for the working classes in a wider program of nationalist industrial development. The emotional speech delivered at the fire corps headquarters, located just off the Praça da República, addressed the firefighter as the peace-waging soldier who faced death in saving property and lives. Offering special praise for João Batista de Castro Morais Antas (d. 1857), first commander of the Provisional Corps, and Aristárcho Pessoa (1879–1949), commander during Vargas's first regime, the president spoke of the salary and benefits due to these self-sacrificing public servants. He took pains to establish himself as a staunch advocate for these urban workers.

It is not incidental that a speech laden with the rhetoric of state protections was delivered in Rio. Brazilian populism began as an urban movement, and Vargas made direct appeals to Carioca workers and voters during his tumultuous second administration. In all likelihood, some of the same firefighters addressed in 1951 were tasked with putting out fires and restoring public order during the highly emotional disturbances that followed the radio announcement that the president had taken his own life in August 1954.

Commander, Officers, Sub-Officers and Soldiers of the Firefighter Corps.

We recall today the anniversary of the creation of the Corpo Provisório de Bombeiros da Corte [Provisional Firefighter Corps of the Court]—an event that signaled a new phase in the quest to guarantee the life and property of the population of the city of Rio de Janeiro. The steady growth of a metropolis so rich in natural beauty and the economic prosperity generated at the center of a vast empire necessitated a new way to put down the fires that so often ended up destroying old structures, especially in times when the water lines that drew from the bay arrived late or when the personnel from public works took too long to provide assistance.

Acting under the command of Major João Batista de Castro Morais Antas, the newly established corps and its 130 soldiers burst onto the pages of Carioca history, to write their chapter of selflessness and heroism. In the name of collective security, many have since fallen victim to a holocaust, to give up their lives in that noble gesture of saving another. To these men, we pay tender homage, for the examples of heroism and altruism that they have bequeathed us.

Exceptional is the fate of the soldier whose duty is not to kill, but rather to be charged with a sacrifice so high that only the strong are able to make—to give up one's own life.

This is not the sole reason that firefighters have peace as their exclusive domain. The scope of modern conflicts that might drag an entire nation toward destruction and death in a total war of disastrous consequences in the countryside and the city places a special obligation on firefighters, who must confront the hard challenges of these difficult times. It is they who must lead in civil defense, and their acts are of the same great importance as acts taken on the battlefront.

As we consider measures to increase take-home pay and upgrade infrastructural support, the Government must recognize that Rio's fire brigade has not kept up with the evolution in benefits extended to similar occupational categories in other large cities. Despite the devotion of all those who have had the good fortune to command the Corps—among whom the unforgettable figure of Aristárcho Pessoa stands apart—this institution has always reflected the poverty of our budgets. Although we are still afflicted by a financial crisis that imposes tight restrictions on public spending, the current administration already can identify some of the ways in which it has served the Firefighters Corps: the complete execution of the Earnings and Benefits Code and the broad legislation that benefits inactive servicemen as well as those about to be decommissioned; the promotion of officers who have served more than ten years at lower ranks; the law determining the time in rank; reform of the regulations related to the award of vacation time; provision of funds to conduct repairs on the barracks; the budgetary request to the national congress that would permit us to accelerate a renewal of firefighting equipment, in addition to other steps of lesser urgency. Such measures show my Government's constant concern not to overlook those who are devoted to the public good.

The plan to improve the situation of the soldiers of fire is being completed and will be sent to Congress this very month. Three exceedingly far-reaching measures will be proposed to the Legislature to benefit this corporation: the adjustment of the earnings of corporals and soldiers, increasing take-home salaries for 1,500 men, and the creation of the rank of sergeant-driver.

This is the substance of my support and my esteem for your dedicated and constant work; I hope that you can take with you the moral energy to proceed with your daily fight and the inspiration that always, and increasingly, the Nation will recognize you as not just soldiers of fire, but also soldiers of the people.

Translated by Amy Chazkel

Censoring Rio, 40 Graus

Ralph Benedicto Zumbano

The opening sequence of Rio, 40 Graus (Rio, 40 Degrees) announced the City of São Sebastião do Rio de Janeiro as the movie's starring character. The seductive sounds of the hit samba "Voz do Morro" (Voice of the Morro) play in the background. A soaring aerial shot pans northwestward from the Zona Sul, past downtown, toward the urban periphery of the Zona Norte, coming to earth in a favela where residents trudge up and down a steep hill. The film's plot unfolds through the eyes of five young boys from the morro, played by nonprofessional actors, whose Sunday afternoon work selling peanuts takes them to the beaches of Copacabana, the Sugarloaf cable car, and Maracanã stadium. In brash colors, this movie poster captured an atmosphere of racial, social, and spatial contrasts that serves as the dramatic foundation for a cinematic classic. In its juxtaposition of iconic Sugarloaf, in the lower right, and the improvised homes of the favela, center, as well as the casual smiles of the white beachgoers against the pained faces of urban youth of color, the poster questions just what is so marvelous about the city of Rio.

Director Nelson Pereira dos Santos (b. 1928) shot Rio, 40 Graus on a shoestring budget, at the moment of political confusion that followed the suicide of Getúlio Vargas. A climate of Cold War anticommunism and middle-class moral panic about delinquent youth informed early reviews. Although the film initially passed the national censorship board, Rio's police chief, Geraldo de Menezes Cortes (1911–1962), halted its release in the federal capital. Santos's ties to the banned Communist Party had already placed him under suspicion, and Cortes censored the film, he claimed, because of its potential to foment disunity. It represented an ugly, distorted view of the Carioca people, he argued. He even alleged that the film's title was a fraud: in an unintentionally comic and patently inaccurate statement, Cortes declared that temperatures in Rio never reached 40°C (104°F).

Ralph Benedicto Zumbano (1925–2001), a lightweight boxing champion who served in the São Paulo state legislature representing the Partido Trabalhista Nacional between 1955 and 1959, joined the fight to release Rio, 40 Graus from censorship. With the backing of figures like Zumbano and a collection of national artists, Rio, 40 Graus was commercially released in January 1956. Zumbano's nationalism—

Rio, 40 Graus. Poster.
Film directed by Nelson
Pereira dos Santos. Rio
de Janeiro: Equipe Mo-
acyr Fenelon, 1955.

*tempered with class consciousness and a suspicion of authoritarianism—comes
through in the speech he delivered to the São Paulo state assembly that pressed for
the movie's commercial release. The movie and its soundtrack, featuring sambas by
Zé Keti (1921–1999) and the storied Portela samba school, met with critical success
in Rio and abroad.*

Mr. President, my fellow representatives, as Mr. President knows, last Wednesday various artists and directors of Brazilian cinema came to this Chamber to ask for your solidarity in the fight in which they are involved for
the free exhibition of the film *Rio, 40 Graus.* Among the persons present,
it can be noted that there were well-known Brazilian film directors: Abí-
lio Pereira de Almeida, Alberto Pieralisse [Pieralisi], Rodolfo Nanni, Tito
Batini, and Cavalheiro Lima; the acclaimed actors Carlos Cotrim, Liana
Duval, Paulo Bueno, and Lola Brah; the best cinematographers, Rui San-

tos and the Frenchman James Dezhelain. The prohibition imposed by the Chief of Police of the Federal District was very well explained. Mr. Menezes Cortes prohibited the film solely and exclusively because, first, in Rio *the heat does not ever reach 40 degrees*, the average temperature being 37.5 degrees [Celsius]. The title, therefore, does not express the truth. Second, the film speaks directly to the reality of the social life among Cariocas, and he could not allow the world to know the sad truth. Third, the film has a political content that could awaken a great deal of sentimentalism in the hearts of the people. Thus, distinguished assemblymen, if all films that demonstrate the social reality of each people must be prohibited, the cinemas of all the world would have to close their doors. Take Italian films, for example. They are so good because they are faithful to reality. North American films show the delinquency that once reigned or that still reigns in that society. They teach how social problems should be solved: by the bullet. Such films are exhibited without restriction to our people.

Brazilian cinema has been so forsaken by the government that, even if one is still able to make a film with exclusively Brazilian artists, this only can happen thanks to the great connoisseurs of national cinema. To make a film, we know that at least three million cruzeiros are necessary, and these self-sacrificing defenders of Brazilian national cinema spend up to the last drop of their blood so that Brazilian cinema does not die. With the greatest difficulties, they were able to make *Rio, 40 Graus*, and when it was all ready to be released, the censors accepted it and passed it on, and Columbia Pictures signed a contract to handle the film's worldwide release. The Chief of Police of the Federal District ran roughshod over all laws and prohibited the film's showing. The Commission of Artists [Commissão de Artistas] was invited to come here, with me as an intermediary, to all of the illustrious assemblymen to watch the screening of the film that was to be carried out in a private session for the state authorities, at the Museu da Arte Moderna on the Rua Sete de Abril, 230, on Friday at 10:30 p.m. There they could see what the film was, in fact, all about, and give their respective opinions. It was important to the artists that all of the representatives be there and, since that moment, they are immensely grateful for all that the assemblymen do for Brazilian national cinema.

It was just this that I wanted to say, Mr. President.

Translated by Amy Chazkel

The Diplomacy of Samba

Jornal do Brasil

Rio's Carnaval festivities took on official, national functions in the twentieth century. From the early 1930s, rules required that each samba school entry in the annual competitions celebrate some aspect of Brazilian national history. As a pageant of the nation-state, the samba school desfiles (parades) also served semiofficial, international diplomatic functions.

During the countdown to Carnaval 1960—the last to take place with Rio as the nation's capital—a curious diplomatic row with Paraguay threatened to derail the festivities. Império Serrano, a samba school headquartered in Madureira, had chosen for its desfile "The Retreat from Laguna," a theme that referenced a famous 1868 episode of the Paraguayan War. When the Paraguayan embassy protested unflattering references to their country, the Brazilian foreign ministry pressured Império Serrano to adopt a new theme, "Confraternization Brazil-Paraguay," to assuage Paraguayan sensitivities. Initially infuriated by government interference in the themed performance for which they had rehearsed for months, the five top-ranked samba schools, known as the Grandes Escolas, and other samba organizations still ended up marching down the city center's main avenues as usual. Império Serrano was well received despite the nail-biting two weeks they had just endured, and the Paraguayan embassy expressed gratitude.

Meanwhile, another delicate diplomatic situation developed on a more local scale. Rio's Association of Samba Schools held contests among samba schools each year at Carnaval; judges voted on the most talented and creative performance for a cash prize. When some of the schools disputed the results of the 1960 competition, unruly street protests erupted. The police reacted with violence. Portela, a school headquartered in Oswaldo Cruz, had been declared the winner, but third-placed Salgueiro, from Andaraí, called the outcome unfair and threatened a lawsuit. Império Serrano, for their part, insisted that the dispute with the Paraguayan government had marred their chances for victory.

Amid these street protests, Portela's president, Natalino José do Nascimento (1905–1975), better known as Natal da Portela, suffered a police beating that left him unconscious. He still managed to finish out the 1960 Carnaval season with the honor of being the "Peacemaker of Samba." This newspaper article recounts his diplomatic prowess among fellow sambistas *and municipal officials in the tourism department. The week after Carnaval, the celebrants paraded in full regalia from Madureira to Jacarepaguá. The "winning" samba schools brought their* passistas, *or suited male percussionists, and* cabrochas, *the elegant, scantily clad female dancers. The large marching percussion sections (* baterias) *trailed behind. With this rousing display of camaraderie among competing groups, the samba schools echoed the words of fraternity spoken by the nation's top diplomats.*

"Samba Schools Annul the Official Result of Carnaval Parade"

Representatives of the samba schools who met yesterday at the Department of Tourism unanimously decided to nullify the results of the Carnaval parade competition that took place on the Sunday of Carnaval Week, and to divide up the prize of 280,000 cruzeiros amicably between the five who performed the best. To demonstrate, in addition, that there was no animosity between the samba schools a parade was scheduled for tomorrow in Madureira in front of the bandshell.

The solution was proposed by Natal, the president of Portela, with the aim of putting an end to the impasse created by the dispute around whether or not the negative points in the scoring of the Carnaval parade, which had robbed Portela of the chance to win first place, would be counted. The decision was met with applause and, once it was approved, the president of Acadêmicos do Salgueiro, Mr. Nelson Andrade, tore up the injunction that he had intended to present to the Court, initiating a fight to the death among his companions and the members of Portela.

GENERAL SUPPORT

The conciliatory proposal presented by Natal—who appeared bandaged and wearing simple beach sandals, because the previous day he had been beaten by guards of the Polícia de Vigilância, in defending his interests and those of his samba school—immediately gained the support of representatives of Império Serrano, Mr. Aldemário Ezequiel dos Santos, and Mangueira, Mr. Pereira.

The president of the Association of Brazilian Samba Schools, Mr. Servan Heitor de Carvalho, came out in favor of the proposal and signed the document annulling the competition in the name of the Unidos da Capela Samba School, ranked fourth, which had entered into the group of the so-called Grandes Escolas de Samba [Great Samba Schools].

A SOLUTION AROSE

It was a during a discussion between the sambistas Calça Larga [Joaquim Casemiro], of Salgueiro, and Natal, of Portela, that this final solution for what to do about competition among the Samba Schools came up. After unsuccessfully attempting to gather the members of the Carnaval Commission to get them to release a statement about the question of the judging of the competition between the Samba Schools, Mr. Mário Saladini began trying to manage the negotiations between the schools' directors, inviting them to his office since early yesterday afternoon. He was nonetheless unable to solve the problem.

Watching the samba school leaders come and go from Mr. Mário Saladini's office, Mr. Calça Larga protested: "At least come and argue here, in front of everyone. Doing it like that, behind closed doors, won't accomplish anything."

Hearing what Calça Larga had to say, Portela president Natal also said in a loud voice: "And you should resolve this problem in a way that does not damage anyone, because as things are going right now, this will not end without some dead bodies. I think that what we should do is to annul everything, with neither victor nor vanquished."

FORMALITIES AND SURPRISE

This suggestion made by the president of Portela, that only Calça Larga and a few others knew about, was received with great excitement by reporters and the staff of the Tourism Department there in Mr. Mário Saladini's office.

Speaking in a serene voice, with his neck bandaged and wearing beach sandals—due to the beating that he had suffered on the day before—the president of Portela proposed that the result of the Carnaval parade competition be annulled, as a means of making peace: "Don't you recognize that we are destroying the fraternity that we have between us?" he repeated several times.

One by one, the representatives of the samba schools showed their support, hearing the Mr. Mário Saladini opine that the sambistas were extraordinary: "You are good and wise people, as very few people manage to be," the Director of Tourism said to them, asking a staff member to serve a cup of iced tea to commemorate the conciliatory act.

Demonstration

Soon after the president of Portela invited the other schools for a demonstration of unity and understanding: "Look," announced Natal, summoning the sambistas who had scattered around to the corners of the room—they had not yet taken down the bandshell in Madureira, erected in special homage to Portela. So, on Sunday, there will be Carnaval up there, and I want to be able to count on all five of the top samba Schools: Acadêmicos, Império, Mangueira, and Capela. Let's march together. After, we'll move on to Madureira and we'll end up in Jacarepaguá, at the Largo do Tanque.

All of the Schools committed to be there, and Natal added: "I've already been promised twenty-five buses, but if transportation proves insufficient I'll provide it myself." Aside from the general joyfulness, only Expedito, Portela's public relations agent, did not agree with the annulment. "I'm going to quit samba," he announced with melancholy, as he exited the Department of Tourism, his head hung low.

Translated by Amy Chazkel

IV

Recent Rio

The city of São Paulo already overshadowed the Marvelous City in economic might when the federal capital was transferred from the shores of Guanabara Bay to the highlands of central Brazil. The new capital, Brasília, was poised to drain away investment, know-how, and international cachet. Yet contrary to the fears of some, post-1960 Rio was not reduced to a sad story of the has-been. With its world-famous sidewalk mosaics and sandy beaches, Copacabana extended its reign as the "Little Princess of the Sea." The breezy bossa nova wave that originated in the Zona Sul grew into an international smash. Compelling telenovela melodramas set in Rio, originally produced in centrally located studios before Rede Globo opened a large production complex in Jacarepaguá in the 1980s, extended the domination of the Carioca culture industries in national media markets. The popularity of the Franco-Brazilian motion-picture tragedy *Black Orpheus* (1959) and the rawness of Glauber Rocha's Cinema Novo classic *Entranced Earth* (1967) expanded a rich cinematic vocabulary about the former national capital. Carnaval remained a mainstay of annual festivity, and the three days leading up to Ash Wednesday grew into a year-round industry. The Parque do Flamengo's juxtapositions of mechanical speed and natural beauty and the happenings held at the Museum of Modern Art assured Cariocas of the 1960s and 1970s that they would not be forced to relinquish bragging rights to cosmopolitan modernity. Throughout the city, Cariocas took up new forms of fitness and athletic competition—footvolley, surfing, and mixed martial arts. No longer the capital of Brazil, Rio renewed its status as a globalizing showcase city of beauty, creativity, and Brazilianness.

Post-1960 Rio also provided a stage for national politics, continuing to serve as home to numerous federal agencies, high-ranking officials, and diplomatic missions. As Carioca newspaper and radio mogul Roberto Marinho (1904–2003) methodically assembled the licenses and equipment to enter the television market, the Rio press modernized its role in shaping national public opinion. Between 1962 and 1964, partisan politicking roiled the State

"A Marcha da Família com Deus pela Liberdade encerrou-se diante do altar da pátria." Photographer unknown. From *Manchete*, Edição Histórica, April 1964, 6–7.

of Guanabara, the political jurisdiction that replaced Federal District status when the Brazilian capital moved to Brasília in 1960. Guanabara's firebrand governor, Carlos Lacerda, led attacks on João Goulart, a former labor minister who had taken the presidency in 1961. The political ferment in Guanabara had reached a critical point by 1964. On March 13, during the "Comício da Central," a huge rally at the main railway station, the embattled president called for "base reforms." Middle-class Carioca women (backed by the Catholic Church and anticommunist industrialists) labeled Goulart a communist. They decried inflation and an erosion of traditional family values. The specter of changes to urban property rights sealed these women's stance in joining Lacerda's call for Goulart's removal. A military coup d'état came on April 1, 1964. The following day, nearly one million people gathered on the Esplanada do Castelo for another mass rally, originally planned to be called the March of the Family with God for Liberty, to be joyously renamed the March of Victory. The political projects espoused at this assembly were numerous, but very few envisioned a dictatorship that would last for the next twenty-one years.

The ephemeral State of Guanabara (1960–1975) brimmed with competing projects. Unfettered from direct federal oversight, the political class of the autonomous "state-city" pressed ahead with local priorities, including aggressive measures to address substandard housing, traffic congestion, and inadequate water supplies. Meanwhile, Carioca university students expressed discontent with the strictures of local university administration. They took to the streets, in concert with global youth protest, to denounce militarism and imperialism. Most student protesters in Rio agitated for democracy and social reform, but some factions took up a call for armed insurgency. Surveillance and policing underwent parallel ideological radicalization, aided by training and hardware from foreign advisors. Under Institutional Act 5 of December 13, 1968 (a measure issued from the Palacio das Laranjeiras, in Rio), all legislative bodies including the Guanabara state assembly were shuttered and civil liberties suspended. The former federal capital became a battleground in an asymmetrical war that the national security apparatus waged against so-called domestic enemies. Supporters of military rule stirred up a moral panic over godlessness, birth control pills, and the counterculture.

This time of extremes reshaped the contours of rule in Rio. Policing of gambling, moral turpitude, and vagrancy fused with national surveillance. An urban geography of moralization and countersubversion spread among preexisting and repurposed prisons and barracks that became processing centers, detention cells, and torture chambers for suspected subversives. While some were sent to penal colonies outside Rio, and several hundred were "disappeared," many detainees were held in the city. For example, the annexes of the former presidential palace in Catete were rumored to be sites of harsh interrogations. Outside the "dungeons of the dictatorship," Rio's street corners were militarized by the presence of police patrols, wanted posters, and the patriotic sloganeering of state propaganda. Even when the harshest measures abated, acts of state terror lingered on. Infamously, covert army intelligence agents botched a car bombing at Rio Centro in 1981, two years after the president had announced a program of *abertura* (opening).

Opposition to the "regime of exception" also shaped urban space and its uses. In the lead-up to the clampdown of December 1968, large street protests—often punctuated by violent clashes with the military police—wended through downtown, in front of the Teatro Municipal and below the columns of the ministry of education on Rua da Imprensa. Bloody clashes with police turned downtown streets into a terrain of martyrdom for the left. (Correspondingly, such conflicts made heroes of the young male soldiers tasked with imposing order.) In the face of the repression, armed guerrilla cells went underground, moving among safe houses to plan pamphleteering, armed robberies, kidnappings, and other "actions" intended to disrupt the dictatorship. The counterculture nurtured gentler forms of resistance and nonconformity: listening to rock music, dancing at the discotheque, or smoking a joint at the beach. Censorship was never complete, opening up the possibility for the city's many art galleries, bookstores, and theatrical stages to serve as platforms for questioning undemocratic practices. Even when violent radicalism diminished, in response to the effectiveness of direct repression as well as rapidly expanding opportunities for the educated urban middle classes, the National Students Union headquarters on the Praia do Flamengo, torched in 1964, remained a potent locale to invoke resistance to militarism. In 1984, after the constraints of authoritarianism had loosened in 1979 and the "Generation of 1968" had aged, chastened radicals joined younger generations, a reinvigorated labor movement, and entertainment celebrities to march in the streets of central Rio in mass rallies in favor of direct presidential elections, and in 1992 for the impeachment of President Fernando Collor. On a smaller scale, throughout the city, the late 1970s through the early 1990s were a time when the clamor for democratic practices and values could be heard at the local bar, in the workplace, and at the church pulpit.

A peculiar companion to the repression of the 1970s was the exceptional rate of economic growth known as the Brazilian Economic Miracle. Massive infusions of foreign credit financed so-called Works of the Pharaohs, including projects that altered the economic landscape of Greater Rio: the Rio–Niterói bridge (built 1968–1974), the nuclear power plant in Angra dos Reis (construction begun in 1972), a new terminal at Galeão International Airport (1977), and the metro system (opened 1979). The Miracle years also ushered in the massification of consumerism, especially among upwardly mobile families who gained access to personal credit and higher education. The cumulative effects of development between 1968 and the global contraction of 1981 brought fundamental changes in everyday life, especially as women's participation in the workforce grew alongside their expanded legal rights to self-determination in employment, wages earnings, marriage separation, and birth control. Other facets of the rapid development of Brazil's second-largest urban economy included the democratization of color televisions, the aspirational dream of taking a holiday package tour to Walt Disney World, and the spread of fast-food dining.

The social gains of this development, which elevated Brazil into the world's top ten economies, were highly uneven. Literacy and health indicators improved, as did spatial and economic disparities. This was particularly evident in Rio, where favelas remained a strong index of inequality. A handful of hillside settlements dated back to the 1890s, but the number of favelas on hillsides and wetlands grew dramatically after 1960 (part of a larger trend of rapid population growth). Guanabara governor Carlos Lacerda had intensified a two-pronged approach, initiated by predecessors, of slum eradication and public housing construction. Results varied by project and locale, but the authorities often confronted resistance to removals. At the same time, some publicly financed housing developments became de facto favelas when unlicensed additions and subleasing overwhelmed inadequate infrastructure. Elsewhere, real estate speculation created new enclaves of the well-to-do, while the poor were pushed onto wastelands or toward the periphery.

A concurrent rise in urban violence led elites to seek personal distance from the poor. First, mid-rise condominiums replaced shuttered diplomatic properties, empty lots, and single-family homes; then walls were erected, common areas fenced in behind iron gates, and private security hired to insulate residents from the perception of dangerous "elements." Fear of crime and the deterioration of middle-class quality of life in Copacabana and the Zona Norte's inner suburbs pushed development toward the Baixada de Jacarepaguá, a region where high-rise condominiums and shopping centers came to dominate a landscape with few signaled crosswalks or public squares. Given the limited transportation options between oceanfront Barra da Tijuca and the city center, private automobiles reinforced the socioeconomic segregation of urban expansion in the Zona Oeste.

Class hostility was symptomatic of the urban malaise that accompanied the economic contraction, underemployment, and hyperinflation that afflicted many Latin American cities in the 1980s. The maladies of urban life grew acute in 1988, when the Rio municipal government declared bankruptcy, amid widespread labor unrest. That same year hundreds died in floods and mudslides that afflicted Greater Rio. The causes of such "natural" disasters must be understood as socioeconomic as well as meteorological. Out of necessity, Rio's poorest residents built makeshift homes on unstable hillsides or flood-prone lowlands. Widespread flooding in 1966, 1996, and 2010–2011 destroyed such homes and took lives, perversely honing the city's abilities to administer disaster relief.

Throughout these hard times, the beach remained the quintessential Carioca space of relaxation, play, and matters of the heart. Federal laws prohibited the commercialization of shoreline real estate, making beaches resistant to privatization. More significantly, a heterogeneous citizenry staked collective claim to the sands, intertidal zones, and waves. Yet the apparent democracy of the beach was still infused with micro-differentiations of sexuality, gender norms, and body cultures. The examples are many: In 1970, telenovela actress Leila Diniz (1945–1972) appeared in a bikini, six months pregnant. (Just nine years prior, the hapless president Jânio Quadros had prohibited the use of bikinis at the beach as part of a wider campaign to police women's sexuality.) The public scandal grew when Diniz expressed her willingness to have sex at all hours of the day. Later, the stirrings of a modern gay rights movement brought homosexual men to the beaches of Ipanema. The public displays of same-sex eroticism, sociability, and camp were part of a wider shift in male body culture on full display at the beach, where the rites of bodybuilding, tattooing, and revealing swimwear upended bourgeois strictures of masculine propriety. On returning from exile during the summer of 1979–1980, former student radical Fernando Gabeira walked Ipanema beach wearing a crocheted thong.

Class and race also shaped the beach and its social meanings. The middle classes, who tended to buy refreshments at beachside kiosks, looked askance at working poor families, often of darker skin, who brought along meals in order to economize. Some of those working poor self-segregated to the beaches of Guanabara Bay (e.g., Flamengo, Botafogo, Ramos) and the fishing spots on the Ilha do Governador—all terribly polluted by urban and industrial waste. But the poor also took advantage of changes in urban mobility that followed direct bus service between the Zona Norte and the beaches of the Zona Sul. Perhaps the most fraught episodes of class conflict at the beach took place during the summer of 1992–1993, when poor black youth were blamed for sowing panic among bathers at Copacabana and Arpoador. A racialized media panic about the social disorder of brawling youth, urban gangs, and *arrastões* (dragnets) played prominently in Cesar Maia's successful law-and-order mayoral campaign against Benedita da Silva, an Afro-Brazilian social worker raised in the Chapeu Mangueira favela.

Benedita da Silva's 1992 mayoral race, though unsuccessful, signaled the arrival of new actors in Carioca public life: evangelicals. Since the 1970s, millions of Brazilians have abandoned Roman Catholicism for the spiritual alternatives of evangelical faiths. Still others are born into Protestant families. Whether formed by lapsed Catholics or intergenerational evangelicals, Pentecostal churches have brought new spiritual demands for moral rectitude in the public square. In the temple and at the ballot box, the faithful have voted with their hearts and Bibles, generally pushing the political conversation to the right. The larger story is one of tremendous religious plurality, where traditional orthodoxies of Roman Catholicism (and Judaism, given Rio's long-standing Jewish minority) compete in an urban marketplace of faith that offers solace, salvation, and community in popular Catholicism, dogmatic Pentecostalism, Spiritism, syncretic religions, Candomblé, and New Age sects. Rio's place of privilege in Latin American religious diversity cannot be overstated, given the Carioca home base of several modern faiths, including the Brazilian Spiritist Federation (f. 1884), the Spiritist Federation of Umbanda (f. 1939), and the Universal Church of the Kingdom of God, founded in 1977 by former public servant Edir Macedo, who started preaching at an open-air bandstand in Méier, a neighborhood in the Zona Norte.

New voters of faith, coupled with the restitution of multiparty politics and the extension of political amnesty (both passed in 1979), reconfigured the Carioca political classes during an extended process of redemocratization that accompanied the economic crises of the 1980s. On his return from exile, Leonel Brizola (1922–1994), a leftist politician from Rio Grande do Sul who had stood alongside Goulart at the fateful Comício da Central, assembled a center-left voting coalition that twice delivered him to the governorship of Rio de Janeiro state (1983–1987 and 1991–1994). Brizola brought former exiles, university-educated social scientists and social workers, progressive sectors of the Catholic Church, and education reformers into public policymaking, which had long been dominated by engineers, sanitarians, and political appointees. The state and city education secretariats built a network of public schools, known officially as Centros Integrados de Educação Pública (CIEPs) but nicknamed Brizolões (Big Brizolas), that extended basic education, sporting, nutrition, and social services into needy communities. Although most CIEPs were later converted to conventional schools, their distinctive precast concrete architecture, designed by Brazilian modernist Oscar Niemeyer, still marks Rio's urban landscape.

The social innovations of the Brizola era were moderated by the widening reach of organized crime. Illicit gambling had already built a base for crime syndicates, and the advent of large-scale narcotrafficking fueled violent clashes between rival criminal factions. A spiral of extreme violence led the journalist Zuenir Ventura to write of a "Cidade Partida"—a Broken (or Divided) City. The drug trade had multiple social ramifications, especially when drug lords built community support through samba school sponsorships, social works, and intimidation. In some favelas controlled by drug lords, many municipal services effectively halted. Police responses were generally ineffective, and rogue elements of an underpaid and overwhelmed police force took the law into their own hands, participating in a series of mass killings that gained international infamy. Drug kingpins ran amok with impunity, thanks to heavy arms, private militias, and rampant corruption in the criminal justice system. In 2002, Fernandinho Beira Mar, a notorious gang leader, while incarcerated in Rio's maximum security prison in Bangu was still able to direct operations that shut down city commerce. A gun buyback program initiated by Rio state, followed by a 2003 ban on civilians carrying firearms, reduced some of dimensions of urban violence. The tide turned more dramatically after 2008, when the military police, working with state and municipal agencies and private-public partnerships, developed muscular policies of "pacification," expelling drug traffickers from favelas and rebuilding frayed social services. The ongoing, controversial pacification program has had a strong impact on urban politics.

Contemporary urban policy is informed by a heterodox set of principles that seek to temper unfettered capitalism and deepen the sense of citizenship. Whereas macroeconomic adjustments have curtailed the welfare state and privatized the once dismal telephone service, Rio city and state have sought active partnerships with international lending agencies and nongovernmental organizations to build a social safety net that provides free health care and universal schooling for children. Human rights advocacy and nongovernmental organizations have become primary vehicles of state-citizen interaction. Such shifts address concerns of the poor, sex workers, street children, people with disabilities, and the LGBT community. New partnerships have restored some of the promise of a democratic social compact imagined by unionists, feminists, students, black activists, and neighborhood associations that flowered in the process of redemocratization, only to falter in the successive crises of the late 1980s and early 1990s. The indicators of economic prosperity in recent Brazil have also played a large role in lifting the working poor, such as domestics and street sweepers, into the lower middle classes. For the established middle classes, the anxieties of economic instability have been replaced by the pressing demands of a competitive global economy that privileges those who can speak English.

With its legal origins in the 1974 law that merged Guanabara and Rio de Janeiro states (the *fusão*), a vast metropolitan area now encompasses many municipalities from the Guanabara Bay watershed to the south. The roads of Greater Rio have grown irredeemably traffic-choked; the bay and its tributaries are terribly polluted. Nonetheless, the engineering feats that have been carried out in a cityscape interrupted by granite mountains and waterways have built a vibrant, interconnected metropolis of commuters, revelers, and lovers whose embrace of mobile communications and social media flatten a famously uneven topography and shorten once insurmountable distances.

In 2014, the population of Greater Rio topped 12 million. When added to Greater São Paulo—another metropolis linked to Rio by highways and air shuttle service—Rio is the coastal anchor to a megalopolis of 45 million.

The wealth of this urban conglomeration powers a marketplace of global enterprises and a high-skill workforce. Rio has benefited from the mining- and energy-sector boom of the early twenty-first century. Alongside the mining conglomerate Vale, petroleum giant Petrobras has grown its operations around Guanabara Bay, including a university research center on the Ilha do Fundão. Nonstop air service to Houston and Dubai signals the importance of the global energy economy in Rio's economic future. Hungry for talent, Petrobras is one of numerous multinationals that entice skilled foreigners to relocate to the Marvelous City. The cosmopolitanism of the Carioca business sector reinforces the reach of international megaevents, including two United Nations Earth Summits (1992 and 2012), the Rock in Rio music festivals (1985–2013), the 2007 Pan American Games, the 2013 World Youth Day, the final match of the 2014 FIFA World Cup, and the 2016 summer Olympics and Paralympics. Brasília may be the political capital of Brazil, and São Paulo the lead engine of the BRIC economy, but the world still passes through Rio chasing global dreams of modernity, competition, and creativity in the so-called Land of the Future. Representing the largest of the city's investments in the business of spectacle and megaevents, the Sambódromo Marquês de Sapucaí (inaugurated 1984, upgraded 2012), a half-mile-long concrete structure used for Carnaval parade competitions, propels the city's global brand.

From the depths of a national debt crisis that included municipal bankruptcy, Rio has emerged as a hot destination for innovation, entrepreneurialism, and the global chic. Yet there have been high costs to this prosperity, which has been driven by overheated demand, indebtedness, and currency overvaluation. In the early 2010s, commentators observed a culture of ostentation, exemplified in exorbitant prices paid for real estate, dining out, and luxury brand goods. Some of this criticism channels old-money biases against *emergentes*, a nickname used to cast aspersions on the nouveau riche of Barra da Tijuca. But deeper social rifts were plainly evident in the massive street protests that swept through Rio and other Brazilian cities beginning in June 2013. A variety of protesters objected to the high cost of living, intractable corruption, and massive cost overruns for marquee projects like the reconstruction of Maracanã stadium, while the city's transportation infrastructure and its public education and health systems crumbled.

At the Port of Rio, there are many reminders of the uneasy shifts in the ways contemporary Cariocas collectively think of themselves and their city.

"A Visão do Morro da Providência, a partir do Morro do Pinto." Photograph by Alexandre de Bragança. Used by permission of Companhia de Desenvolvimento Urbano da Região do Porto do Rio de Janeiro (CDURP).

The massive renewal project called Porto Maravilha embodies the hopes and misgivings of revitalization, public good, urban memory, and wealth creation. It elicits a reckoning with the ongoing challenges of social exclusion and environmental degradation. Politicians and planners dream of razing an outdated, ugly transportation and industrial infrastructure to open the port district for redevelopment. Motorists are less enthused by the disruptions to daily commutes. The working poor fear the pressures of real estate speculation, gentrification, and the pasteurization of culture. An early rehearsal of these tensions at the port played out in 1996, when human remains were discovered in the backyard of a private home in Gamboa, near the site of the former slave markets at Valongo. Archaeological digs, archival work, and oral history confirmed the existence of an abandoned cemetery where thousands of slaves had been unceremoniously buried in mass graves in the nineteenth century. The partially excavated cemetery, the Memorial dos Pretos Novos (Memorial of the New Blacks), and the neighborhood of Valongo have become part of a self-guided tour of the port region, but their place in the urban landscape have caused certain tensions for advocates of a modern, forward-looking city. The construction of the Museu de Amanhã (Museum of Tomorrow) provides an interesting counterpoint to the recovery of a city's slave past. The audacious look of this science and technology museum, designed by the Spanish architect Santiago Calatrava, will reshape the meanings and uses of a region that encompasses a working port for container shipping and luxury cruise liners, as well as the Morro do Livramento, birthplace of Rio's greatest writer, Machado de Assis, and the Morro da Providência, where the urban poor have made their lives for nearly 125 years.

The Ephemeral State of Guanabara

Federal Congress

Sixteenth-century European explorers mistakenly supposed a great bay to be the mouth of a river, making the "River of January" into a place-name. Tupi toponyms roughly translated as "bosom of the sea" (guana and bara) also stuck. The terms' indigenous roots, as well as the close historical connections between the bay and city, made "Guanabara" a natural choice for the political jurisdiction that replaced the Federal District when the Brazilian capital moved to Brasília in 1960. Yet the State of Guanabara turned out to be ephemeral. In 1975, Guanabara and Rio de Janeiro states were joined together into a unitary jurisdiction known as Rio de Janeiro. In the fusão (fusion), Rio city became the two combined states' capital, depriving Guanabara Bay's second city, Niterói, of the political and administrative oversight of Rio state exercised since the early nineteenth century.

Two federal laws, excerpted here, chart the making and unmaking of Guanabara. The 1960 law, named after San Tiago Dantas (1911–1964), a Brazilian Labor Party congressman born in Rio, created the State of Guanabara out of the former Federal District. But Guanabara electoral politics proved to be an irritant to the military rule, and the Dantas law was undone in 1974. Antônio de Pádua Chagas Freitas (1914–1991), a Carioca politician who served as the last governor of Guanabara, stepped down on March 15, 1975.

The fusão of Guanabara and Rio states provided an administrative vehicle for the poorer municipalities of Greater Rio to benefit from the wealth generated in Rio city. The fusion also wove strong ties between city and state. Nonetheless, at least two small political movements grew up in the first decade of the twenty-first century, organized around the call for returning the municipality of Rio to an autonomous status in the federative republic. One movement, originating online in 2008, O Rio Decide (Rio Decides), called for a popular plebiscite on a reseparation of Rio city and state, jurisdictions that the movement's organizers describe as unique, with different interests and distinct cultures. Such movements have been unsuccessful, in part due to the very structure of the original 1974 law that created the Metropolitan Region of Rio de Janeiro, popularly known as Grande Rio. The close integration of Rio city with surrounding municipalities presents tremendous disincentives to *dismembering regional transportation, urban planning, education, and social services. With the outsize role that Rio city has come to play in the technological and financial administration of the huge offshore oil fields in the state's north, the movement for* desfusão *(de-fusion) appears even less likely to take hold.*

Law No. 3.752 (San Tiago Dantas Law)

President of the Republic, let it be known that the National Congress decrees, and I sanction, the following law:

Article 1 On the date upon which the Federal Capital is relocated, as mandated in Article 4 of the Transitory Constitutional Guidelines, the present Federal District will then constitute the State of Guanabara, in observance of Section 4 of that same article, maintaining the same geographical limits, and having as Capital and center of government the City of Rio de Janeiro.

Article 2 On the date of its constitution, the State of Guanabara will, independent of any other official acts of transfer, assume the rights, duties, and obligations of the current Federal District, as well as the dominion and possession of all fixed and moveable property belonging to the Federal District, and the public services rendered or maintained by the Federal District.

Article 3 To the State of Guanabara, on the date of its constitution, will be transferred without any indemnity the local public services rendered or maintained by the Union, including the personnel, property, and rights comprised by and involved in those services.

Section 1 The transferred services and associated personnel, whether civil or military, will be under the jurisdiction of the State of Guanabara and be subject to state authority, with respect to both the organization of these services and the laws that regulate relations between the state and workers. Included in these services are Justice, the Office of the Public Prosecutor, Military Police, firefighters, penal institutions, and the administration and activities of the Federal Department of Public Security, which is charged with policing in the present Federal District.

Article 6 The Legislative Assembly will be installed by convocation and under the presidency of the President of the Regional Electoral Tribunal, in a locale designated in advance, within ten days following official notice, and

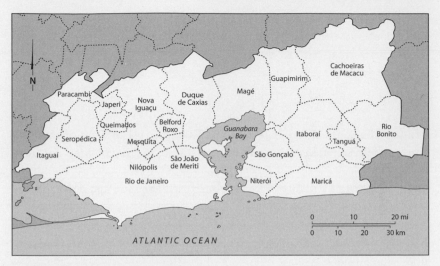

Greater Rio de Janeiro, 2014.

proceed to elect its Board. The Governor-elect will assume office before the Regional Electoral Tribunal.

Article 7 Legislative powers in the State of Guanabara will continue to be exercised until the dissemination of the Constitution by the Municipal Council, elected by the people on October 3, 1958, a document which confers the right, beyond the powers recognized in Law 217, of January 15, 1948, to approve the vetoes imposed by the provisional governor or to reject them by a majority of two thirds of members.

Section 1 The members of the Constituent Assembly and the current municipal councilors will compose, upon the promulgation of the Constitution and according to the form it dictates, the Legislative Assembly of the State of Guanabara, in compliance with the duration of their respective mandates.

Section 2 Until the promulgation of the Constitution it shall fall to the Legislative Assembly, in addition to its representative functions, to legislate regarding the administrative and judicial organization of the State of Guanabara.

Article 8 Until the Governor-elect assumes office on October 3, 1960, the Executive Power shall be exercised by a Provisional Governor nominated by the President of the Republic, with the approval of the Federal Senate.

Supplementary Law No. 20, July 1, 1974
CHAPTER II: REGARDING THE FUSION OF THE STATES
OF RIO DE JANEIRO AND GUANABARA

SECTION I
On the Organization of Public Powers

Article 8 The States of Rio de Janeiro and Guanabara shall form one unitary State, to be designated the State of Rio de Janeiro, starting on March 15, 1975.

Single paragraph: The City of Rio de Janeiro shall be the Capital of the State.

Article 9 The Representative Assembly of the new State shall be elected on November 15, 1974, and will be installed on March 15th of the following year, under the presidency of the President of the Regional Electoral Tribunal of Guanabara until the election of its Board.

Article 10 For the first four years of existence of the new State, the President of the Republic will nominate its Governor, according to the conditions of Article 4 of this Supplementary Law.

Single paragraph: The Governor, nominated on October 3, 1974, in a manner according to this article, will assume office on March 15, 1975.

SECTION IV
On the Metropolitan Region of Rio de Janeiro

Article 19 Following Article 164 of the Constitution, the Metropolitan Region of Rio de Janeiro is established.

Single paragraph: The Metropolitan Region of Rio de Janeiro is composed of the following municipalities: Rio de Janeiro, Niterói, Duque de Caxias, Itaboraí, Itaguaí, Magé, Maricá, Nilópolis, Nova Iguaçu, Paracambi, Petrópolis, São Gonçalo, São João de Meriti, and Mangaratiba.

Translated by Jerry D. Metz

Recreation in the Parque do Flamengo

Ethel Bauzer de Medeiros and Others

The ambition of the Parque do Flamengo outstrips nearly all other interventions into the shoreline of Guanabara Bay. A space of contrasts, the park (officially named Parque Brigadeiro Eduardo Gomes but commonly called the Aterro do Flamengo) is bisected by an expressway that allows cars and buses to transit between downtown and Botafogo at high speeds. Bayside, elderly people and small children amble along winding footpaths lined with palms and flowering plants. On the other side of the highway, fronting a stretch of upscale apartment buildings and the grand Hotel da Glória, soccer fields are in constant use. Expansive lawns are used for sunrise tai chi, weightlifting, and interval training. Notoriously high levels of water pollution do not prevent sporting competitions and swimming at the park's sandy beaches.

The park's execution is credited to Maria Carlota "Lota" de Macedo Soares (1910–1967), a self-educated urban planner who shared her life with American poet laureate and Brazilophile Elizabeth Bishop (1911–1979). Lota assembled a team of top-flight urbanists, engineers, and landscape architects (including Roberto Burle Marx, whose initial sketch appears here) to carry out a high-modernist vehicular expressway surrounded by tropical greenery and multimodal recreation. With the political muscle of Guanabara governor Carlos Lacerda, Lota's Work Group repurposed the rocky earth taken from the Morro de Santo Antônio to construct a greenway that came to be intimately associated with the city's iconic vistas. In the article excerpted here, Ethel Bauzer de Medeiros (b. 1924), a member of the Work Group and former head of the International Recreation Association, wrote about the benefits of the recreation facilities, performance spaces, and public lavatories in this public park, which was designated a national landmark in 1965.

The park's post-landmarking history reflects certain dynamics that Lota and Medeiros hoped to moderate. Park funding and administration have been perpetually embroiled in local politics. The park's "natural" environment and its social uses have evolved, often out of synch with original plans. Poor maintenance of recreational facilities left some areas semidesolate. The dense tree canopy and sweeping overpasses have been appropriated as makeshift homeless encampments or sites for illicit drug use and cruising for sex. The Marina da Glória (center of the photo

"Projeto do Parque do Flamengo." Illustration by Burle Marx, 1961. Used by permission of Burle Marx & Cia.

here) has been especially controversial, as preservationists loyal to Lota's vision have squared off against private commercial interests, event planners, and economic development consortiums that have floated various proposals to privatize an ostensibly public area. In such tensions, we see how urban Rio constantly renews itself in the struggles over the allocation of recreation space in a metropolis set within a spectacular landscape.

One Million Square Meters for Public Recreation

A vast public park is set to open in Guanabara on a plot of land reclaimed from the sea. Its most remarkable characteristic, however, is not its expanse—one hundred hectares—but its prime location. In a four-hundred-year-old city, with a population of almost four million inhabitants concentrated in an area of slightly less than 1,300 square kilometers, the dedication of such a centrally located space to public recreation is especially noteworthy.

THE MEGALOPOLIS AND ITS PROBLEMS

Recreational activity is today understood to be a basic human necessity, particularly for the residents of large cities. If technological progress has ushered in higher standards of living and greater material comfort, it has

"Marina da Glória 4." Photograph by Rodrigo Soldon, 2009. Licensed under Creative Commons Attribution 2.0 Generic license.

also resulted in greater automation, routine, and tedium for man, who has seen his labor progressively subdivided and his tasks further specialized. The extraordinary acceleration of social change following the Industrial Revolution has resulted in even more tension and conflict in the face of the challenges inherent to life in urban centers where living space itself is contested. Competition in cities permeates every activity; the bureaucratic machine had to expand and interpersonal contact has become increasingly less personal. To all of this was added increased leisure time, now available not only to children and adolescents, but to adults as well. Compounding all of these issues is the heightened rate of acts of delinquency, especially acute on Sundays and holidays.

In an interdependent society such as ours, each day has become a succession of challenges: the need to earn a living, to feed oneself, schooling, transportation; the physical distances to traverse, the means of communication between people; the space in which to move about, the need for rest and recreation. The latter two are recognized as crucial not just to the individual but to the well-being of the broader community, which benefits from its members' fruitful use of leisure time so that they attain greater mental health and, ultimately, productivity.

Previously, entertainment meant leaving the small town to go into the city in search of the lights, sounds, commercial novelties and excitement only it could provide. The authorities' concern with providing recreation centered on mitigating abuses and preventing disruptive acts during public commemorations, sometimes elevating the profile of certain celebrations with their personal attendance. Today the idea of a holiday is escaping the city in search of natural beauty unmarred by civilization. Thus, on weekends the roads exiting major cities are packed with vehicles filled with people chasing after sunlight, fresh air, and open space, seeking ways to revitalize their spirits and temperament to make up for the emotional exhaustion of fighting for their lives on a daily basis. Yet cities continue to grow larger, encroaching into their surrounding countryside, making the weekend journey ever more noisome, stressful, and costly.

CONCLUSIONS FROM RECENT RESEARCH ON RECREATION

It is worth mentioning here some results from a survey about recreation conducted in the United States by the Census Bureau. Between 1959 and 1961, 16,000 people from various socioeconomic backgrounds, age groups, and geographic regions were interviewed on the subject. Among the results were the following findings:

1. Opportunities for open-air recreation are most pressing near metropolitan areas.
2. There is a considerable amount of land available for such recreation, however it is not utilized, being deemed too distant from areas of high population density.
3. Water is a focal point of open-air recreational activities.
4. Offering facilities for open-air recreation results in economic benefits for the broader community.
5. Simple activities (e.g., going for a car ride or a walk, swimming, and enjoying panoramic vistas) are the most popular activities regardless of socioeconomic background, age, or occupation of those surveyed.

THE URBANIZATION PLAN FOR THE ATERRO GLÓRIA-FLAMENGO

Recognizing, for the aforementioned reasons, that it is imperative to offer easily accessible facilities for open-air recreation in major cities, sites that can be frequented not just on weekends but every day and by people of various ages and social classes, the Plano de Urbanização do Atêrro Glória-Flamengo took shape. The Work Group headed by Lota Macedo Soares—

architects, botanists, engineers, and landscape designers—relied on advice from specialists in urban planning and recreation.

The broad swath of reclaimed land has two car lanes, enough to handle some of the traffic between the center of the city and the Zona Sul without creating bottlenecks in the affected area. Since pedestrians ought to encounter tranquility and freedom in the park, vehicles are not allowed to enter, parking instead along the periphery in six lots with the capacity for 1,200 cars.

Six pedestrian bridges and an equal number of underground passageways, the latter housing public restrooms, guarantee visitor safety.

A little less than half of the total area will be covered in turf, with gardens alongside the Museu de Arte Moderna, the large pergolas around Glória, and the Morro da Viúva. The central part is being turned into wooded areas, planted along artificial undulations in the terrain. Numerous concrete benches, distributed along the graveled paths throughout the work, will serve those seeking contemplative and restful activities in an area of great scenic beauty. In the gardens, designed by Burle Marx and his team, large groups of plants of the same species are used to create the effect of contrast between the masses of vegetation. The plants were brought from various areas of the country to the nursery where they were acclimated before being set in the soil, keeping in mind the aim of utilizing varied species of plants, blooming at distinct times of the year, to ensure the constant presence of flowers in the garden.

Beneath the pergolas there is an orchid house as well as permanent exhibits of birds, fish, and plants native to Brazil which will complement the calmer recreational activities.

The only vehicle to traverse the entire park will be the *tremzinho* [little train]—a tractor pulling four cars—with a total capacity of one hundred seated passengers. Four such vehicles will cover a three-kilometer circuit on a five-meter-wide concrete track, which at night will operate as a service road. The train station will also have public restrooms (the total number of which will exceed ten).

An area of approximately 40,000 square meters, intended for picnics, will have concrete benches and tables in shaded areas, close to the water.

Two areas for model airplanes—one regulation sized, fifty meters in diameter, and another smaller one, forty meters in diameter—are now functioning, attracting numerous participants and spectators. The latter sit on a long cement bench, coated in oxicrete (painted blue), encircling the area and enclosed by a metallic cover.

Before the end of this year, an eighteen-by-fifty-meter reflecting pool, sixty centimeters deep, surrounded by bleachers and a protective strip, will be opened for model boats.

Sports facilities include eight freestyle soccer fields, six small ones (thirty by sixty meters) and two large ones (eighty by forty meters); paved courts, two for basketball and six for volleyball. Sidelines for futsal were also drawn on the latter so as to maximize the use of each court, servicing varying interests.

A puppet and marionette theater, designed by Carlos Werneck de Carvalho, will seat two hundred spectators to watch shows unfold on a three-hundred-square-meter stage suited to various activities. Its walls will be of exposed brick covered with panels by Enrico Bianco.

Teachers specializing in various recreational activities will serve visitors of all age groups in two "playgrounds," sized roughly 30,000 square meters each. As with everywhere else in the Park, the main idea behind these areas is to stimulate the active involvement of visitors in activities as opposed to mere spectatorship so as to foster true recreation. One playground is situated where Flamengo neighborhood begins and the other on the Morro da Viúva, each with a pavilion (designed by A. E. Reidy) for stationary activities as well as convenient shelter on rainy or exceedingly hot days. Each "playground" is composed of the following sections: toddlers, primary school children, adolescents and adults, and the elderly. One of the parks will have a small village with little houses, a school, stores, streets, squares and an overlook designed by Maria Laura Osser.

The equipment for the recreational units is intended to be cost-efficient and easily maintained but also resistant to intensive use and weathering.

The overriding concern has been to offer varied equipment to stoke the imagination at the same time as it, through the simplicity and beauty of its design, inspires aesthetic appreciation.

The anchorage for visiting boats will be in the Glória cove; abutting the Morro da Viúva will be a restaurant designed by Jorge M. Moreira. Throughout the entire Aterro there will be extensive signage to guide the public.

Plans for an artificial beach at Flamengo, 1,500 meters long and about 50 meters wide, are in the early planning stages.

BANDSTAND

Project designed by architect Affonso Eduardo Reidy.

A platform approximately 80 square meters, situated 100 meters off the ground, is dedicated to musical performances. It is sheltered by a quadrangular cover atop a concrete slab. Along the two diagonals is the cover resting on a single central pillar. Underneath the structure there is a supply depot.

DANCEFLOOR

Project designed by architect Affonso Eduardo Reidy.

The dancefloor will be composed of two circular platforms, respectively, sixteen and thirteen meters in diameter, at differing heights. The first will be encircled by a seven-step grandstand, below grade. It will be able to seat 500 people.

2 DE DEZEMBRO PAVILION

Project designed by architect Affonso Eduardo Reidy.

The structure will be made of reinforced concrete and composed of a 391-meter platform, situated 100 meters above the surrounding land above which two slightly curving walls will support the roof made of four inverted domes.

The pavilion will have an expansive hall, balconies, workrooms for caretakers, a first-aid clinic, pantry, dressing room, and lavatories for different age groups and sexes.

PUPPET AND MARIONETTE THEATER

Project designed by architect Carlos Werneck de Carvalho.

Auditorium with an average capacity of 200 people.

Roof—a concrete slab supported by eight pillars interlaced by two exposed beams.

Stage—with the following annexes: Performance space; Restroom; Storeroom; Basement.

Its outer walls are covered with panels by painter Enrico Bianco.

The theater will be located among trees so as to improve the acoustics for performances and to make the ambience as agreeable as possible.

MORRO DA VIÚVA PAVILION

Project designed by architect Affonso Eduardo Reidy.

The playground installed at the Morro da Viúva Pavilion will be circular with a 22-meter diameter and an internal garden.

Its concrete shell structure will be composed of a perimeter curtain wall.

The pavilion will have an expansive hall, a room for nannies, a first-aid clinic, pantry, dressing room and storerooms, and lavatories for different age groups and sexes.

Translated by Andre Pagliarini

This House Is Yours!

Carlos Lacerda

Carlos Lacerda (1914–1977), the irascible center-right journalist who served as the first governor of Guanabara, embraced improvements in housing the working poor and the eradication of substandard dwellings, especially favelas. During Lacerda's gubernatorial tenure (1960–1965), the state housing authority established in 1962, named Companhia de Habitação Popular do Estado da Guanabara (Guanabara State Popular Housing Company; COHAB-GB), took the lead in constructing popular housing intended for poor Cariocas, especially those displaced during parallel programs of favela clearance. The marquee projects of COHAB were Vila Progresso (renamed Vila Kennedy in honor of the slain U.S. president), located in Bangu; Vila Aliança, also in Bangu; and Vila Esperança, in Vigário Geral. The planning stages for a popular housing project in the Cidade de Deus, located in Jacarepaguá, also originated during Lacerda's term.

The early phases of popular housing construction and favela removal achieved some notable gains: nearly forty thousand working poor and public servants gained access to about eight thousand housing units. Yet the shortcomings were evident: few of the city's poor secured access to these homes; some actively resisted removals. Those who did move found the new housing to lack adequate infrastructure and public services. Transportation to the centers of employment was precarious. Official recognition of such shortcomings, in conjunction with the drawdown of Alliance for Progress funds that had originally guaranteed the construction loans, would alter local and national housing policies after 1967. Yet the future of publicly financed low-income housing still looked bright in 1965, when Lacerda prepared to make a bid for the national presidency. The governor brimmed with optimism as former favelados took up residence in orderly rows of modest brick homes. He envisioned a new economic arrangement that enabled the poor to acquire title to their homes, transforming the impressionable rabble into respectable, democratic, market-oriented citizen-consumers. Lacerda also saw the transfer of home title as a didactic moment, when the lower classes were instructed on the practical aspects of household management as well as the responsibilities of civic engagement and moral propriety.

The Manual do Proprietário, a homeowner's manual distributed by COHAB to the new residents, opens with the promise as well as the cautions of popular housing. This brief letter from Lacerda to the new homeowners makes the direct appeal to an emergent political class of citizens, who are reminded of their duties to themselves, to God, and to the less fortunate. The second page echoes the legal registry of homeownership. The third page gives a visual identity to a new ideal of housing for the poor—the well-maintained, single-family house that elevates the working poor into middle-class respectability, conferred by the rights and efforts of property ownership.

Fellow Property-Owner

Life was made for everyone, such that each family should HAVE A HOUSE. But it is not merely that. It is also that each house HAVE A FAMILY. The understanding of the duties owed by each person to the next is just as important as the understanding of the rights of each individual. That person next to you is your relative and your neighbor. That person is like us. Our duties to that person are great. For this reason, this house has been built.

I hope that the owner of this house, under God's protection, thinks of those who still do not have this opportunity, and I hope that the owner assists in giving this opportunity to all.

Congratulations.

Carlos Lacerda

Year of the Fourth Centennial [1965]
COHAB-GB Social Service

I, _____, AM THE PROPERTY

OWNER OF THE HOUSE LOCATED AT _____,

NUMBER_____

IN THE_____RIO DE JANEIRO,

STATE OF GUANABARA

I HAVE SIGNED THE REGISTRY OF PURCHASE

DAY_____

REGISTRY_____

BOOK_____ PAGES_____

THIS HOUSE IS YOURS!

IT IS YOUR DUTY TO
PRESERVE IT
EXPAND IT
BEAUTIFY IT

DO EVERYTHING AT YOUR DISPOSAL THAT WILL HELP TRANSFORM
THIS HOUSE INTO A CHERISHED HOME.

Translated by Daryle Williams

"Esta Casa é Sua!" Guanabara State Popular Housing Company, from *Manual do Proprietário* (manual) (Rio de Janeiro: Secretaria de Serviços Sociais, 1965).

An Act of Student Protest

Correio da Manhã *Staff Photographer*

A wave of discontent swept global youth in the late 1960s, especially among university students. In Brazil, students agitated against restrictions on the right to organize; they voiced broader concerns over political process and generational authority. The strong, often contradictory forces of Cold War paranoia, radical nationalism, rock 'n' roll music, sexual liberation, and consumerism brought educated young adults to air their dreams and outrage in the streets of Paris, Mexico City, Berkeley, and Rio. In Brazil, the National Students' Union (União Nacional dos Estudantes; UNE) played an outsize role in organizing student voices against a series of reform measures enacted by military generals eager to contain student activism. The UNE headquarters, located on the Praia do Flamengo, was torched and the organization declared illegal, stoking the radicalization of some student leaders. On March 28, 1968, Edson Luís de Lima Souto, a high schooler who had migrated to Rio from northern Brazil, was killed in a police action against a downtown student hangout. Mourned as a martyr, Edson Luís became a rallying cry for a youth movement that took to the streets in protest of the harsh measures employed by police and state security officers. Protest marches, strikes, denunciatory pamphleteering, and countercultural chants were integral to these student mobilizations, which often faced violent repression.

The Correio da Manhã, a major morning daily, dedicated ample photojournalistic coverage to student upheaval in Rio. This photograph from the paper's October 23, 1968, edition captures a dramatic moment as a young woman is poised to hurl a pedra portuguesa, one of Rio's ubiquitous cobblestones, during what appears to be a youth riot. The debris-strewn street contrasts sharply with the utter normalcy of parked cars, a lamppost, and street trees. The protesters' target is unseen, but it is easy to imagine that the mixed-gender, university-age protesters clashed with a group of all-male army recruits of about the same age. Race and class differences were a noted difference between such groups, as student protesters were typically middle-class and white, whereas security and police officers were drawn largely from the ranks of working-class men of color.

The woman's attire captures the intersections of gender and student protest in

"Manifestação estudantil contra o regime militar." Photograph by staff photographer. From *Correio da Manhã*, October 23, 1968. Courtesy of Arquivo Nacional, Rio de Janeiro.

1968 Rio. The ensemble is conventional, down to the low-slung pumps and sensible handbag. Yet the length of a belted dress veers close to the minidress, a shocking fashion import. Body movement reveals bare thighs. Such suggestive, modish dress was fodder for a moral panic that developed around behaviors deemed by conservatives as unwomanly and against bons costumes *(good manners). Another unsettling aspect of this sort of scene, for many, was that an unnamed woman was participating in brazen acts of violence. The totality of the photo evokes a range of actions associated with student rebellion in the fateful year 1968.*

Dancin' Days

Nelson Motta with Ruban Sabino

The prodigious output of the movie studio dream factories headquartered in Rio (e.g., Cinédia, f. 1930; Atlântida, f. 1941; Cinedistri, f. 1949) was rarely screened outside Brazil. The advent of videotaped television, introduced in 1960, changed the scenario, and a new vehicle for export-quality programming took off: the telenovela (commonly known as novela). The city's sizeable television production facilities (including repurposed film studios) churned out serialized dramas set in the Marvelous City. The nightly soap operas, repackaged and dubbed, traveled easily across borders. In its loss of political capital status, Rio became Brazil's novela capital, and the unbounded success of Brazilian soaps maintained the city's stature on the global stage in the age of television.

Dancin' Days, a hit novela originally broadcast on the Globo network between July 1978 and January 1979 and subsequently rebroadcast in dozens of countries worldwide, exemplified the type of story lines, characters, values, and scenery that grew the Rio-centric novela industry and its global fan base. Each primetime episode added a compelling twist to the tumultuous relationships between Júlia (Sonia Braga), an ex-con who abuses alcohol, her frigid millionaire sister Yolanda (Joanna Fromm), and Julia's estranged teenage daughter Marisa (Glória Pires). An early work by the accomplished Carioca novela writer Gilberto Braga (b. 1946), Dancin' Days delighted audiences with its dramatizations of the intimate lives, moral excesses, and cultural tastes of an urban middle class coping with modernity. The most memorable scenes were set in Dancin' Days, a neon-lit discotheque that took its name from a short-lived club with a similar name that operated in the Shopping da Gávea, an enclosed mall in the Zona Sul. Sonia Braga's character scandalized television audiences with her writhing moves on the club's dance floor. The sound track pulsated with disco hits, from Ronaldo Resedá's "Kitch Zona Sul" to covers from the sound track of Saturday Night Fever (1977). Racy clothing set fashion trends in real-life discotheques that sought to capture the look and sound of the fictional Dancin' Days.

Nelson Motta (b. 1944), a Paulista musical producer, cowrote (with Ruban Sabino [Rubens de Queiroz Barra]) the song that accompanied the opening credits.

Recorded by As Frenéticas (The Frenetic Women), a group of former nightclub host-esses, "Dancin' Days" was a smash in its own right. Strong sales of the novela's sound track helped seal the song's place in a global imaginary of Rio as forever fabu-lous. In their celebration of reckless abandon and eroticized bodies in motion, the lyrics transport the listener into a special world of pleasure and self-fulfillment. The song has managed to maintain its appeal for more than three decades. Yet "Dancin' Days" is also a song very much of a specific time and place. Well before the formal start of the "opening" that eventually led to a return to civilian democracy, Cario-cas, real and fictional, pushed back at the moralism of authoritarian rule—feeling, suffering, dancing, and partying to the disco beat.

"Dancin' Days"

Open up your wings,
release your wild beasts,
let loose,
come join this party
And bring with yooooooou
your craaaziest dreams
I want to see your body,
beautiful, light, and loose

Sometimes, we feel, we suffer, we dance
even without wanting to dance
In this party anything goes
it's just important to be yourself,
just as you are

[Repeats]

Sometimes, we feel, we suffer, we dance
even without wanting to dance
In this party anything goes
it's just important to be yourself,
just as you are

Dance well, dance badly, dance without stopping
Dance well, dance badly, dance even if you don't know how to dance   ·

[Repeats]

In this party anything goes
It's just important to be yourself,
just as you are

[Repeats]

[Abra suas asas,
solte suas feras,
caia na gandaia,
entre nessa festa
E leve com vocêee
seu sonho mais loouuco
Eu quero ver seu corpo,
lindo, leve e solto

A gente as vezes, sente, sofre, dança,
sem querer dançar
Na nossa festa vale tudo
vale ser alguém como eu,
como você

A gente as vezes, sente, sofre, dança,
sem querer dançar
Na nossa festa vale tudo
vale ser alguém como eu,
como você

Dance bem, dance mal, dance sem parar
dance bem, dance até sem saber dançar

Na nossa festa vale tudo
vale ser alguém como eu,
como você]

Translated by Daryle Williams

Burger Wars of 1979

Jornal do Brasil

A key episode of Rio's long-running romance with consumer trends hit the scene on February 13, 1979, when the first McDonald's franchise in South America opened its doors. The restaurant was not the first to sell hamburgers with fries to Cariocas, but the arrival of the global brand that stood behind the smiling face of Ronald McDonald traded on the appeal of a dining experience purportedly superior in taste, comfort, and efficiency to the early innovators in the Brazilian fast-food market. One of the many rivals to McDonald's was Bob's, a fast-food restaurant founded in 1951 by Robert Falkenburg (b. 1926), an expat American tennis champion who introduced soft-serve ice cream to Brazilian consumers. Falkenburg had turned an American-style menu of cheap eats originally sold at luncheonettes and vending carts—hot dogs, hamburgers, and milkshakes—into a successful, scaleable business that included its own domestic suppliers. Competitors Gordon and Mab's also angled for market share. Cariocas of means had already experienced the McDonald's brand during their travels abroad, priming the market for the arrival of the Golden Arches in Rio. At the same time, the McDonald's corporation was ready to build on its success in countries outside the United States, adapting to local palates a core menu built around the Big Mac, McFries, and a soft drink.

Brazil's first McDonald's opened in Copacabana, as the first Bob's had done more than twenty-five years earlier. The beachside neighborhood's density and lifestyle held promise for building a successful business to satisfy changing urban dining tastes, including the ascendant habit of eating lunch away from home and dining options specifically targeted at children. In making the restaurant successful, investors sought to change the managerial, technological, supply chain, and labor dimensions of food service, molding the restaurant's kitchens on Rua Hilário de Gouveia to standards taught at a corporate training facility in Chicago.

As this Jornal do Brasil *article reveals, the established fast-food outlets were poised to mount an aggressive response to their new competitor. With the immediate success of the McDonald's brand, a veritable "Hamburger War" was in the making. In reality, consumer behavior demonstrated that there was plenty of room for everyone. As more McDonald's restaurants opened, Bob's began its own franchising in 1984. Not all Cariocas were enamored with such novelties, and Rio's widely read social columnist Zózimo Barroso do Amaral (1941–1997) wryly wondered elsewhere in the* Jornal do Brasil *how it could be that Cariocas would wait in long lines for such pedestrian food.*

With McDonald's in Rio, the Hamburger War Begins

With the arrival of McDonald's onto the Carioca market, the War of the Hamburger has been declared: Bob's, Gordon, Mab's and other luncheonettes are in danger of losing regular clients who might be tempted to try out a taste of the renowned king of hamburger products, whose fare is known to be of the absolute same quality in more than four thousand establishments spread across the entire world. For example, not only the hamburger, *but also fries and apple pies—all menu items most characteristic of McDonald's—will have the same taste here as found in a restaurant in Frankfurt. This could be an advantage or not, everything depending on the refinement of the consumer's palate.*

In operation for about a month on Rua Hilário de Gouveia, in Copacabana, and selling on average three thousand hamburgers per day, McDonald's appears to prove that very soon it will dominate the market in Brazil, even though it has yet to do any kind of advertising. The idea to bring the McDonald's brand to Brazil originated four years ago, when Peter Rodenbeck, an American who has lived here for twelve years and is now managing partner of the business, initiated market surveys and communications with McDonald's, which for its part had already expressed an interest in the Brazilian market. This initial contact was followed by face-to-face meetings; Peter attended the so-called "Hamburger University," a course created and maintained by McDonald's in Chicago that specializes in technical training for its executives. The preparations for the opening of the restaurant in Rio were under way. The contract was a *joint-venture*, with 50% domestic capital, and included the creation of Empresa de Alimentos e Turismo [the Food and Tourism Company], a Brazilian subsidiary of McDonald's.

The McDonald's company works through a system of franchises. Around 70% of its restaurants belong to different franchisees licensed to use the name McDonald's that receive all the company's technical support and *know-how*. According to its manager in Rio, substantial technical work precedes the restaurant's opening, such as equipment licensing and worker training. "Our equipment supplier spent one month visiting the American machine manufacturers and thus was able to transfer some of their technology here. With time, then, we will change out equipment that is initially imported," explains Peter Rodenbeck.

The choice of Rio to be the first location for McDonald's, which intends to expand rapidly to other Brazilian cities, principally São Paulo, was due to the city's very casual lifestyle, oriented to the open air and the beach. Copacabana was initially chosen for the traffic, especially among pedestrians, thus bringing every type of customer to McDonald's. But the plan is to expand to other neighborhoods of the city; two other restaurants in different locations are already being negotiated and should open by the end of the year.

RONALD MCDONALD

For Peter Rodenbeck, four basic points link McDonald's restaurants to the community where they are located. The first is the supply of food products, equipment, and service acquired through local providers under the supervision of McDonald's, whose rigorous oversight guarantees quality. "Then, a fixed clientele, in large part drawn from neighborhood residents. In addition, children are always welcome: for them, we promote special events and create a series of characters like the clown Ronald McDonald, known throughout the world," he says. Another factor responsible for the global success of McDonald's is its system of staff recruitment among students and housewives. "The short and flexible work schedule gives them work opportunities compatible with their other activities. Although unfamiliar to Brazilian conditions, we will set up the same system," said Peter.

In Brazil, the menu will initially have 13 items. In sandwiches, hamburgers are the strong point: the Big Mac—two patties, onion, pickles, cheese, lettuce and a secret-recipe special sauce—is the favorite. But there is also the cheeseburger, the common hamburger and the fish filet, also with sauce and pickles. For a side, french fries. To drink: Coca-Cola, orange juice, and the milkshake. Beyond these, McDonald's also offers in Rio the hot apple pie and the ice-cream sundae. Despite the passion for standardization, McDonald's is flexible enough to add new items to its menu, when this becomes a positive for the local consumer. Its menu includes wine in France, tea and fish and chips in England, beer in Germany, soup in Japan, and in Brazil, a tropical country, the idea was to include orange juice.

"Everything in a McDonald's restaurant follows rigid standards, this is one of the secrets of the business," says Peter Rodenbeck. "And it is because of this that going once, the customer always returns. The consumer can be certain that in any place in the world where he enters a McDonald's, he can eat a hamburger with fries and a milkshake, always with the same standard of quality."

The restaurant in Copacabana boasts air-conditioning, sit-down tables and 80 employees of both sexes. It will serve products that are 100% Brazilian-made. According to McDonald's world objectives, prices are low and accessible for most people.

The restaurant has been full during its entire first month—despite having not yet launched any kind of advertising or had any formal inauguration—with lines forming primarily on weekends and during lunch hours. For Peter Rodenbeck, this demand is due to the Cariocas' great ability to spread good news—beyond being a novelty. "A good part of the clientele always returns. I think that is due to the quality, not only of the food, but also of the ambiance itself. We only regret that space is limited: many arrive and encounter a packed restaurant. Based on the experience with the first, we plan to make other restaurants much larger," he says.

The inauguration of the store will take place tomorrow at 5 p.m. in a very informal ceremony, according to Thomas Gruber, McDonald's international marketing director, who has come from company headquarters in Chicago especially to prepare the inauguration party and to make contact with Rodenbeck and advertising agencies, in preparation for a future publicity campaign in the Brazilian media. At the inauguration, on a stage set up at Copacabana beach, at the intersection of Hilário de Gouveia, the Number One personality in McDonald's lore throughout the world will be introduced to the Carioca public: the clown Ronald McDonald. Ronald McDonald will perform a show, accompanied by the American School of Rio de Janeiro band. A parade will follow. Children will receive plastic presents and balloons, in addition to special McDonald's hats.

"It will be the first appearance of Ronald McDonald in South America. Ronald is our public relations for children throughout the world and, according to research performed in the United States, he is the second most popular person in the United States among children."

Translated by Shawn Moura

Barra da Tijuca, Boomtown (but Not for All)

Israel Klabin; Angela Coronel and Heloisa Perez

Israel Klabin (b. 1926), the scion of a prominent Jewish Brazilian industrialist family, was appointed mayor of Rio in March 1979, just as a liberalization of military rule began to bring meaningful reforms to national political life. Klabin left office fifteen months later over disagreements about the legacies of the fusion of Guanabara and Rio de Janeiro states. He subsequently went on to a prominent career in environmental activism, including organizational responsibilities for the United Nations Earth Summit held in Rio in 1992.

About five months into his short mayoral tenure, Klabin paid homage to Lucio Costa (1902–1998), the world-renowned architect and urbanist, in remarks that were reprinted in Cidade, a periodical of the municipal secretariat of planning (reproduced here). Klabin spoke in praise of a large-scale plan for the region of western Rio popularly known as "Barra": the Pilot Plan for Barra da Tijuca, completed June 22, 1969. Costa's plan laid out the orderly urbanization of a large swath of the Baixada de Jacarepaguá, a lightly inhabited area separated from the central city by high forested mountains, the Atlantic Ocean, and limited transportation links. When Francisco Negrão de Lima, governor of Guanabara between 1965 and 1970, had pushed massive public works in tunnel and highway construction to overcome these physical obstacles, Barra had opened to residential and commercial development.

Costa and his political backers, in concert with real estate developers, were animated by the idea of preventing Barra from becoming another Copacabana: a world-famous beach neighborhood whose cachet had been eroded by verticalization without adequate infrastructure, by overpopulation, and by the spread of low-cost housing. The Barra plan regulated building height, massing, and lot size. It projected an infrastructure for high-speed car traffic. The plan envisioned housing the poor, especially in areas covered by a "Parallel Plan," yet the bias tilted toward middle-class residents with private automobiles. Other elements of the plan included the preservation of inland waterways and ocean vistas that made Barra a tropical paradise set within a large urban conglomeration. Klabin's remarks—delivered ten years after the Barra plan had been put in place—included glowing references to the scope and rapid pace of development in the region.

The second article here, which appeared in the same issue of Cidade, offers a tonic to Klabin's enthusiasm. Angela Coronel and Heloisa Perez profile poor Rio residents living in the shadows of tony high-rises. The testimonies taken from the local working classes imply that standards of living had been declining for Barra's poor. The article also features Constantino Mandarino (b. 1938), an Italian-born priest. Popularly known as "Frei Dino," Mandarino led Barra's São Francisco de Paula parish between 1973 and 1985, and his duties were closely tied to the social and spiritual needs of poor Roman Catholics who resided in Barra and the adjacent neighborhood of Recreio dos Bandeirantes. The Rio state legislature honored Mandarino for his pastoral works with the title Honorary Citizen in 2010. Three decades prior, Frei Dino's parishioners had known him to speak in frank terms about the unevenness of urban planning at this time when western Rio boomed.

Remarks in Tribute to Lucio Costa and the Plano Piloto da Barra da Tijuca

Around 80% of the city's population, which is today more than five million inhabitants, is concentrated in only 20% of the city's territory. Of the 1,771 square kilometers (the area occupied by our city), only 480 square kilometers can be potentially urbanized. This by itself explains the Baixada de Jacarepaguá's importance as doubtlessly the most noble expansion of the city, with its 165 square kilometers, of which eighty-two square kilometers can be urbanized—around one fifth of the total available area.

The expansion to the west, already irreversible, will receive state and municipal oversight to deter overpopulation of already saturated areas and neighborhoods. The pace of construction in Barra da Tijuca and throughout the Baixada de Jacarepaguá relieves pressure on the Zona Sul and provides a new style of housing and higher quality of life for those who are opting to live in this area, the natural extension of the Zona Sul.

The growth projections for the year 2000 estimate a population of 9.4 million inhabitants in Rio. At this level, the Baixada de Jacarepaguá will be practically occupied by all segments of the population, as we will also promote the so-called Parallel Plan, coordinated through the National Housing Bank, destined for those classes with an income of between three and seven times the minimum salary.

This planned and orderly growth, directed to the west, can be credited to the Lucio Costa Plan—perhaps the only or one of the few examples of urban planning recorded in the country. Until the 1960s, this beautiful large plain was still a wild landscape dominated by lagoons, mountains, and twenty kilometers of oceanfront beaches. That natural state was a result of the physical barriers of the Tijuca and Pedra Branca massifs, which effectively isolated the region from the rest of the city. The opening of the Estrada Lagoa-Barra, during the gubernatorial tenures of Negrão de Lima and Chagas Freitas, back in the times of the State of Guanabara, created first-rate access to the Zona Sul—thanks to the opening and construction of tunnels, elevated roads, and a bridge. Due to insufficient urban planning, the threat existed that this entire region would be occupied in a way similar to Copacabana and the rest of the Zona Sul, whose inadequate planning the city resents even today.

Thanks to the Lucio Costa Plan and to the projects that municipal and state public departments are conducting in the region to provide it with adequate infrastructure, the Baixada de Jacarepaguá grows in a disciplined and harmonious manner. And thanks to business interests that are making important investments here and providing for an aggressive expansion of the workforce, the region will have a brilliant future within the city of Rio de Janeiro. It is projected to reach 250,000 inhabitants.

The standard adopted by the urbanist Lucio Costa to create two principal urban centers—one in Barra and another in Sernambetiba—complete with apartments, offices, commercial buildings, cultural activities and leisure areas, beyond a large planned municipal civic and administrative center, will transform this region into the greatest center of density and expansion in the city over the coming decades.

The Contrasts of Barra

"Favela in Barra? Where?"

This is the reaction of the majority of people when they learn that we are doing a piece on the favelas in Barra. Moreover, in all honesty, we were also surprised by the number of small favela communities we encountered. Or discovered. Because arriving at a favela in Barra is truly a discovery: whether situated between dunes or casuarina trees, they are always so well hidden that it is necessary to have in hand reliable directions to reach the settlements—be it on foot, descending, climbing, crossing rudimentary bridges, or by canoe.

There are eight larger settlements. And these, as incredible as it may seem, are more hidden than the smaller ones. There you find recent arrivals, who moved to Barra in search of work building the complexes planned to provide the middle and upper classes with more comfort than the Zona

Sul can offer. That is, according to the developers. According to Barra's parish priest, however, "this new elitist concept of living well is creating a serious social problem."

"Barra is the neighborhood with the most absolute contrasts," affirms
Brother Constantino Mandarino. "It begins with men who hang from scaf-
folds to construct the middle-class paradises and who then can't even come
close to the lobby. This, added to the fact that these same men have to live
temporarily in builder's shacks or in favelas hidden from the eyes of the large
real estate developers, already creates conditions ripe for social problems."

LONG-STANDING INHABITANTS

"It is in the favelas that you can find the original inhabitants of today's Barra.
They know how to tell the history of the neighborhood from the beginning,
when the bridge that links the Estrada do Joá to the road to Itanhangá was
built by the Army," as Dona Maria Sebastiana Dias, who has lived in Barra
since 1940, remembers.

"At that time, I was already taking in clothes, washing them at the edge
of the canal, then perfectly clean. We leveled all this ground you see, using
the clothes money to pay the dump trucks, transformed this area from a
swamp for crabs, into solid ground for children to play on," she affirms,
pointing in the direction of the edge of the Lagoa da Tijuca canal.

At that time, the obstacles in getting to a simple pharmacy were enormous. Medical assistance was available in canvas tents, once per week, in
the main square.

"But it was much better, ma'am. The doctors had less work with us than
they do today. You know," explains Fátima Viera, "it seems that the water
was better, cleaner. Children didn't get cuts on their legs just from playing
in the water like they do today."

STILL A RURAL ZONE

Due to the fact that the favelas are by and large horizontal, it is common to
find farmyards and even small herds of cattle, there "just to give a little milk
to the children," explained a recent arrival in Piabas, on the 21 kilometer
mark of Avenida das Américas, who talked with us while he cared for his recently born calf. On the Estrada do Itanhangá, around street number 2000,
between many shacks and some fields, the response we obtained when we
asked the name of the favela was another question:

"Favela here, missus? This is all ours, our property," a group of suspicious men affirmed emphatically and, on perceiving the presence of a blue city government Volkswagen, took quick action to remove a dead dog from the pavement.

The others, like the majority of favela inhabitants in Barra, refused to provide information for fear of a possible removal.

"This word 'favela' is a permanent threat for all the inhabitants," affirms Brother Constantino. "They no longer believe anyone, or anything. They have grown tired of politicians' election-eve promises. And now they are suspicious, fearful."

Translated by Shawn Moura

State Terror in the Early 1980s

James J. Blystone and Joaquim de Lima Barreto

*General João Figueiredo (1918–1999) oversaw the gradual drawdown of military au-
thoritarianism during a six-year presidential tenure that began in 1979. Nonetheless, incidents of state terror continued into the early 1980s, as right-wing extremists inside state intelligence services undertook a series of violent acts in hopes of
disrupting the political "opening" (abertura). Some activities were coordinated by
security officials based in Rio, secretly organized under the code name Operação
Cristal (Operation Crystal). Other incidents formed part of an international campaign of countersubversion, coordinated by security forces throughout the Southern
Cone, called Operation Condor. The documents here cover two episodes of state terror contemporaneous with these notorious operations.*

*The first document is a declassified 1980 dispatch by James J. Blystone, regional
security officer (RSO) at the U.S. embassy in Buenos Aires. Blystone references information on the fate of fugitives from an Argentine rebel group named the Montoneros,
two having been kidnapped in Rio with the coordination of Brazilian intelligence.
As the U.S. diplomat takes a global perspective on Argentine security operations
against a Montonero strike force called the Tropas Especiales de Infantería (Special
Infantry Troops; TEI), he reveals Brazil's second city to be a place of central importance for state-sponsored countersubversion in the hemispheric dirty wars of the
1970s and 1980s.*

*The second document here comes from the official investigation into a brazen act
of domestic state terror that unfolded the night of April 30, 1981, at the Riocentro (also
known as Rio Centro) convention center. As twenty thousand spectators gathered
in Jacarepaguá for a musical performance to commemorate International Workers'
Day (see the advertisement pictured), a bomb inside a car driven by security agents
prematurely exploded. The botched bombing killed an army sergeant and wounded
a parachutist who served in the Information Operations Detachment of the Internal
Defense Operations Center (DOI-CODI), an army strike force known for its central
role in political repression. Shortly after the first blast, a second bomb exploded at a
substation supplying power to the convention center. The official investigation into
the bombings was handled through a military police inquest conducted by the First*

Army Command, based in Rio. This technical report, written in the dispassionate voice of the special investigative unit of the Rio State Secretariat of Security, synthesized the facts as they were known immediately after the bombings. Years after the Superior Military Tribunal shelved the case, investigations were reopened in 1999, and additional evidence of military involvement was considered. The case was closed yet again, as the 1979 political amnesty law limited the state's punitive power for past political crimes. Recently discovered documents add further proof to allegations that the bombing was planned by right-wing extremists hoping to extend the scope of the national security state.

DATE: 7 April 1980
REPLY TO ATTN OF: RSO/James J. Blystone, American Embassy, Buenos Aires
Subject: Conversation with Argentine Intelligence Services
TO: The Ambassador
Through: DCM/Maxwell Chaplin

On April 2, 1980, the RSO had a meeting with a member of the Argentine intelligence services to discuss various topics. In the beginning the RSO jokingly asked what had happened to the two Montoneros that disappeared between Mexico and Rio. The source answered that he would tell me but only in the strictest of confidence as this information was top secret. Source stated that Force 601 had captured a Montonero and during the interrogation learned that this Montonero was to have a meeting with the two Montoneros from Mexico and the meeting was to take place in Rio de Janiero [*sic*]. The two Montoneros from Mexico are Horacio Campiglia (warname Peter) and Susana de Binstok. Horacio Campiglia (number 4 or 5 in the Montonero structure) has overall charge of the TEI operations and manages these forces from Mexico. Source advised that during the interrogation they told the Montonero that they had captured, that if he cooperated with the forces he would live. This Montonero knew he was in no position not to cooperate, provided the date and time for the meeting in Rio. The Argentine military intelligence (601) contacted their Brazilian military intelligence counterparts for permission to conduct an operation in Rio to capture two Montoneros arriving from Mexico. Brazilians granted their permission and a special team of Argentines were flown under the operational command of Lt. Col. Román, to Rio aboard an Argentine airforce C130. Both of the Montoneros from Mexico were captured alive and returned to Argentina aboard the C130. The Argentines, not wanting to alert the Montoneros that they had conducted an operation in Rio, utilized an Argentine woman and man to register at a hotel using the false documents obtained from the two captured Montoneros, thereby leaving a trail that the two Montoneros from Mexico had arrived in Rio, registered at a hotel and then departed. These two Montoneros are presently being held at the army's secret jail, Campo de Mayo.

Regarding another subject, the source advised that within the last ten to 15 days security forces had captured alive 12 members of a TEI group which was reinfiltrating the country. Source stated that they had captured some time ago, the Montonero who was the TEI training instructor in Libya (previously reported by the RSO) and who is now working with the Argentine services. This Montonero who is cooperating with the Argentines, received information that 12 members of the TEI would be re-entering Argentina via bus routes from Paraguay, Uruguay, and Brazil. The Argentine security services, with the cooperation of the police set up a trap to capture all 12 members. The police performed documentation and drug control procedures in the bus terminals in Buenos Aires and the intelligence services with the cooperation of this Montonero, were able to apprehend the TEI members arriving by bus. Once the Montonero member was identified, the police would ask to check their documents and advise the individual he would have to go to the police station for routine police matters. Once the Montonero was placed in a car for transportation to a police station, military intelligence took over and transported the Montonero to their secret jail in Campo de Mayo. All 12 members of the TEI group were captured with documentation which indicated that they would place under surveillance 10 targets of the Ministry of Economy and of the 10 targets under surveillance, decide which three would be the easiest to attack. The Argentine intelligence service is upset as none of the 12 TEI members apprehended were armed. Logistically the Argentines are confused as to where and how the Montoneros are obtaining their weapons.

Regarding the TEI, the Argentines have further learned that a group of TEI members are to infiltrate the country to reorganize their political structure, which is a drastic change from previous operations. This for the Argentines signifies a change in the Montonero thinking in that they have decided to give up armed attacks and try to gain their objectives through political means.

On the last subject, the RSO inquired whether the source had any additional information regarding Jarara de Cabezas. Source stated that he hadn't any new information beyond the fact that she is still alive and being held by the Navy. (Note, the RSO was not previously informed that this individual was being held by the Navy, just that she was being held.)

The RSO questioned the source regarding the disappeared who are able to communicate and visit their families. Source advised that this is true. The forces sometimes capture Montoneros but during investigation and interrogation, learn that the individual is a sympathizer, not a full-fledged member or combatant. These individuals, after a period of time are allowed limited liberty by the forces to contact their families until their paperwork is ready. At that time they are sent out of the country. An agreement is made with them that they will not contact their families for a period of months. Source stated that it would be detrimental to the services if these individuals were granted limited liberty and then killed.

THIS INFORMATION IS NOT TO BE USED WITHOUT
PRIOR PERMISSION OF THE RSO.

STATE PUBLIC SERVICE
SECRETARIAT OF PUBLIC SECURITY
D.G.I.E. D.I.G D.A.O.
SPECIAL RESOURCES SERVICE
TECHNICAL REPORT

HISTORY

At 21:45h on 30 April 1981, on orders from "Elmo Zero," Team Falcon 11, consisting of Joaquim de Lima Barreto and Jorge Cortes Rezende, departed for the Rio Centro parking lot in Barra da Tijuca, a location where there had been an explosion with victims.

Arriving at the location, the Team entered in contact with Detective Gilberto from the 16th Police District who was already there and informed the team that there had been two (2) explosions, one in the parking structure and the other in the power substation in Rio Centro. He also related that there had been one fatality in the interior of a car and another victim had been sent to Lourenço Jorge Hospital.

EXAMINATION OF THE 1ST LOCATION

It is an area of approximately 2,000 square meters, with various traffic lanes, used for parking at Rio Centro in Barra da Tijuca.

With the inspection under way, it was determined that there had been a car, make Puma, license plate RJ OT 0297, partially damaged and in its interior, seated in the front-left seat (observer in front of the vehicle), lay the

body of a man. Later identified as being Guilherme Pereira do Rozario, 3rd Sgt. of the Brazilian Army.

The car, built with a fiberglass body, was found laterally stopped, outside the center of the lane, with the forward tires partially turned to the left (as seen in front of the vehicle), more than half of its rear inside the lane and another part on top of the line marking the parking spaces (vertical orientation).

It had its right door (as seen from behind the vehicle) totally destroyed, the left door dislocated, ceiling partially dislocated and crushed, front windshield totally broken, rear windshield jettisoned behind, landing four meters from the vehicle, totally shattered, side windows dislocated along with their respective seals. Driver's side rear window torn off. The front and rear of the vehicle remained intact. The rear lights, right and left, flashed uninterrupted.

The explosion caused the shattering of the front windshield of a Chevette, license plate RJ MY-4609, found parked approximately 10 meters from the location.

Fragments and bent pieces of the clockwork case from an alarm clock were found and collected by this Team outside and near the vehicle.

The DPPS Team, consisting of Dr. Pedro Cardoso and Detective Inspector Magalhães and the team from the Instituto de Criminalística Carlos Éboli with Engineer Pires also arrived at the location.

EXAMINATION OF THE 2ND LOCATION

Examining the 2nd location (Power Substation), along with Dr. Pires from Instituto de Criminalística Carlos Éboli, it was determined that there had been an explosion in the interior and on the ground of said substation. The explosion, which did not result in casualties, produced a crater of approximately 1m (one meter) in diameter by 30cm (thirty centimeters) in depth.

CONCLUSION

After thorough examination of the effects produced, the damage caused and the fragments encountered, we find that the 1st (first) Bomb, exploded in the interior of the vehicle, was *a home-made alarm clock* being part of the same.

The explosive utilized can only be identified through a chemical lab test.

As concerned the 2nd (second) Bomb, the one placed in [the] power substation, did not cause damage because it exploded on the ground, nothing has been found to aid in its identification.

Rio de Janeiro, 3 May 1981

Joaquim de Lima Barreto

Attached: Pieces and fragments of the alarm clock collected at the location

Translated by Shawn Moura

The Consumer Spectacle of BarraShopping

Cora Rónai

The enclosed shopping mall adapted the shopping arcade (galeria) to an age of middle-class suburbanization and consumption. As a privatized space open to the general public, the mall, known by the English-language loanword "shopping," enticed Carioca consumers to set aside worrisome street crime, the hassles of limited parking, and the declining appeal of traditional retail. The dynamic interplay of middle-class relocation to the Zona Oeste and the socioeconomic decline of the urban core further accelerated the shift away from traditional shopping habits, once concentrated downtown. The mall invested heavily in the discrete pleasures of air-conditioning, an abundance of options, and the new.

Rio's first major enclosed mall, Shopping Rio Sul, opened in April 1980. The office-and-retail development in Botafogo brought the city up to speed with São Paulo, where the shopping center concept had grown steadily since the first in the nation opened there in 1966. Another mall, larger than any other in Brazil, opened in Barra da Tijuca in 1981. Surrounded by an ocean of parking lots, BarraShopping was anchored by four large tenants connected by two levels of indoor shopping "streets" decorated with touches of Belle Époque Rio and modernist gardens. BarraShopping would eventually grow into a mega retail complex, with hundreds of shops and restaurants, an ice-skating rink, a movieplex, and adjacent medical offices surrounded by significant engineering feats of automobile infrastructure and wetlands reclamation. Retailers continually refined offerings for meeting basic needs while stoking consumer dreams. Together, merchandiser and consumer justified the large capitalization, speculative real estate development, and corporate licensing necessary for the success of a shopping center built for habits once associated with the public street, small-scale retailers, and walking outdoors.

News coverage about the inauguration of BarraShopping included this story by Cora Rónai (b. 1953), a Carioca journalist, blogger, and author. Rónai adopts a slightly tongue-in-cheek tone, notably in her description of Lojas Americanas, a low-cost, general merchandise retailer founded in Niterói in 1929 that operated in other locales throughout Greater Rio.

"And now, for you, BarraShopping!"

EVERYTHING is ready, ladies and gentlemen, for tomorrow's sensational spectacle: the inauguration of the biggest *shopping center* in all of Brazil. Promotional exaggeration? None whatsoever, a fact rigorously proven with measuring tape: the building is 150 thousand square meters in size. When the entire complex is functioning next year, there will be almost 300 stores to tempt the respectable public's spirit of consumption.

In other words (or other numbers, as you prefer), more than one thousand, five hundred meters of display cases, which could even inspire the creation of revolutionary sporting practices. Who can spend the most in the shortest distance? Or, to the contrary, who can spend the least in the most kilometers?

The shopping center does not want for other playful attractions. There is a carousel for children, an ice-skating rink for the more daring athletes, three movie theaters, and a small children's theater that will be ready in about four months' time. For those who prefer to chat while having some nibbles and a drink, there are many restaurants, luncheonettes, and tea rooms, not to mention the chocolate and candy shops.

The better part of these chow houses are located in a space called Rio Antigo, a type of clearing between the avenues of shops that reproduces an old-fashioned plaza, with a fountain and everything. The chandeliers are in the colonial style, the shop signs similar to each other in their *fin-de-siècle* look; little tables and chairs in the middle of the plaza try to give the consumer (in the most visceral and strict sense of the word), the idea that car horns, robberies, and pollution are things of another world.

And besides, inside the Shopping, they really are. The stores were set up astride one another, forming long avenues; in the middle of these avenues there are gardens designed by [Roberto] Burle Marx, full of ferns, tropical plants, and improvised gardens that cover the spaces that, in the future, will hold escalators linking the shopping center's two floors.

On the lower floor, for now, only the large stores, like Sears, Mesbla, C&A, and Lojas Americanas—whose commercial spaces span both floors— will be open. Smaller stores, which total 140, will only open in 1982. One of the three movie theaters will also be on this floor; it will be inaugurated next November.

"We wanted to create an atmosphere integrated with nature," explains José Isaac Peres, general-manager of Embraplan and president of Multishopping, two companies directly linked to the project. "For this reason we have these plants, all this greenery; for this reason, also, we use natural light. With the skylights that we placed along the entire shopping center, we will only need artificial light after six in the evening. It came out beautiful, didn't it? But that's just what we wanted, a pleasant place, to bring people in just to see it all, to become an attraction."

An economist, forty years old, with four children, Peres began his career when he was twenty-three by founding Veplan, a real estate business; in 1975, he sold off his share and created Embraplan, Multishopping, and Multiplan, three businesses that also function in the real estate sector, but specialize in *shopping centers*. In the last three years, he has opened five *shoppings*, one in Morumbi [São Paulo city], one in Ribeirão Preto [São Paulo state], one in Belo Horizonte [Minas Gerais], the one in Barra da Tijuca and one to be opened in Brasília. Embraplan does all the market research, the plans, projects, all the conceptual work; Multishopping comes in on the investment side. In the case of BarraShopping, it collaborated with other associated businesses: Bozano Simonsen, Esta, and Shell.

For Peres, the principal concern in the realization of a shopping center is its conceptualization phase, when errors come at the modest costs of pencil, paper, and erasers. For this reason, that is the part that takes the most time. Once it is definitively decided what is to be done, construction goes rapidly. Prototype of the successful executive, José Isaac Peres laments not being an architect. Yet he has a hobby: fishing. He can be found on the seashore, rod in hand, every Saturday (when he isn't inaugurating a *shopping center*).

But say what you will, the large, formidable spectacle of BarraShopping isn't exactly integration with nature; it is consumption and the temptations that surround it. There is nothing excessively pretentious in the construction that necessitated about six billion cruzeiros; but the stores!

There are mirrors everywhere, neon signs, colored lights, all the lures possible in the display cases made of chrome, showy plastics, acrylic, wood, and more mirrors. The boutiques distinguish themselves through competition; the display designers play with creativity, rediscover the old, search for the exceptional.

At this party, attracting the public is everything. Even the large stores, which have for years maintained a lack of imagination as a carefully cultivated tradition, enter into the game, and shine like never before. Lojas Americanas, which, from what could be expected, doesn't have much that is not on display, decided to import special miniature carts from Japan so that the clientele can go shopping. The carts are similar to those that are found in supermarkets, but smaller, to be compatible with the moderate size of the merchandise. What fascinating playthings!

The comparisons to Rio Sul, the city's other large shopping center, are inevitable. In brilliance and luxury, in the concentration of famous labels per square meter, the competition is tough: but in space, BarraShopping wins hands down. Its total area represents nothing less than the entire commercial space of Leblon, plus half the commercial space of Ipanema.

"Well," says Peres, "it happens that Rio Sul lives on the past, in a region that was already developed before it was constructed, and is characterized by the lack of space. We live in the present and, especially, the future, since there can already be no doubt that the Rio of the future will be in Barra. Only one more comparison: Barra has an area 20 times larger than all of Zona Sul. Can you imagine what this will be like in 20 years?"

If the attempt to imagine it is difficult, the respectable public shouldn't be ashamed; it's enough to imagine what BarraShopping will be like in one year, when both floors will be operational and all their attractions (including a small marina) will be going at full steam. There will be help with this beginning Tuesday, when it will be open to the public after 10 in the morning; the inauguration tomorrow is reserved for authorities and special guests. In the end, with all the spectacle that it values, the shopping center also has its preview . . . [1]

Translated by Shawn Moura

Note

1. Ellipsis points are original to the article.

A Weekend at Maracanã

João Baptista Figueiredo

The weekend of August 28–29, 1982, was a busy time at Maracanã stadium. That Saturday, Nilson Fanini (1932–2009), the charismatic Protestant pastor who led the First Baptist Church of Niterói (f. 1892), joined Brazilian president João Baptista Figueiredo and other prominent officials on a temporary stage mounted on the playing field. Fanini had aggressively courted the Brazilian political class, and Rio's sporting venues provided space for hosting mass gatherings that combined religious and political messages of engaged, righteous conservatism. Figueiredo, a Roman Catholic, addressed a crowd of Baptists, evangelicals, and lapsed Catholics estimated to number two to three times larger than the forty thousand that Fanini had assembled in 1981 when the governor of Rio state spoke at Maracanãzinho, an indoor venue adjacent to the behemoth stadium. Assembled under the banner "Deus Salva a Família" (God Saves the Family), Fanini's followers listened to the president's prepared remarks on the defense of family in times of change. The day's events were then picked up on Reencontro (Reencounter), Fanini's thirty-minute daily television program.

On Sunday, Maracanã returned to its more familiar usage. An estimated crowd of 122,000 watched Flamengo (f. 1895) handily defeat crosstown rival Fluminense (f. 1902). Flamengo's three goals came quickly, leaving scoreless Fluminense to struggle through the bitter end. Flamenguistas deliriously cheered as their storied team took the lead in the Guanabara Cup tournament. Again, television extended the physical and emotional reach of events taking place at the famed stadium.

The photo here captures the contained emotions of Figueiredo's Saturday remarks. Fanini (left) stands with his wife, Helga, and their daughter behind the president, who speaks with a Bible at his right hand. Joining the president is Arolde de Oliveira (b. 1937; center), an aspiring politician from the Partido Social Democrático, a party closely associated with the military regime. Oliveira was part of a rising slate of Protestant politicians who sought office on the basis of the appeal of embracing Christian family values, moral rectitude, and hard work in bridging the messy transition from authoritarian to democratic rule. In the background, thousands stand in the upper deck, just above the green-and-white banner advertising financial services offered by

"Reencontro no Maracanã em 1982." Photograph by Ismail Cavalcanti. August 28, 1982, Flickr, http://www.flickr.com/photos/32341837@N05/6166485942/.

the Rio state bank, Banerj. Although Brazilian evangelicals are known for emotionally charged church services, the crowd assembled at Maracanã surely shared with the dignitaries an earnestness of purpose, forbearance, and modesty in dress that characterized an ascendant faith movement with rising political ambitions. Such attire contrasted sharply with the bold red-and-black jerseys, shorts or jeans, and casual shoes worn by Flamengo fans, who raucously celebrated the following day with chants, drumming, fireworks, vulgarities, and copious amounts of beer.

Dearest friends

The world today is marked by the acceleration of historical processes. Human societies evolve faster than Man can adapt. Humanity finds itself overwhelmed by changes in traditions and way of life.

This widespread phenomenon is evident in Brazilian society. Our population is growing. The demands of both countryside and city are growing, as are those of Brazilians and residents of the most remote places on Earth. Our knowledge grows and our spirits are tested by experiences previously unknown that today are part of our everyday life.

As the natural foundation of human society, the family prepares the individual—socially and morally—for adult life. As childhood fades, the family presents the surest path to personal fulfillment for men and women to achieve balance and happiness in life. Preserving the broader values of our society and respect for the dignity of human life requires that the family be protected along with the ethical principles it represents. The defense of the family is the duty of every individual and every citizen. It is also one of the responsibilities of the State, and a duty from which my administration has not shied away.

The lessons of Scripture, which "Reencontro" has broadcast for the past seven years, are the surest guide for man to develop his talents in the fields of science, engineering, and economics, without enslaving himself to material advancement and the impositions of consumer culture. In today's tumultuous world, those lessons preserve the fundamental values of the human being, its dignity, and its spirituality.

May God bless our people and allow us to develop, in a climate of peace and security, the open, democratic, and fair society we all seek, rewarding the generosity of the Brazilian heart and its devotion to the ethical principles that inspire our every interaction.

Translated by Andre Pagliarini

The Spider Woman Kisses Rio

Tânia Brandão

Rio de Janeiro has always been a city of voluntary and involuntary exile, and the 1970s and 1980s were a time of transit and resettlement for Spanish Americans displaced by political extremism, economic instability, and social strife. One such figure was Manuel Puig (1932–1990), an Argentine writer who took up residence in the fashionable beachside neighborhood Leblon between 1980 and 1988. Puig's Rio was transnational. He traveled often; much of his time was spent on translations and adaptations of his novels and plays. Yet he still managed to set down local roots, earning permanent residency and enjoying the pleasures of Carioca beaches and men.

Puig's novel El beso de la mujer araña *(Kiss of the Spider Woman), published in 1976, led to international acclaim that included a 1985 feature-length film adaptation directed by Hector Babenco, another Argentine residing in Brazil. Set in a dreadful Buenos Aires prison, the novel is about two archetypes of the Cold War man—a tough-minded political prisoner held on charges of Marxist subversion (Valentín Arregui) and an effeminate, frivolous window-dresser arrested for the corruption of a minor (Luís Molina). Amid innovative tricks of narrative form, the action moves forward in dialogue, as each character passes the time by recounting movie plots. During Puig's residence in Rio, he wrote a Portuguese-language theatrical adaptation of* El beso, *staged in 1981 at the Teatro Ipanema and again in 1983 at the Teatro Glache Rocha, on Avenida Rio Branco. The play could not have been performed in Argentina, where Puig's works were censored for purported moral and political offenses against the highly repressive regime installed in 1976. (By the 1983 staging, that regime was in shambles, having led the Argentine armed forces to humiliating defeat in the Falklands/Malvinas War.)*

Tânia Brandão (b. 1952), a respected Carioca theater critic, reviewed the 1983 performance starring Rubens Corrêa (1931–1996), an actor prominent in Rio's theatrical counterculture, and directed by Ivan de Albuquerque (1932–2001), a pioneer in experimental staging. Brandão's review offers a glimpse of the mind-set and sentiments of progressive-minded theatergoers at the time that the Brazilian military regime was entering its twilight. With large doses of existentialist reflection, Brandão explores what Puig's characters have to say about heroism, masculinity, and agency at a transitional moment when Brazilian society was exiting its prisons of militarism and machismo. The unspoken context was the dismantling of a national security apparatus that had once encompassed torture cells at the army police barracks in Tijuca and the political police headquarters on downtown's Rua da Relação. Puig, Valentin, Molina, and the seductive Spider Woman invited Cariocas to explore the imagination (or delirium) of postauthoritarian life.

When man discovered that he was a minor piece of dust adrift in space, it was a revolution. The dissemination of this truth led to the creation of superheroes. Flying over cities, imposing order in interstellar space, forever triumphant over the greatest villains, the comic book superheroes of the twentieth century are irresistible. Whether in the comics, in movies, or in books, we are drawn to the allure of overcoming, even if only for a moment, the fragile state of the mere mortal. As he follows the exploits of the superhero, the most ordinary man can feel that he is among the most powerful. Such adventures neutralize a feeling of nothingness, making it possible to believe in reason as a superpower. Poetry ceases to be only that and becomes everything.

Certain literary pieces of the twentieth century seek to accomplish the inverse. These seek to discuss man by broaching his essential nothingness. No magic words, no utility belt, certainly no super cars or aerodynamic spaceships. The person is only his body. Or less than that. He cannot even follow the impulse of his body to come and go. He is a prisoner, for example. Reduced to feelings and speech. He is a number.

This is precisely what happens in "The Kiss of the Spider Woman," currently on a new run in Rio at the Teatro Glauce Rocha. The play consists of two conflicting faces of nothingness in our time, a guerrilla and a homosexual. Their names, Valentín and Molina, are laden with meaning. The guerrilla symbolizes man as pure rational impulse, pure intellect. The homosexual—passive, out of the closet—is pure submissiveness and emotion. Through conversation these two characters establish an increasingly deep relationship. By the play's end, they prove that man, in whatever situation, is the opposite of self-centered solitude. Man may be dust, he may be nothingness. But that nothingness is love of one's own species.

The plot begins with a beautiful lighting effect at the back of the stage. Illuminating the back and the top of the stage, the frailty of man is the first sentiment offered by the play. As the spectator watches on, Valentín and Molina demonstrate in fast-paced scenes and with minimal staging how little there is to man and yet how that little bit is the deliverance of the human race. The play is a great showcase of acting. Rubens Corrêa and José de Abreu are exquisite in the interpretation of dialogue. Rubens Corrêa is a consummate actor, of the kind that can summon the most powerful urges of emotion with the slightest gestures. His interpretation of Molina is much beyond the standard. He is moving, flawless. It's a must-see. The play is an actor's showcase.

The script is current, though it is not great. It was adapted by the author from the best-selling novel of the same name. The novel's structure is not entirely theatrical, so the play must rely on recorded lines to construct its plot development. The dialogue is nimble and cinematic. In another theatrical piece, "Quero," also produced by Teatro Ipanema, author Manuel Puig was able to make a more effective translation from text to stage. In "Kiss of the Spider Woman" seduction does not happen clearly as delirium. The character of the guerrilla presents some flaws as constructed by the author. There is a certain sensationalistic, exhortative tone to this recent literature in which political concerns are central. The choice of the characters alone is indicative of this trend. But the handling of the matter in quick, dry scenes neutralizes the possibility of a superficial currentness. The text ends up with a strong tinge of agitprop, to convince the spectator that he is merely the superhero of nothingness.

Director Ivan de Albuquerque happily opts for fast pacing. The excellent timing leads a spiral of emotion toward a complete crescendo. Abreu and the director developed the Valentín role as the perfect counterpoint to the plot's major hero—a homosexual who must take on all manners of danger and suffering for love. It is selfless love, the love of the most complete and profound surrender, the greatest feeling that can define humans. This is the text's most important idea, and what makes the play so powerful. Many in the audience become emotional and cry as they witness such profound affirmation of love in such selfish and troubled times.

The set, trapping the actors in a small box, heightens the sensation that they are reduced to the many manifestations of nothingness. The prison-box imagined by Anísio Medeiros transforms the performers into living marionettes. The scenery moves about at the sides of the stage, allowing for a continuous exploration of this sensation. There is a sense of light and airy realism that suggests a certain elegance. The costumes are perfect. The lighting by Eldo Lúcio is inspired, achieving precise emotional effects. The lighting and music punctuate the transitions between scenes. The story develops through scenes that show the growing affection between two completely different people. In this way, the use of the color red and the playing of the music of Buenos Aires underscore with great joy man's inexorable trajectory toward love.

"Kiss" returns to Rio after a successful tour of various capitals. As we watch this performance, we are taken to see ourselves in our essential insignificance. We are dust, without a doubt. But in the smallest part of ourselves, mixing our commitment to reason and affection, we can yet discover the wondrous chance to be superheroes. Through love, of course, man is able to overcome the worst conditions that life, being the unpredictable game that it is, can impose on him. We are dust, but transcendental dust. The Spider Woman is an artifice that invites each of us to spin our own web of life with what is best in us. And the best of every one of us does not depend on superpowers, rather it is present even in nothingness, even when life seems little more than an inglorious prison.

Translated by Andre Pagliarini

Rallying for Direct Elections

Ricardo Kotscho

Rio's long tradition of mass public demonstrations was evident during the first half of 1984, amid a noisy national debate about the path out of military rule and severe economic contraction. As a cloistered Congress met in Brasília to debate a constitutional amendment about presidential succession, the streets and plazas of downtown Rio filled with citizens calling for the direct election of the next chief executive. The national campaign, known as Diretas Já (Direct Elections Now), included organized mass meetings, pamphleteering, and celebrity appearances. A public rally in favor of direct elections—the largest in Brazilian history to that moment—took place along Rio's central streets on April 10, 1984. In a partial defeat of the more progressive prodemocracy voices, the Congress ultimately charted an indirect path to replace the ailing general João Figueiredo (1918–1999). Tancredo Neves (1910–1985), a politician from Minas Gerais state and an outspoken proponent of the Diretas Já movement, was chosen to serve as the first civilian president since 1964. Tragically, Neves fell gravely ill and subsequently died before taking office.

Ricardo Kotscho (b. 1948), a prize-winning reporter born in São Paulo who worked at several of the most important outlets of print journalism before serving as a campaign aide and press secretary to president Luiz Inácio "Lula" da Silva, published the account excerpted here of the Diretas Já campaigns shortly after the actual events. Writing in a style that combines essayism, investigative journalism, and man-on-the-street reporting, Kotscho captures the broad scope and the dynamic energies mobilized in favor of direct democracy. He makes reference to other mass rallies in the history of Rio, including the ones that preceded the coup of 1964, as well as smaller rallies in favor of direct presidential elections held in state capitals throughout Brazil. He captures the popularity of Milton Nascimento (b. 1942) and Geraldo Vandré (b. 1935), two Brazilian singers whose lyrics became the anthems of generations yearning for democratic freedoms. With optimism and hope, Kotscho points to the various indicators of the exhaustion of the authoritarian model of state governance. The narrative marvels at the transformation of Rede Globo, a mass media conglomerate historically aligned with conservative interests. Such perspectives on the big political players are tempered with a sincere sympathy for a citizenry who found the streets of central Rio to be, yet again, the stage of the Brazilian nation.

Rio's Grand Rally: The Apotheosis

April 11—Rio de Janeiro
A Great Country rediscovers the Nation

"É o Rio de Janeiro, velho . . ." [That's Rio de Janeiro, my old man . . .]

Looking at that crowd, the friend neither said nor was asked anything else. Nothing needed to be said after that embrace between two teary-eyed, grown men in Rio de Janeiro, but above all in Brazil, the stage for the greatest and most fantastic popular demonstration of all time.

After that rally in Rio de Janeiro, the apotheosis of a journey that began timidly in São Paulo with some 15,000 people demanding direct elections in front of Pacaembu stadium in November of last year—only six months ago—nobody will ever dare speak of consensus or negotiation unless it is the consensus around direct elections now, here and now.

If there were any doubts before this historic April 10, let it be known that Brazil has once again confronted its destiny at the great nexus of the human sea that, beginning at Candelária [Church] and flooding Avenida Presidente Vargas, from there to Praça da República and down Avenida Rio Branco to Cinelândia in one direction, and to Praça Mauá in the other, erupting in a single cry that hung in the air for far too long of enough is enough and hope.

Who could have imagined only six months ago that Rio de Janeiro, famous for its beaches, beautiful women, samba schools, and the *jogo do bicho*, nostalgic for the time when it was still the capital of the Republic, would see its people come together in the streets as far as the eye can see, clapping, hands held high, to the beat of the song "Nos bailes da vida" [In the dances of life; 1981], sung by performers such as Milton Nascimento and Wagner Tiso?

"Todo artista tem de ir / onde o povo está . . ." [Every artist must go / where the people are . . .]—besides the artist, they might sing of the worker, teacher, liberal professional, the unemployed, businessman, white-collar worker, farmer, student, journalist, poet; people of all colors, sizes, anxieties, and illusions who yesterday released their righteous indignation as well as the certainty that, despite everything else, there is still pride in being Brazilian.

It is a pity that [recently deceased, pro-redemocratization senator] Teotônio Vilela and all those who have fallen along the way were not alive to see how it was worth it to believe, to resist, to keep pushing until the day that we could no longer be held down. Brazil went back twenty years in the span of just a few hours, able to look forward once again, its future in its own hands, its people in the streets yearning to forgive but never forget.

One handmade banner created by an unnamed Brazilian among the mass of people, held high alongside thousands of others, perhaps captures the spirit of what all those people had to say better than the weary journalist's sentimentality: "Se alguns pediram 64, agora todos pedem diretas" [If some called for (the coup of) 64, today all are calling for direct elections].

Ironically, a documentary film called *Jango*, directed by Silvio Tendler, is currently playing in Rio, with long lines at the movie theaters ever since its premiere. Without discussing the merits of either the film or the protagonist, I am after all neither a critic nor a political commentator, I can say only that this coincidental meeting of past and present is pointing to a future that is close by, around the next corner, as if the people were carrying out an autopsy on the live body of a regime that did not work and that nobody, as of right now, wants to see continue.

To those who missed the joy of being here or of seeing it on television yesterday, only one thing needs to be said: at six o'clock in the evening no major political figure had arrived, no governors, and the artists were the same as always, yet the rally in Rio had already gotten its message across. Even if no one had used the microphones at the lectern, even if not a single word had been uttered, this period of Brazilian life marked by "64" would still have been buried forever in the eyes of each and every person, by the confetti raining down, by the parties in the streets and on balconies of all the buildings on Avenidas Presidente Vargas and Rio Branco, by the green and yellow that waved more than on any independence day celebration in recent memory.

Brazil was no longer the same even before the first national leader began speaking, when the sun set in the limpid Rio sky of that Tuesday afternoon that nobody will forget. The speakers' platform—there was another behind it that ended up serving as a waiting room—was invaded by journalists from Rede Globo who, from one minute to the next, wanted to see, hear, and cover everything having to do with the rally. The boycott by the most powerful television station, accompanied by almost all major press outlets through these many months, crumbled before the mass of people, who no longer need a formal invitation to know where they ought to go.

It is better this way than in the rallies at the outskirts of Brazil where one would not find a single journalist until a few weeks ago to chat with and kick around estimates over the number of attendees in the streets, as reporters tend to do.

It took a while but it was nice to once again see journalists from all the newspapers, radio stations, and television channels covering our country's most important events.

For a moment, seeing that whole celebration, Rede Globo announcing on special live broadcasts of "Jornal Nacional" from Candelária that the rally had already amassed over one million people, my mind turned to the videotaped images of other rallies in Teresina, São Luís, Macapá, Rio Branco, Cuiabá, where this whole apparatus was nonexistent, with smaller crowds due to the size disparity with Rio de Janeiro, but where the same expressions could be seen, the same yearning, the same purity of believing in something to fend off despair.

Yes, the campaign for direct elections carried on, paying no mind to the cynicism of so many allies who may have appreciated the party but had little faith in a happy ending. Until the moment when, among so many luminaries of the opposition, Eduardo Portela, president Figueiredo's former minister of education, famous for an utterance while falling from a horse, was spotted at the rally. Congressmen of the Partido Democrático Social are applauded just for being on the platform even though nobody really pays much attention to what they have to say. Indeed, the impression one had from walking through that multitude was that nobody was interested in listening so much as in talking. There were fifty-two official speakers but hundreds of thousands on the ground spoke nonstop, as if it were a Mass with the liturgy handed out at the entrance to the church.

General Ernesto Geisel, who works at Norquisa [Nordeste Química], in the Banco Econômico building (the same as his minister Calmon de Sá, who left Banco do Brasil for the Ministry of Industry and Commerce due to the mysterious case of an administrative check), does not know what he missed. From his window right in front of Candelária he could see, if he was at work yesterday, a Brazil that he could not imagine in his time as president—a Brazil with dignity.

In the hours before this grand affirmation of national pride, however, the climate in Rio was more tense than festive. Everyone knew something historic was about to happen, but many feared that moment not on account of the people, of course, but for what the survivors of the Rio Centro episode might attempt next in a final desperate act to stop the national will from becoming reality.

The agents of the federal police stationed at the Hotel Guanabara on balconies with optimal vantage points of the rally, following orders from Minister of Justice Abi Ackel, are the best witnesses the bunkered inhabitants of the Palácio do Planalto will have when they return from their vacations to hear about what took place on this Tuesday, April 10, 1984, in the city of Rio de Janeiro. But if they want to know sooner, reading this newspaper, they can be certain: it was nice to see—Brazil has never seen anything like it. In the streets of Rio de Janeiro, this great Country once again made itself into a Nation.

When everyone joined hands at the end of the rally, on the platform and in the streets, to sing the national anthem, Rio de Janeiro had returned to being the Rio of Brazil, cheerful and spunky, serious when necessary but always generous. And then the crowd went away, beneath a light rain tasting of new life, boldly singing the musical verses of Geraldo Vandré, which had become an anthem in its own right: "Vem / vamos embora / que esperar não é saber / quem sabe faz a hora / não espera acontecer" [Come / let's go / he who waits is not knowing / he who knows makes the moment / not waiting for it to happen].

Translated by Andre Pagliarini

A Summer Up in Smoke

Chacal

In August 1987, the cargo ship Solana Star took on twenty-two tons of marijuana while docked in Singapore. Drug traffickers intended to offload some of the illicit cargo near Rio before proceeding to the United States. When the crew learned of a collaborator's arrest, they tossed thousands of vacuum-sealed aluminum cans packed with marijuana into the Atlantic, about one hundred nautical miles from the southeastern Brazilian coast. Fishermen and beachgoers soon spotted the discarded cans floating in the waves. By January 1988, at the height of summer in the Southern Hemisphere, "hunting for cans" became a popular pastime for Rio's beach crowd. Many Cariocas who lived through that summer still remember a city buzzing with irreverent excitement.

Ocean currents may have carried cans as far south as Santa Catarina. Yet what soon became known as the Verão da Lata (Summer of the Can) was a distinctly Rio phenomenon. Nowhere else in Brazil did so many urban dwellers socialize at the beach, and the idea of marijuana providentially washing ashore resonated deeply. Some observers attribute the shared excitement to the last gasp of hippie counter-culture. Others see it as the product of the combination of a city's iconoclastic self-image, the prevalence of drugs in youth culture, and a collective sense of relief in the recent consolidation of democracy. Enduring memories of the Verão da Lata were animated by skepticism toward drug interdiction. What better way to parody and criticize corrupt and ineffectual policing than to allude to that event in which the people joyfully partook of the bounty of the sea while the bumbling police managed to recover only 150 cans?

In 1995, the Carioca singer Fernanda Abreu (b. 1961) released Da Lata (From the Can), a hit album containing two tracks that make direct references to the Verão da Lata. One track, "A Lata" (The Can), is credited to Abreu and to Chacal (Ricardo de Carvalho Duarte, b. 1951), a Carioca poet involved in the bohemian counterculture and happenings of the 1970s. Abreu's musical interpretation combined samba-funk, Brazilian Popular Music, and rap. Chacal's poem of the same title (which follows here) playfully riffs on that summer of 1987–1988, when aluminum cans of pot circulated in the tough alleys of the Borel and Tabajaras favelas, in the Cruzada São

Sebastião housing complex in Leblon, and in Marambaia, the paradisiacal coastline of far southwestern Rio. Rhythmic references to percussion styles and to kicking the can invoke the improvised musical instruments made out of cheap found objects often used by gatherings of poor musicians. The phrasing "vira lata" plays on slang for a stray mutt. Filled with local references, the poem highlights another character-istic aspect of Carioca culture: its inventive and liberal use of language. The Verão da Lata introduced a piece of local slang, "da lata" ("of" or "about" the can), to denote something of high quality.

"The Can"

In the darkness of deep night
In the silence of the hush
Suddenly a kick
In the rhythm
The drumming started up
And the hollow sound of this can
It was a funk dance over in Lapa
It was the Wailers in Jamaica
It was a jam session in Nigeria
It was the *morro* readied for battle

Say it kick the can flip the can
Say it by hand say it by foot say what you'll say

In the can
The black dude says
And it does not stick in his throat
Finally, good man
It's the streetcar, it's the train
From Estácio to Pavão
There's no space for anyone
From Borel to Tabajaras
In Mangueira, in Cruzada
Already at the Morro Dona Marta
From the can
Emerges the genie of smoke
That came from the sea to the sand
A sure good thing came up at the beach

To set one's hair on end
From the crew that sets things on fire
In the pan, up in smoke
Frying pan *agogô*
Grumari, Arpoador
From *macumba* to *macumbada*
In the Restinga da Marambaia

Say it kick the can flip the can
Say it by hand say it by foot say what you'll say

All power goes astray
All power kicks the can
All the power to the can

[No fundo da madrugada
No silêncio na calada
De repente foi chutada
Na batida
Começou a batucada
E o som seco dessa lata
Era um funk lá na Lapa
Era o wailers na Jamaica
Um pagode na Nigéria
Era o morro em pé de guerra

Diz na lata chuta lata vira lata
Diz na mão diz no pé diz que diz

Na lata
Nego diz
E não entala
Demorou, sangue bom
É o bonde, é o trem
Do Estácio ao Pavão
Não tem pra ninguém
Do Borel ao Tabajaras
Na Mangueira, na Cruzada
Já no morro dona Marta
Da lata

Sai o gênio da fumaça
Que do mar veio pra areia
Coisa boa deu na praia

Pra fazer a cabeleira
Da galera que incendeia
Na panela, no vapor
Frigideira agogô
Grumari, Arpoador
Da macumba à macumbada
Na restinga marambaia

Diz na lata chuta lata vira lata
Diz na mão diz no pé diz que diz

Todo o poder vira lata
Todo o poder chuta lata
Todo o poder para lata]

Translated by Daryle Williams

Female Planet

Claudia Ferreira

Rio de Janeiro was the host city for the 1992 United Nations Conference on Environment and Development (colloquially known as the Earth Summit or ECO-92) and the Fórum Global, a parallel assembly of international organizations representing civil society. The official proceedings of the Earth Summit took place at Riocentro, a massive convention center in Jacarepaguá. The Fórum Global assembled in temporary pavilions erected along the Parque do Flamengo. A huge contingent of soldiers and police maintained tight security at both venues.

A standout at the Fórum Global was Planeta Fêmea (Female Planet), an assembly of women's and feminist organizations seeking to incorporate the resolutions of the World Women's Congress for a Healthy Planet (Miami, 1991) into the values and action plans to come out of the Earth Summit. Planeta Fêmea became a space for women to articulate their views on the paths toward sustainable development; it was a space for an open critique of the official Rio Declaration on Environment and Development. Various events held at the pavilions pointed to the many downsides of the multilateral environmentalism: the perpetuation of gender inequalities, the displacement of families in green energy projects, and the threats to traditional foodways in the commercialization of sustainable farming. The activists assembled at Planeta Fêmea also challenged the Rio Declaration's silence on militarism and nuclear testing.

Claudia Ferreira, a prize-winning Carioca photojournalist noted for her documentation of global women's social movements, captured the many faces of Planeta Fêmea. In the first photo shown here, a male soldier stands watch near the pavilions of the Fórum Global. In the second, a nun sits alone, quietly watching the conference proceedings in a telecast over a handwritten sign that reads "WHY MILITARISM HAS TO GO." In the third, Benedita da Silva (center), an Afro-Carioca social worker and city council member who would eventually rise to be governor of the State of Rio de Janeiro, participates in a panel discussion with other women. In the fourth photo, two women wearing traditional garb from Africa and South Asia share a light moment outside the pavilion. In all these images, the viewer notes how ECO-92 meant many things for women attendees. The Earth Summit allowed Rio to be a stage for global exchanges of feminism and environmental advocacy. In addition, ECO-92 presented opportunities for Carioca women, like Ferreira and Benedita (as da Silva is commonly known), to further their careers as public figures. In such contexts, Rio was a venue for the articulation of women's understandings of their place in global development and local politics.

Untitled. Photograph by Claudia Ferreira. Collection: "Conferência das Nações Unidas para o Meio Ambiente e Desenvolvimento / ECO 92—Fórum Global / Planeta Fêmea." Used by permission of Claudia Ferreira.

Untitled. Photograph by Claudia Ferreira. Collection: "Conferência das Nações Unidas para o Meio Ambiente e Desenvolvimento / ECO 92— Fórum Global / Planeta Fêmea." Used by permission of Claudia Ferreira.

Untitled. Photograph by Claudia Ferreira. Collection: "Conferência das Nações Unidas para o Meio Ambiente e Desenvolvimento / ECO 92—Fórum Global / Planeta Fêmea." Used by permission of Claudia Ferreira.

Untitled. Photograph by Claudia Ferreira. Collection: "Conferência das Nações Unidas para o Meio Ambiente e Desenvolvimento / ECO 92—Fórum Global / Planeta Fêmea." Used by permission of Claudia Ferreira.

From Favela to Bairro

Fernando Cavalieri

In the 1980s, the synergistic effects of a transition to civilian democratic rule and the passage of a new federal constitution shifted the grounds of debate about the appropriate ways to remedy the very real problems associated with the range of irregular and unlicensed land occupations lumped together under the term "favela." Secular and religious-based social movements promoted the idea that the favela should be understood as a creative, imperfect solution to long-standing urban challenges. The recognition of shantytowns as an integral part of the city, rather than threatening spaces at the margins, developed alongside affirmations that all the city's residents had equal rights to the city. Favela advocates led calls to strengthen citizenship among the urban poor. Out of these reformist initiatives evolved municipal policies in urban development and popular housing aimed at improving the quality of life for the working poor through planned urbanizations in favelas. Core projects included the extension of educational facilities, basic sanitation services, and child care. Such innovations built on a gradual engagement between Rio's favelas and municipal administrations, brokered by various actors, notably the public officials associated with Rio state governor Leonel Brizola's Partido Democrático Trabalhista, the Catholic Church, and the daily O Dia (f. 1951).

A generation of city officials, including sociologist Fernando Cavalieri, participated in the paradigm shifts in city–favela–favelado relations. The experiences of Cavalieri and others form part of an oral history project about the history of urbanism in Rio that was conducted by the Centro de Pesquisa e Documentação de História Contemporânea do Brasil, a pioneering research center within the Fundação Getúlio Vargas, located in Botafogo. These excerpts from Cavalieri's interview highlight two initiatives: Projeto Mutirão (the Volunteer-Collective Project) and Programa Favela-Bairro (the Favela-Neighborhood Program). The latter, funded by a 1995 Inter-American Development Bank loan of US$180 million, targeted about 25 percent of Rio's favela dwellers across seventy-three communities, including Andaraí in the Zona Norte.

Cavalieri's recollections emphasize the challenges faced by reform-minded public administrators working to adapt to the realities of favelas, their residents, and innovative forms of organizational activity, including residents' associations. The logistical, technical, and political stressors were substantial. Fundamentally, observes Cavalieri, the projects required state and municipal officials to grapple with the problem of strengthening the democratic character of the city.

Projeto Mutirão

In 1981, the Secretariat of Social Development began a pilot project in Rocinha to develop certain targeted urbanization initiatives. Another program, Projeto Urbanização Comunitária/Mutirão, was created that same year. Its work in the favelas was intended to be broader in scope. Members volunteered their time on the weekends, but earned some wages during the week when they helped out in various public works going up in the favelas. The city donated material and technical assistance, but the initial projects were pretty limited in scale. The number of communities served was also small. . . . But Projeto Mutirão grew significantly, especially by 1983 or 1984. It received more resources, its budget increased, it expanded its reach. But it still remained mostly focused on a few types of activity, principally the construction of sewer systems and enhancing accessibility: improvements to stairs and streets and the installation of concrete pavement. There was very little headway with aqueducts to bring water to homes. . . . Mutirão was designed to be rooted in the community and in resident associations, even down to using locally sourced labor, a specific requirement of the program. . . . Ultimately, Mutirão grew quite a bit in the area of nurseries and preschools, meeting a significant and vital need. . . . Over ten years of action the project acquired a critical mass of specialists—a dedicated team of engineers, architects, and social workers who really understood favelas. They were able to devise alternative technical solutions to what we might call the insuperable problems facing the favelas, even with the limited resources they had available.

Programa Favela-Bairro

So, Favela-Bairro, along with the project to survey neighborhood land into parcels, emerged from the Grupo Executivo de Programas para Assentamentos Populares (GEAP). The GEAP was an old dream many of us in city government had always maintained to create an entity composed of representatives from diverse agencies that could debate ideas and establish parameters for action in the favelas. . . . GEAP came to include various public officials or their representatives, quickly gaining momentum. It had an audience with the mayor, who approved its first official documents. Those were regulations for urbanization, planned initiatives of the housing department, and so on. A temporary housing secretariat was put in place, and things evolved from there. Later a permanent secretariat was created by law, in December of 1994. But before all of that, Favela-Bairro was getting under way, though in embryonic form. It was listed in the *Diário Oficial*, together with the other programs of the housing secretariat. So what happened? With the participation of the city as well as the Institute of Brazilian Architects, we held public forums on ideas and methods for urbanizing favelas. We opened a competition, selecting fifteen teams to work in twenty-three favelas. Then the Andaraí community, where an early internal pilot project like Favela-Bairro was already in place, joined forces with us. The winning teams were contracted to implement their projects. That began a new phase of action in the favelas, from an urban planning perspective. Instead of the way it had been—as we used to call it, piecemeal, in which an engineer would show up and say, "Well, I'll lay some asphalt over there, and build some stairs over here." No, there was now a comprehensive vision of the favela as neighborhood. This was a first major difference.

With this it became possible to get a loan from the Inter-American Development Bank. . . . Of course, that was a long process of negotiations and discussions, of revisions and improvements, of hearing from lots of consultants. The program really evolved through all that. I'd call it a major turning point, and another important distinction. We established a methodology different from that of Mutirão, and it kept growing and getting better over time. It became a source for government policy that I long thought, and still do think, is the definitive approach to favelas. . . .

The program's philosophical pretexts are also fundamental. The principal one is the idea of integration with the city. The favelas should be consolidated, their areas of risk diminished. These neighborhoods already make up part of the daily life of the city, and their residents have constructed an important, valuable private patrimony there—but it's public patrimony as well, since the public has contributed to it. Many local governments have contributed significant public investment, even if it hasn't always been consistent or well organized. No one speaks anymore of reforming, modifying, or transforming the favelas. . . .

The new paradigm is to take advantage of the city as it is, with its own dynamics, and build on that, without razing everything and trying to reconstruct it from the ground up. This is the main concept, to create that integration through urban elements including a functional street system, even maybe starting with just an outer ring of roadways that allows for people to enter and exit by car. All the smaller interior streets should link up with that ring. There should be new spaces of public integration, which typically include plazas and areas for sports and leisure. These would be intended not only for the local residents but for people from adjacent neighborhoods. This sort of public infrastructure, the sporting equipment, is extremely necessary. Look, there's a soccer field in every single favela, but soccer is played by adult males. Favela-Bairro had some serious difficulty convincing the community that the soccer field would still exist, but we could do other things such as parks or playgrounds for young kids, leisure areas for the elderly, and even basketball and volleyball courts. The methodology emphasizes greater social inclusion, an inclusion that goes beyond the question of sports. Even sporting activity has to be rethought in terms of just occupying physical space. There is now a series of organized sporting activities in the neighborhoods, with a very important goal: to try to attract young people to healthy pursuits, to get them away from the clutches of drug use or drug trafficking. Another significant dimension of this is the daycare centers, which are intended to both offer better service to the children and allow their mothers to keep working.

And clearly—I didn't say this before, but it should be obvious—another major focus of the program was developing the infrastructure for basic sanitation: water, sewage, storm drains. And other services. There was hardly any public lighting, trash collection, maintenance of the slopes, or pedestrian circulation systems. Favelas did not have real sidewalks, although some roads had narrow footpaths where pedestrians could try to avoid cars and motorcycles. Summing it all up, the concern of Favela-Bairro was to create a city out of what was already there—to create an urban space that kept its own unique characteristics, but with all the formal elements of an organized city that facilitate the movement of people, and foster social engagement.

Translated by Jerry D. Metz

Adeus 2-2-6!

Paulo Mussoi

In 1975, the telephone services for Rio city and state were merged into a single state-owned enterprise, Telerj. High demand for new phone service and the need to upgrade existing lines continuously outstripped capacity for two decades. As service progressively declined, Telerj won the ignoble distinction of being the worst performer in national customer satisfaction surveys. By the early 1990s, the company averaged 180 days to transfer a line; a repair service call could take two months. Installations could take years. The overheated secondary market for new lines priced many lower-income households out of phone services. Limited supply also constrained service in neighborhoods experiencing rapid growth, notably the Zona Oeste. For those who had landline phones and for users of the iconic public phones known as orelhões (big ears), dropped and misdirected calls became the norm.

By November 1996, frustrations with deteriorating phone service had prompted Rômulo Fritscher (1962–2010), a Carioca photographer and videographer who owned an internet school and webpage-building service, to launch a website called "Eu Odeio a Telerj" (I hate Telerj). The site quickly became a forum for Fritscher and thousands of fellow Cariocas to vent about the poor services offered by "Telerda"—a word play on "Telemerda" (Tele-shit)—that they found left them second-class citizens. In their criticisms of the abysmal service provided by many publicly owned enterprises, Fritscher's website and sister blogs represented new forms of popular democracy in the internet age, particularly the power of consumer rights movements. Telerj tried to improve services, offering new telephone exchanges, investing in cellular service, and making hapless forays into prepaid internet service. Another gesture toward improved service was to retire the archaic three-digit analog exchange "2-2-6." In its place came the almost fashionable digital prefix 539. This Jornal do Brasil article covers, with a touch of ironic nostalgia, the death of 226, the target of numerous complaints on Fritscher's website.

In 1998, privatization of phone services in Brazil took the maligned Telerj out of business; it was replaced by Telemar. Telerj's cellular services were absorbed into another company now known as Vivo. Although telephone and internet services in Rio *continued to be the object of online complaints, capital investment in fixed telephone lines, expansion of cellular service, the rise of private internet providers, including satellite and cable, and more savvy customer service departments eventually did in the need for "Eu Odeio a Telerj." Yet the website (now defunct) still holds folkloric status in the memories of Cariocas who lived through the difficult era of neoliberal privatizations.*

Dois, dois, meia, cala a boca e não chateia [Two, two, six, shut up and don't be a pain]. For every Telerj customer still suffering with the precarious services of Rio's worst phone exchange, the nonsensical childish chant has made sense for some time. Among this unfortunate group there is not a single person who does not anxiously await the moment when the 226 prefix will be silenced forever. Especially since talking on that line, for several years, has not been its strong point. "Knowing that the phone number is going to change renews my hope. I have had no greater difficulty in my life during the last few years than speaking on the telephone," declares philologist and academic Antônio Houaiss.

The owner of an authentic 226 exchange for no less than 27 years, Houaiss today is one of the line's oldest users. Yet he still recalls a time when picking up the phone was not an adventure with an unpredictable ending. "Not so long ago, my phone worked well. Over the last five years problems have mounted. Today, I sometimes spend an entire day trying to make a call but I cannot," he complains.

Relief

Another wordsmith, however, had more luck: the venerable journalist Barbosa Lima Sobrinho, who had the same phone number in his Botafogo home for over thirty years, was among the first to receive the new 539 prefix. The scholar could not speak to the *Jornal do Brasil* but, according to one of his assistants, the change was "a relief." The same relief is already felt by former mayor Saturnino Braga, model Monique Evans, comedian Bussunda [Cláudio Besserman Vianna] and musician Daniel Gonzaga, son of Gonzaguinha, all happy owners of new digital extensions after years of suffering with the hated 226.

The change in prefix also excited singer Marcelo D2, of the group Planet Hemp. "Finally, I can access the internet," he exclaimed, on hearing the news. According to D2, his problematic 226 phone line forced him to keep unopened the box containing a new modem he bought to connect his personal computer to the net. "If there is nothing worse than 226 for simply talking on the phone, imagine trying to connect to the internet. I preferred to wait so as not to become even more irritated," he explains.

Leader

The internet, in fact, is where one finds the most detailed portrait of the 226 line's inefficiency. On the already famous home page of *Eu odeio a Telerj*, created by designer Rômulo Fritshner [*sic*], the prefix leads the rankings of most complaints. "I don't have any concrete statistics on this, but of the more than one thousand emails that I've received since the site was created, the vast majority are complaints about 2-2-6. Thank God that will soon be over," he exclaimed.

Translated by Andre Pagliarini

In Praise of a Modernist Monument

Gilberto Gil

The Palácio Gustavo Capanema, a modernist skyscraper in the heart of downtown Rio, is among the most pioneering structures built in the twentieth century. The main building is a sixteen-story tower covered by glass curtain walls. Row on row of moveable louvers (brise-soleil) protect the building's occupants from the intensity of the tropical sun. The tower stands on columns (pilotis) that open a ground-level plaza to the free circulation of pedestrians. A secondary structure, low-slung and perpendicular to the skyscraper, encloses the plaza. Against the muted colors of stone and concrete glisten blue-and-white ceramic tiles executed by Cândido Portinari (1903–1962), a Brazilian modernist. Tropical gardens grace a roof garden built atop an exhibition space surrounded by a ribbon of glass. Originally constructed to serve as the headquarters of the Ministry of Education and Health (see the photo here), the Palácio Gustavo Capanema is a testament to the remarkable confluence of domestic and international currents in modernist art, architecture, and urbanism; modern techniques in steel-frame construction; and state cultural programming during the Estado Novo dictatorship (1937–1945).

Gustavo Capanema (1900–1985), an enthusiastic reformer from Minas Gerais who served as minister of education and health between 1934 and 1945, nurtured the intellectuals who were drawn to the design competition for the ministerial headquarters. Capanema's protection facilitated the collaboration between Brazilian architects Lucio Costa (1902–1988) and Oscar Neimeyer (1907–2012) and the radical Swiss-French urbanist Le Corbusier (1887–1965). In rewarding the modernists, Capanema marginalized competing currents in Brazilian architecture, especially neocolonialism and eclecticism, whose practitioners also sought state favor in public architecture. At its inauguration in 1944, the ministry edifice stood as a triumph for the proponents of Brazilian variants of the International Style.

In 2003 and again in 2007, minister of culture Gilberto Gil (b. 1942), an Afro-Bahian musician of international renown, delivered remarks, reproduced here, on the enduring innovation of the building, renamed for Capanema. On both occasions, Gil summarized the list of notable architects, artists, landscape designers, and engineers who collaborated on the project. In his 2003 remarks, he made special *mention of poet Carlos Drummond de Andrade (1902–1987), who wrote on a spectacular yet unusual workplace in which the interior design and furnishings were intended to induce new forms of disciplined white-collar productivity. In 2007, Gil singled out the work of the Instituto do Patrimônio Histórico e Artístico Nacional (National Historical and Artistic Heritage Institute; IPHAN) and its special relationship to this edifice, which had been designated a national heritage site in 1948 and was then under consideration for inclusion in the UNESCO World Heritage List. He concludes his 2007 remarks on a note that demonstrates a particular sensibility toward the cultural needs of the people of Rio. In hopeful optimism, the federal minister envisions a world in which Cariocas find in the monumental structure the inspiration for cultural sustenance, engagement with the state, and bold innovation capable of producing other local spaces of international distinction.*

Remarks on the Capanema Building, February 6, 2003

> Days of adapting to the intense, natural light that replaced artificial bulbs during the day; to the short wooden dividers there in the place of walls; to the standardized furniture that once catered to the fantasies of directors or the weight of provisions. New habits are rehearsed . . . The room they put me in did not work out well. The day before yesterday I moved to a place with better accommodations. From the wide windows of the tenth floor the Bay is revealed, beating back the grey mass of buildings. Down below, in the Ministry's suspended garden, Celso Antônio's statue of a nude woman, reclined, holding between her stomach and thighs some water from the last rainfall which the birds come to drink, a charming conversion of the granite's sex into a natural fountain. The unforeseen utility of works of art.

My friends:

Those words, written by Carlos Drummond de Andrade in *O Observador no Escritório* [The observer in the office; 1985], recount the first days of April 1944, when minister Gustavo Capanema and his staff moved into what was then called the Ministry of Education and Health headquarters. It is fascinating to hear Drummond write not just of the natural light that flooded the offices, but of the spatial sensation of being in a radically new building, and the subsequent rehearsal of new habits. That is the gift, the virtue and the truth of great architecture. Built space being able to renew the way we experience forms and habits.

Yet this edifice designed by Lúcio Costa and Oscar Niemeyer, based on Le Corbusier's original sketches, is not solely that. The building is founda-

"Aspectos do edifício-sede do Ministério da Educação e Saúde, bem como dos seus arredores." Photographer unknown, c. 1943–1956. Arquivo Gustavo Capanema (GC), foto 496_22. Courtesy of Centro de Pesquisa e Documentação da História Contemporânea do Brasil / Fundação Getúlio Vargas, Rio de Janeiro.

tional, the mark of Brazil's and the world's new architecture, a landmark of invention in Brazilian cultural history. And it offers us fundamental lessons for the moment that we are living.

Here is clear proof of our capacity to creatively assimilate international languages, imprinting upon them our own original mark to a point that we outdo foreign achievements. Because the truth is that this building, an example of tropical boldness and refinement, caught the world centers of culture by surprise. That being the case, I cite Lúcio Costa himself:

"The building constructed as the old headquarters for the Ministry of Education and Health appeared as if out of nowhere, and its serene beauty was surprising when, after the war, the world became aware of its remarkable presence. The defining example of the new Brazilian architecture was revealed in a similar way, to an international standard of architectural reconceptualization that demonstrated that our native ingenuity is up to the task of learning from foreign experiences while no longer serving as an eternal ideological impersonator, but in fact anticipating them in actual achievements."

Another lesson that this grouping and this building affords us resides in the alliance that was woven between the traditional and the innovative. That is not what happened in Europe, where groups divided themselves, as adversaries, in the name of a purported dichotomy between memory and invention—and the pamphleteer Le Corbusier wanted to make a *tabula rasa* of the past. The Instituto do Patrimônio—created by a handful of young innovators, under the leadership of Rodrigo Melo Franco de Andrade—was housed right here, in this cutting-edge building. Lúcio Costa worked for the same government agency. We can therefore say that this group had one foot in Ouro Preto and one in the future, which would one day come to be called Brasília.

This building also teaches us the need for a sense of responsibility in urban construction. Social and cultural responsibility. Because every building is important, rising into the landscape, profoundly marking the city's body with its physical dimension, with its symbolic weight, and with its message. That is why we should look upon every proposal to build gigantic structures with critical reservation, those large in proportions but culturally superfluous, devoid of meaning.

Finally, I would like to recall the historical context in which this building was erected. It was constructed during the Second World War, thus generating an eloquent counterpoint to the war. While technology in Europe was being used to destroy, in Brazil it was being used to build. And let that also serve as a lesson today, as the prospect of a new war appears ever closer. May technology, for us, always be a constructive instrument for peace.

After all, it is necessary to show Rio and the entire nation the meaning of this building. It is necessary to inform, illuminate, and use its beautiful spaces. To recover what is needed from its installations. That is something the Ministry of Culture will do such that this edifice may be reborn in the city for the heart of the nation.

Remarks on the Inauguration of Information Kiosks
at the Palácio Gustavo Capanema, April 13, 2007

His Excellency Carlos Fernando de Andrade, regional representative of the Instituto do Patrimônio Histórico e Artístico Nacional; Elza de Souza, representative of the Ministry of Education; Adair Rocha, head of the Ministry of Culture's regional representation in Rio de Janeiro state; all present dignitaries.

To speak of this building, this edifice, this palace of arts and utopias, goes beyond the subject of modern Brazilian architecture; we venture toward the territory of global renown.

Designed during the tenure of minister Gustavo Capanema to house the former Ministry of Education and Health, the sixteen-story building inaugurated by President Getúlio Vargas was the first modernist building of its size anywhere in the world.

It takes up an area, along with its gardens designed by Burle Marx, of 27,536 square meters.

The project of designing the Palácio Gustavo Capanema, drawing from the early studies conducted by Le Corbusier, involved a number of esteemed architects including Lúcio Costa, Oscar Niemeyer, Affonso Eduardo Reidy, Jorge Machado Moreira, Carlos Leão and Ernany de Vasconcelos. Under the supervision of engineer Emílio Baumgart, the building was erected between 1937 and 1943. Gneiss was used to coat the gables, per the suggestion of Le Corbusier himself. The glazed wall tiles—a traditional element of Brazilian architecture—used to sheath the surfaces and walls at ground level were designed by Cândido Portinari. Both inside and out, the building possesses other works of art representative of the modernist movement in our country to be appreciated in the mosaics, paintings and murals by Portinari, and sculptures by Bruno Giorgi, Vera [Adriana] Janacopoulus, and Celso Antônio. The roof garden is another standout, created by the aforementioned landscape artist Roberto Burle Marx.

This building became an icon of world architecture and represents a watershed in the history of civil construction.

Preserved as a national historic landmark since 1948, the Palácio Gustavo Capanema could very well be Brazil's first building recognized by UNESCO as a World Heritage Site. The request, with over two thousand signatures, was submitted to the Ministry of Culture by the Institute of Brazilian Architects on August 5, 2003.

More than a monument, the Palácio Gustavo Capanema is a center equipped with various cultural capabilities. It has auditoriums for shows and conferences, galleries for art exhibits, and several research archives. Its numerous floors still house the regional offices of the Ministries of Culture and Education as well as the Fundação Cultural Palmares, the headquarters of Funarte [the National Art Foundation], along with other divisions of IPHAN and the Fundação Biblioteca Nacional.

The fact that the Palácio is a historical monument that houses administrative offices of various functioning entities leads to the challenge of creating an unparalleled infrastructure for public visitation that allows for expanded access to the building's rich artistic archive.

The measures proposed by the Ministry of Culture through its regional representation in Rio de Janeiro aim to grant the Palácio Gustavo Capanema with a basic level of support for visitation, commensurate with the building's historical, cultural, social, educational, and touristic importance.

Headed by IPHAN, the other organs of the Ministry of Culture in partnership with universities and other research bodies are forming a study center to maximize the potential accumulated in this space, place, and time.

For now, we turn over to the population this simple multimedia space as a symbolic and concrete way of sharing the commons that impel the construction of public policy, here in its cultural expression.

The city of Rio de Janeiro must have access to itself. In this way Brazil and the world benefit.

Translated by Andre Pagliarini

Venerating Escrava Anastácia

Kelly E. Hayes

Escrava Anastácia—Anastácia the Slave—is a highly popular figure in the devotional life of Rio de Janeiro, especially among Cariocas who follow the spirit, if not the doctrinal laws, of Roman Catholicism. Anastácia's distinction draws from many sources, but the image of a blue-eyed, black woman in an iron collar, whose mouth is covered by a heavy mask that prevents her from eating, has been a powerful element of urban iconography for the past half century. Some consider the legends that surround Anastácia to be truthful narratives of the horrors visited on enslaved women in Portuguese America. Others argue that the story of Anastácia's birth in West or West Central Africa, enslavement in Bahia, and an attempted rape by her master are apocryphal, without substantiation in documented evidence. All agree her sufferings brought on miraculous powers to heal others.

The heartrending stories about this manacled woman may have influenced the decision of the Nossa Senhora do Rosário e São Benedito dos Homens Pretos church, a legendary temple in downtown Rio popular among the city's men and women of color since the seventeenth century, to include an image of Anastácia in an exhibition about slavery mounted in a church annex in 1968. By the 1970s, that image, whose origins can be traced to an illustration of an unnamed male slave propagated by the nineteenth-century French traveler Jacques Arago (1790–1855), had become an object of intense popular devotion. The storied church on Rua Uruguaiana became a shrine to the popular slave saint. A subsequent ban on devotional works to Anastácia at the church dispersed the cult to various spots throughout the city.

The cult of Anastácia the Slave is now citywide, in household niches, online, and in performance. Variations of the Arago portrait are available for purchase in neighborhood shops that sell religious items. Anastácia has also been incorporated into the pantheon of saints and spirits venerated in umbanda, a syncretic religion that originated in Rio. In the Zona Norte neighborhoods of Penha and Vicente de Carvalho, sanctuaries named for Anastácia offer Masses held Wednesdays and

"Santuário Anastacia." Photograph by Kelly E. Hayes, 2006. Vicente de Carvalho, Rio de Janeiro. Used by permission of Kelly E. Hayes.

Sundays. These three photographs, taken by U.S. scholar Kelly E. Hayes, document one such sanctuary and two makeshift shrines. Here we see Escrava Anastácia and glimpse a gritty streetscape of metal security bars, litter, telephone and electric lines, satellite dishes, graffiti, and pedestrians navigating around private cars that partially block the public sidewalk.

"Anastácia Bust." Photograph by Kelly E. Hayes, 2006. Vicente de Carvalho, Rio de Janeiro. Used by permission of Kelly E. Hayes.

"Anastácia Penha." Photograph by Kelly E. Hayes, 2006. Penha, Rio de Janeiro. Used by permission of Kelly E. Hayes.

Campaigning for a "Rio without Homophobia"

Rio de Janeiro State Secretariat for Human Rights

Carioca writer João Paulo Emílio Cristóvão dos Santos Coelho Barreto (1881–1921), better known as João do Rio, flouted the social conventions of bourgeois male sexuality during the First Republic. He played the dandy, penned homoerotic verse, and promoted Oscar Wilde. By midcentury, Rio's Carnaval celebrations had grown famous for extravagant cross-dressing pageants and an open tolerance for nonnormative sexual escapades. Outside of Carnaval, many homosexuals made their lives transiting between the conventions of straight society and the spaces of same-sex sociability. Nevertheless, laws against moral offenses empowered the criminal justice system and public health services to detain transgressive men and women on suspicion of deviant acts and mental disturbance. By the 1970s, a self-conscious gay rights movement had arisen in Rio. Situating itself in dialogue with international struggles to decriminalize consensual same-sex relations and delist homosexuality as a mental disorder, the movement embraced in equal measures the disruptive ribaldry of queer sexualities and the importance of social acceptance and equal protection for sexual minorities. In the 1980s, this movement set deep roots in local struggles over the transition from military to civilian rule and the response to HIV/AIDS.

Since the 1990s, a raft of judicial and administrative decisions have extended protections to lesbians, gays, bisexuals, and transgenders (formerly known by the acronym GLS—"gays, lesbians, and sympathizers"—but now commonly called "LGBT") in areas including civil partnerships and same-sex marriage, survivor benefits, adoption rights, and nondiscrimination in employment and housing. In 2007, the state of Rio de Janeiro formally incorporated gay and lesbian concerns into statewide human rights administration. More recently, Rio municipal schools have embraced antibullying policies. Yet the general trend toward the mainstreaming of LGBT life has not erased persistent strains of popular, religious, and official prejudice against the erotic and affective lives of LGBT Cariocas. A pernicious pattern of violent assaults on travestis—a capacious term that goes well beyond the male cross-dresser—is a sobering tonic to the festive self-affirmation of the Rio Gay Pride Parade, held annually in July.

In partnership with the city of Rio and other municipalities, the state government developed a publicity campaign, Rio Sem Homofobia (Rio without Homophobia), which promotes social services for LGBT citizens while combating prejudice, denouncing hate crimes, and promoting LGBT tourism. Here is the campaign's brief account of its history, along with two public awareness posters. The first image is unmistakably set in downtown Rio, where the clock tower of the Central do Brasil railway station stands tall over Avenida Presidente Vargas. The second, marking National Trans Visibility Day, deftly captures the cultivated glamour of Carioca travestis and transgenders.

Rio Sem Homofobia

OUR HISTORY

In January 2007, the government of the State of Rio de Janeiro made a number of commitments to the state's lesbian, gay, bisexual, travesti, and transgender community. By March of the same year, finding the measure unconstitutional, the state high court overturned Law 3786/01, a measure drafted by Sérgio Cabral and Carlos Minc that had extended to public employees the right to request a same-sex partner's pension in event of the partner's death.

Since the law called for resources to be allocated in the state budget, the executive branch had to take the lead in crafting a bill. And so it did. The governor submitted a new bill to the state legislature. However, the law was not enforced due to, among other factors, bigotry and the nonrecognition of the LGBT community's rights. Considering that this law was an amendment to a piece of draft legislation originating from the executive, presented by the government of the state, Governor Sérgio Cabral, committed to human rights, decided in March 2007 to introduce a new bill to ensure that this abrogated right would be respected.

On the afternoon of May 15, 2007, the state legislature passed a bill recognizing the same-sex partners of state employees for the purposes of social security benefits. Bill 215/07 was approved in emergency session with an up or down vote, 45 votes in favor and 15 against, becoming Law 5034 of 2007.

In a letter to the state legislature, Governor Sérgio Cabral affirmed that the alterations in the law fulfilled the aims of Article 1, Section III and Article 3, Section IV of the national constitution, that identify human dignity, the reduction of social inequality, and the promotion of the well-being of

UM LUGAR TÃO MARAVILHOSO COMO O RIO NÃO COMBINA COM HOMOFOBIA.
RESPEITE LÉSBICAS, GAYS, BISSEXUAIS, TRAVESTIS E TRANSEXUAIS.

RIO SEM HOMOFOBIA É UMA INICIATIVA DO GOVERNO DO RIO DE JANEIRO. MAS PODE SER A SUA TAMBÉM.
Como qualquer forma de preconceito, a homofobia deve ser combatida em todos os lugares e, por isso, o Governo do Rio está lançando o Rio sem Homofobia. Uma iniciativa inédita que vai contar com vários setores do governo e promover a cidadania e a conscientização da sociedade. Afinal, respeitar a diversidade é um dever de todos. Faça parte do Rio sem Homofobia. A População LGBT merece seu respeito.

DISQUE CIDADANIA LGBT
0800 0234567
www.riosemhomofobia.rj.gov.br

 RIO SEM HOMOFOBIA

 GOVERNO DO Rio de Janeiro
SOMANDO FORÇAS

SECRETARIA DE ASSISTÊNCIA SOCIAL E DIREITOS HUMANOS

SUPERINTENDÊNCIA DE DIREITOS INDIVIDUAIS, COLETIVOS E DIFUSOS

"Rio Sem Homofobia." Campaign by Governo do Estado do Rio de Janeiro, Secretaria de Assistência Social e Direitos Humanos / Superintendência de Direitos Individuais, Coletivos e Difusos. Licensed under Creative Commons Attribuio 2.0 Brasil license, http://www.riosemhomofobia.rj.gov.br/campanha/ver/8_rio-sem-homofobia.

all, regardless of origin, race, sex, color, or age, as fundamental objectives of the Federative Republic of Brazil.

THE CREATION OF THE SUPERDIR WITHIN THE SEASDH

In a large ceremony held on May 28, Governor Sérgio Cabral signed law 5034 and with then-Secretary of Social Welfare and Human Rights Benedita da Silva officially inaugurated the team that would compose the Super-intendência de Direitos Individuais Coletivos e Difusos da Secretaria de Estado de Assistência Social e Direitos Humanos [Superintendency of In-dividual, Collective, and General Rights of the State Department of Social Welfare and Human Rights], which, among other things, had the challenge of devising and implementing LGBT policy for the State of Rio de Janeiro.

But we did not stop there. On June 28, 2007, we made yet another ad-vance in the fight for LGBT citizenship. In a public ceremony, Governor Sér-gio Cabral and his cabinet launched a technical committee to develop the statewide program—"Rio Sem Homofobia"—composed of fourteen rep-resentatives of the LGBT and human rights movements as well as scholars from various universities.

The governor's charge to the technical committee via Decree 40.822/07 was celebrated with a ceremony in the Salão de Inverno in the Guanabara Palace. The goal behind the appointment of twenty-eight representatives was the development of the statewide Rio Sem Homofobia program, in-tended to reduce discrimination and promote LGBT rights.

That was the starting point for the collective construction of a set of poli-cies dedicated to the state's LGBT community. The technical committee met for six months and presented a report with proposals and recommended ac-tions that were discussed and approved at the first state conference for LGBT policy and human rights, held between May 16 and 18, 2008.

FIRST STATE CONFERENCE FOR LGBT POLICY AND HUMAN RIGHTS

For the first time in Rio de Janeiro state, a conference was held solely for the purpose of discussing public policy devoted to the LGBT community. The conference was held between May 16 and 18, 2008, at the Odylo Costa Filho Theater on the campus of the Universidade do Estado do Rio de Janeiro (UERJ) in the city's Zona Norte. Activities extended into Saturday and Sun-day and were attended by activists and members of the state government.

The principal aim of the conference was to define strategies and ways to implement actions taken by the statewide Rio Sem Homofobia program.

"January 29 / National Trans Visibility Day. / Reassess norms. / Change your perspective. / Respect travestis and transgenders." "Rio Sem Homofobia: Dia da Visibilidade Trans." Campaign by Governo do Estado do Rio de Janeiro, Secretaria de Assistência Social e Direitos Humanos / Superintendência de Direitos Individuais, Coletivos e Difusos. Licensed under Creative Commons Attribuio 2.0 Brasil license, http://www.riosemhomofobia.rj.gov.br/campanha/ver/9_dia-da-visibilidade-trans—29-de-janeiro.

A city as wonderful as Rio is no place for homophobia. Respect lesbians, gays, bisexuals, travestis, and transgenders.

Rio Sem Homofobia is an initiative of the state government of Rio de Janeiro. But it can be yours as well. As with any form of bigotry, homophobia must be confronted everywhere, so, for that reason, the state of Rio is launching Rio Sem Homophobia. This innovative program will rely on the participation of various sectors of the state government to promote citizenship and raise social awareness. After all, everyone has a duty to respect diversity. Take part in Rio Sem Homofobia. The LGBT community deserves your respect.

Translated by Andre Pagliarini

The Last Night at Help

Flávia Lima

Copacabana stretches along a 3.7-mile expanse of beach between the Copacabana and Duque de Caxias forts. The densely populated Zona Sul neighborhood extends inland from the beach, but it is best known for oceanfront Avenida Atlântica. All types of Cariocas and visitors gather and stroll, day and night, along the wide sidewalk (calcadão) of patterned black-and-white cobblestones that follows this bustling thoroughfare lined with palm trees, food stands, and lifeguard towers. Midway down Avenida Atlântica, a massive beachfront nightclub once stood below a neon sign that flashed dancing feet and the English word "Help." This article, published on the final day before Help permanently shut down in 2010, expresses a mixture of nostalgia and pragmatic acceptance of the economic importance of the shadowy goings-on at this once bustling night spot.

Nightclubs open and close frequently, and it is not every day that the event is covered in a national newspaper. But Help was emblematic of Copacabana's recent history of faded glamour, seediness, and renewal. Opened in 1984, Help was first a dance venue for the upper-middle class. As Copacabana experienced a loss of its former glitz, the streets surrounding Help saw increasing indicators of urban poverty and homelessness. The sex industry expanded, and sex workers used the club to cultivate clients, often foreign tourists. Help appeared in such guidebooks as the Brazilian edition of The Lonely Planet *with coy but obvious suggestions of its fame as a place where one could pay for sex. The closure of Help was the fruit of a long-standing project of moralization and redevelopment led by Sérgio Cabral (b. 1950), a Rio state legislator who won the governorship in 2007. On the site formerly occupied by the nightclub, now demolished, rises the Museu da Imagem e do Som (Museum of Image and Sound), relocated from its former location in Rio's historic downtown.*

With a digital camera in his hands, an amateur photographer clicks his last shots. Stationed in front of Help for eight years, Marcos (who did not want to give his last name) makes his living photographing people in front of the nightclub Help and the restaurant Terraço Atlântico, in the Copacabana neighborhood in the Zona Sul. This Wednesday, the nightclub's last day of operations, he could not hide his apprehension.

"I made lots of money working here, taking photos of gringos, of the people. Sometimes I take in 300 reais [about US$168 in January 2010] per night. With the closing of the club, it's really going to hurt me. I'm going to miss it," he lamented.

Yesterday afternoon, in the main room of the nightclub around two hundred people participated in an auction that offered for sale all of the products that were used at the establishment. According to marketing director Bruno Cruz, the appliances, furniture, and electronic equipment that formerly illuminated the dance floor as well as about two thousand vinyl records used by the club's DJs were all put up for auction. The organizers hoped to recover around 300,000 reais.

At night, the activity at the entrance to the nightclub remained intense until dawn. Regular patrons and tourists took pictures of the neon sign, with the registered trademark "Help" that imitated dance steps with flashing light.

Regulars at the nightclub for five years, escorts [*garotas de programa*] Selma and Camila, who gave fictitious names, were also worried.

"There's going to be one less tourist attraction, and one less source of income for the city. Internationally, the Zona Sul will stop. Tourism in Rio is over," lamented Selma.

Camila was more nostalgic. She didn't hide her disappointment in knowing that the club would be closed, and that the space would be used as the new headquarters of the Museum of Image and Sound.

"It's going to be sad to arrive here tomorrow and find everything all closed down, without the neon sign lit. Today I came to say good-bye," she said, visibly upset.

Translated by Amy Chazkel

(Re)Constructing Black Consciousness

Benedito Sérgio and Ailton Benedito de Sousa

Established in 1974, the Instituto de Pesquisas das Culturas Negras (Institute for Research on Black Cultures; IPCN) positioned itself as a leading voice of black activism in Rio. In its early years, the founders prided themselves on a commitment to the serious study of postcolonial Africa as a foundation for a wider engagement with the vitality and diversity of Afro-Brazilian life. Led by a team of educated middle-class professionals, the IPCN developed links with academic circuits throughout the African diaspora to question the guiding myth of Brazilian racial democracy. The efforts of the IPCN in the twenty-first century have included advocacy for the construction of a monument to the slave trade near the site of the old slave market in Valongo.

The IPCN is a standout among the affiliates of the pioneering Movimento Negro Unificado (United Black Movement) for holding property title to its administrative headquarters. The two-story building, located adjacent to the Praça da Cruz Vermelha, stands in close proximity to middensity working- and middle-class neighborhoods where sociability revolves around quintessentially Carioca spaces like the botequim *(corner bar), small-scale commerce, and* gafieiras *(dance halls). Nearness to the skyscrapers of downtown had its downside, as the IPCN headquarters shared the physical deterioration seen throughout the residential areas of the Centro. Physical decline was an ironic reflection of the financial difficulties and infighting that weakened the organization's stature in the era of postauthoritarian democracy. In the first decade of the twenty-first century, a building that had once brimmed with engaged activities confronted the threat of squatters.*

In October 2010, a handful of IPCN founding members launched a campaign to save the dilapidated headquarters. The campaign included periodic streetside social gatherings (confraterizações) that promised feijoada, beer, dance and musical performances, and capoeira for a modest price (see the invitation shown here). A blog was launched to raise funds for restoration work. The blog's entries, like the one excerpted here—"Manifesto to the Brazilian People," dated November 20, 2010 (the Day of Black Consciousness, an official holiday in the state of Rio de Janeiro since 2002)—narrate the IPCN's place in the history of black politicking while making the larger case for a particular "black" critique of race and racism in Brazil. Efforts to address the sad state of the institution's headquarters are a platform for a wider agenda of constructing consciousness well beyond the Praça da Cruz Vermelha. As of 2015, work to stabilize and restore the building has been slow—akin to the pace of efforts to build black citizenship in the city as a whole. Nonetheless, the manifesto shows that the pathways of Afro-Brazilian consciousness run through the shabby streets of downtown Rio.

Manifesto to the Brazilian People

I. GENERAL PROPOSALS

1. Confident in the belief that after much reflection we will reach a consensus regarding the issues here presented, and confronted with the neglect that for decades has characterized the IPCN, a pioneer in the fight for the political, economic, and cultural consciousness of the Brazilian people, especially those of African descent, a group of partners and friends have authored this manifesto to invite one and all to participate in a joint effort to reinvigorate the IPCN, beginning with the restoration of the external façade, thereby salvaging the building's role as a productive hub for knowledge and as a meeting space for our people bound together by the Black Diaspora, a historical phenomenon that between the fifteenth and nineteenth centuries dispersed African peoples and cultures around the world as a source of labor. As enslaved warriors we became protagonists in the history of mankind and established our presence globally through our music, our culture, our color. We therefore reaffirm that for us the diaspora is the dispersion across the world of the black man and black woman, their art, their culture, not as slaves but as warriors, contributing to culture and civilization, an attribute maintained by an enduring commitment. We repudiate to its very core the racist proposition that we and other colonized peoples are parasites of a purported European civilization.

2. It is generally understood that humanity, over the course of centuries, has undergone an intense and accelerated process of change, unparalleled in history for its breadth. The Brazilian people cannot remain passive during this process of transformation. The old world is being reshaped right before our eyes, ushering in a different world of heightened anxiety. From a social policy standpoint, the new historical conditions call for new covenants between peoples with which to solve the impasses inherited from both the recent and distant pasts. New ethics are called for. It can no longer be said that there are primi-

tive peoples disconnected from mankind, frozen in time. When these do appear, as was the case recently in the Peruvian jungle, they are hailed as wonders. No longer can men of this or that ethnicity be humiliated and enslaved to applause or generalized indifference. There are no longer any "unclaimed" lands to "discover," "unexplored" seas to explore, civilizations to destroy. Today everyone realizes that the real conquerors of Mount Everest are the sherpas from the mountains of Nepal, without whom nobody could climb Everest. Today Tarzan would be a buffoonish character, even in a traveling circus in some African village. Today there is no more Superman. Faced with new tactics of resistance employed by the oppressed, it is clear that so-called supermen are terrified of death, that they are also men of flesh, bone, and soul.

Today, seeing the statues of the pharaohs on the internet, we can attest from their physical traits that the esteemed Senegalese anthropologist Cheikh Anta Diop was right: Egyptian civilization was black or negroid, a fact never disclosed in any history textbook. Finally, if today slavery persists here or there, physical labor, not economically sound in virtually the entire world, is headed toward obsolescence. Like patriarchy itself, slavery sanctioned by law and custom is a mere vestige of the past. . . .

8. Brazil is a nation composed of men and women from all branches of humankind, each contributing to a synthetic cultural DNA from which material and spiritual legacies are derived. This shared cultural and material inheritance is how each branch contributes to the national project. Each branch has played, and continues to play, an important role in this project, justifying collaborative efforts here and around the world. These individual roles are important not only because the protagonists may be black, indigenous, or white, but also because they are human. What is at stake going forward is the unanimous recognition of this obvious historical fact: Brazil as a nation belonging to everyone, formed by disparate cultural legacies, where racism and religious intolerance are serious crimes. Where inequality—a condition inherent to society—persists, it cannot be based on one's sect, color, religion, or sexual orientation. . . .

IPCN, HISTORY AND PLAN OF ACTION

The IPCN was founded in the early 1970s at the height of the military dictatorship. Confronted with the inflexibility of political institutions at the time, a handful of young people—men and women from almost every walk of life, including government workers, bankers, business owners, journalists, athletes, artists, actors, dentists, musicians, songwriters, *sambistas*, coaches, small business owners, poets, students, self-employed workers and the unemployed—mobilized as one under a banner reading "We want to change the situation of the black Brazilian."

It was at the time a nearly impossible aim. After all, ever since the Frente Negra Brasileira [Brazilian Black Front] had been proscribed at the start of the Estado Novo regime [1937–1945] no other collective black organization had been able to flourish. We lived under the fourth version of republicanism—evidently its most cruel form since the first dictatorial republican experiments that followed the end of slavery. In a way, it was yet another attempt to create another Christian European utopia in this tropical paradise thereby fulfilling so many prophecies of a New World—the Promised Land for this or that ethnicity but not all of them.

One by one, every form of resistance to a project of national exclusion had been put down: Dom Obá [Cândido da Fonseca Galvão, also known as Obá II D'África], advisor to the emperor and defender of the poor, was transformed into a farcical character of our past; the Guarda Negra [Black Guard], originally decimated and dispersed, was vilified once again after 1964; Canudos and so many other stifled uprisings. Such had been the case after independence, when it was widely believed that the nation and freedom itself would be for all Brazilians—the Malê Revolt [Salvador da Bahia, 1835] belied that notion. After the Paraguayan War what had we won? Our first favela, today the Morro da Providência, the birthplace of Machado de Assis and the origin of Pequena África [Little Africa, a nickname for Rio's Cidade Nova], rich in characters that marked our history and culture. There, in the spaces of black sociability—the homes of our Tias Ciatas—samba was born. The head of the army has long ceased to be in the same mold as Henrique Dias who, alongside Felipe Camarão, gave national purpose to the fight of a few plantation owners to expel the Dutch from the northeast.

That was the Brazil those young people dared to challenge. One name among the ideologues engaged in that fight is the lawyer Ives Mauro Silva da Costa. Another is the first corresponding member of our organization, who in a way will become our safest bet: Colonel Octávio Nicol de Almeida, spokesperson, according to him, for President General Ernesto Geisel. After that others would come in disguise, from DOPS, CENIMAR, PARASAR [agencies of the state security apparatus during the post-1964 military regime], etc.

Jumping from "safehouse" to "safehouse," home to home, including the headquarters of a few institutions—the Brazil-Germany Cultural Institute,

NESTE DOMINGO, 8 DE JULHO, NÃO PERCAM:
FESTA DE ANIVERSÁRIO DO IPCN
FEIJOADA, CAPOEIRA, MÚSICA E DANÇA AFROS

Domingo, 8 de Julho, a partir de 10h, entrem na grande roda de capoeira do IPCN, Rua Mem de Sá, em frente ao número 208.

Além da roda de capoeira teremos a apresentação do Grupo Ilê Ofé comandado por Charles Nelson, como um dos pontos alto dos festejos pelo 37º aniversário do IPCN - marca histórica da Resistência Negra no Brasil e no mundo.

ESPERAMOS VOCES LÁ! Para muita confraternização em frente ao Instituto de Pesquisa das Culturas Negras (IPCN), Rua Mem de Sá, 208, Lapa

Conheça mais acessando o nosso blog:
www.recuperacaodoipcn.blogspot.com

"Convite." Unsigned handbill. Instituto de Pesquisa das Culturas Negras (IPCN). Used by permission of Ailton Benedito de Sousa.

Teatro Opinião, the Associação dos Servidores da Comlurb—we were finally able to obtain financial support from the Inter-American Foundation of the United States Democratic Party to purchase the property next to the Red Cross building on Rua Mem de Sá, 208 in Rio de Janeiro, officially beginning operations on June 8, 1975.

There were prosperous years, but the story would not end there. The democratic opening came and with it several leaders came to the fore. We believed yet again that the *abertura* would belong to everyone. Beginning in the 1980s we began to experience a series of challenges that would result in the violent degradation of our property and values, a process that would accelerate in the ensuing two decades.

At the sight of a once-imposing building in ruins and the Institution practically shuttered, a group of original members decided to take action, seeking out their directors and informing them of their plan to restore at least the exterior of the building and resume operations. Toward that end, OCRES Arquitetura Ltda. was hired at a cost of R$48,000. Given the urgency of the situation, the first step was taken to bring together twelve individuals willing to contribute 4,000 reais apiece, divided into four installments, according to what was agreed on at the first meeting. Many were called on but the actual number of contributors, notwithstanding the myriad declarations and promises of support, is currently far below what is necessary. Still, work on the renovation project was started and the first installment, the product of a new financing plan with five installments, has been settled by a loan. For the resumption of activities it is necessary to restore the ceiling and interiors. To do that, we must immediately begin organizing preliminary actions. We are thinking of bringing together 120 people tasked with contributing 400 reais, divided into four installments and deposited in checking account "CAD RECUP DO IPCN" at the Banco do Brasil, Branch 3260-3 and account number 9297-5. Once involved, these benefactors, at the discretion of a General Assembly and statutory procedures, will become part of the Advisory and Governance Board which will form jointly with an active existing fiscal council in accordance with the norms approved by the slate of associates, principally the moral recuperation of IPCN.

Abandoned as it has been these past few years, the IPCN is left with several possibilities: (a) have its headquarters occupied by the homeless, as has already happened in the past; (b) have its headquarters revert back to the state or local government due to the accumulated debts; (c) have the leadership boards that have met irregularly in the past few years recognized as heroes, which in some way would correspond to the facts; (d) recognize fallacious accounts of the history of the black movement in Rio de Janeiro; (e) establish a precedent so that what has happened to the IPCN can happen to any entity of the people; (f) finally, give confirmation to the racist interpretation that views us as incapable blacks unable to successfully manage our collective undertakings.

Do not stand on the sidelines, we have already decided: RECOVER IPCN NOW: WE WANT IT!

Day of Black Consciousness, November 20, 2010

Benedito Sérgio
Ailton Benedito de Sousa

Translated by Andre Pagliarini

A *Quilombo* in Lagoa

Marcelo Fernandes

In the 1920s, an Afro-Brazilian family named Pinto took possession of some land located on the sparsely inhabited, forested eastern bank of the Lagoa Rodrigo de Freitas, in the Zona Sul. That settlement now plays a part in a long history of runaway slave communities (quilombos) in Greater Rio that dates back to the colonial era. In the 1970s, twenty-two luxury condominiums were built adjacent to the Pinto settlement. Tensions gradually increased between the Pintos and their neighbors, to the point that descendants of the original Pinto settlers petitioned federal authorities to protect their properties, named Quilombo Sacopã. Their claims drew from provisions in the 1988 constitution that extend collective property titles to lands occupied by the descendants of runaway slaves. In making such claims, the Pinto community made use of the legal redefinition of maroon history, as it evolved from the strictly historical establishment of family lineage to anthropological questions of self-identity. (The Pintos, after all, had settled the land three decades after the abolition of slavery and could not claim to be direct descendants of a historic maroon community.) To be the quilombola *descendant meant staking claim to longstanding black traditions, even if an actual maroon community had not existed on the particular site to be protected.*

Sacopã's longtime Afro-descendant residents received federal recognition as re-manescentes (descendants of quilombolas) in 2004, and Rio's municipal chamber approved a measure to designate Sacopã a "Special Area of Cultural Interest" in 2012. Meanwhile, conflict brewed over the cultural and land rights of these long-established Afro-Cariocas who lived alongside newer arrivals who were much whiter and wealthier. The latter, organized in neighborhood and condominium associations, lodged complaints about bothersome loud noises that accompanied Sacopã's well-known rodas de samba *(samba circles) and* feijoada *feasts. The municipal chamber tried to impose a total prohibition on music at Quilombo Sacopã. This* Jornal do Brasil *feature captures the multiple dimensions of the tense climate.*

The article is not overtly politicized, yet its title implies that "quilombolas" and "residents" are two separate, opposing groups. Such perspectives on remanescentes reflect a strain of unease in contemporary Carioca society about the legitimacy of black communities' claims to land rights. The well-off may not dispute the worthiness of black cultural heritage, and academics substantiate the long history of maroon communities in Rio's once-remote suburbs. All parties appear to be invested in the protection of natural resources. Yet the Lagoa well-to-do channel class and racial concerns that a landmarking craze, fueled by loose rules and opportunism, might be under way.

One of the toniest parts of Rio de Janeiro is the object of a long-running court dispute, which now begins another round. Twenty-two condominiums in the area called Fonte da Saudade—an area with the most expensive square footage in the Marvelous City on the edge of the Lagoa Rodrigo de Freitas—were notified in 2008 by the National Institute for Colonization and Agrarian Reform (INCRA) that their homes were located in an area that had been designated as part of the Quilombo Sacopã. With this news, the residents began to fear for their property rights.

Some of the area residents question the legitimacy of the quilombo. For the president of the Residents' Association of Fonte da Saudade, the physician Ana Simas, the land was the property of the Darke de Mattos family, whose matriarch departed the country, leaving behind some household employees.

"That place was never a quilombo. Luís is the descendant of Manoel Pinto, who stayed there after his employer traveled never to return. Today, it's part of an Área de Proteção Ambiental [Area of Environmental Protection; APA]. It's a public place, and they cannot build anything there; they cannot even live there. And now they want the help of INCRA to take over the area where the condominiums stand. This infringes on our property rights," Ana insists, adding that the residents of the quilombo would contribute to deforestation.

According to Kátia Vasconcellos, who heads the condominium association at Chácara Sacopã, one of the buildings that received notice from INCRA, the aim of the quilombo would be to take over the vacant areas that are under the control of the municipal government.

"They are claiming areas that are under municipal control that have been set aside for conservation, and they want to construct more residential buildings. They simply cannot use this land, which is not theirs," she affirms.

The musician Luís Pinto Júnior, known as Luís Sacopã and representative of the quilombo where twenty-six people reside, denies that his community is deforesting the area. He admits that the land was a gift from the Darke de Mattos family to his father, who would not have registered ownership. With respect to the Area of Environmental Protection, he says that the José Guilherme Merchior Park was created after the residents already lived there.

"Our family has lived in this region for a hundred years. At first, we made legal claims to the land based on squatters' rights [*usucapião*], but we lost the legal case with a three to zero vote in 2005. Currently, the process is in the third level of appeal at the Supremo Tribunal de Justiça [Supreme Court]. Coincidentally, when we lost this case, the judge who rendered the decision was removed from his position," he says in his defense, quoting the supreme court judge Roberto Wider, who reported on the proceedings and was removed from his post by the Conselho Nacional de Justiça [National Council of Justice] under suspicion of involvement in a scheme to issue judgments in exchange for pay.

Luís denies that he intends to construct new buildings and also denies the charges of deforestation. "We did not tear down one tree and we are under the strong oversight of the municipal government, both the Municipal Institute of Geotechnology of Rio de Janeiro (Geo-Rio) and the environment secretariat."

With respect to the legitimacy of the Quilombo, this designation is the responsibility of the Fundação Cultural Palmares [Palmares Cultural Foundation], connected to the Ministry of Culture. The agency affirms that the community self-identifies as quilombola, and the certification is not specifically related to the geography of the place, but rather is related to the cultural ties that the community has with the place of residence.

"The concept of the quilombo as a place where runaway slaves gathered no longer applies. Now, if a group with presumed slave ancestry claims the status of being from a quilombo, we grant the title, because many communities have to move because of agribusiness, and in the case of Sacopã, because of real estate speculation," Maurício Jorge dos Reis, the director of the Department of Protection of Afro-Brazilian Heritage of the Fundação Cultural Palmares, explains.

Institute Says That Condominium Residents Will Not Be Harmed

Regarding the notice given to the twenty-two condominiums, INCRA announced that the initial designation as a quilombo was faulty, and that the work is now being redone.

"A new map is being drawn up. We are not going to take one centimeter away from the condominiums. And with respect to the park, the quilombo community members were already here before its creation," explains the anthropologist Miguel Pedro Alves, coordinator of INCRA's Grupo de Serviço de Quilombos [Quilombo Service Group].

The self-recognition certificate for the quilombo was issued in 2004, four years after the creation of José Guilherme Merchior municipal park during the administration of the former mayor [Luiz Paulo] Conde. The Secretary of the Environment announced that he attempted to remove the residents from that location, with no success, and that he currently is seeking a solution from the Secretary of Housing to relocate the inhabitants. The Secretary added that within the APA there would be no occupation, according to Federal Law 9985/2000, and he consulted again with the municipal attorney general regarding INCRA's proceedings.

The businessman Darke de Mattos, who is a descendant of the land's original owner, Astréia Darke de Mattos, explained that years ago his father sold a part of the property to a group of lawyers, and the rest was donated to the city to become an ecological preserve.

"I was against the sale, because I thought that it would result in real estate speculation. Our family is against any type of occupation of that land, including by the Pinto family, which only had made a word-of-mouth agreement with my great-aunt Astréia," he explains.

The lawyers were forced to sell off the lots to a real estate developer that operated in Torre Rio Sul, according to Luís Sacopã. The office tower's management does not list any developer by the name given to us.

According to Flávio Gomes, history professor at the Federal University of Rio de Janeiro (UFRJ), there have been innumerable quilombos in the area of Lagoa Rodrigo de Freitas, where the favela removals that took place in the 1960s resulted in real estate speculation. It would be easy for anthropologists to prove that the population established there is made up of descendants of land occupations in that area dating from the nineteenth century.

"There is no doubt that Sacopã, which is organized around a family, has descended from these types of black, semi-urban land occupation in the nineteenth century," he stated.

Translated by Amy Chazkel

An Oral History of Brazilian Jiu-Jitsu

Ben Penglase and Rolker Gracie

Brazilian jiu-jitsu, like Brazilian capoeira, is a globalized martial art that has taken specific local forms. Whereas the well-known Afro-Brazilian fight-dance originated in popular culture and slave resistance, Brazilian jiu-jitsu first took hold among the urban middle classes. The impresario Paschoal Segreto sponsored demonstration matches during the Carioca Belle Époque, before Hélio Gracie (1913–2009) took the combat form and its related philosophical tenets to widespread prominence. In this translation of an oral history interview from 2010, the U.S. cultural anthropologist Benjamin Penglase speaks about the sport's development in Rio with one of Hélio Gracie's seven sons, Rolker (b. 1964). The interview took place at the famed Gracie Academy in the Zona Sul neighborhood of Humaitá, but Rolker speaks of the school's origins in downtown Rio and its later move to Lagoa. In this regard, he maps the transience of sporting habits among Rio's middle class.

Brazilian jiu-jitsu initially took root when Hélio and his older brother Carlos (1902–1994) studied judo with Mitsuo Maeda, a Japanese fight champion and immigration advocate who arrived in northern Brazil in 1914. In 1925 the two Gracie brothers moved from Belém do Pará to Rio, where they innovated on the basis of what they had learned with Maeda. In the Brazilian capital, Hélio and Carlos assiduously cultivated connections with the local elite: some of their early students included the politician Carlos Lacerda, future president João Figueiredo, rising media mogul Roberto Marinho, playboy Jorge Guinle, and architect Oscar Niemeyer. In this interview, Rolker Gracie speaks of another connection forged between his family and the Wernecks, a dynasty from the state of Rio de Janeiro whose influence dates to the colonial period.

The sport has developed along a number of paths, some led by the Gracie dynasty and others by Luiz França, another disciple of Maeda, and Oswaldo Fadda (1921–2005). (França and Fadda led the popularization of Brazilian jiu-jitsu among Rio's working poor.) The Gracies transformed a proscribed subculture of no-holds-barred challenge matches, called vale tudo, into a highly publicized, formal aspect of Rio's sporting scene. Many maneuvers shared with mixed martial arts (MMA) continued to be associated with disorderly behaviors, but the innovative Gracie style of jiu-

jitsu grew to international prominence in the 1990s, when Carioca native Royce Gracie (b. 1966), Rolker's younger brother, won three of the first Ultimate Fighting Championships.

BENJAMIN PENGLASE: So . . . could you tell me about your connection to jiu-jitsu?[1]

ROLKER GRACIE: Okay, let's go. I'm the son of grand master Hélio Gracie. I've been doing jiu-jitsu since I was born. I was practically born on the *tatame* [training mat]. My older brothers are Rorion, Relson, and Rickson. Rickson is four and a half years older than me. I was born 1964. My younger brothers are Royler and then Royce and Robin. And ever since I can remember I've been like this, like you see me now, on the tatame wearing a kimono [the uniform used for jiu-jitsu].

BP: And who taught you? Was your dad your teacher?

RG: No . . . all my brothers were teachers. So I was taught not just by my father, but by all my older brothers, by Rorion, Relson, and Rickson, who were also my teachers. . . . But I really learned the most from my brother Rickson. My partner here in this academy has always been Royler. This academy has always been mine and Royler's. And I also learned a lot from Royce. Even though he was younger, Royce was always an enlightened guy. In the world of vale tudo he's a big star, probably the biggest star ever in vale tudo.

BP: But what was it like, did you help to teach classes in your dad's school, or . . .

RG: My dad's school was first on [Avenida] Rio Branco. When I was a little kid, I'd go there every day, and my dad would be teaching classes, he and my brothers Rorion and Rickson. . . . That's how I learned: watching the older members of the family and helping them with their classes.

BP: And this academy here, when did it open?

RG: Here in this exact location? Twenty-two years ago. But this academy . . . at first it was on Rio Branco on the seventeenth floor. Then we moved to Vasco da Gama club [Lagoa], and we were there for a few years. Then it moved here. But all the students from there continued to train here. I have students who started training with us all that time ago when we were on Rio Branco, they're still training with us here today.

BP: Wow, that's a long time.

RG: Yeah, I have students here who are in their sixties. The Gracie school is the oldest in Rio. So we have some of the students who've been training jiu-jitsu longer than anywhere else.

BP: And why did you come here to this building?

RG: Well, it's like this: after we went to Vasco, the club had a change of leadership, and we had to leave. And we have a strong connection with the Wernecks. Members of the Werneck family were our students when we were on Rio Branco. And the Werneck family owns the building that this school is located in. So they invited us to come in as partners. This floor here is too loud for classes, and the school wanted to move further back. So they let us use these floors during lunch time and in the evenings, when there are no classes.

BP: And how would you define jiu-jitsu? Is it a martial art, a sport . . .

RG: It's the *arte suave* [gentle art], the arte suave. Listen: it's a method of self-defense that my father . . . he founded the jiu-jitsu federation just to take it out of illegality [*tirar da ilegalidade*]. There used to be no competitions. My dad set up a federation to be able to say that it's a legal sport. Understand? Jiu-jitsu is an art for you to be able to fight in the street and not get beat up.

BP: So do you teach jiu-jitsu as a sport or for self-defense?

RG: No . . . what I always say . . . here in our school we have students who are interested in jiu-jitsu as a sport and jiu-jitsu for their daily lives. So here we teach the three: sport jiu-jitsu, self-defense jiu-jitsu, and the jiu-jitsu aspect of vale tudo. Whenever there's an MMA fight and someone used a lot of jiu-jitsu, we always have a class about that, making that the focus of the class and showing what they did, what they used correctly. You see, originally when my family had the first vale tudo fights, it was as a test of one martial art against another. Now it's not that any more. Now it's an athlete against another athlete.

BP: What do you try to pass on to your students? What do you think that it's important for them to learn?

RG: Respect, good judgment [*bom senso*]. Knowing how to respect others, respect the elder student, the more advanced student. That's fundamental in martial arts.

BP: Jiu-jitsu is really becoming very popular internationally. Why do you think this is happening?

RG: Because of its technique. It's a sport that allows a small person to deal with anyone [*fazer frente com qualquer um*] through technique. It's a sport for a smaller person, a weaker person to win through skill. And you don't need strength. Strength isn't here [points to arm], it's here, in your mind.

BP: When I was living here in Rio in the 1990s, jiu-jitsu was very visible, it was always in the newspapers . . .

RG: There was a time, at the end of the 1990s and beginning of the 2000s, the time of the so-called bad boys, about ten years ago, when there was lots of confusion. Any time anything bad happened, the media tried to connect it to jiu-jitsu. But that wasn't true. When there were fights in the street, it was up to the police to sort it out.

BP: With so many foreigners training jiu-jitsu, do you think that it will change?

RG: Sure. It will change *them*. It will improve their lives. My father and my uncle Carlos, they were ahead of their time. They saw in the sport something that they loved, and they embraced it, and this transformed the whole family. We are now a martial arts clan. Jiu-jitsu in the U.S. still involves using a lot of strength. American culture is very competitive. Americans always want to be the best, want to know more. That's why they need to come straight to the source, to come here to Brazil, this is the headquarters, the root of jiu-jitsu. So there you have it!

Translated by Ben Penglase and Amy Chazkel

Note

1. In this selection, ellipsis points indicate a pause.

Whatever Your *Fantasia,* Always Use a Condom

Ministry of Health

The State of Rio observed World AIDS Day 2011 by administering rapid-results HIV tests at the bustling Central do Brasil railway station at the edge of downtown Rio. Working in coordination with the federal health ministry's HIV/AIDS public awareness campaign, Fique Sabendo (Be in the Know), state health workers distributed condoms free of charge and answered questions about the transmission and treatment of HIV. Of the 711 tests administered, sixteen came back positive. Officials offered counseling and directions on accessing a public health system of regular checkups and antiretroviral medications.

An accompanying public relations campaign publicized the incidence of HIV/ AIDS infections in Rio city, where 85 percent of the 70,656 cases reported since the start of the epidemic in the early 1980s had been registered. Two messages predominated in the coverage of the tests administered in the railway station: HIV prevention was the responsibility of all citizens, and regular testing was a key part of prevention efforts.

Several months prior to this testing, a similar joint effort of federal, state, and municipal health agencies launched a campaign to promote condom use during Carnaval. The national campaign had distinctly Rio inflections, using scenery and situations familiar to a Carioca's vocabulary of pre-Lenten revelry. The print campaign included posters that presented a smiling, attractive young Afro-Brazilian woman—the archetype of sex appeal in samba school parade competitions— wearing a costume made of condoms. The caption for this poster, and others that featured women of a rainbow of skin complexions, reads, "Whatever your fantasia, always wear a condom." (Fantasia has the double meaning of "fantasy" and "costume.") The appeal of this facet of the larger public health campaign, both serious and tongue-in-cheek, was the message conveyed to women of all colors that the personal power to engage in sexual activity included the social responsibility to lower HIV risk by insistence on condom usage. Other parts of the campaign offered a decidedly sex-positive message aimed at teenage schoolgirls who mix gossip about

"Sem camisinha não dá!" Poster by Ministério da Saúde, Departamento de DST, Aids, e Hepatites Virais.

the sexual conquests of Carnaval with the acknowledgment that it is their right and responsibility to seek out free, confidential testing for HIV and other sexually transmitted infections. The slogan "Fique Sabendo" was the parting message of a thirty-second video clip, transcribed here, that featured an interracial group of three high schoolers, dressed in outfits that took their cues from the blue-and-white public school uniforms worn in Rio. In the background, the viewer observes a school built in the neocolonial style that could easily be located in Rio's close-in Zona Norte neighborhoods, such as Tijuca or Vila Isabel.

SCHOOLGIRL 1: Carnaval was good, huh?

YOUNG SCHOOLGIRL 2: Good? I made out a lot . . . [1]

[laughter]

SCHOOLGIRL 2: . . . and did a whole lot more. You two didn't miss out on the fun, right?

SCHOOLGIRLS 1 AND 3: Yeah . . .

SCHOOLGIRL 3: Too bad it's over, huh?

SCHOOLGIRL 2: Ah, but all good things must come to an end.

SCHOOLGIRL 1: They sure do. And the end was good!

[laughter]

SCHOOLGIRL 2 [TO CAMERA]: For those who used a condom, now there is nothing but happy memories. But if you forgot to take care of yourself it is important to get tested for AIDS and syphilis at a health clinic. It is free, fast, and confidential.

VOICE-OVER: Always use a condom for sex. Anything else just won't do.

Translated by Andre Pagliarini

Note

1. In this selection, ellipsis points indicate a pause.

"Pacification"

Adam Isacson and Observatório de Favelas

Shortly after taking office in 2007, Rio state governor Sérgio Cabral (b. 1963) adopted a new model of public security and policing in communities overwhelmed by narcotraffickers and private militias. In November 2008, a special unit of the military police called a Unidade da Polícia Pacificadora [Pacifying Police Unit; UPP] took Morro Dona Marta in Botafogo. As other occupations followed, officials replaced the bellicose "war on crime" with a coordinated project of "pacification." The mainstream press immediately declared the governor's policy of community engagement and open-ended police occupation successful. Violence and disorder, while still common, declined in "pacified" communities. State services were strengthened, and public utilities gained reliability. Even the policy's detractors acknowledged an improved sense of security resulting from coordinated attempts to impose order and to nurture civil society among favela residents. Yet the UPPs also generated resentment and strife. The pacifying units, answering to the Rio state secretariat of security, have been criticized for their intrusive attempts to control daily life in poor communities. Some residents of pacified communities decry the financial strains of real estate speculation that has accompanied improved security, especially in communities located in the Zona Sul. Above all, critics denounce the continuation of police violence, exemplified by the 2013 case of UPP officers charged with acts of brutality leading to the death of Amarildo Dias de Souza, a stonemason's assistant in Rocinha, Rio's largest favela. In solving some serious problems, the UPPs have generated new ones involving the rights of Rio's poorest citizens.

International human rights organizations have voiced serious concerns about the underlying organizational logic of pacification. In 2011, Adam Isacson of the Washington Office on Latin America (WOLA) wrote about pacifications within a hemispheric context of state-sponsored security operations. The Isacson piece (reproduced here, with accompanying photos) drew from the insights of classified documents released on Wikileaks in 2009 that suggested that Rio's pacification program derived from counterinsurgency tactics developed in the post-9/11 "War on Terror." Rio-based social movements have also voiced their misgivings about pacification as policy and practice. Social media have served as an especially popular vehicle *for discussion of this type. One example is the Facebook page created in 2012 by residents of the Complexo da Maré (also known as Maré), a neighborhood of about 130,000 in the Zona Norte that sprawls between the Linha Vermelha and Avenida Brasil. The imminent arrival of a UPP and the long-standing complaints about police infringements on civil, political, and collective rights prompted the formation of a campaign named Somos da Maré e Temos Direitos (We Are from Maré and We Have Rights). In partnership with the Redes de Desenvolvimento da Maré (the Maré Development Networks) as well as local and international human rights organizations, the campaign's supporters make deft use of social media and traditional communication channels to monitor police activity and to combat misconduct. A posting to the organization's Facebook page is reproduced here. Such online activism exposes how even well-intentioned programs might harmfully perpetuate the "divided" city.*

Rio de Janeiro's Pacification Program

Just before the holidays I accompanied WOLA colleagues on a week-long research trip to Brazil. While in Rio de Janeiro, I saw a scenario that's starting to look very familiar around Latin America, and that may recur elsewhere in 2011.

It goes something like this:

1. Decades of government neglect effectively cede a piece of territory, and its population, to violent groups. This neglected territory could be a discrete urban neighborhood; it could be a vast rural region. The violent groups—whether insurgents, pro-government militias, mafias or gangs—recruit unoccupied youth and fund themselves by drug trafficking, extortion and kidnapping. The illegal groups corrupt and penetrate the very government institutions that are supposed to confront them: the security forces, the judicial system, local and sometimes national government.

2. The violence and illegality worsen, eventually becoming so intolerable that they affect daily life in wealthier, more central territories—if not national security as a whole.

3. The government responds by sending in large numbers of security forces, including army troops, to clear the violent groups from the neglected zone and hunt down their members.

4. Past experience or current frustrations make clear that a military/police occupation won't be enough. Instead, officials present an innovative-looking, sequenced and coordinated "whole of government" plan. The

idea is to bring in more trustworthy police, have civilian government agencies provide basic services, and integrate the zone's residents as full citizens who are no longer excluded from national life.

5. At the end, the plan calls for the security forces to withdraw to normal levels, leaving behind a functioning civilian state, a legal economy and an engaged citizenry.

If you follow Latin America, you've seen this scenario playing out, with varying degrees of success, in Ciudad Juárez (the "Todos Somos Juárez" program) and some other Mexican border cities; in the slums ringing Medellín, Colombia ("Operación Orión" and its aftermath); and in rural Colombian zones like La Macarena, where an ambitious "Consolidation" program is now completing its fourth year. If you follow Afghanistan, this narrative also probably applies to territories like Marjah or Kandahar since the Obama administration increased troop levels a year ago.

This list now includes Rio de Janeiro, a mega-city that will host some of the soccer World Cup in 2014 and the Olympics in 2016. A "Favela Pacification Program" begun at the end of 2008 is now accelerating as Rio seeks to regain control of pockets of statelessness—decades-old shantytowns and slums called favelas, dispersed throughout the city.

Impoverished, violent, poorly governed neighborhoods are common in Latin America, where rapid urbanization began in the second half of the twentieth century. In most of the region's cities, though, slums concentrate on the outskirts. The poor neighborhoods blanketing the hillsides around downtown Medellín are a classic example.

Rio de Janeiro is different. A legacy of freed slaves relegated to what was then the city's worst land—hilltops and swamps—Rio's shantytowns are scattered throughout the city's geography, including alongside some of its most exclusive neighborhoods. For generations, the favelas were tolerated but ignored. City government made little or no effort to provide services like electricity or water, which are pirated, or even trash collection. Notoriously corrupt police provided little or no protection, if they were present at all.

In last 20 years, these pockets of urban lawlessness were taken over by violent drug-trafficking gangs who carry weapons and deal drugs openly, with a cocaine-on-display brazenness not equaled in Colombian or Mexican cities. Today, most of the violent competition for control of the drug trade takes place between three gangs: the "Red Commandos" (Comando Vermelho), the "Friends of Friends" (Amigos dos Amigos), and the "Pure Third Command" (Terceiro Comando Puro). In addition, some favelas have seen the drug gangs displaced by "militias"—vigilante groups usually led by off-duty police—who rival the gangs in brutality and corruption.

Rio's Military Police have been part of the problem. (Despite their name, the Military Police are no longer a part of Brazil's armed forces, as they were during the country's 1964–1985 dictatorship. Today, Military Police forces are constabularies subordinated to state governments, but with a military-style organization and subject to the military justice system.) With "resisting arrest" the most frequent pretext, the Rio and São Paulo police kill over 1,000 people each year, making them probably the most lethal police forces in the world. Between their reputation for brutality and their reputation for corruption—including collusion with the drug-trafficking gangs—the Military Police are widely distrusted, if not hated, in the favelas.

In December 2008, Rio's state and city governments under Governor Sergio Cabral and Mayor Eduardo Paes (whose PMDB party [Partido do Movimento Democrático Brasileiro] is part of Brazil's ruling coalition) embarked on a new strategy, the Favela Pacification Program. Under the program, the Rio Military Police's elite unit (the Police Special Operations Battalion or BOPE, featured in the "Elite Squad" movies) sweeps into a favela, chasing out—or chasing underground—the gangs. This operation often includes intense urban combat. Immediately afterward, the BOPE are meant to give way to government officials offering social services and a brand-new police force, the Pacification Police Units or UPP.

The UPP is a key piece of this puzzle. Though part of the Military Police, it is a force-within-a-force being created from scratch. It recruits only brand-new police, untainted by association with the old, troubled force, and prefers college graduates. Recruits to the new force receive training with a large component of human rights and community policing skills. Afterward, UPP members are closely monitored for signs of corruption or abusive behavior.

A confidential 2009 WikiLeaks cable from the U.S. Consulate in Rio (worth a read) explains further.

> UPP commander Colonel José Carvalho—a former United Nations Peacekeeping Commander—told us on August 25 that only new police academy recruits are selected into the UPP program. "We need fresh, strong minds, not a Rambo," Carvalho stated. "The older generation of cops is more oriented to kicking down doors and shooting people."

The UPP received glowing praise in an October 2010 *New York Times* article about its operations in the notorious City of God favela, one of the first to be occupied in late 2008.

"Armored personnel carrier at an entrance to the Complexo de Alemão favela." Photograph by Adam Isacson, 2010. From "Rio de Janeiro's Pacification Program," Washington Office on Latin America, blog entry, January 5, 2011, http://www.wola.org/ rio_de_janeiro_s_pacification_program. Used by permission of Adam Isacson and the Washington Office on Latin America.

Even with violent challenges ahead, many Rio residents are rooting for the program. Dilma Rousseff, the leading candidate to be Brazil's next president, has proposed expanding the model to other cities. Millions of dollars in donations from companies like Coca-Cola and a billionaire businessman, Eike Batista, are also pouring in, paying for things like police equipment.

With 1,000–1,500 members and presence in a few dozen favelas—most of them small communities near some of the wealthiest tourist beaches—the UPP is still a small force, though recruitment and training are accelerating. The goal is to arrive at about 12,000 UPPs, present in 160 communities, by 2014, according to Rio state public security secretary José Mariano Beltrame.

While the new police force is barely online, coordination of security with social services has also been a challenge. A program of "quick impact" projects called UPP Social is able to offer some assistance, but lacks the authority to encourage the rest of the federal, state and city governments to make long-overdue investments in education, health, sanitation and similar

"Soldiers posted at an entrance to the Complexo do Alemão Favela." Photograph by Adam Isacson, 2010. From "Rio de Janeiro's Pacification Program," Washington Office on Latin America, blog entry, January 5, 2011, http://www.wola.org/rio_de_janeiro_s_pacification_program. Used by permission of Adam Isacson and the Washington Office on Latin America.

services. Officials said that persuading the Rio government's *"Secretarias"* to coordinate with the Pacification Program has been difficult.

Still, the Favela Pacification Program is moving ahead very quickly— perhaps more rapidly than originally planned.

In October, Security Chief Beltrame told the *New York Times* that gang leaders fleeing "pacified" favelas were moving to larger, more dangerous "mothership" favelas, particularly the sprawling Complexo de Alemão series of favelas in the northern part of the city (population approximately 200,000), not far from Rio's airport. However, Beltrame said at the time, "he probably did not have the manpower" to move the Pacification Program into the Complexo de Alemão during 2010, as it would be a "complex operation."

Yet a month and a half later, the Complexo de Alemão operation had begun. On November 28, hundreds of BOPE and military police agents entered the Vila Cruzeiro part of the complex and moved through the rest of Alemão, chasing out the Comando Vermelho leaders who had been controlling it. The operation for the first time included regular Brazilian Army soldiers and Marines, who drove armored personnel carriers into the neighborhood and continue to guard its perimeter.

The operation was very popular in Rio. It came a week after a wave of bus burnings and other violence that, officials believed, was the gangs' attempt to derail the Pacification Program through intimidation. News footage showed gang leaders running for their lives; Rio residents celebrated.

But now comes the hard part, and it's going to be particularly difficult because as of now there are none of the "new" police—the UPPs—yet recruited, trained and available for duty in Alemão. The disliked Military Police are in charge, along with the Army and Marines, which may stay deployed in the favela until June or even October.

The neighborhood has seen some hints of social services to come—at least, a major campaign by private utilities (electric, phone, cable television) to sign residents up for legal connections. But for now, many Alemão residents we spoke with are wary, if not downright fearful.

We heard allegations of police abuse during the takeover operation, though some civil-society leaders we spoke with contended that the extent of abuse was far less severe than a 2007 offensive in Alemão that killed at least two dozen people. That offensive—ostensibly to secure the city for the upcoming Pan American Games—was not accompanied by public services, community policing or any other effort to improve governance.

One of the most serious allegations, detailed in a December *New York Times* article, is that the Military Police may have allowed as many as 400 gang members to escape. The *Times* piece echoes allegations that the Military Police kept for themselves money confiscated from the drug dealers during the Alemão offensive. During our visit to the Complexo de Alemão, we spoke with residents who told of police kicking in their doors, ransacking their homes and stealing cash and valuables.

This is a crucial moment for winning the favela populations' trust and support. It is of great concern, then, that—for at least the next several months—the "old" Military Police are the main authority, and the much-promoted "new" UPP units aren't ready yet. And beyond policing, the arrival of other social services is still uneven and uncertain, with plans and commitments notably more vague.

Meanwhile Rio has 600 favelas, plus even poorer and more violent slums on its distant outskirts. Some of these favelas may indeed be brought into the city's civic life for the first time. But while political will seems to exist, resource and manpower limitations make it likely that only a relative handful—chiefly those in more central zones of the city—will see much improvement in governance between now and the 2016 Olympics.

Our Rio visit was another reminder that these operations—call them "counterinsurgency," "clear, hold and build," "stabilization and development," "consolidation"—are becoming ever more common in today's Latin America.

Establishing a state presence after a long absence from a territory is a worthy goal, but these ambitious, complex operations don't have universal support. Opponents on the left argue that they are an example of wealthy residents seeking to evict the poor from key zones. Those on the right argue that a civilian component is unimportant, that the state needs only to provide security and enforce the law, and the free market will take care of the rest. Civil-society groups, even those who share the programs' goals, worry about militarization, human rights abuse, and the likelihood that the government's commitment won't be sustained.

Where these programs have been tried, there have been early successes in some cases, and frustrations in all cases. The process requires a level of patience and coordination uncommon in any government. A list of lessons and best practices to keep these programs on track could go on for an entire publication. Four general principles, though, would be the following.

1. The state presence must become civilian as soon as security conditions allow. A military or police occupation alone, in which citizens get few other government services, will fail once the security forces draw down their numbers, as security demands elsewhere will require them to do.

2. Citizens of these zones must be included in decision-making. Security and development plans cannot be imposed from without. If there is a lack of consultation, not only won't there be "buy-in," but populations may oppose the plan outright, fearing that its real goal is their removal.

3. The justice system must be able quickly and transparently to investigate and punish corruption and abuse. A greater state presence can do more harm than good if government representatives steal from or abuse the population with impunity. The resulting damage to the state's credibility can undermine the whole effort.

4. Before claiming security successes, ensure that improved security is truly a result of public policy. Recent past drops in crime have sometimes resulted from either a pact between criminal groups, or one

criminal group's dominance and monopoly over illegal activity. Recent examples include Medellín in the mid-2000s, Nuevo Laredo in the late 2000s, and perhaps São Paulo today. While reduced murder and violent crime rates are welcome, if they are not a result of government institutions' performance, they will be as temporary as the balance of power between competing organized crime groups.

"We Are from Maré and We Have Rights"

The campaign by Redes [de Desenvolvimento] da Maré, a joint initiative of Amnesty International and the Observatório de Favelas [Favela Observatory], calls for the distribution of stickers and folders with instructions for residents.

The action takes place next Tuesday, November 6, at 10:00 AM in front of the Redes headquarters (Rua Sargento Silva Nunes, 1012—Nova Holanda —Maré).

The campaign "Somos da Maré e temos direitos" [We are from Maré and we have rights] is a new initiative by Redes da Maré, Amnesty International, and the Observatório de Favelas to protect the right of local residents to security and to prevent abuses and disrespectful actions on the part of police forces. This initiative is especially significant since Maré is one of the communities about to receive a UPP (Unidade de Polícia Pacificadora).

About fifty thousand flyers with instructions on how to act if approached by police officers, whether on the street or at home, will be distributed among the many favelas of Maré. A schedule of demonstrations in the sixteen neighborhood communities will be released shortly by the organizations responsible for the campaign.

The first event will take place next Tuesday, the sixth, at 10:00 AM, in the Nova Holanda community. The meeting point will be in front of the Redes headquarters (Rua Sargento Silva Nunes, 1012). Along with tips on how to avoid abusive treatment by the police, residents will also receive stickers to put on the doors of their homes that read: "We know our rights! Do not enter this house unlawfully."

"This is not an impromptu movement. We already have an established track record of consciousness-raising among residents of Maré regarding their rights," explained the director of Redes, Eliana Silva. "What we seek to accomplish with this campaign is to include residents as active agents in the process of securing the right to public safety. They are central actors and the raison d'être of the pacification policy, not mere spectators to the whole process."

The instructions of the organizations is that residents utilize existing services to denounce police abuses, such as the Internal Affairs Division of the Military Police and the Human Rights Commission of ALERJ [Assembléia Legislativa do Estado do Rio de Janeiro], the state legislature. Redes da Maré also offers residents a support hotline: (21) 3105-5531.

"We want to break with the logic that we are at war and that anything goes, including violating the rights of residents in communities where UPPs are established," stresses the executive director of Amnesty International in Brazil, Átila Roque. "Pacification is only justified insofar as it guarantees the rights of all citizens, beginning with the residents of favelas."

The campaign makes clear, moreover, that police officers are public servants acting on the people's behalf and thus deserve to be supported so that they can do their work in the best possible manner. All the instructions of the responsible organizations point in this direction and base themselves on the need for clarity when it comes to the rights and duties of local residents.

"The city should belong to everyone; this is a basic tenet. We cannot tolerate the fact that a police officer might approach a resident on the basis of his or her skin color, sexual orientation, physical appearance, or social class, be it in Maré or the Zona Sul," concludes Jaílson Silva, coordinator of Observatório de Favelas. "We want people to take ownership of their city and being aware of their rights is a first step toward everyone being able to circulate freely and safely, beginning with their own neighborhood."

Translated by Andre Pagliarini

An Open Letter from a Massacre Survivor

Wagner dos Santos

Deep fissures in civil society fueled a spate of mass killings (chacinas) that outraged metropolitan Rio in the 1990s. Award-winning journalist Zuenir Ventura's 1994 best seller Cidade Partida *(Broken [or divided] city), explored a chacina that took place August 29, 1993, in a Zona Norte favela named Vigário Geral. Several weeks prior to the shameful events discussed by Ventura, approximately seventy youths had been violently attacked while sheltering in the commercial arcades that face the landmark Igreja da Candelária, in downtown Rio. Eight youths—males aged between eleven and nineteen—were slain; dozens more were injured. Wooden coffins, later replaced by a cross bearing the victims' names, appeared on the Praça Pio X to denounce the attacks and pay homage to the dead. The culprits were later identified as Rio civil and military policemen acting in disguise. Some commentators characterized their alleged motives as retribution for a prior assault on an officer's mother. Others identified the callousness of an undisciplined, underpaid, and corrupt public safety force hostile to street children and other "marginal" elements of a fractured urban society. By 2014, some of the accused culprits of the tragic events at Candelária had been imprisoned, some had been exonerated, and others awaited sentencing.*

The Chacina da Candelária (Massacre at Candelária) provoked indignation among local and international human rights groups; the incident has been the subject of numerous popular treatments, academic studies, and human rights reports. Since the tragic events of 1993, forty-four of the seventy youths involved—largely impoverished black males—have been reported dead. The tragic story of Sandro Barbosa do Nascimento (1978–2000), one of the survivors to come to a violent end, is told in the gripping, if sensationalist, 2002 documentary Ônibus 174 *(Bus 174). Wagner dos Santos, a young man in his early twenties at the time of the incident, was another survivor. His eyewitness testimony was central to the prosecution of nine assailants. Yet Santos's victimization, like Nascimento's, did not end at Candelária. He has never fully recovered from gunshot wounds to the head, and he fears reprisals for his testimony. With the support of human rights advocates, including Amnesty International, Santos left Brazil to reside in Switzerland under the cover of witness protection.*

Santos's 2013 open letter to the Brazilian governing classes, republished in various outlets including Rede de Comunidades e Movimentos Contra a Violência (Communities and Movements Against Violence Network) and reproduced here, recounts his terrifying experiences on the night of July 23, 1993, and his disillusionment with Brazilian society. The letter circulated during the widespread public protests against social inequality and institutional corruption that swept Rio and other Brazilian cities in the middle months of 2013, loosely grouped under the umbrella of the Passe Live (Free Bus Fare) movement. Santos's letter added the poignant voice of historical memory to the human costs of social exclusion, state violence, and impunity. More than twenty years on, Candelária still stains Cariocas' moral consciousness.

To the Governing Classes of Brazil,

For me, twenty years after the Candelária Massacre, little has changed. On the night of July 23, 1993, I was walking down Rua Dom Geraldo to buy cigarettes when a car passed by. I continued walking. I looked back and saw two young men coming over. That's when I realized that the car was returning. Right after that I was seized and put in the car. Inside the automobile an argument broke out between the people who were there. One of them had a gun pointed at my head. Then I felt something entering my head. I ended up losing consciousness, only awakening near the Museu de Arte Moderna.

And then, as everyone knows, my martyrdom began, as I had to stay at the hospital and be denigrated by all. I received every kind of threat, pushing me to the point of leaving a farewell note to those helping me before I slit my wrists. After all this time I, Wagner, consider that in that moment the Brazilian government had the opportunity to make a profound change, but it did not want to, preferring to carry on and leave everything as it was.

I even faced discrimination during the trial as the authorities did not trust the word of a street-dweller, which is what I was considered. I was not even granted an indemnification from the state as I did not have the means to sustain myself. To this day I await facial reconstruction surgery. For twenty years there has been a lack of respect on the part of rulers, a lack of public policies dedicated to poor and black youth. There is no investment in children. It is easier to kill than to care for. I follow the news out of Brazil and see that the country is still far from being a nation oriented toward the poorer population. To the contrary, it directs its actions to privilege the population of high economic means.

Now, with these demonstrations, the rulers are being forced to respond to a populace that is fed up with corruption and the way in which they are treated by the State. Funds for health care are inadequate, as are monies for better wages for teachers. Rulers continue to innovate as with the so-called forced internment policy which takes people to places without the capacity to attend to individuals in need. This happens precisely because the rulers do not ask what people want, instead appearing with some readymade measure. In other countries, rulers listen to the population.

I have noticed that in recent years people who say they are survivors have emerged but have never appeared in any part of the process over this whole period. But I reaffirm that the only people with permission to speak in my name are my family, especially my sister Patrícia de Oliveira.

I do not believe in change in Brazil. I would very much like to, but returning to my country is something that will take a long time, if indeed this will even someday be possible. Unfortunately, I am treated with more respect outside Brazil.

I sincerely hope that the rulers of Brazil put an end to the massacres that continue to take place, whether the violence is against street-dwellers or communities across the country. If that does not happen it will be very difficult to continue saying that Brazil is a democracy.

Wagner dos Santos
Geneva, July 22, 2013

Translated by Andre Pagliarini

Reading and Writing the Suburbs

Biblioteca Parque de Manguinhos;

Samuel M. Silva and Alex Araujo

Manguinhos is a suburban neighborhood that straddles Avenida Brasil, a congested highway in the Zona Norte. Rail lines bisect the area, fragmenting the neighborhood. Home to the sprawling campus of the Fundação Oswaldo Cruz, Brazil's leading biomedical research institute, Manguinhos encompasses a few formal housing tracts situated among a complex of densely populated favelas. Just as police were undertaking a pacification action in October 2012, the Rio state government embarked on an experiment in postindustrial urbanism in Manguinhos: a pioneer "library-park." State officials reimagined the library, traditionally a temple for the silent worship of the printed word and the preservation and storage of printed books. This experiment was predicated on the idea that memory, creativity, and culture are held not only in books but in the relationship between individuals and the place where books are read and written.

The Biblioteca Parque de Manguinhos (Manguinhos Library-Park) is modeled on pioneering efforts in Colombia, where reenvisioned public libraries have been built in geographically marginal, underserved urban communities plagued by violent crime and drug trafficking (like suburban Rio). A sun-drenched, open space with clean modernist lines, the site is a laboratory for learning and expression. A similar import from Colombia is the Teleférico do Alemão, a cable-propelled transit system in the Complexo do Alemão (a community that has seen a new library accompany "pacification") that provides low-cost transportation to residents of the communities that neighbor Manguinhos. Such initiatives imagine new ways to enable Rio residents to exercise the right to the city. They represent a sharp departure from past public policies of favela eradication, or abandonment to narcotraffickers.

The first document here, taken from the institution's homepage, introduces the Biblioteca Parque de Manguinhos to the online public. Vera Saboya, a state official, shows enthusiasm and ambition for the project's social aims in the communities of the subúrbio. The piece offers a glimpse into the cross-city collaborations that have accompanied pacification, as the venerable Brazilian Academy of Letters joined forces with state education agencies and favelados to build a new space and sentiment for the written, spoken, and performed word. The second document, appearing in the library-park's online journal, Setor X, *features an interview with Manguinhos resident Alex Araujo, a locksmith and aspiring writer. It speaks to the multiple paths of creativity and self-expression that wend their way through the books and media that are increasingly available to the residents of Rio's vast suburbs as part of their basic cultural rights to the city.*

Introducing Manguinhos Library-Park

The Biblioteca Parque de Manguinhos is the first in a network that the Secretariat of Culture of the State of Rio de Janeiro has implemented, with the goal of creating a new level of services for the communities in the state.

Inaugurated in April of 2010, its main point of reference is the highly successful experiments implemented in Medellín and Bogotá in Colombia; it is a cultural and shared community space that offers broad accessibility to the population, in physical plant, staffing, and services offered.

In its 2,300 square meters, the Parque de Manguinhos library has a comfortable main room, a large reading room for study and classes, a multimedia space, a play room, and, soon, a literary café and an auditorium that seats 200. The "My Neighborhood" room attends to the need for meeting rooms and community forums.

In these spaces, one can freely access the bookshelves and the internet, watch films, listen to music, participate in innumerable cultural activities, or put in a request to borrow books and films among the over 27,000 titles available in its holdings.

Based on the idea that libraries should not only be silent spaces and should, even more, be something like cultural centers with broad accessibility, the Parque de Manguinhos library will carry out cultural activities and will promote reading through the most diverse range of support, envisioning its role as also that of stimulating the production, enjoyment, and diffusion of artistic production and, especially, making possible access to culture.

In this sense, crucial to the development of the library has been WordLab (PalavraLab)—the Word Laboratory Program. Aimed at the development of language in the most diverse forms of textual production, WordLab is based on two principal axes: laboratories for the development of language and the production of content, and the promotion of creative writing courses and workshops.

According to the Superintendent of Reading and Knowledge of the State

"Favela de Manguinhos." Photograph by Junius, 2009. Licensed under Creative Commons Attribution Share-Alike license.

"Inauguração da Biblioteca Parque de Manguinhos." Photograph by Pedro França/MinC, 2010. Licensed under Creative Commons Attribution 2.0 Generic license.

Secretariat of Culture, Vera Saboya, this space plays an important role in the communities that it serves.

"The Parque Library is a multifunctional public library in an at-risk area and, thus, it plays a role in the reduction of violence, creating a space for the community to gather together. Culture has a decisive role to play in the construction of a citizen who is both critical and confident in his or her role as a creator in society. In this way, it transforms through reflection, through creation, and through joy," says Vera.

The Brazilian Academy of Letters is the patron of the Parque de Manguinhos Library, which it helps through the donation of books, with consultations regarding the acquisition of new titles for updating its collection and advisement concerning scheduling seminars. In the future, we will launch, in partnership with the State Secretariat of Culture, the Manguinhos Library-Park / Brazilian Academy of Letters literary prize.

Translated by Amy Chazkel

Interview with a Local Writer

SAMUEL M. SILVA: What is your occupation?

ALEX ARAUJO: I am a locksmith, and I work as a commercial representative, and besides that, I am also a writer.

SMS: How long have you been working as a locksmith?

AA: I have been a locksmith for twenty-seven years. I never had any other profession. I started out at a boarding school for boys, Funabem, when I was eleven.

SMS: And what brought you to take up writing?

AA: After many years, in 2008 I purchased the business where I worked. I took on the debts. The company was already running in the red with the banks and suppliers, and I contracted even more debts. This is without even saying anything about the various problems with clients, employees, and suppliers. The problems snowballed to the point that by the end of 2011 I could not take it anymore and I closed down my locksmith shop, though I still continued to work in the business. I had shut down the shop but its problems continued to follow me and in January of 2012 I decided to write about what I was going through, beginning to write a book with the working title "Boomerang." In truth I had told myself: if I write a book and publish it that will be the best business deal of my life as I will be earning a living making use of my imagination, and I will not have the problems of buying and selling, and beyond that, my imagination will be my stockroom for ideas.

SMS: What is your preferred genre?

AA: I write all kinds of genres.

SMS: You write diverse literary genres, why is that?

AA: Because despite being a locksmith, I create and invent a variety of things, and some people call me a crazy professor, perhaps that's why I have such diverse literary ideas.

SMS: And why do you called yourself an *escritor da pesada* [weighty writer]?

AA: First off, because I was overweight, and second because the place where I live, Manguinhos, was known as *barra pesada* [rough-and-tumble] because of the drug traffic, and third for the inspiration from characters in the media: *Um Tira da Pesada* [*Beverly Hills Cop*], "Tio da Pesada" [*The Bernie Mac Show*], et cetera.

SMS: And how do you find the writer's life?

AA: I know that it is difficult to live off one's writing, but I intend to do so. That's the reason I write different genres for diverse readers.

SMS: Do you believe that there is a readership for your books?

AA: Yes, I was never much one for reading and today I cannot live without reading and writing.

SMS: How do you intend to have your books published?

AA: I am going to try various paths: through a publisher, which I know to be difficult; or I edit it on my own and take my chances with an ebook.

SMS: Does your family support you in your new career as a writer?

AA: Yes, though there was some discord at the beginning.

SMS: Do you have any sense of how much you might earn as a writer?

AA: I never much thought about that, but I intend to earn enough to sustain myself.

SMS: You also compose funk music and produce videos. What's the inspiration for this?

AA: It all came about from the need to create a sound track for my films.

SMS: Alex, thank you very much for this interview and please be sure to let us know when you have published one of your books. Much success in your new career!

Translated by Daryle Williams

A Century of Change at the Port

Halley Pacheco de Oliveira and Unknown Photographer(s)

Over the past five centuries, the Port of Rio de Janeiro has remained a central part of the city and its sense of self. The contemporary port installations that run from Praça Mauá to Santo Cristo, specializing in container freight and transoceanic cruise ships, still bear signs of bygone activities of warehousing, the commodity trade, and immigrant arrivals. In recent years an ambitious project named Porto Maravilha (Port Marvel, a word play on Rio's "marvelous" nickname), has embraced a sweeping renovation of the zona portuária (port zone), updating the region's obsolete infrastructure, demolishing the elevated highways that separated the bay from the city, and creating new spaces of commerce, residence, and sociability.

For all of its sweeping ambition, Porto Maravilha is hardly unique; Rio's evolving port zone has experienced numerous (highly disruptive) readaptations, especially over the past century. Until the early twentieth century, smaller vessels ferried cargo from ship holds to various piers built along the bay shore. In the absence of a centralized port authority, private owners oversaw activities at each pier. Cargo was hauled on the backs of stevedores or with the aid of manual hoists and winches. Inadequate facilities impeded the arrival of large ships and the speedy transit of goods and people between ship and shore. In 1903, the federal government approved a project to modernize and urbanize an immense area reclaimed from the bay. Lauro Müller (1863–1926), the minister of roads and public works, and another engineer, Francisco de Paula Bicalho (1836–1913), oversaw works carried out by the C. H. Walker Company, an English firm. The first two photographs here, taken from an album held by the Rio state archive that documents the port improvements of 1905–1913, reveal the contrast between the nineteenth-century storehouses (first photo) and the new installations that handled large cargo and passenger steamships (second photo). These images capture the modernized port installations that transformed the port region, erasing the traces of earlier facilities where enslaved Africans were disembarked en route to nearby barracoons. We also glimpse the ambitious urbanistic and visual changes adjacent to the hilly neighborhoods where dockworkers and their families built communities closely associated with Carioca working-class life.

Twenty-first-century reforms once again remake the port and its surroundings.

"Antigos trapiches da Saúde." Photographer unknown, 1913. From *Álbum das Obras do Porto do Rio de Janeiro.* Courtesy of Arquivo Público do Estado do Rio de Janeiro, Rio de Janeiro.

Today's renovation project, however, takes a different approach to the historical uses and the communities of the maritime district. Porto Maravilha planners envision the recuperation of the vestiges of a city that nearly vanished in the early twentieth century. Archeological excavations have revealed remains of the Cais da Imperatriz, a wharf built for the 1843 arrival of Emperor Pedro II's Italian bride Teresa Cristina. The digs have also uncovered vestiges of the Cais do Valongo, an even older wharf that served as one of the most important points of entry for enslaved Africans in the Americas (third photo). The exhibits at the Memorial dos Pretos Novos, an organ of the Instituto de Pesquisa e Memória Pretos Novos (Newly Arrived Blacks Research and Memory Institute), interpret the slave past, including a mass grave of the enslaved that functioned through the 1830s (fourth photo). Porto Maravilha is a large-scale, architectural-urbanist undertaking sensitive to the importance of urban memory, relating the city's past and present throughout the streets, piers, waters, and memories of the port.

"Um trecho do caes concluido." Photographer unknown, 1913. From *Álbum das Obras do Porto do Rio de Janeiro*. Courtesy of Arquivo Público do Estado do Rio de Janeiro, Rio de Janeiro.

"Cemitérito dos Pretos Novos." Cais do Valongo / Cais da Imperatriz. Photograph by Halley Pacheco de Oliveira, 2013. Licensed under Creative Commons Attribution Share Alike 3.0 license.

"Cemitérito dos Pretos Novos." Memorial dos Pretos Novos. Photograph by Halley Pacheco de Oliveira, 2013. Licensed under Creative Commons Attribution Share Alike 3.0 license.

Suggestions for Further Reading and Viewing

What follows is a list of published works about the city of Rio de Janeiro directed to anyone interested in exploring the city beyond *The Rio de Janeiro Reader*. With an Anglophone readership primarily in mind, the suggestions that follow omit works that are only available in Portuguese and other languages. We include, however, some of the small but growing number of translated classics of Brazilian scholarship about the Marvelous City. This list also includes a select number of subtitled feature-length motion pictures and documentaries set in Rio, as well as a sampling of canonical literary works by Carioca authors available in English translation. Readers with a working command of Portuguese can expand their knowledge by consulting the online catalogues of the Arquivo Nacional (the Brazilian National Archive), the Arquivo Histórico Ultramarino (the Portuguese colonial archive), the Arquivo Nacional Torre do Tombo (the Portuguese National Archives), the Fundação Biblioteca Nacional (the Brazilian National Library), the Instituto Moreira Salles (exceptionally strong in photography), the Museu de Imagem e Som (a tremendous resource on video and music), and other cultural centers and museums located in Rio. For more information on such institutions, see the municipal government's multilingual official guide at http://www.rioguiaoficial.com.br/.

Websites and General Works about Rio de Janeiro

The Brazilian National Library, located in the heart of downtown Rio since the early nineteenth century, makes available a growing collection of digitized periodicals, photographs and prints, maps, and rare books. Most titles are in Portuguese, but the library's digital collection also contains important foreign-language items, especially illustrated traveler accounts. Visit http://bndigital.bn.br. Hundreds of full-text digitized serials, including titles from the small Carioca English-language press, can be accessed through the library's Hemeroteca Digital, http://hemerotecadigital.bn.br/.

The Instituto Brasileiro de Geografia e Estatística (Brazilian Institute of Geography and Statistics) regularly updates demographic and other statistical data on the city of Rio de Janeiro, drawing from statistical modeling, household surveys, census data, and other sources. Visit http://cod.ibge.gov .br/RIJ.

Porto Maravilha, the consortium responsible for the renovation of the port zone, has an English-language website that highlights the port's past, present, and future. Visit http://www.portomaravilha.com.br/web/esq/ mnuBrieFing.aspx.

The Rio Secretariat of Urbanism maintains a site featuring maps and illustrations with animated graphics showing the city's changing physical and human geography. Visit http://portalgeo.rio.rj.gov.br/EOUrbana/.

Synthetic works on the city include Ruy Castro, *Rio de Janeiro: A City on Fire*, translated by John Gledson (New York: Bloomsbury, 2004), and Beatriz Jaguaribe, *Rio de Janeiro: Urban Life through the Eyes of the City* (New York: Routledge, 2014).

Part I. Colonial Rio

Boxer, C. R. *Salvador de Sá and the Struggle for Brazil and Angola, 1602–1686.* London: Athlone Press, 1952.

Edmundo, Luiz. *Rio in the Time of the Viceroys.* Translated by Dorothea Harneker Momsen. Rio de Janeiro: J. R. de Oliveira, 1936.

Lara, Silvia Hunold. "Customs and Costumes: Carlos Julião and the Image of Black Slaves in Late Eighteenth-Century Brazil." *Slavery and Abolition* 23:2 (2010), 123–146.

Léry, Jean de. *History of a Voyage to the Land of Brazil.* Translated by Janet Whatley. Berkeley: University of California Press, 1993.

Luccock, John. *Notes on Rio de Janeiro, and the Southern Parts of Brazil; Taken during a Residence of Ten Years in That Country, from 1808 to 1818.* London: S. Leigh, 1820.

Schultz, Kirsten. *A Tropical Versailles: Empire, Monarchy and the Portuguese Royal Court in Rio de Janeiro, 1808–1821.* New York: Routledge, 2001.

Soares, Mariza de Carvalho. *People of Faith: Slavery and African Catholics in Eighteenth-Century Rio de Janeiro.* Translated by Jerry Dennis Metz. Durham, N.C.: Duke University Press, 2011.

Wilken, Patrick. *Empire Adrift: The Portuguese Court in Rio de Janeiro, 1808–1821.* London: Bloomsbury, 2004.

Part II. Imperial Rio

Almeida, Manuel Antônio de. *Memoirs of a Militia Sergeant* [*Memórias de um Sargento de Milícias*]. Translated by Ronald W. Souza. New York: Oxford University Press, 2000.

Azevedo, Aluísio. *Mulatto* [*O Mulato*]. Translated by Murray Graeme Macnicoll. Texas Pan-American Series. Austin: University of Texas Press, 1993.

Barbosa, Rosana. *Immigration and Xenophobia: Portuguese Immigrants in Early Nineteenth-Century Rio de Janeiro*. Lanham, Md.: University Press of America, 2008.

Barman, Roderick. *Citizen Emperor: Pedro II and the Making of Brazil, 1825–1891*. Stanford, Calif.: Stanford University Press, 1999.

Cowling, Camillia. *Conceiving Freedom: Women of Color, Gender, and the Abolition of Slavery in Havana and Rio de Janeiro*. Chapel Hill: University of North Carolina Press, 2013.

Dent, Charles Hastings. *A Year in Brazil, with Notes on the Abolition of Slavery, the Finances of the Empire, Religion, Meteorology, Natural History, etc*. London: K. Paul Trench and Company, 1886.

Frank, Zephyr. *Dutra's World: Wealth and Family in Nineteenth-Century Rio de Janeiro*. Albuquerque: University of New Mexico Press, 2004.

Hahner, June E., and Adèle Toussaint-Samson. *A Parisian in Brazil: The Travel Account of a Frenchwoman in Nineteenth-Century Rio de Janeiro*. New York: Rowman and Littlefield, 2001.

Holloway, Thomas. *Policing Rio de Janeiro: Repression and Resistance in a Nineteenth-Century City*. Stanford, Calif.: Stanford University Press, 1993.

Karasch, Mary C. *Slave Life in Rio de Janeiro, 1808–1850*. Princeton, N.J.: Princeton University Press, 1987.

Kraay, Hendrik. *Days of National Festivity in Rio de Janeiro, Brazil, 1823–1889*. Stanford, Calif.: Stanford University Press, 2013.

Lauderdale Graham, Sandra. *House and Street: The Domestic World of Servants and Masters in Nineteenth-Century Rio de Janeiro*. Austin: University of Texas Press, 1992.

Machado de Assis, Joaquim Maria. *Dom Casmurro: A Novel*. Translated by Helen Caldwell. New York: Farrar, Straus and Giroux, 2009.

Machado de Assis, Joaquim Maria. *Posthumous Memories of Brás Cubas* [*Memórias Póstumas de Brás Cubás*]. Translated by Gregory Rabassa. New York: Oxford University Press, 1998.

Machado de Assis, Joaquim Maria. *The Psychiatrist and Other Stories*. Berkeley: University of California Press, 2000.

Magaldi, Cristina. *Music in Imperial Rio de Janeiro: European Culture in a Tropical Milieu*. New York: Scarecrow Press, 2004.

Silva, Eduardo. *Prince of the People: The Life and Times of a Brazilian Free Man of Color*. Translated by Moyra Ashford. New York: Verso, 1993.

Spatial History Project, Stanford University. "The Broken Paths of Freedom: Free Africans in Nineteenth-Century Slave Society." http://web.stanford.edu/group/spatialhistory/cgi-bin/site/project.php?id=1069.

Spatial History Project, Stanford University. "Terrain of History." http://web.stanford.edu/group/spatialhistory/cgi-bin/site/project.php?id=999.

Part III. Republican Rio

Azevedo, Aluísio. *The Slum* [*O Cortiço*]. Translated by David H. Rosenthal. New York: Oxford University Press, 2000.

Barreto, Alfonso Henriques de Lima. *The Sad End of Policárpo Quaresma* [*O Triste Fim do Policarpo Quaresma*]. Translated by Mark Carlyon. New York: Penguin Classics, 2015.

Carvalho, Bruno. *Porous City: A Cultural History of Rio de Janeiro*. Liverpool: Liverpool University Press, 2013.

Caulfield, Sueann. *In Defense of Honor: Sexual Morality, Modernity, and Nation in Early Twentieth-Century Brazil*. Durham, N.C.: Duke University Press, 2000.

Chazkel, Amy. *Laws of Chance: Brazil's Clandestine Lottery and the Making of Urban Public Life*. Durham, N.C.: Duke University Press, 2011.

Fischer, Brodwyn M. *A Poverty of Rights: Citizenship and Inequality in Twentieth-Century Rio de Janeiro*. Stanford, Calif.: Stanford University Press, 2010.

Hahner, June E. *Poverty and Politics: The Urban Poor in Brazil, 1870–1920*. Albuquerque: University of New Mexico Press, 1986.

Hertzman, Marc A. *Making Samba: A New History of Race and Music in Brazil*. Durham, N.C.: Duke University Press, 2013.

Love, Joseph. *Revolt of the Whip*. Stanford, Calif.: Stanford University Press, 2012.

McCann, Bryan. *Hello, Hello Brazil: Popular Music in the Making of Modern Brazil*. Durham, N.C.: Duke University Press, 2004.

Meade, Teresa. *"Civilizing" Rio: Reform and Resistance in a Brazilian City*. University Park: Penn State University Press, 1997.

Needell, Jeffrey. *A Tropical Belle Époque: Elite Culture and Society in Turn-of-the-Century Rio de Janeiro*. New York: Cambridge University Press, 1987.

Portal Augusto Malta, Arquivo Geral da Cidade do Rio de Janeiro. http://portalaugustomalta.rio.rj.gov.br/.

Rio, João do. *The Enchanting Soul of the Streets* [*A Alma Encantadora das Ruas*]. Translated by Mark Carlyon. Rio de Janeiro: Cidade Viva Editora, 2010.

Soares, Jô. *A Samba for Sherlock* [*O Xangô de Baker Street*]. Translated by Clifford Landers. New York: Vintage, 1998.

Sussekind, Flora. *Cinematograph of Words: Literature, Technique, and Modernization in Brazil*. Translated by Paulo Britto. Stanford, Calif.: Stanford University Press, 1997.

Vianna, Hermano. *The Mystery of Samba: Popular Music and National Identity in Brazil*. Translated by John Charles Chasteen. Chapel Hill: University of North Carolina Press, 1999.

White, Richard Dunning. *Sketches of Rio de Janeiro and Environs*. Exeter, England: William Pollard and Company, 1897.

Williams, Daryle. *Culture Wars in Brazil: The First Vargas Regime*. Durham, N.C.: Duke University Press, 2001.

Part IV. Recent Rio

Alberto, Paulina. "When Rio was *Black*: Soul Music, National Culture, and the Politics of Racial Comparison in 1970s Brazil." *Hispanic American Historical Review* 89:1 (February 2009), 3–39.

Arias, Enrique Desmond. *Drugs and Democracy in Rio de Janeiro: Trafficking, Social Networks, and Public Security*. Chapel Hill: University of North Carolina Press, 2006.

Conde, Maite. *Consuming Visions: Cinema, Writing, and Modernity in Rio de Janeiro*. Charlottesville: University of Virginia Press, 2012.

Evenson, Norma. *Two Brazilian Capitals: Architecture and Urbanism in Rio de Janeiro and Brasília*. New Haven, Conn.: Yale University Press, 1973.

Fonseca, Rubem. *The Taker and Other Stories*. Rochester, N.Y.: Open Letter, 2008.

Gaffney, Christopher Thomas. *Temples of the Earthbound Gods: Stadiums in the Cultural Landscapes of Rio de Janeiro and Buenos Aires*. Austin: University of Texas Press, 2009.

Garcia-Roza, Luíz Alfredo. Inspector Espinosa Series. Vols. 1–7. London: Picador, 2003–2010 [1996–2007].

Gay, Robert. *Bruno: Conversations with a Brazilian Drug Dealer*. Durham, N.C.: Duke University Press, 2015.

Gay, Robert. *Lúcia: Testimonies of a Brazilian Drug Dealer's Woman*. Philadelphia: Temple University Press, 2005.

Goldstein, Donna. *Laughter Out of Place: Race, Class, Violence, and Sexuality in a Rio Shantytown*. Berkeley: University of California Press, 2013.

Green, James N. *Beyond Carnival: Male Homosexuality in Twentieth-Century Brazil*. Chicago: University of Chicago Press, 2001.

Guillermoprieto, Alma. *Samba*. Reprint ed. New York: Vintage, 1991.

Hanchard, M. G. *Orpheus and Power: The Movimento Negro of Rio de Janeiro and São Paulo, 1945–1988*. Princeton, N.J.: Princeton University Press, 1998.

Langland, Victoria. *Speaking of Flowers: Student Movements and the Making and Remembering of 1968 in Military Brazil*. Durham, N.C.: Duke University Press, 2014.

Lins, Paulo. *City of God*. Translated by Alison Entrikin. New York: Bloomsbury, 2006.

Lispector, Clarice. *Hour of the Star*. Translated by Giovanni Ponteiro. Manchester: Carcanet, 1986.

Magalhães, Rosa. *Fazendo Carnaval / The Making of Carnival*. Rio de Janeiro: Lacerda Editores, 1997.

McCann, Bryan. *Hard Times in the Marvelous City: From Dictatorship to Democracy in the Favelas of Rio de Janeiro*. Durham, N.C.: Duke University Press, 2014.

Melo, Patrícia. *Inferno*. Translated by Clifford Landers. New York: Bloomsbury, 2003.

Neate, Patrick, and Damian Platt. *Culture Is Our Weapon: Making Music and Changing Lives in Rio de Janeiro*. New York: Penguin, 2010.

Penglase, R. Ben. *Living with Insecurity in a Brazilian Favela: Urban Violence and Daily Life*. New Brunswick, N.J.: Rutgers University Press, 2014.

Perlman, Janice. *Favela: Four Decades of Living on the Edge in Rio*. New York: Oxford University Press, 2011.

Perlman, Janice. *The Myth of Marginality: Urban Poverty and Politics in Rio de Janeiro*. Berkeley: University of California Press, 1976.

Rochester, Julia. *The Candelária Massacre: How Wagner dos Santos Survived the Street Children's Killing That Shook Brazil*. New York: Vision, 2008.

Silva, Benedita da, Medea Benjamin, and Maisa Mendonça. *Benedita da Silva: An Afro-Brazilian Woman's Story of Politics and Love*. Oakland, Calif.: Food First Books, 1997.

Testino, Mario. *Mario DE JANEIRO Testino*. Los Angeles: TASCHEN America, 2009.

Treece, David. *Brazilian Jive: From Samba to Bossa and Rap*. London: Reaktion Books, 2013.

Weber, Bruce. *O Rio de Janeiro: A Photographic Journal*. New York: Knopf, 1986.

Rio de Janeiro on the Big Screen

O Amor Natural. Dir. Heddy Honigmann. First Run Features, 1996.

Another Love Story [*Maré, Nossa História de Amor*]. Dir. Lúcia Murat. Wide Management, 2007.

Babilônia 2000. Dir. Eduardo Coutinho. Riofilme, 2002.

Black Orpheus [*Orfeu Negro*]. Dir. Marcel Camus. Lopert Pictures Corporation, 1959.

Bossa Nova. Dir. Bruno Barreto. Sony Pictures Classics, 2000.

Bus 174 [*Ônibus 174*]. Dirs. José Padilha and Felipe Lacerda. THINKfilm, 2002.

Carnaval Atlântida. Dirs. José Carlos Burle and Carlos Manga. Sagres Filmes, 1952.

Casa Grande. Dir. Fellipe Barbosa. Migdal Filmes, 2015.

Central Station [*Central do Brasil*]. Dir. Walter Salles. Sony Pictures Classics, 1998.

City of God [*Cidade de Deus*]. Dirs. Fernando Meirelles and Kátia Lund. Miramax Films, 2002.

City of Men [*Cidade dos Homens*]. Dir. Paulo Morelli. Miramax Films, 2009.

Edifício Master [Master building]. Dir. Eduardo Coutinho. VideoFilmes, 2002.

Elite Squad [*Tropa de Elite*]. Dir. José Padilha. IFC Films, 2007.

Entranced Earth [*Terra em Transe*]. Dir. Glauber Rocha. Mapa Filmes, 1967.

Flying Down to Rio. Dir. Thornton Freeland. RKO Radio Pictures, 1933.

Four Days in September [*O que É Isso, Companheiro?*]. Dir. Bruno Barreto. Miramax Films, 1997.

It's All True. Dirs. Orson Welles and Norman Foster. Paramount Pictures, 1993.

Lucio Flavio [*Lúcio Flávio, O Passageiro da Agonia*]. Dir. Hector Babenco. Unifilms, 1981.

Madame Satã. Dir. Karim Aïnouz. Wellspring, 2002.

The Music according to Antonio Carlos Jobim [*A Música segundo Tom Jobim*]. Dir. Nelson Pereira dos Santos. Sony Pictures, 2012.

Notorious. Dir. Alfred Hitchcock. RKO Radio Pictures, 1946.

Orfeu. Dir. Carlos Diegues. New Yorker Films, 1999.

The Other Side of the Street [*O Outro Lado da Rua*]. Dir. Marcos Bernstein. Strand Releasing, 2006.

Pixote [*Pixote: A Lei do Mais Fraco*]. Dir. Hector Babenco. Unifilms, 1980.

Possible Loves [*Amores Possíveis*]. Dir. Sandra Werneck. Cineluz, 2001.

Reaching for the Moon [*Flores Raras*]. Dir. Bruno Barreto. Wolfe Video, 2013.

Rio. Dir. Carlos Saldanha. 20th Century Fox, 2011.

Rio Breaks. Dir. Justin Mitchell. Breadcrumb Trail, 2009.

Rio Sex Comedy [*Rio, sexe et (un peu de) tragi-comédie*]. Dir. Jonathan Nossiter. Océan Films, 2011.

Rio, Zona Norte. Dir. Nelson Pereira dos Santos. Lívio Bruni Produções Cinematográficos, 1957.

Road to Rio. Dir. Normal McLeod. Paramount Pictures, 1947.

Subway to the Stars [*Um Trem para as Estrelas*]. Dir. Carlos Diegues. FilmDallas Pictures, 1987.

Summer Showers [*Chuvas de Verão*]. Dir. Carlos Diegues. Unifilms, 1978.

Via Appia. Dir. Jochen Hick. Strand Releasing, 1991.

Waste Land [*Lixo Extraordinário*]. Dirs. Lucy Walker, João Jardim, and Karen Harley. Arthouse Films, 2010.

The Xango from Baker Street [*O Xangô de Baker Street*]. Dir. Miguel Farias Jr. Columbia TriStar, 2001.

Acknowledgment of Copyrights and Sources

Part I. Colonial Rio

"A Navigator's Diary," by Pero Lopes de Sousa, from *Diário da navegação da armada que foi á terra do Brasil em 1530 sob a Capitania-Mor de Martin Affonso de Souza* (Lisbon: Sociedade Propagadora de Conhecimentos Utéis, 1839), 25–26.

"On 'Brazilian Savages,'" by Jean de Léry, from "Of the natural qualities, strength, stature, nudity, disposition, and ornamentation of the body of the Brazilian savages, both men and women, who live in America, and whom I frequented for about a year," in *History of a Voyage to the Land of Brazil, Otherwise Called America*, translated by Janet Whatley (Berkeley: University of California Press, 1990), 56–68.

"Channeling the Carioca River," minutes of the Municipal Council of the City of Rio de Janeiro, project for the Arcos da Carioca, presented April 25, 1648, printed in *O Rio de Janeiro no século XVII: Accordãos e Vereanças do Senado da Camara, copiados do livro original existente no Archivo do Districto Federal, e relativos aos annos de 1635 até 1650* (Rio de Janeiro: Oficinas Graficas do *Jornal do Brasil*, 1935), 160–161.

"The Cachaça Revolt," (1) by Agostino Barbalho Bezerra, written on November 8, 1660, from "Excerpto de uma memoria manuscripta sobre a história do Rio de Janeiro durante o governo Salvador Corrêa de Sá e Benevides, que se acaha na Bibliotheca publica d'esta côrte," reprinted in *Revista do Instituto Histórico e Geográfico Brasileiro* 3:9 (Rio de Janeiro: Imprensa Americana, 1841), 3–28; (2) by Salvador Correia de Sá e Benevides, "Extracts of the Announcement of the Election and Acclamation of Governor Agostinho Barbalho Bezerra, Rio de Janeiro, November 8, 1660," from "Excerpto de uma memória manuscripta sobre a história do Rio de Janeiro durante o governo Salvador Corrêa de Sá e Benevides, que se acaha na Bibliotheca publica d'esta côrte," reprinted in *Revista do Instituto Histórico e Geográfico Brasileiro* 3:9 (Rio de Janeiro: Imprensa Americana, 1841), 31–33.

"French Corsairs Attack," (1) by René Duguay-Trouin, in *The Memoirs of M. du Gué-Trouin, Chief of a Squadron in the Royal Navy of France, and Great Cross of the Military Order of St. Lewis . . ."* (London: J. Batley, 1732), 216–218; (2) by Jonas Finck, from "To the Reverend Mr. Boehm at London: From the Printer who was sent from England to India. He gives an Account of his Voyage to, and Arrival at St. Sebastian . . . ," in *Propagation of the Gospel in the East: Being a Collection of Letters from the Protestant Missionaries and Other Worthy Persons in the East-Indies*, by Bartholomaeus Ziegenbalg, pt. 3, 1st letter (London: J. Downing, 1718), 6–8.

"The Wages of Indigenous Labor," by André Soares de Souza, in "Copia de requerimento em que os oficiais do Senado da Cidade do Rio de Janeiro pedem a Sua Majestade que não se altere a forma de pagamento do jornal devido aos indios que trabalham na obra de condução da agua do Carioca para a cidade," Arquivo Nacional, Rio de Janeiro, Fundo Vice-Reino, Diversas Caixas, n.d.

"The Customary Rights of Market Women," (1) by public attorney, from "Questão das quitandeiras, com um requerimento delas, datado de 29 de maio de 1776, e outros documentos," Arquivo Nacional, Rio de Janeiro, Diversos Códices [Fundo NP], Códice 807, vol. 19, folhas 62–68, Procurador e demais oficiais municipais, May 29, 1776. (2) by Municipal Officials, "Questão das quitandeiras, com um requerimento delas, datado de 29 de maio de 1776, e outros documentos," Arquivo Nacional, Rio de Janeiro, Diversos Códices [Fundo NP], Códice 807, vol. 19, folhas 62–68, Procurador e demais oficiais municipais, June 11, 1776.

"Valongo, a Notorious Slave Market," by Bráz Hermenegildo do Amaral, from "Os grandes mercados de escravos africanos; As tribus importadas; sua distribuição regional," in *Annaes do 1º Congresso internacional de Historia da America*, vol. 5 (Rio de Janeiro: Imprensa Nacional, 1925–30), 467–468.

"Lettered Men under Investigation," (1) letter from Conde de Resende [José Luiz de Castro] to Antônio Diniz da Cruz e Silva, "Ofício de 11 de junho de 1794 escrito pelo vice-rei Conde de Resende ao desembargador-chanceler Antônio Diniz da Cruz e Silva," written June 11, 1794, in *Autos da devassa: Prisão dos letrados do Rio de Janeiro* (Rio de Janeiro: Ed. UERJ, 2002), 71; (2) statement by José Bernardo da Silveira Frade, from "Devassa Ordenada pelo Vicerei Conde de Resende, 1794," in *Anais da Biblioteca Nacional de Rio de Janeiro* 61 (1939): 262–265.

"Cultivating Cinnamon in Late Colonial Rio," by Bernardino António Gomes, from *Memoria sobre a canella do Rio de Janeiro: Offerecida ao Principe do Brazil nosso senhor pelo Senado da Camara da mesma cidade no anno de 1798* (Rio de Janeiro: Impressão Régia, 1809), 7–23; 39–40.

"Eagerly Awaiting the Royal Family," by Padre Luiz Gonçalves dos Santos [Padre Perereca], from *Memorias para servir a historia do reino do Brasil: Divididas em tres epocas da felicidade, honra, e gloria, escriptas na Corte do Rio de Janeiro no anno de 1821, e offerecidas à S. Magestade El Rey Nosso Senhor o Senhor D. João VI*, tomo 1 (Lisbon: Impressão Regia, 1825), 1–19.

"'Infectious Disorders' of the Port," by William Sidney Smith, from The National Archives of the U.K. (TNA): Kew, ADM 1/19: Letter from W. Sidney Smith to W. W. Pole, British Admiralty, July 24, 1808.

"The Passeio Público," by John Luccock, in *Notes on Rio de Janeiro and the Southern Parts of Brazil* (London: Samuel Leigh, 1820), 87–89.

Part II. Imperial Rio

"The Feast of the Holy Spirit," by Henry Chamberlain and G. Hunt, from "The Feast of Espirito Santo," in *Views and Costumes of the City and Neighbourhood of Rio de Janeiro* (London: T. McLean, 1822), unpaginated.

"The Emperor Dissolves the Constitutional Assembly," by Henry Chamberlain, from The National Archives of the U.K.: Kew FO 63/261, fs. 87–113: Dispatch from Henry

Chamberlain to George Canning (and enclosure of a translation of the handbill "Proclamação" by Pedro I, printed by Imprensa Nacional), November 15, 1823.

"Views of the Palace Square," by Jean-Baptiste Debret, from *Voyage pittoresque et historique au Brésil, ou Séjour d'un artiste français au Brésil, depuis 1816 jusqu'en 1831 inclusivement*, vol. 3 (1839) (Paris: F. Didot, 1834–1839), 111–118.

"The Night of the Bottle-Whippings," unsigned, from "Pertubassões," *O Republico*, no. 48 (March 21, 1831), 222–223.

"The Slave Dance Called Candomblé," by Eusébio de Queiroz, Arquivo Geral da Cidade do Rio de Janeiro, Policia da Corte [Fundo OE], Códice 6.1.25, folha 12 [Request from Police Chief Eusebio de Queiroz Coutinho Mattoso da Camara to the Câmara Municipal], June 1, 1833.

"From the Dungeon to the House of Correction," by Eusébio de Queiroz, Arquivo Nacional, Rio de Janeiro, Polícia da Côrte, Códice 339, 1837, vol. 1 [Chief of Police Eusébio de Queiroz Coutinho Mattoso Câmara reports on Prisoner Removal from the Calabouço], May 30, 1837.

"Photography Arrives in Rio," unsigned, from "Noticias Scientificas. Photographia," *Jornal do Commercio*, no. 1 (January 17, 1840), 1.

"Transient Laborers of the Fazenda Santa Cruz," by Paulo Barboza da Silva, Arquivo Nacional, Rio de Janeiro, Diversos Códices [Fundo EM], Códice 572, "Ofícios e outros papeis da Casa Imperial sobre os seguintes assuntos: Coutada da Ilha do Governador, escravos que foram libertos para servirem no exército, Fazenda Santa Cruz, Inventários e funcionários da Casa Imperial, Mordomia e solenidades da Côrte, 1801–1868," February 5, 1844, and April 30, 1844.

"Recollections of Nineteenth-Century Women," by Adèle Toussaint-Samson, from *A Parisian in Brazil*, translated by Emma Toussaint (Boston: James Earle, 1890), 43–45; 118–120.

"Workers, for Sale or Rent," in *Diário do Rio de Janeiro*, no. 29 (February 27, 1850), 4.

"Maria Angola Denounces Illegal Enslavement," (1) by Maria Angola, The National Archives of the U.K.: Kew, FO 128/48, fs. 158–161; 198–205: Miguel Hoz de la Sierra, writing on behalf of Maria Angola [Rebola], to British Minister Henry Howard, August 1853; (2) by Miguel Paes Pimenta, Arquivo Nacional, Rio de Janeiro, Diversos [Fundo OI], 6D-101, Miguel Paes Pimenta to the emperor, August 1853.

"The Capoeira Gangs of Rio," by João Jacintho de Mello, Arquivo Geral da Cidade do Rio de Janeiro, Códice 40-3-78, folha 3, "Capoeiras: Communicação do administrador dos africanos, à cerca da aggressão soffrida, de um capoeira, produzindo ferimentos," João [Jacintho] de Mello, November 25, 1858.

"French-Language Classifieds," in "Annonces," *Courrier du Brésil*, November 20, 1859, 8.

"Public Entertainment in Imperial Rio," by Joaquim Manoel de Macedo, in "Labirinto," *Jornal do Commercio*, November 19, 1860, 1.

"Sex Trafficking in the Imperial Capital," by 759 Citizens, Arquivo Geral da Cidade do Rio de Janeiro, Códice 48-4-63, folhas 2–5, Petition to Chamber of Deputies, June 2, 1879.

"A City Celebrates Slave Emancipation," by [Joaquim Maria] Machado de Assis, in "A Semana," *Gazeta de Notícias*, May 14, 1893.

Part III. Republican Rio

"Making the Federal District," by Assembléia Constituent, Presidência da Republica, Portal da Legislação, Constituição da República dos Estados Unidos do Brasil, February 21, 1891.

"The Legendary Festival of Our Lady of Penha," by Alexandre José de Mello Moraes Filho, from *Festas e tradições populares do Brasil* (Rio de Janeiro: Fauchon e Cia, 1895), 141–153.

"The Animal Game," by Francisco José Viveiros de Castro, from *Jurisprudência Criminal: Casos julgados, jurisprudencia estrangeira, doutrina juridica* (Rio de Janeiro: H. Garnier, 1900), 314–317.

"An Allegation of Infanticide," (1) by Margarida Rosa da Assumpção, Arquivo Nacional, Rio de Janeiro, Pretoria do Rio de Janeiro, Freguesia de Santa Ana, 8 (1895–1911) [Fundo OR], OR.0.IQP.3065, in "Inquerito exame do parto de Antonia China," 1904; (2) by Margarida Rosa da Assumpção, Arquivo Nacional, Rio de Janeiro, Pretoria do Rio de Janeiro, Freguesia de Santa Ana, 8 (1895–1911) [Fundo OR], OR.0.IQP.3065, in "Inquerito exame do parto de Antonia China," 1904; (3) by Henrique Pereira de Mello for the Delegacia de Policia na 10a Circumscripção, Arquivo Nacional, Rio de Janeiro, Pretoria do Rio de Janeiro, Freguesia de Santa Ana, 8 (1895–1911) [Fundo OR], OR.0.IQP.3065, in "Inquerito exame do parto de Antonia China," 1904; (4) by Henrique Pereira de Mello for the Delegacia de Policia na 10a Circumscripção, Arquivo Nacional, Rio de Janeiro, Pretoria do Rio de Janeiro, Freguesia de Santa Ana, 8 (1895–1911) [Fundo OR], OR.0.IQP.3065, in "Inquerito exame do parto de Antonia China," 1904; (5) by Henrique Pereira de Mello for the Delegacia de Policia na 10a Circumscripção, Arquivo Nacional, Rio de Janeiro, Pretoria do Rio de Janeiro, Freguesia de Santa Ana, 8 (1895–1911) [Fundo OR], OR.0.IQP.3065, in "Inquerito exame do parto de Antonia China," 1904. Translations © Cassia Roth.

"The Hotel Avenida," unsigned, *Brasil-Moderno* 9, nos. 12–13 (June–July 1908), no pagination.

"The Cult of Nostalgia," by João do Norte [Gustavo Dodt Barroso], in "O Culto da Saudade," *Jornal do Commercio*, December 22, 1912.

"Anarchists under Arrest," by Corpo de Investigação e Segurança Pública do Distrito Federal, Arquivo Nacional, Rio de Janeiro, Série Justiça [Fundo AM], Policia, 1J6, Pasta 657, letter from Corpo de Investigação e Segurança Pública do Distrito Federal to Aurelino Leal, Chief of Police, September 17, 1918.

"Demolition of the Morro do Castelo," by Carlos Sampaio, in "Ofício dirigido ao Exmo. Sr. Presidente da República" (October 31, 1922), from *Discursos e notas* (Rio de Janeiro: Typographia da S. A. Gazeta da Bolsa, 1925), 67–73. [Instituto Histórico e Geográfico Brasileiro, Miscelânea 180.1.3, n. 1–14.]

"Exhuming Estácio de Sá," by various notables, Arquivo Nacional, Rio de Janeiro, Códices Diversos [Fundo NP], Códice 792, vol. 2, in "Acta da exhumação dos restos mortais do fundador da Cidade de S. Sebastião do Rio de Janeiro e seu primeiro Capitão Mór, Estácio de Sá," January 15, 1922.

"'Flying Down to Rio,'" by Louis Brock, in "Flying Down to Rio," Louis Brock, May 8, 1933, UCLA Performing Arts Special Collections, RKO Studio Collection, box S-282, folder 687.

"Bertha Lutz Goes to Congress," by Bertha Lutz, in "Discurso de Posse," *Diário do Poder Legislativo*, July 29, 1936, 14512–14513.

"The Fount of the Queen," by Armando Magalhães Correa, in "Chafariz do Largo do Capim, de Catumbi, e Bica da Rainha," from *Revista do Instituto Histórico e Geográfico Brasileiro* 170 (1935): 73–81, reprinted in *Terra carioca: Fontes e chafarizes* (Rio de Janeiro: Imprensa Nacional, 1939).

"A Writer's Brazilian Diary," by Stefan Zweig, in "Brazilian Diary," from *The Living Age*, vol. 351 (Boston: Littell, Son and Company, 1937), translated by Ruth Norden, 384–392.

"A Fond Farewell to Praça Onze," by Herivelto Martins, 1942. Used by permission of Editora Mangione.

"Avenida Presidente Vargas," by Helio Alves de Brito, from "As Obras da Avenida Presidente Vargas," *Revista Municipal de Engenharia* 9 (April 1944): 100–111.

"Introducing the 'Civilized Indian' João José Macedo," by Cândido Mariano da Silva Rondon, Arquivo Geral da Cidade do Rio de Janeiro, Série Gabinete do Prefeito, Ofício n. 286, Letter introducing João José Macedo, from Cândido Mariano da Silva Rondon to Mayor Ângelo Mendes de Moraes, June 9, 1949.

"Madame Satã, a Grifter in Lapa," (1) Police Report by Commissioner Gilberto Paiva de Lacerda, Occurrence no. 1645, Processo, 481, 20a Vara Criminal, September 25, 1949, Arquivo Nacional, Rio de Janeiro, Ministério Publico (Fundo D3) cx. 979; (2) "Walfrido Andrade Deposition," Police Report by Commissioner Gilberto Paiva de Lacerda, Term of Declarations, Processo 2230, 20a Vara Criminal, January 19, 1949, Arquivo Nacional, Rio de Janeiro, Ministerio Publico [Fundo D3], cx. 979; (3) "Madame Satã Deposition," Police Report by Commissioner Gilberto Paiva de Lacerda, João Francisco dos Santos Act of Qualification, Processo 2230, 20a Vara Criminal, January 19, 1949, Arquivo Nacional, Rio de Janeiro, Ministerio Publico [Fundo D3], cx. 979.

"A City's Crushing Defeat at the World Cup," (1) by various, in "A Cidade do Rio de Janeiro na véspera das partidas finais da 'Taça Jules Rimet,'" *Jornal do Brasil*, July 16, 1950, 9. Used by permission of *Jornal do Brasil*; (2) unsigned, "Merecida a vitória dos uruguaios," *Correio da Manhã*, July 18, 1950, 2° caderno, 1.

"Soldiers of Fire," by Getúlio Vargas, Presidência do Brasil, Casa Civil, in "Discurso Pronunciado pelo Presidente Getúlio Vargas em Homenagem ao Corpo de Bombeiros do Distrito Federal em 2-7-1952," July 2, 1952.

"Censoring *Rio, 40 Graus*," by Ralph Benedicto Zumbano, speech delivered to São Paulo state assembly, *Diário Oficial do Estado de São Paulo* 65, no. 228 (October 14, 1955), 46.

"The Diplomacy of Samba," by anonymous, in "Escolas de samba anulam o resultado oficial do desfile," *Jornal do Brasil*, March 3, 1960, 1° caderno, 9. Used by permission of *Jornal do Brasil*.

Part IV. Recent Rio

"The Ephemeral State of Guanabara," (1) Lei No. 3.752 [Lei San Tiago Dantas], April 14, 1960; (2) Lei Complementar No. 20, July 1, 1974.

na inauguração de totens informativos no Palácio Gustavo Capanema," April 13, 2007.

"Campaigning for a 'Rio without Homophobia,'" by Governo do Estado do Rio de Janeiro, Secretaria de Assistência Social e Direitos Humanos / Superintendência de Direitos Individuais, Coletivos e Difusos, from "Nossa História," http://www .riosemhomofobia.rj.gov.br/secao/sobre/nossa-historia. Licensed through a Creative Commons License (Attribuio 2.0 Brasil).

"The Last Night at Help," by Flávia Lima, from "Lamentos no adeus à Help," *O Globo*, January 8, 2010. Used by permission of *Agência O Globo* and Flávia Lima.

"(Re)Constructing Black Consciousness," by Benedito Sérgio and Ailton Benedito de Sousa, from "Manifesto ao Povo Brasileiro," Instituto de Pesquisa das Culturas Negras (IPCN) Blog, November 20, 2010, http://recuperacaodoipcn.blogspot .com/2010/11/manifesto-ipcn.html. Used by permission of Ailton Benedito de Sousa.

"A *Quilombo* in Lagoa," by Marcelo Fernandes, from "Terras em área nobre abre polêmica entre moradores e quilombolas," *Jornal do Brasil*, March 6, 2010, accessed October 30, 2013. Used by permission of *Jornal do Brasil*.

"An Oral History of Brazilian Jiu-Jitsu," interview with Rolker Gracie (Gracie Humaitá school), August 17, 2010, Rio de Janeiro, by Benjamin Penglase. Used by permission of Benjamin Penglase.

"Whatever Your *Fantasia*, Always Use a Condom," by Ministry of Health [Departamento de DST, AIDS, e Hepatite Virais], from "Após o carnaval" Campaign, Episode 3, February 25, 2011, http://www.youtube.com/watch?v=BkH4glnYL4Y. Transcribed by Andre Pagliarini.

"'Pacification,'" (1) by Adam Isacson, Senior Associate for Regional Security, WOLA, from "Rio de Janeiro's Pacification Program," Washington Office on Latin America (January 5, 2011). Used by permission of Adam Isacson and the Washington Office on Latin America; (2) by Observatorio de Favelas, "Somos da Maré e Temos Direitos" (Facebook page), accessed November 6, 2012, https://www.facebook.com/ events/381831921896885. Used by permission of Observatorio de Favelas.

"An Open Letter from a Massacre Survivor," by Wagner dos Santos, in "Carta de Wagner dos Santos, único sobrevivente vivo da Chacina da Candelária," Rede de Comunidades e Movimentos contra a Violência, July 23, 2013.

"Reading and Writing the Suburbs," (1) from "Apresentação: A Biblioteca Parque de Manguinhos," licensed through a Creative Commons License (Atribuio 2.0 Brasil); (2) by Samuel M. Silva, interview with Alex Araujo, *Setor X* 2 (September 2013): 40–41. Used by permission of Alex Araujo.

Every reasonable effort has been made to obtain permission. We invite copyright holders to inform us of any oversights.

Index

abertura. See redemocratization

Abreu, Fernanda, 297

advertisements, 121–125; for slaves, 112–115. *See also* newspapers

Affonso VI, 27–29

Africans, 5, 7, 11–13, 41–43, 74–76, 99, 112–113, 116–120, 327–329, 363

Afro-Brazilian culture, 149–150; identification with African diaspora and, 327–329; Reis do Congo and, 171; spirituality and, 99–100, 241, 317–319

airports and aviation, 145, 147; Galeão, 4, 238; Santos Dumont, xiv, 205

Almeida, Hilária Batista de, 149–150

Alvarenga, Thomé Correia de, 26–28

Amnesty International, 352–354

anarchists, 174–178

Andrade, Carlos Drummond de, 312

animal game (*jogo do bicho*), 155–157, 293

anticommunism, 146, 236–237

Araujo, Alex, 360–361

architecture, 11–12; eclectic, 163–164; Fluminense School of, 74; modernist, 143–144, 251, 311–315; neoclassical, 74, 103; vernacular, 167–168; verticalization of, 163

Arcos de Lapa, 12, 168–169

Argentina: Montoneros from, 275–278; Operation Condor and, 275–277

armed forces of Brazil: 1964 coup and, 236; politics and, 83–84, 139, 143, 185–186

Assis, Machado de, 134–137, 245

Assumpção, Margarida Rosa da, 158–160

Astaire, Fred, 187

Aterro do Flamengo. *See* Parque do Flamengo

authoritarianism, 146, 237–238

automobiles and automobility, 208–209, 211–212, 254–255, 270

Avenida Atlântica, 325

Avenida Central. *See* Avenida Rio Branco

Avenida Presidente Vargas, 208–210

Avenida Rio Branco, 163; monumental obelisk at, 185–186

bahianas, 108–109

Baixada de Jacarepaguá, 239, 270–271

Barbalho Bezerra, Agostinho, 26–29

Barbalho Bezerra, Jeronimo, 26, 28

Barra da Tijuca, 270–274, 281

Barroso, Gustavo Dodt, 170

beaches, 200, 227, 325; beach culture, 239, 297–298; sexuality and, 240

Bezerra, Antonia Mendes, 158–162

Bica da Rainha (Fount of the Queen), 195–197

black culture. *See* Afro-Brazilian culture

Blystone, James J., 275–278

Bob's (restaurant), 266–267

Bonaparte, Napoleon, 14, 60

bondes, 141

bossa nova, 146, 235

botany, 55, 57

Bragança monarchy. *See* João VI; Pedro I; Pedro II

Brandão, Tânia, 288–289

Brasílisa, transfer of capital to, 146–147, 235

Brazilian empire, 77–78, 82–85, 97

Brazilian independence, 74, 79, 82; commemoration of, 136–137, 179–180; movement for, 74

Britain: antislavery interventions by, 116–118; Royal Navy of, 64, 66–67

Brito, Hélio Alves de, 208

Brizola, Leonel, 304; Brizolões (educational centers) created under, 241

Brock, Louis, 187

Burle Marx, Roberto, 255, 315

Cabral, Sérgio, 321, 323

Cachaça Revolt, 26–29

calçada (cobblestoned walk). *See* Avenida Atlântica

candomblé, 99–100

Canning, George, 82–84

Capanema, Gustavo, 144, 311

capoeira (martial art and dance), 119

capoeiras (gangs), 119–120

Carioca, definition of, 1, 9

Carioca, A (painting), 132–133

"Carioca, The" (musical number and dance), 187–190

Carioca, Zé (cartoon character), 203

Carioca River, 12, 24–25, 35–36

Carmelite convent, 86–88

Carnaval, 1–4, 145, 171, 206–207, 341–343; of Denunciations, 146

"Ca Room Pa Pa" (musical number), 222

Castro, José Luiz de, 50–52

Catholicism, 11; Feast of the Holy Spirit and, 79–80; Festival of Our Lady of Penha and, 149–154; pluralization of religious belief and, 240–241. *See also* Jesuits

Cavalieri, Fernando, 304–305

censorship, 227–229

Centro (neighborhood), xiii–xiv, 327

César de Oliveira Sampaio, Carlos, 179

Chacal (Ricardo de Carvalho Duarte), 297–300

Chamberlain, Henry, 79–80, 82–84

children and youth, 116–118, 128, 158–162, 227, 354–355; recreation for, 255–257, 307; youth rebellion, 237, 240, 261–262

"Cidade Maravilhosa" (song), 1

Cidade Nova, 206

cinema. *See* film

cinnamon, cultivation and trade of, 55–58

citizenship, 76, 82, 191–194, 241–242, 258–259, 304, 320–324, 327–332

Cold War, 146, 227; culture shaped by, 288–290

commodities trade, 12–14, 75; brazilwood and, 9–10

Compte, Louis, 103–104

conservative moralism, 285–287

Conspiracy of Rio de Janeiro, 50–54

Constitution of 1824, 76, 82, 93–95, 99

Constitution of 1891, 147–148

consumerism, 238, 281–282; fast food and, 266–269

Copacabana (neighborhood), 141–142, 266, 270, 325

Copacabana Beach, 200

Corcovado, 89, 135, 137

Cortes, Geraldo de Menezes, 227, 229

Costa, Lúcio, 270–272, 311, 313–314

coups d'etat. *See* armed forces of Brazil

crime, 240; narcotrafficking and, 241–242, 344–347, 357. *See also* legal proceedings; police

crônica, 126, 134–135

Cruz, Oswaldo, 140

Cunha Salles, José Roberto da, 155–157

Daguerre, Louis-Jacques, 103–104

dance, 76, 187–190, 222; capoeira as, 119; disco, 263–265

"Dancin' Days" (song), 264–265

Dancin' Days (telenovela), 263

Debret, Jean-Baptiste, 41, 86; artwork of, 43, 90

Demiciano (Free African), 119–120

democracy, 7, 148, 191–194, 236, 241, 292–296, 304–305

Diário do Rio de Janeiro, 112
Diniz, Leila, 240
diplomacy: between Britain and Brazil, 116–118; between Paraguay and Brazil, 230; between United States and Brazil, 203–205. *See also* France: corsairs from
Disraeli, Benjamin: Primrose Day and, 135–136
domestic workers, 114, 119
Drummond, João Batista Viana, 155
Duclerc, Jean-François, 30–31
Duguay-Trouin, René, 30, 32

Earth Summit, 301–302. *See also* Forúm Global
education, 241, 304, 358–360
electricity, modern conveniences and, 163, 165
England. *See* Britain
entertainment. *See* leisure activities
environmental conservation, 195, 197, 334–336
Ernesto, Pedro, 142
Escrava Anastácia, 317–319
Estado Novo, 208, 311, 330. *See also* Vargas, Getúlio
evangelism, 240–241, 285–286

Fanini, Nelson, 285
favelas, 144, 201–202, 207, 239, 272–274; city services extended to, 304–307; Complexo da Maré, 352–353; "pacification" programs in, 344–353; Programa Favela-Bairro and, 304–307; Projeto Mutirão and, 304–305; removal of, 258; Rocinha, 6, 344
Fazenda Imperial de Santa Cruz, 106–107
feminism, 191–194, 301–303
Ferreira, A. Luiz, 134
Ferreira, Claudia, 301–303
Festa do Divino Espírito Santo (Feast of the Holy Spirit), 79–80

Figueiredo, Carlos Honorio de, 116–118
Figueiredo, João Baptista, 285
Figueiredo e Melo, Pedro Américo de, 132–133
Filho, André, 1
film: *Black Orpheus*, 235; *Entranced Earth*, 235; *Flying Down to Rio*, 187–190; *Nancy Goes to Rio*, 222; *Ônibus 174*, 354; *Rio, 40 Graus*, 227–229; *Saludos Amigos*, 203–204
Finck, Jonas, 30–32
firefighters, 224–226
First Republic, 78; fall of, 185; proclamation of, 139
Flores da Cunha, Luís, 185–186
Floresta da Tijuca (Tijuca Forest), 24
Fluminense, definition of, 73
Fonseca, Antônio Borges da, 92, 94
football. *See* soccer
fortifications and defense, 30–34, 89–91, 203–205
Forúm Global, Planeta Fêmea (Female Planet) and, 301–303
France: artists from, 73; Brazilian politics influenced by, 50–54; commercial community in Rio de Janeiro from, 88, 108, 121–125; corsairs from, 30, 33; culinary influences of, 73–74; France Antarctique, 10, 19; invasion of Portugal by, 59–61
Fritscher, Rômulo: Eu odeio a Telerj (website), 308, 310

gender relations, 45, 76; elite, 108, 110–111; HIV/AIDS prevention and, 341–343; law and, 158
Gil, Gilberto, 311–312
Gomes, Bernardino António, 55
Goulart, João, 236
Gracie, Hélio, 337–338
Gracie, Rolker, 337–339
Great Britain. *See* Britain
Guanabara (state), 237; creation of, 247–250; *fusão* (fusion) with Rio de Janeiro (state), 247, 250

Guanabara Bay, 2–7, 12, 19–20, 89–91;
European discovery and naming of,
9–10, 17; islands of, 199–200; landfill
projects in, 142, 179; whaling in, 48–49

Help (nightclub), 325–326
Hermenegildo do Amaral, Bráz, 41
homosexuality, 213–214, 240, 288; LGBT
rights movement and, 320; Rio Sem
Homofobia campaign and, 321–324
hotels: Copacabana Palace, 187; Hotel
Avenida, 163–166; Hôtel Pharoux, 123;
Hôtel Ravot, 122–123
housing, 208; Companhia de Habitação
Popular do Estado da Guanabara
(COHAB), 258–259; *Plano Piloto da
Barra da Tijuca* and the Parallel Plan,
270–274. *See also* favelas
Howard, Henry, 116–118
Hoz de la Sierra, Paulo Manoel, 116–118
human rights, 242, 320–324, 344–345, 347,
351, 353–356. *See also* citizenship
Hunt, G., 79–80

Igreja de São Sebastião, 182–183
Ilha das Enxadas, British naval hospital
proposed at, 66–67
immigrants, 73, 76, 140–141; anarchist
movement supported by, 174–178;
Portuguese, 149–150, 152; slave labor
replaced by, 106
Imperial Chapel, 87–88
Indians. *See* indigenous peoples
indigenous peoples, 9, 17–18; appearance
and customs of, 20–22; assimilation of,
211–212; government policies toward,
211; labor of, 11–12, 35–36; Tamoio, 9–10,
35; Temiminós, 19; Tupinamba, 19, 35
industrialization, 142, 145–146
infanticide, 158–162
Instituto de Patrimônio Histórico e
Artístico Nacional (IPHAN), 312, 315–316
Instituto de Pesquisas das Culturas Negras (IPCN), 327–332

internet, 308–310; social media, 345
Isabel, Princess: abolition of slavery by,
134–135

Jesuits, 11, 35–36
João, Prince Regent. *See* João VI
João VI, 15, 59–65, 73–74, 82, 87–89
Joaquim, Leandro, 48–49, 69
Joaquina, Carlota, 87
journalism. *See* newspapers
Julião, Carlos, 37, 39

kiosks, 167–169
Klabin, Israel, 270
Kotscho, Ricardo, 292
Kubitschek, Juscelino, 146

labor, wage, 112
labor movements, 142; anarchist involvement in, 174–178
Lacerda, Carlos, 258–259
Lagoa (neighborhood), 142, 333–336
Lapa (neighborhood), 79–81; Afro-
Brazilian men and, 213
Largo do Paço (Palace Square), 86–91,
103–104
Lavradio, Marques do (Luís de Almeida
Portugal Soares), 41–44
Le Corbusier (Charles-Édouard
Jeanneret-Gris), 311, 314–315
legal proceedings: civil, 38, 334–335; criminal, 50–54, 155–157; police investigations and, 213–217
leisure activities, 126–129, 144; class
distinction in, 126–129; nightlife, 145;
outdoor recreation, 251–257. *See also*
beaches
Léry, Jean de, 19
liberalism, 7, 50–54, 82, 92–96, 139,
147–148, 258–259
Lima Souto, Edson Luís de, 261
literature. *See crônica*; print culture
Luccock, John, 69
Lutz, Bertha, 191–194

Macedo, João José, 211–212

Macedo, Joaquim Manuel de: "Labirinto," 45, 126

Madame Satã (João Francisco dos Santos), 213–217

Magalhães Corrêa, Armando, 195

Malta, Augusto, 167–169

Mandarino, Constantino, 271, 273

Manguinhos (neighborhood), 357, 361; Biblioteca Parque de Manguinhos and, 357–360

maps, 2, 97–98, 203–205, 249

Maracanã stadium, 218–220, 285–286

"Maracanazo" (The Blow at Maracanã), 219

Maria Angola, 116–118

Maria I, 62–65, 196

marijuana, Summer of the Can and, 297–298

Marina da Glória, 251–252

Martins, Herivelto, 206

Massacre (*chacina*) at Candelária, 354–355

Massé, João, 33

mass media, 142, 144–145; Rio de Janeiro's prominence in production of, 235

McDonald's, 266–269

Medeiros, Ethel Bauzer de, 251

Mello, João Jacintho de, 119–120

Mello Morais Filho, Alexandre José, 149

Metropolitan Region of Rio de Janeiro, 247, 250

Michellerie, Eugène de la, 97

military regime, 236–238; conservative moralism of, 285–287; direct elections movement to end, 292–296; state terror committed by, 237, 275–276; suppression of Afro-Brazilian institutions by, 330; suppression of student protests by, 26

Ministry of Culture, 315–316; Fundação Cultural Palmares and, 335

Ministry of Education and Health, 143–144

Miranda, Carmen, 222

monarchism, 78, 82–85, 92–95

monuments, 182–186, 195. *See also* Maracanã stadium; Palácio Gustavo Capanema

Moraes, Ângelo Mendes de, 211–212

Morro do Castelo, demolition of, 142, 179, 181–182

Municipal Chamber, 24–25, 35–36, 37–40, 99–100

Museu Histórico Nacional, 170–171

Nascimento, Natalino José do, 230–233

National Congress, 191–194

national government: constitution of, 76, 82–85, 92–95, 99, 147–148; urban space shaped by, 139, 143–144, 170, 238, 311–316

national identity, 5–6, 74, 82, 85, 92–96, 136–137, 170–173, 230

National Institute for Colonization and Agrarian Reform (INCRA), 334–336

National Students' Union (União Nacional dos Estudantes, UNE), 261

nativism and xenophobia, 74, 92, 97, 154, 174

natural disasters, social inequality and, 239

natural environment and resources, xv, 9–10, 12, 75, 150, 195–197, 199; flora, 55–58, 69–70, 181, 251, 255, 282. *See also* beaches; environmental conservation; water management

newspapers: anarchist, 174–177; *Correio da Manhã*, 261; *Courrier du Brésil*, 121–125; French immigrant owned, 121; politics influenced by, 92–96, 235–236; *O Republico*, 92–96; sports coverage in, 218–221

Night of the Bottle-Whippings (Noite das Garrafadas), 92–96

Niterói, transfer of state capital from, 247

Noronha e Britto, Marcos de, 60–62

Nossa Senhora do Parto (church), 45–47

Oliveira, Saturnino Alves de, 158–162

Olympics. *See* sports

Operation Condor, 275–276
Ouro Preto, 173

Paço Imperial, 103
Padre Perereca (Luiz Gonçalves dos
    Santos), 59
Paes Pimenta, Miguel, 116–118
Palácio Gustavo Capanema, 311–316
parliament, 130–131. *See also* National
    Congress
Parque do Flamengo, 251–257
Passeio Público, xiv, 69–71
Patrocínio, José de, 134
Pedro I, 87, 92–94; constitutional assem-
    bly dissolved by, 82–85
Pedro II, 78
Peixoto, Francisco Cabral, 163–164
people of color: free, 75–76; illegal en-
    slavement of, 116–118; multiculturality
    and, 12; religious processions and, 80
Pereira Passos, Francisco, 139, 167
Peres, José Isaac, 282–283
performing arts, 76, 126; theater,
    288–291
Pessoa, Cândido, 191–192
photography, 103–105, 167–169, 301–303
Pinto Júnior, Luís, 334–335
pirates. *See* France: corsairs from
police, 76–77, 99–100, 155, 158–162, 230–231;
    curfew for people of African descent
    enforced by, 119; favela pacification
    and, 242, 344–353; killings by, 347, 354,
    356; Military Police, 347, 350; Pacifying
    Police Units (UPPS), 344–353; political
    repression by, 146, 174, 237–238; Public
    Security and Investigation Bureau,
    174; Riocentro bombing investigated
    by, 278–280; riots and, 93–94; vagrancy
    laws enforced by, 141; vice regulated
    by, 214. *See also* crime
political activism, 50–54, 191–194, 236–238,
    241, 261–262, 285, 292–296, 304–307, 320,
    327–332. *See also* nativism and xeno-
    phobia; Revolution of 1930; riots and
    revolts

populism, 142; working-class appeal of,
    224
port of Rio de Janeiro, 55, 66–67, 75,
    89–90, 141; Porto Maravilha renewal
    project and, 243–245, 362–365; rebuild-
    ing of, 170
Portuguese colonial administration, 7,
    24–29, 33–44, 50–54
Portuguese Royal Court, relocation to
    Rio de Janeiro of, 14–15, 59–66
Praça D. Pedro I, 134
"Praça Onze" (song), 206–207
Praça Onze (square), 206
print culture, 74; *crônica* and, 126; travel
    narratives and, 108, 198. *See also*
    newspapers
prisons: Aljube, 101–102; Calabouço,
    101–102; House of Correction, 101–102,
    117; House of Detention, 101; political
    penal colonies, 146
prostitution, 110, 213–214, 325–326; sex
    trafficking and, 130–131
public health and sanitation, 42–44,
    66–67, 139–140, 179, 181, 307; HIV/AIDS
    prevention, 341–343; vaccination, 140
public illumination, 48, 74
Puig, Manuel: *El beso de la mujer araña*
    (Kiss of the Spider Woman), 288–291

Queiroz Coutinho Mattoso da Camara,
    Eusébio de, 99–102
quilombos, 75; Quilombo Sacopã, 333–336
quitandeiras, 37–40

race: gendered stereotypes and, 108–110;
    public relations campaign representa-
    tions of, 341–342
racial democracy, critiques of, 327
Recolhimento do Parto asylum, 45–47
redemocratization, 238, 241; direct elec-
    tions movement and, 292–296
Redes de Desenvolvimento da Maré,
    Somos da Maré e Temos Direitos
    campaign against police abuses by, 345,
    352–353

religious beliefs, pluralization and diversity of, 240–241
religious processions and festivals, 79–81, 149–155, 171
republicanism, 53, 78; political tensions and, 139
Revolution of 1930, 142, 185–186
Rio Branco, Baron of (José Maria da Silva Paranhos), 134–135, 137
Riocentro convention center, bombing of, 275–276, 278–280
Rio de Janeiro (city): as capital city, 4–5, 13, 15, 74, 139, 147; climate of, 56–57, 227, 229; economy of, 9–10, 12–14, 48, 75–76, 106, 112, 121, 142, 145–146, 238–239, 242–243, 281, 362; as Federal District, 147–148; finances of, 180–181; foundation of, 10, 17; globalization and, 243; international sporting events and, 214, 218–221, 243, 346; as Neutral Municipality, 147–148; other cities compared to, 171–172, 200–201; population of, 6, 73, 243; socioeconomic conditions of, 242–243
Rio de Janeiro (state): *fusão* (fusion) with Guanabara (state), 247, 250; LGBT rights legislation and policies enacted in, 321–324
riots and revolts, 92–96, 237–238
River of January. *See* Guanabara Bay
Rodenbeck, Peter, 267–269
Rondon, Cândido Mariano da Silva, 211–212
Rua Direita (a.k.a. Rua Primeiro de Março), 108–109
Rua do Ouvidor, 78

Sá, Estácio de: exhumation of, 182–184
Sá e Benevides, Salvador Correia de, 26–29
samba, as symbol of Rio de Janeiro, 145
samba schools, 145, 206–207, 230–233
Sambódromo, 208, 243
Santos, Wagner dos, 354–356
São Gonçalo, 26–28

São João de Ypanema ironworks, 106
São Paulo (city), 235, 243
São Paulo (state), 106
São Sebastião do Rio de Janeiro. *See* Rio de Janeiro (city)
Segreto, Paschoal, 155–156
Senado da Câmara. *See* Municipal Chamber
Sertão Carioca, 195. *See also* suburbs
sex and sexuality, 12, 76, 109–110, 145, 158, 187, 222, 240, 251, 261–262, 341–343. *See also* homosexuality; prostitution
shopping centers, BarraShopping and, 281–284
Silva, Benedita da, 240, 301
Silva, Paulo Barboza da, 107
Silva Alvarenga, Manoel Inácio, 50, 52–54
Silveira Frade, José Bernardo da, 50, 52
slavery: abolition of, 134; agriculture and, 106–107; contemporary iconographical representations of, 317; Law of the Free Womb and, 134–135; postindependence continuity of, 74
slaves: African, 7, 11–13, 41–43; cemetery for, 41, 244, 365; fugitive, 115; government-owned, 106–107; incarceration of, 101–102; regulations imposed on, 77, 99–100; resistance by, 75; spirituality of, 99; treatment of, 41–44, 101, 106–107, 110; urban, 75, 112–115
slave trade: Africans freed from, 116, 119–120; illegal, 75; Valongo slave market and, 13, 41–43
Smith, William Sidney, 66–68
Soares, Maria Carlota de Macedo, 251
soccer, 285; World Cup and, 214, 218–221, 243
social inequality, 4, 13, 201–202, 227–229, 238–240, 271–273, 355
social media, 345
Sociedade Literária do Rio de Janeiro, 50
Society of Jesus. *See* Jesuits
socioeconomic segregation, 239
Sousa, Martim Afonso de, 17
Sousa, Pero Lopes de, 17–18

Sousa, Washington Luís Pereira de, 185
Souza, José Ignácio de, 163–164
Souza Prata, Sebastião Bernardes de, 206
sports, 144, 256; Brazilian jiu-jitsu,
    337–340. *See also* soccer
student protests, 237; radical left and, 238;
    shifting gender norms and, 261–262
suburbs, 140–142, 195, 357–361; access to
    water and, 196–197
Sugarloaf Mountain, 200

Teixeira, Escalartina, 158–162
telephone services: complaints about,
    308–310; privatization of, 308–309;
    Telerj and, 308–310
television: Rede Globo and, 292, 294; tele-
    novelas, 263. *See also* mass media
Tiradentes (Joaquim José da Silva Xavier),
    50, 173
tourism, 219–220, 325–326. *See also* hotels
Toussaint-Samson, Adèle: *Une Parisienne
    au Brésil*, 108
transportation, 12, 76, 163, 208, 272; street-
    cars and, 141. *See also* automobiles and
    automobility

United States: alliance between Brazil
    and, 203–205; films produced in, 187–
    190, 203–204, 222; Operation Condor
    and, 275–277

urbanization and urban planning, xiv,
    7, 33, 74, 139–143, 145–146, 163, 205, 238;
    Barra da Tijuca as site of, 270–272;
    demolition of old structures and, 167,
    170, 179, 206–210; land disputes and,
    333–336; natural setting of, 201–202. *See
    also* favelas; housing

Valongo slave port and market, 13, 41–43;
    mass grave near, 244; Memorial dos
    Pretos Novos and, 363, 365
Vargas, Getúlio, 142, 146, 185–186, 208, 224
Villegagnon, Nicolas Durand de, 10,
    19–20
Viveiros de Castro, José, 155

water management, 11–12, 24–25, 35–36,
    208–210
welfare state, 224–226
women, 45, 108–111, 116–118. *See also* femi-
    nism; gender relations
World War II, 198, 203–204

Zona Norte, xiv–xv, 208–210
Zona Oeste, xv, 195, 281. *See also* Baixada
    da Jacarepaguá; Barra da Tijuca
Zona Sul, xiv, 271–273; land reclamation
    in, 179
Zumbano, Ralph Benedicto, 227–228
Zweig, Stefan, 198